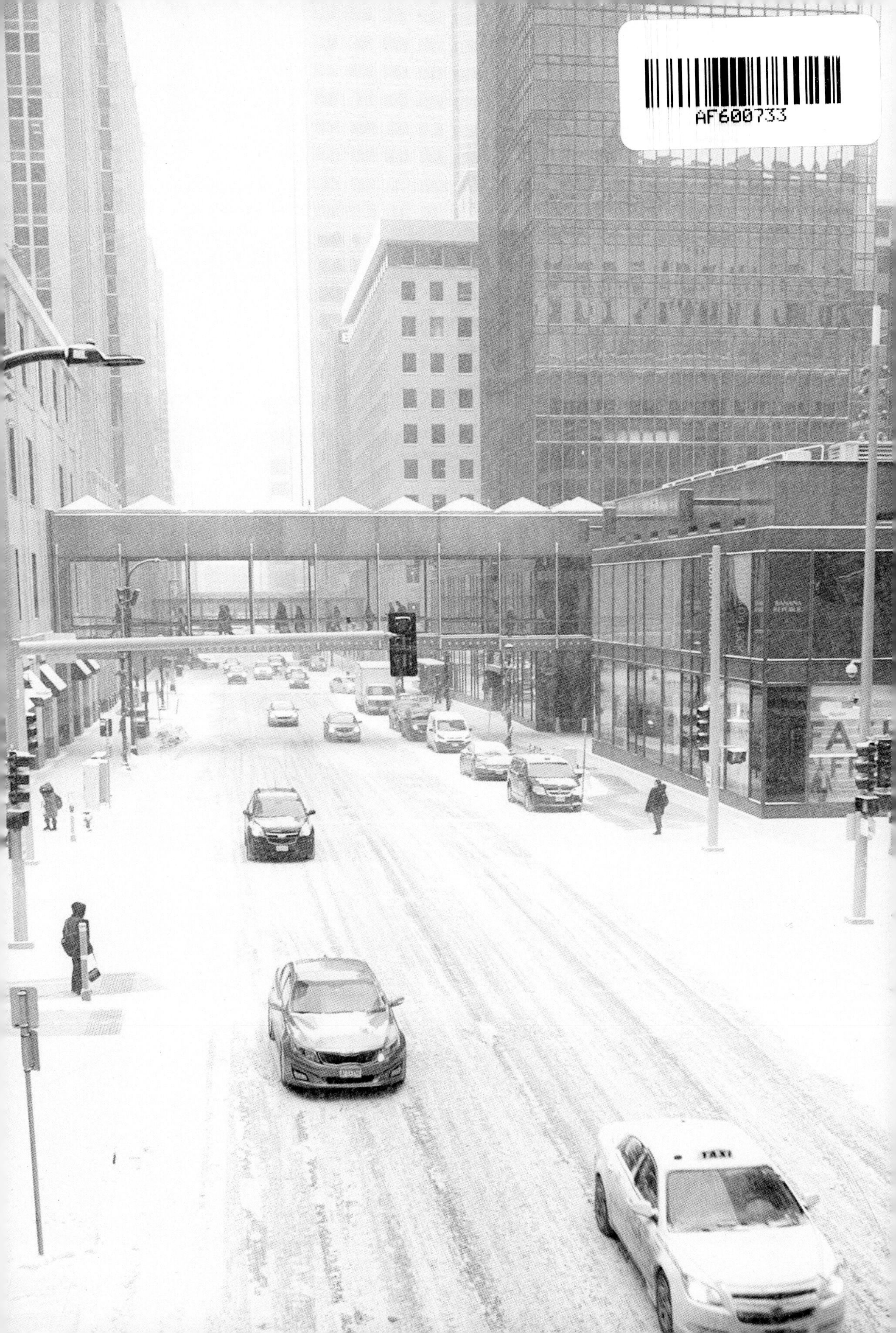
TAXI

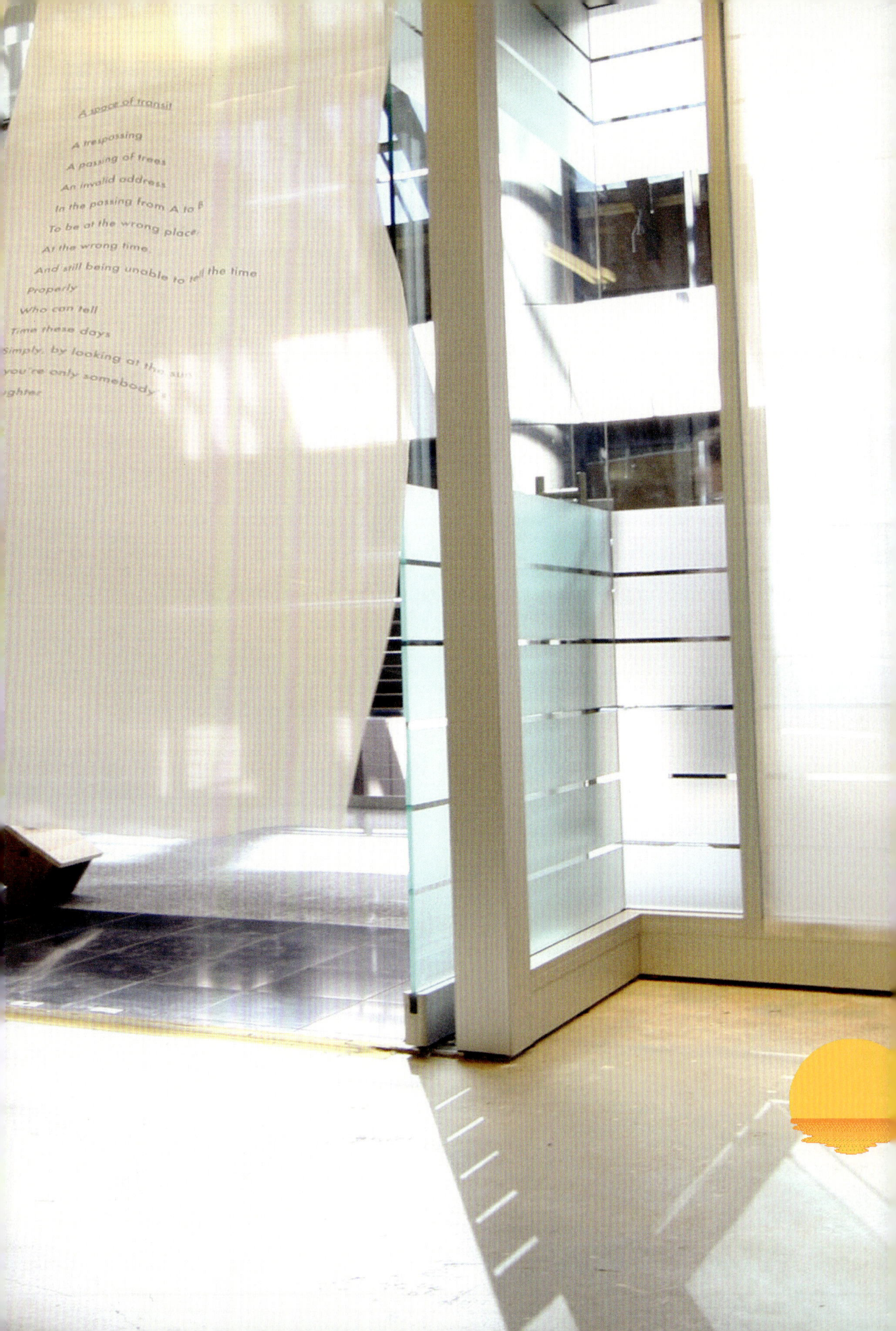
A space of transit
A trespassing
A passing of trees
An invalid address
In the passing from A to B
To be at the wrong place
At the wrong time
And still being unable to tell the time
Properly
Who can tell
Time these days
Simply, by looking at the sun
you're only somebody's
ughter

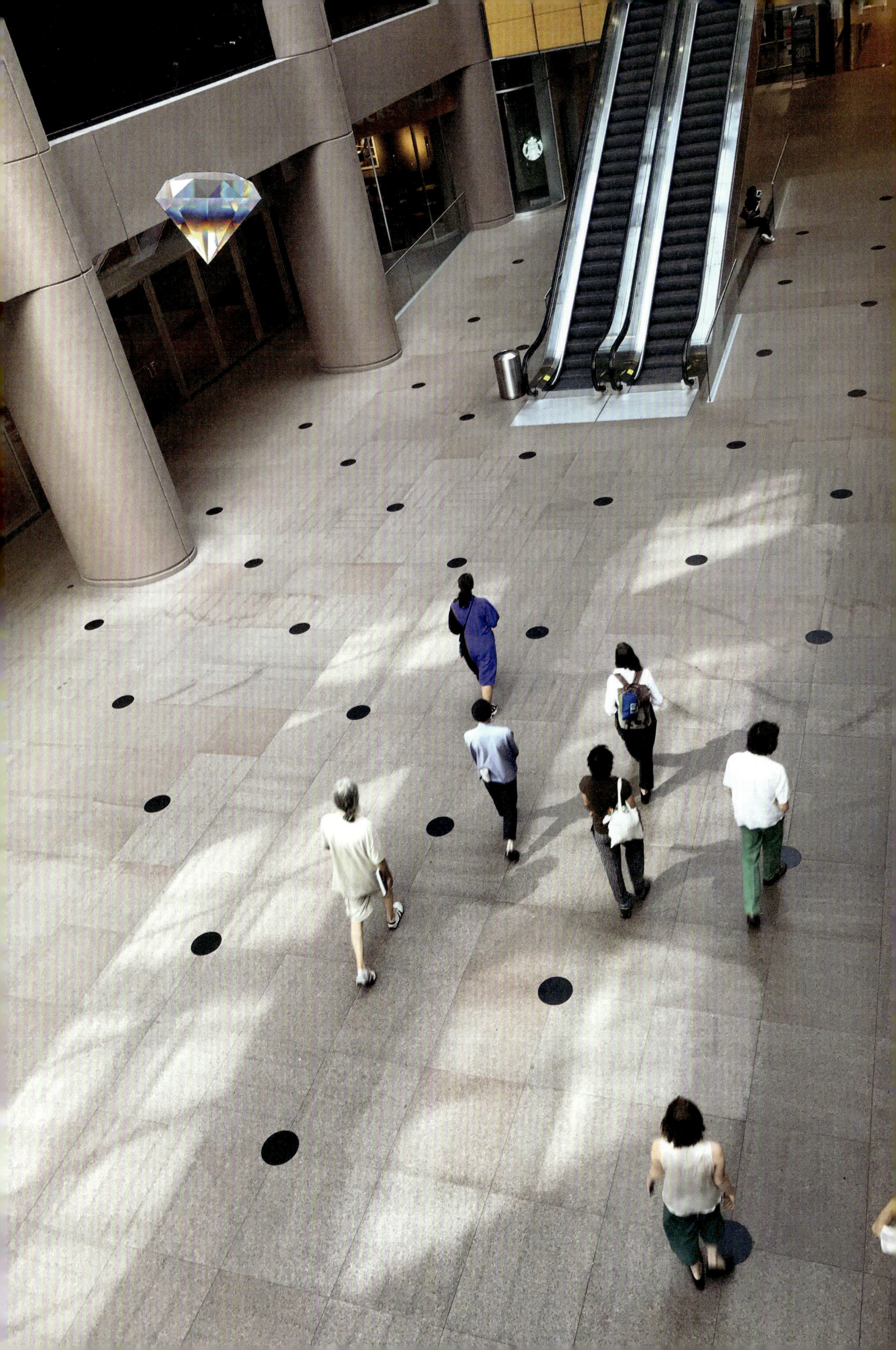

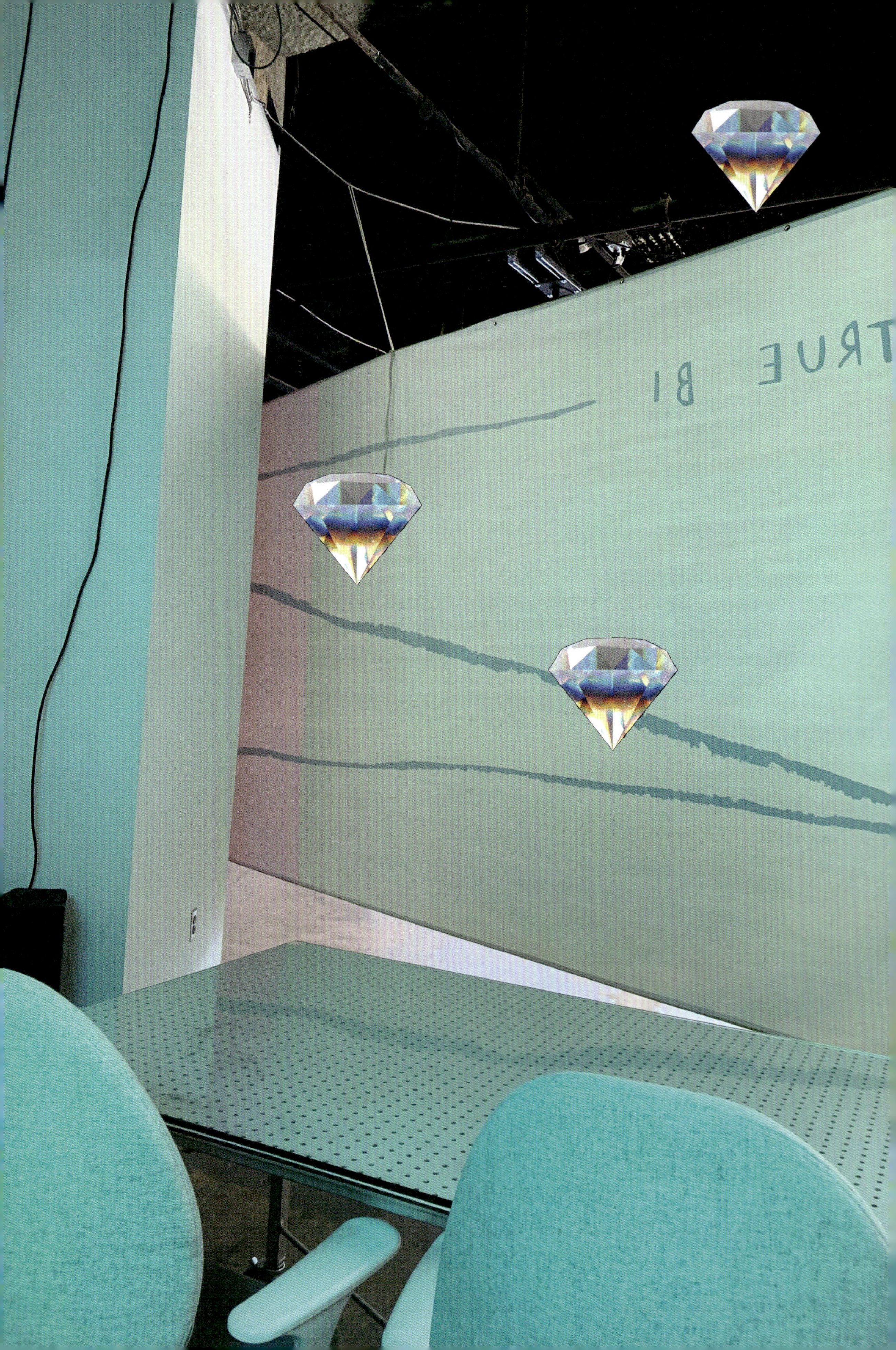

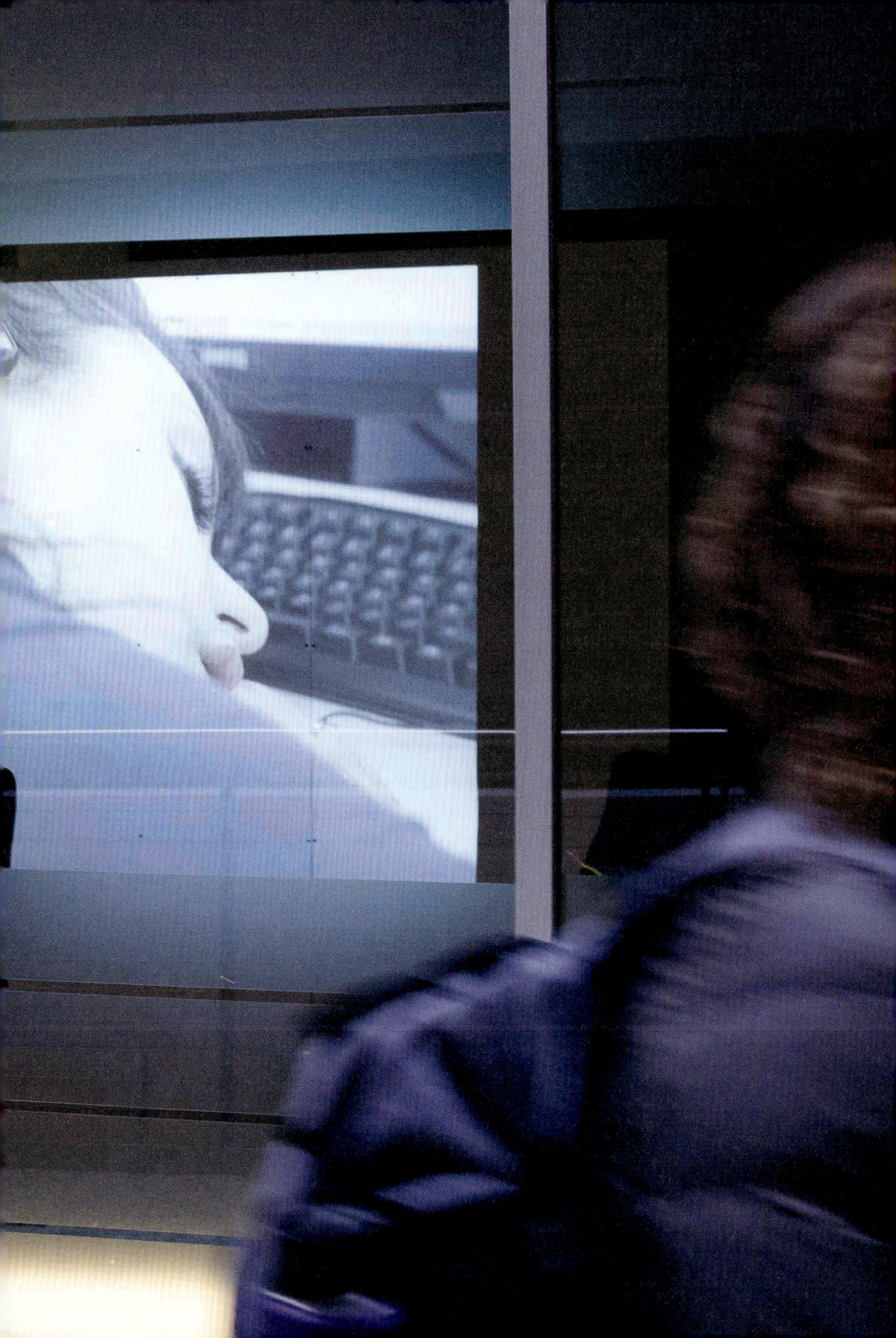

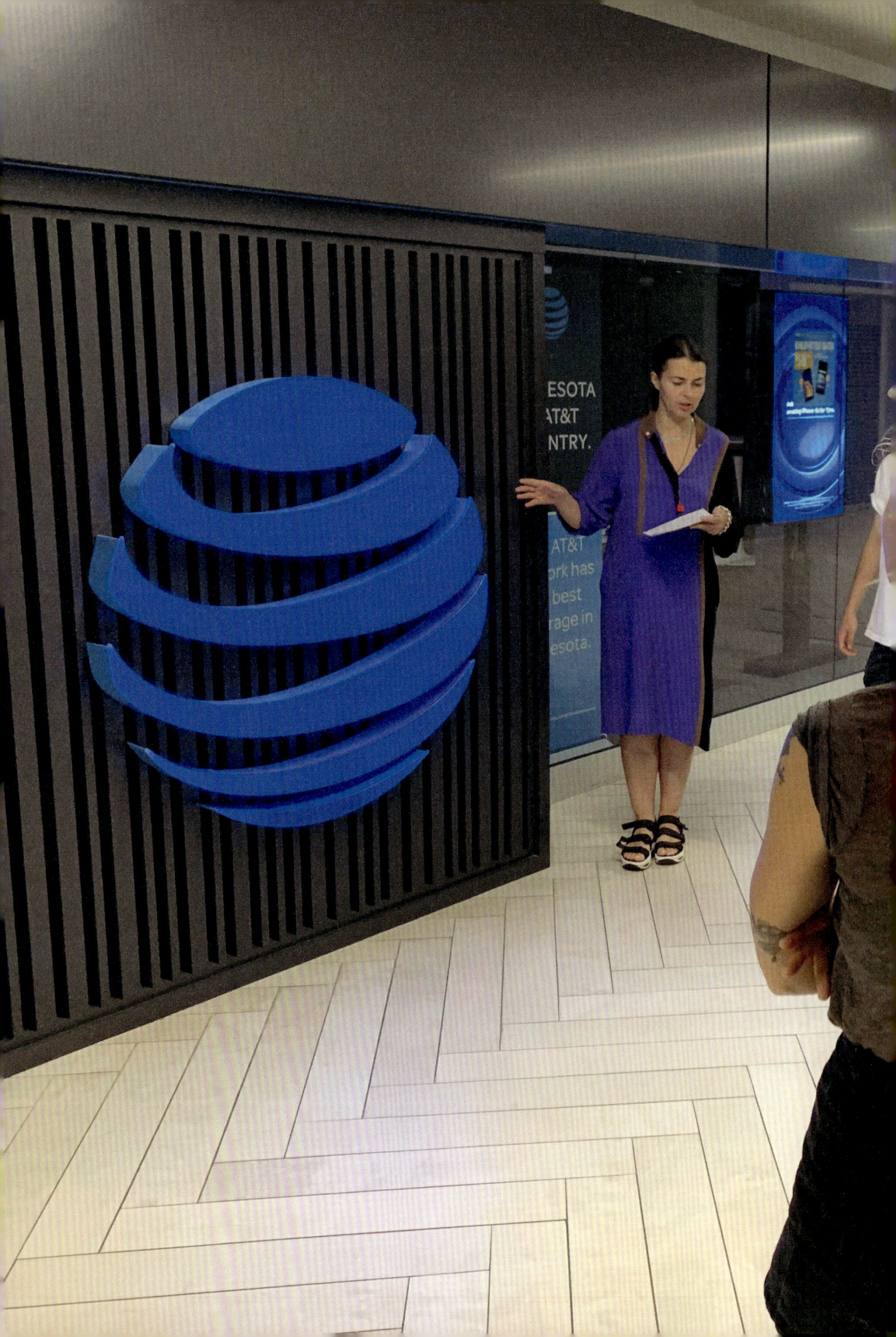
ESOTA
AT&T
NTRY.
AT&T
ork has
best
rage in
esota.

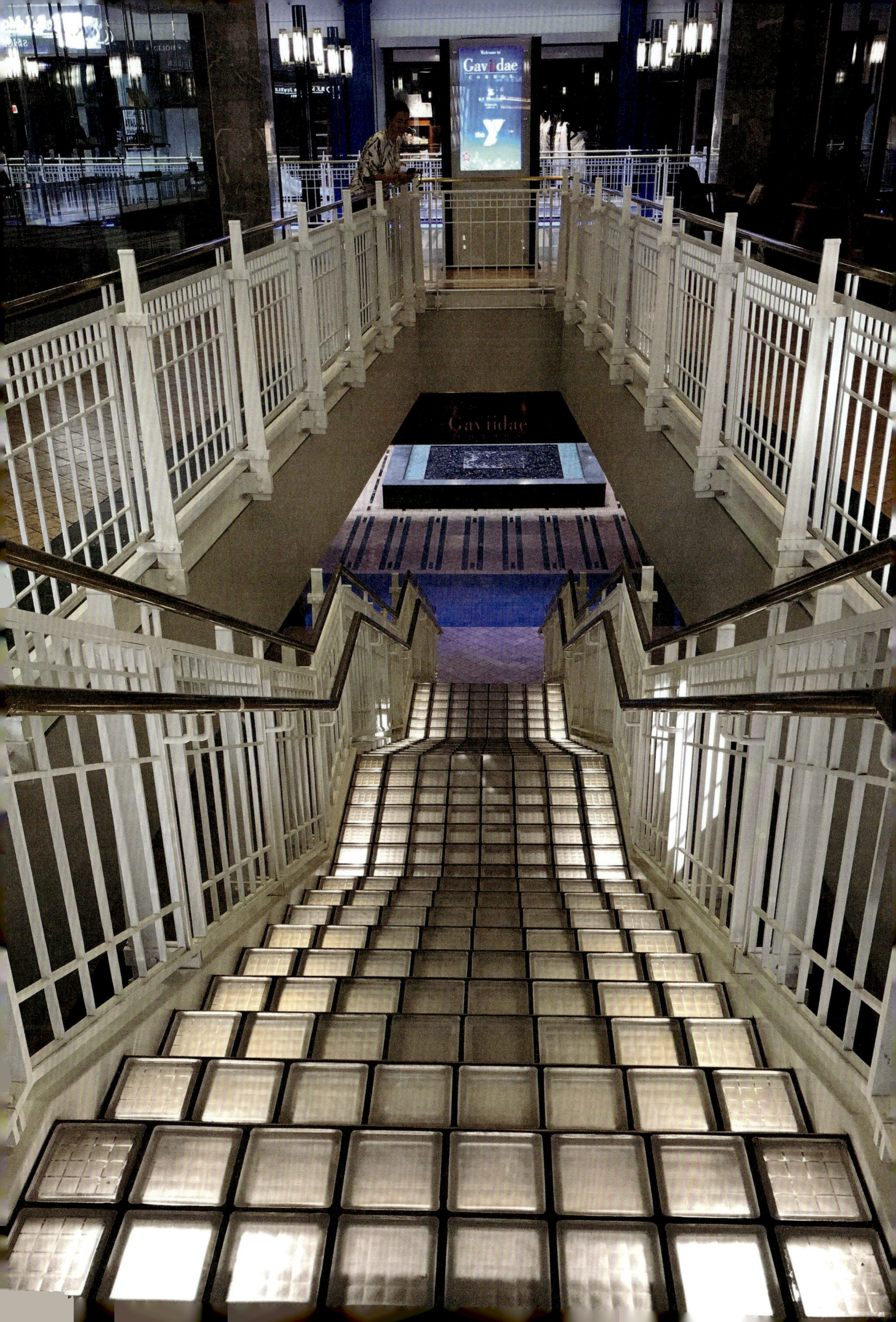
Gaviidae
Gaviidae

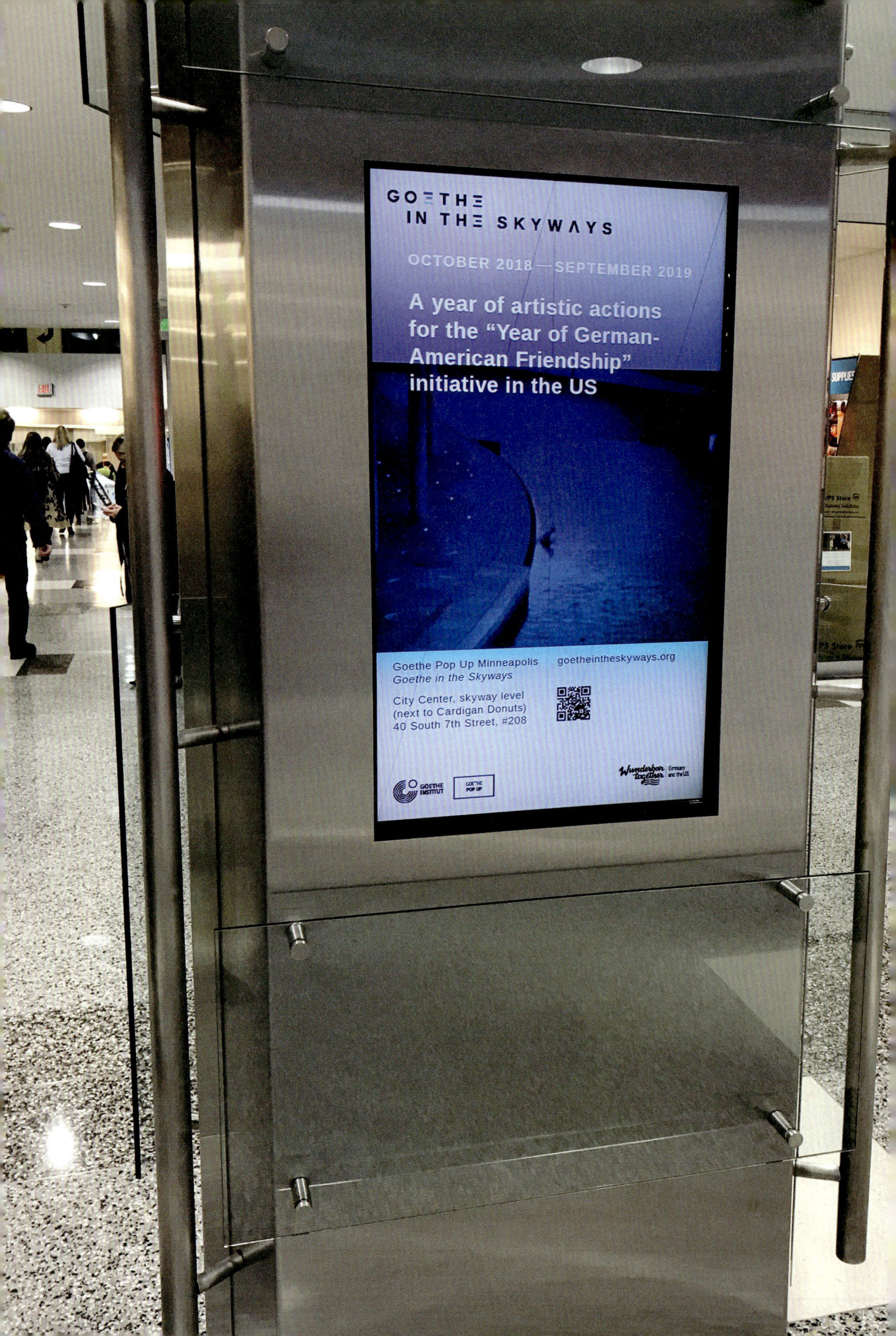
GOETHE
IN THE SKYWAYS
OCTOBER 2018 — SEPTEMBER 2019
A year of artistic actions for the "Year of German-American Friendship" initiative in the US
Goethe Pop Up Minneapolis
Goethe in the Skyways
City Center, skyway level
(next to Cardigan Donuts)
40 South 7th Street, #208
goetheintheskyways.org

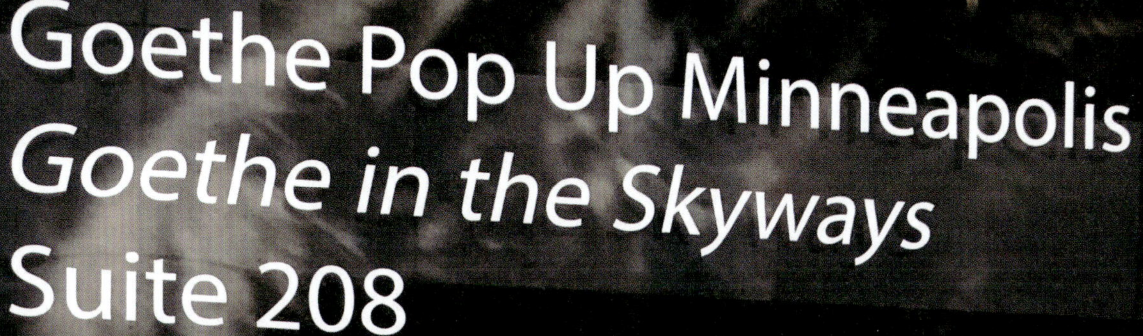

Mon–Fri 10am–6pm
(subject to closure)

www.goetheintheskyways.org
info@goetheintheskyways.org

GOETHE
POP UP

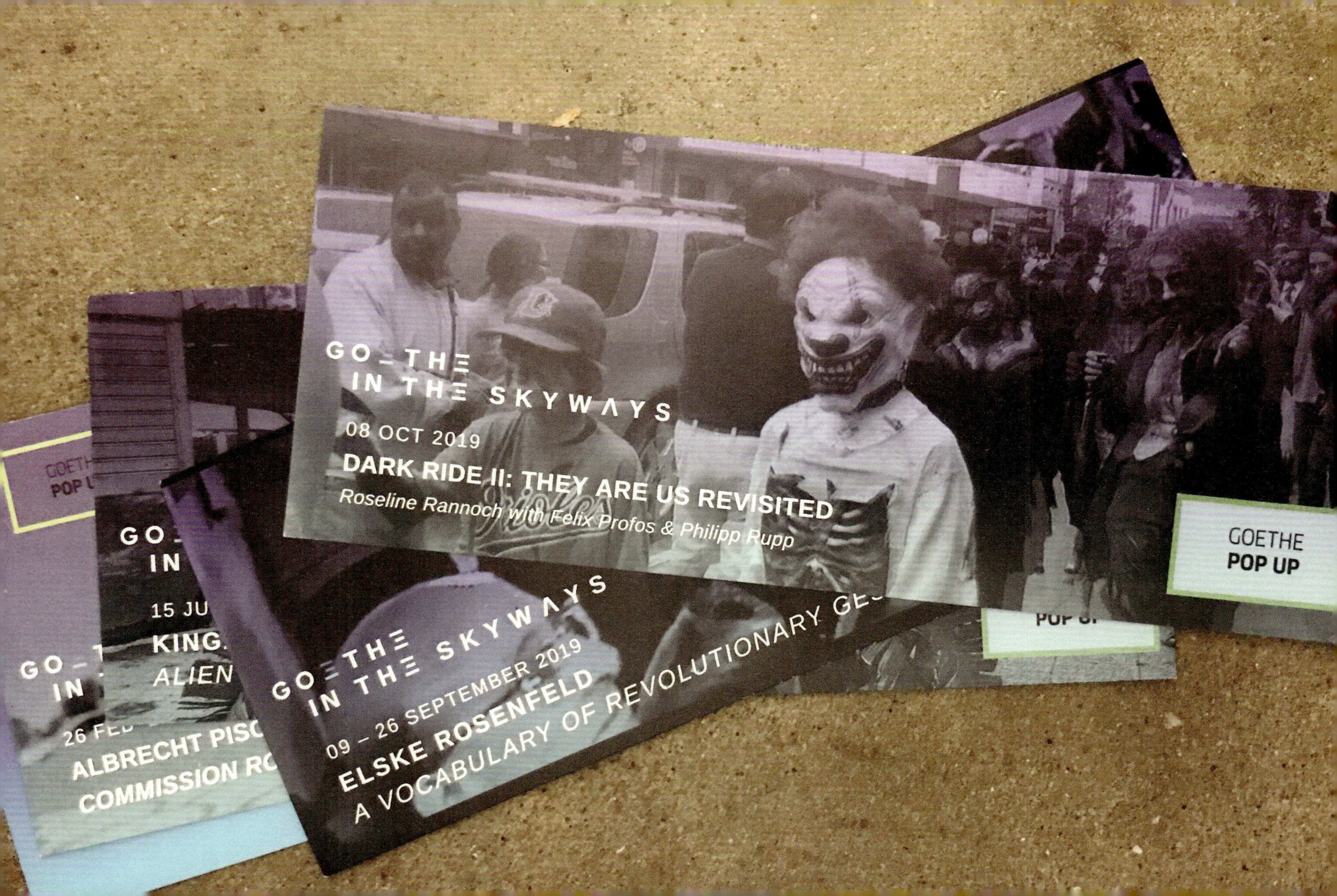

GO_THE
IN THE SKYWAYS
08 OCT 2019
DARK RIDE II: THEY ARE US REVISITED
Roseline Rannoch with Felix Profos & Philipp Rupp
GOETHE
POP UP

GO_THE
IN THE SKYWAYS
09 – 26 SEPTEMBER 2019
ELSKE ROSENFELD
A VOCABULARY OF REVOLUTIONARY

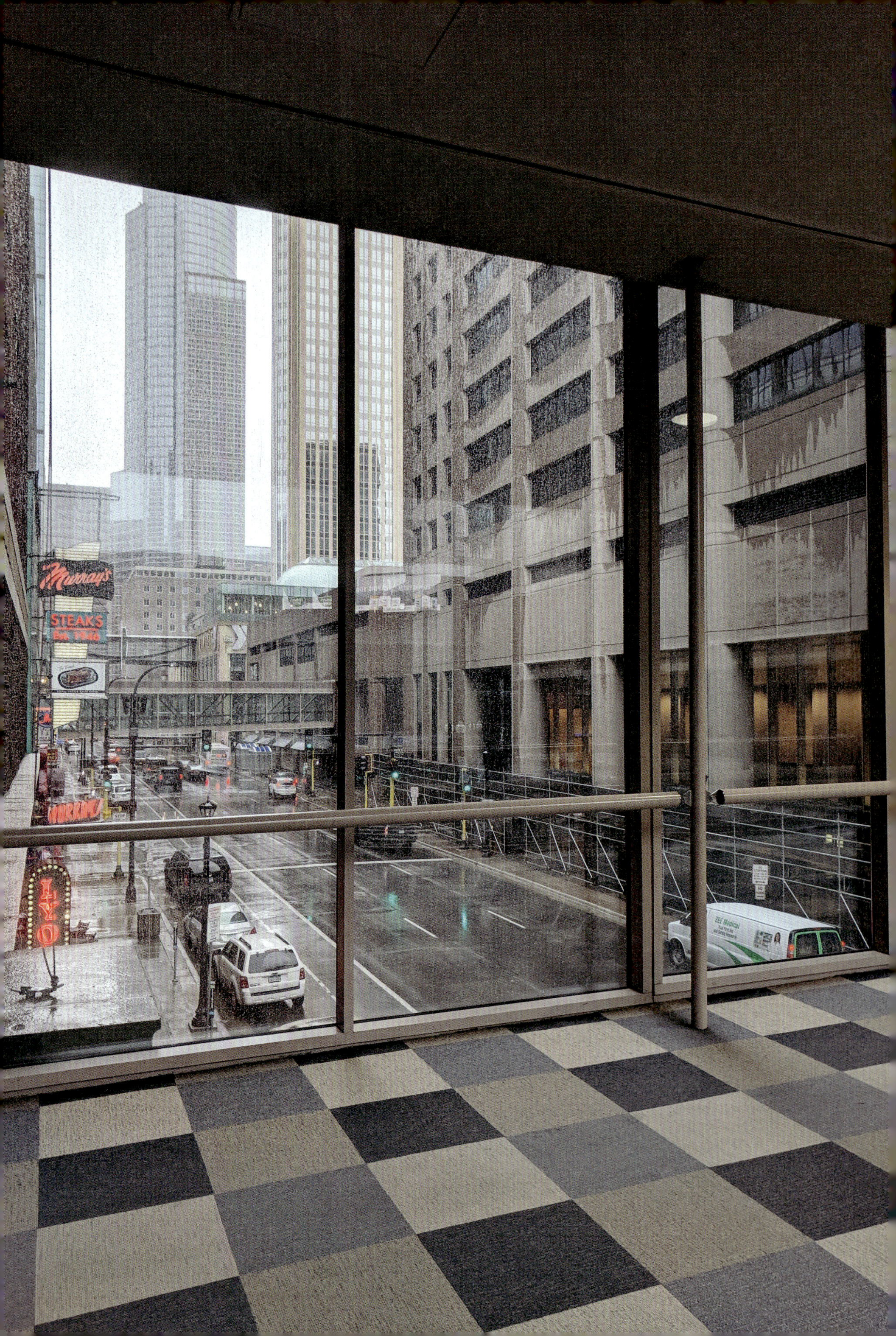
Murray's
STEAKS

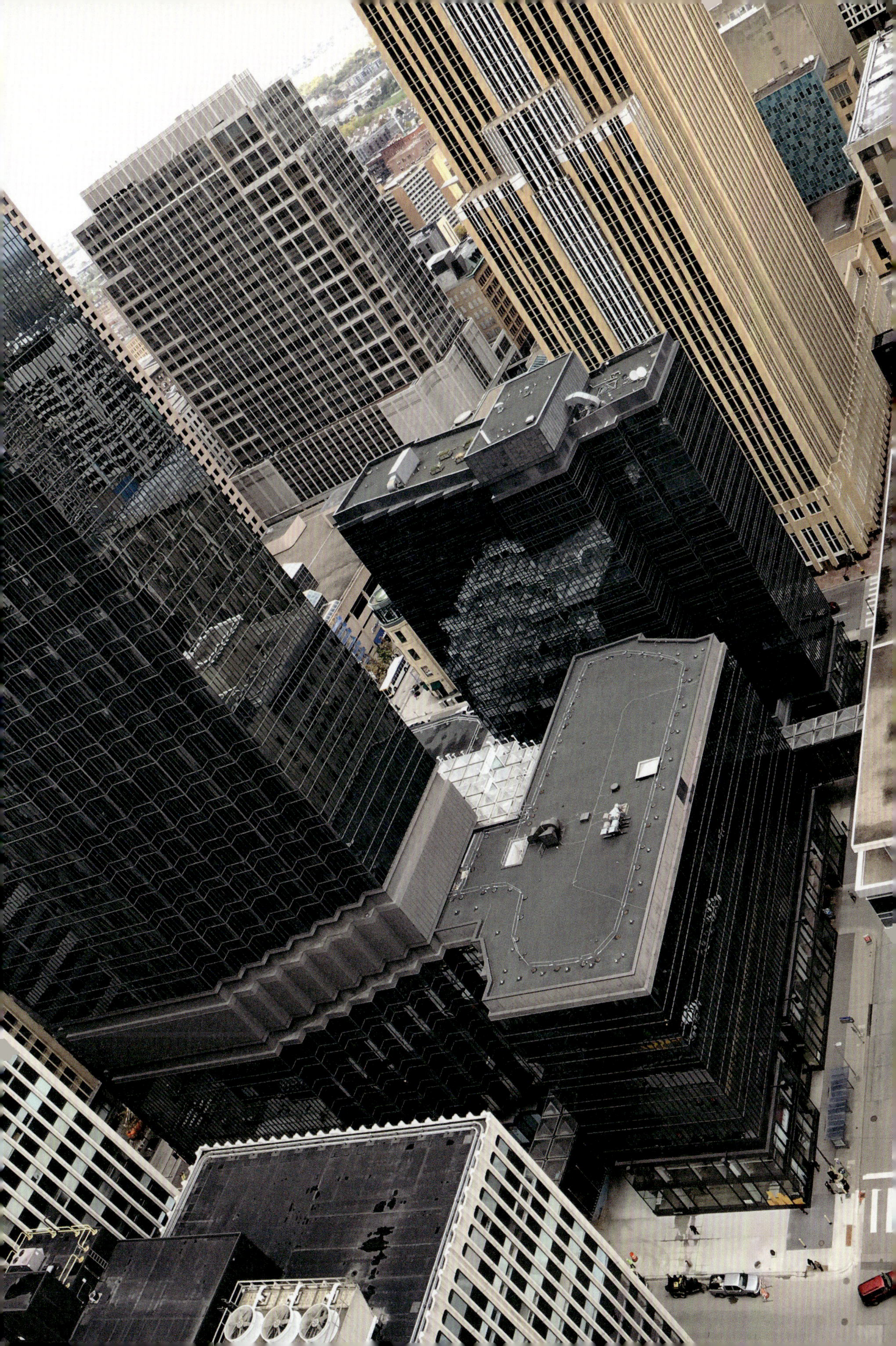

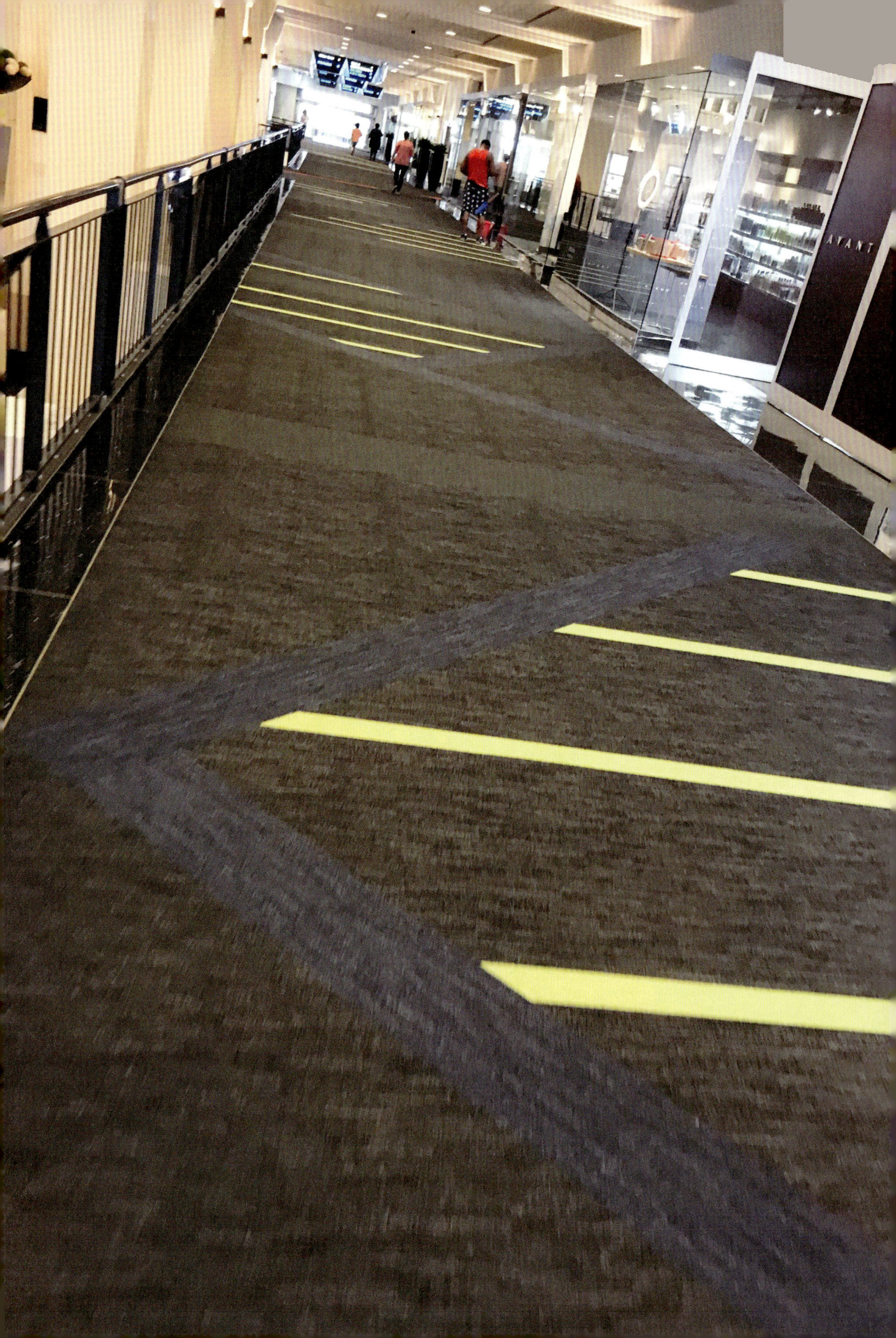
AVANT

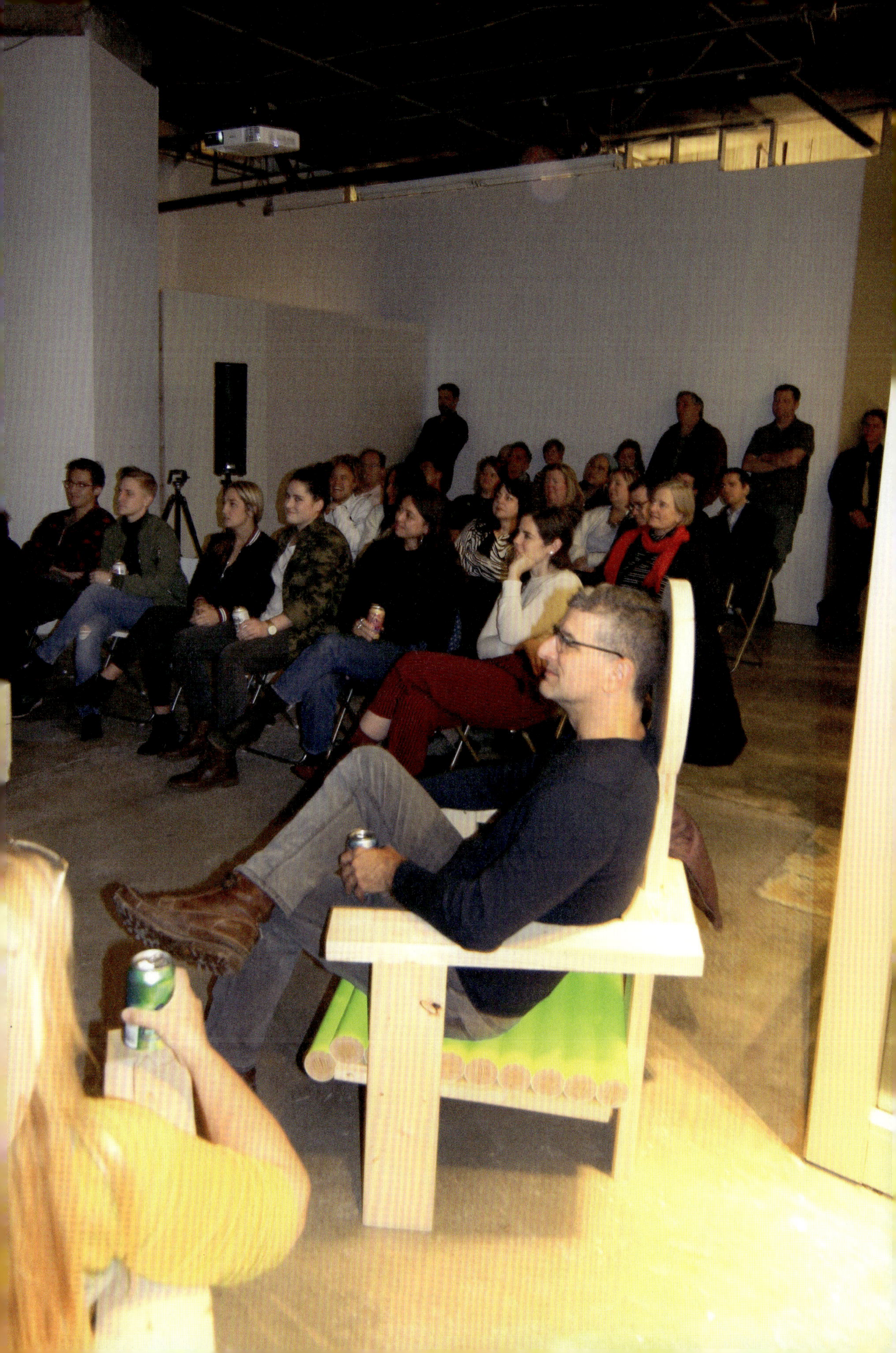

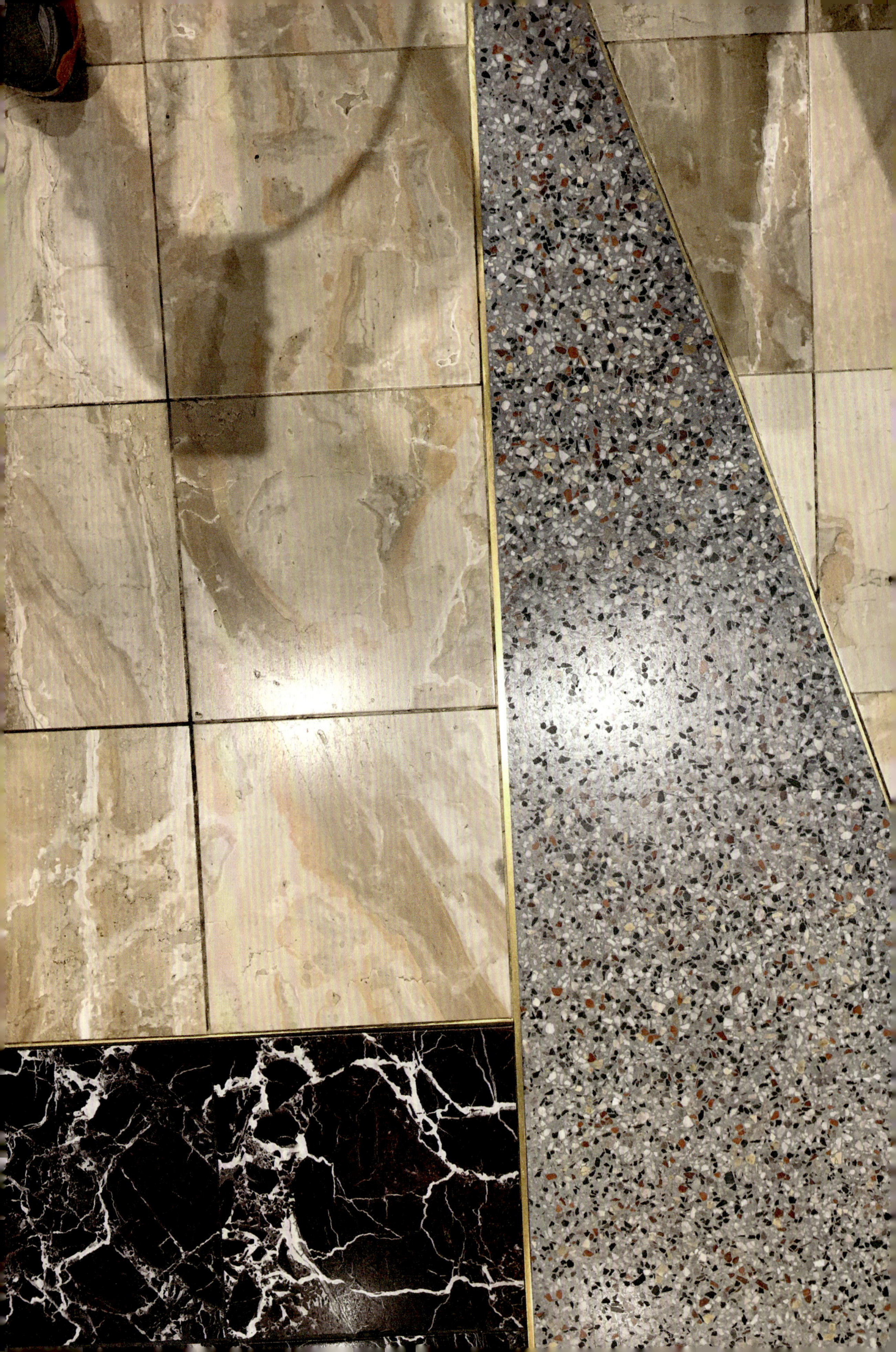

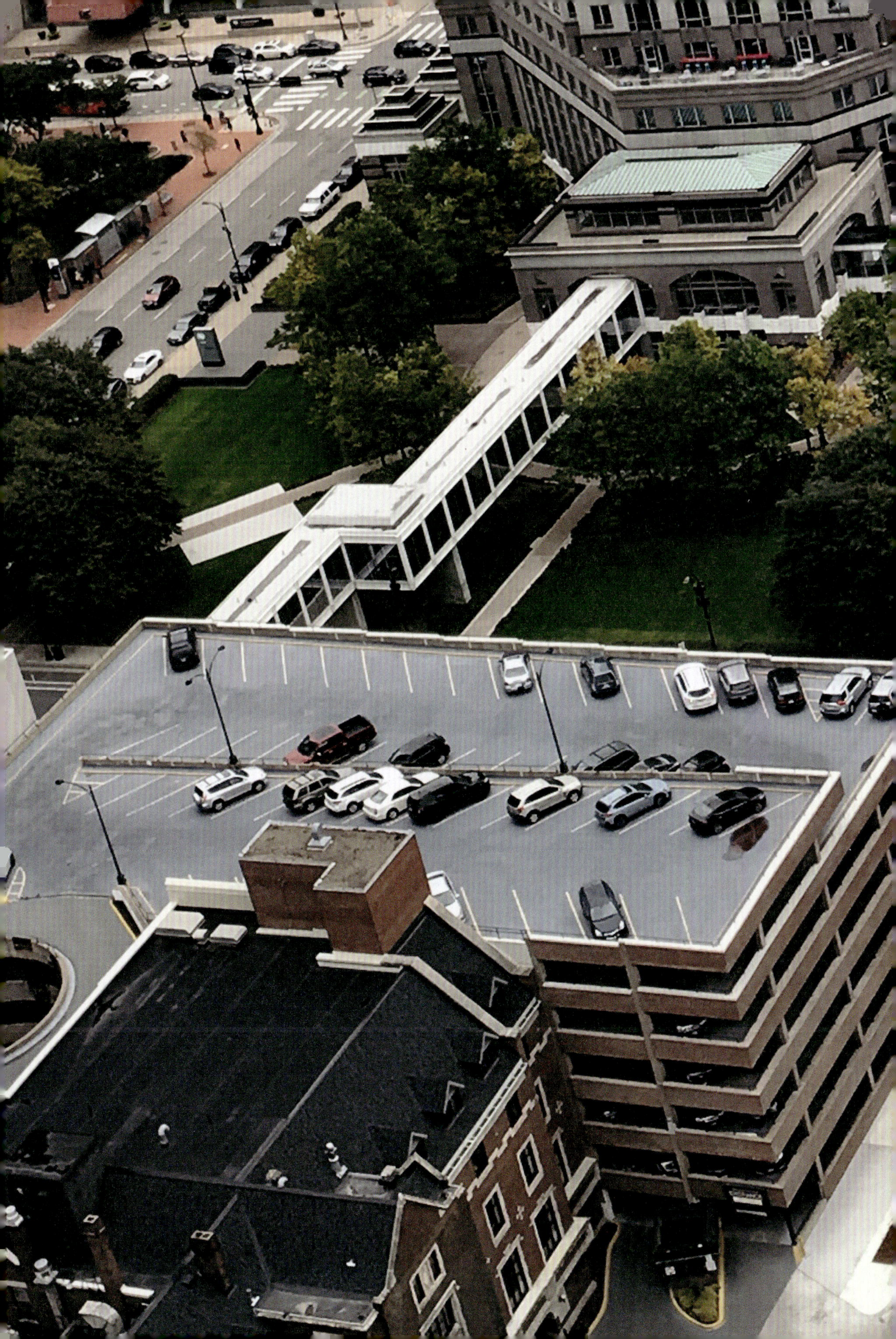

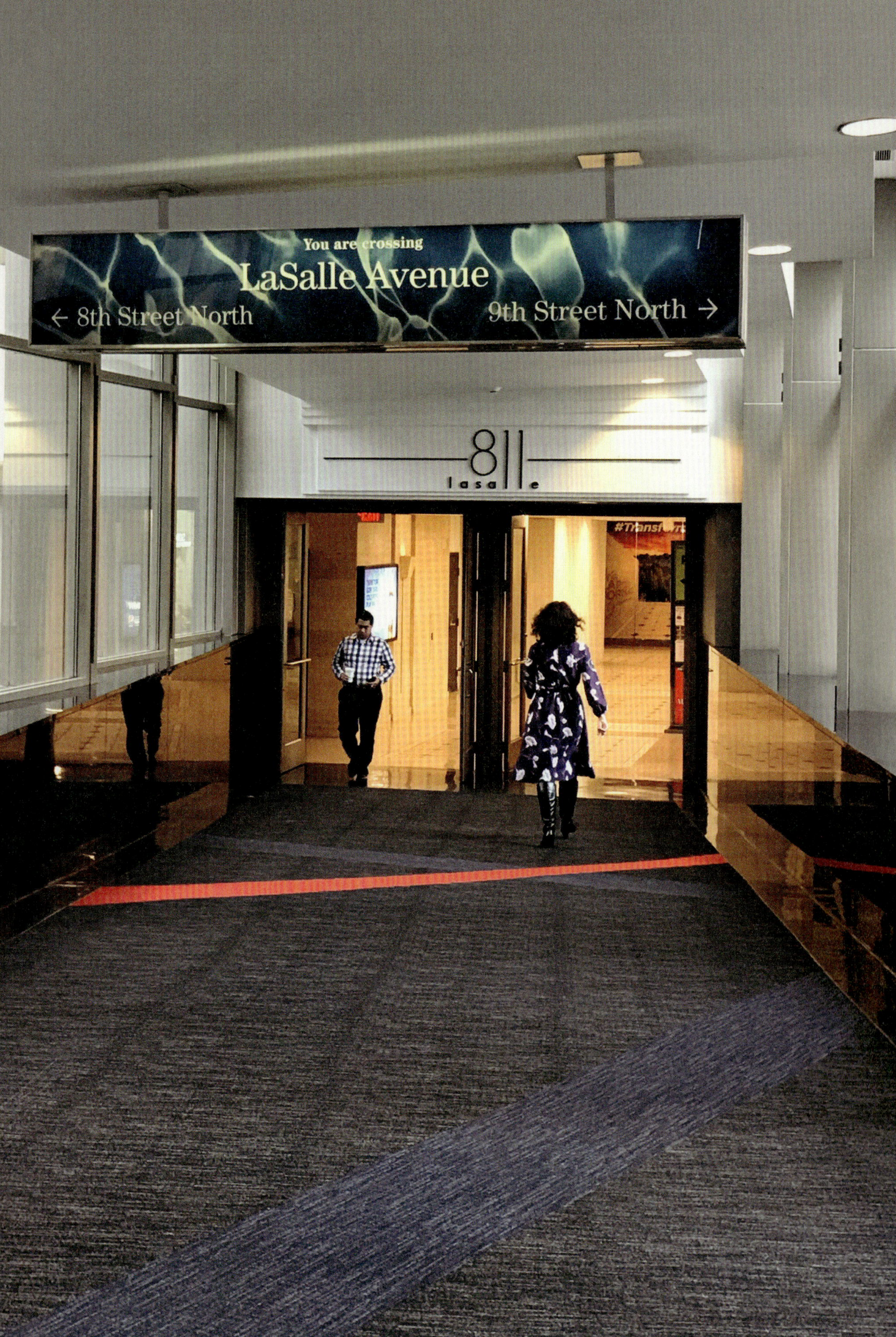
You are crossing
LaSalle Avenue
← 8th Street North
9th Street North →
811
lasalle

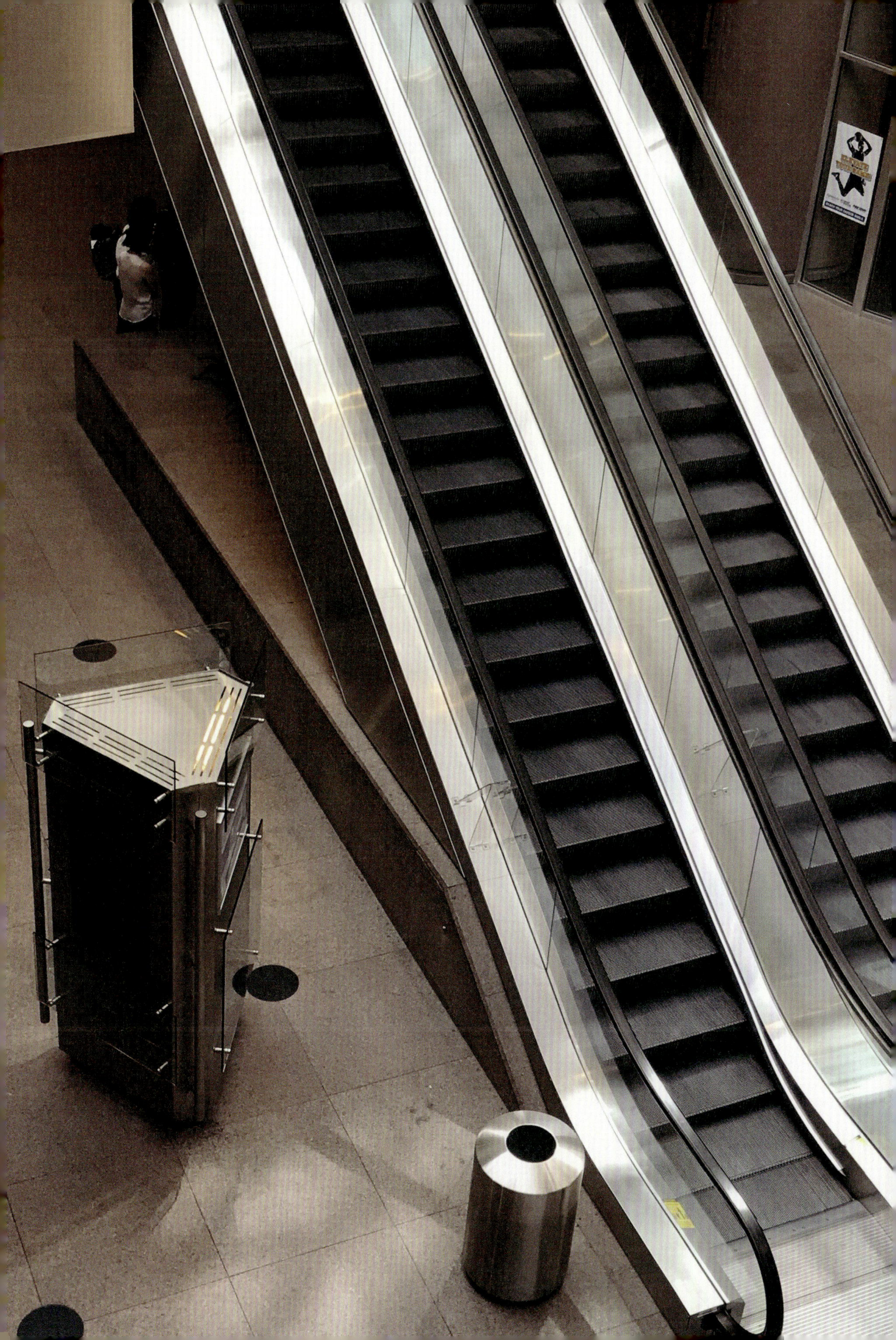

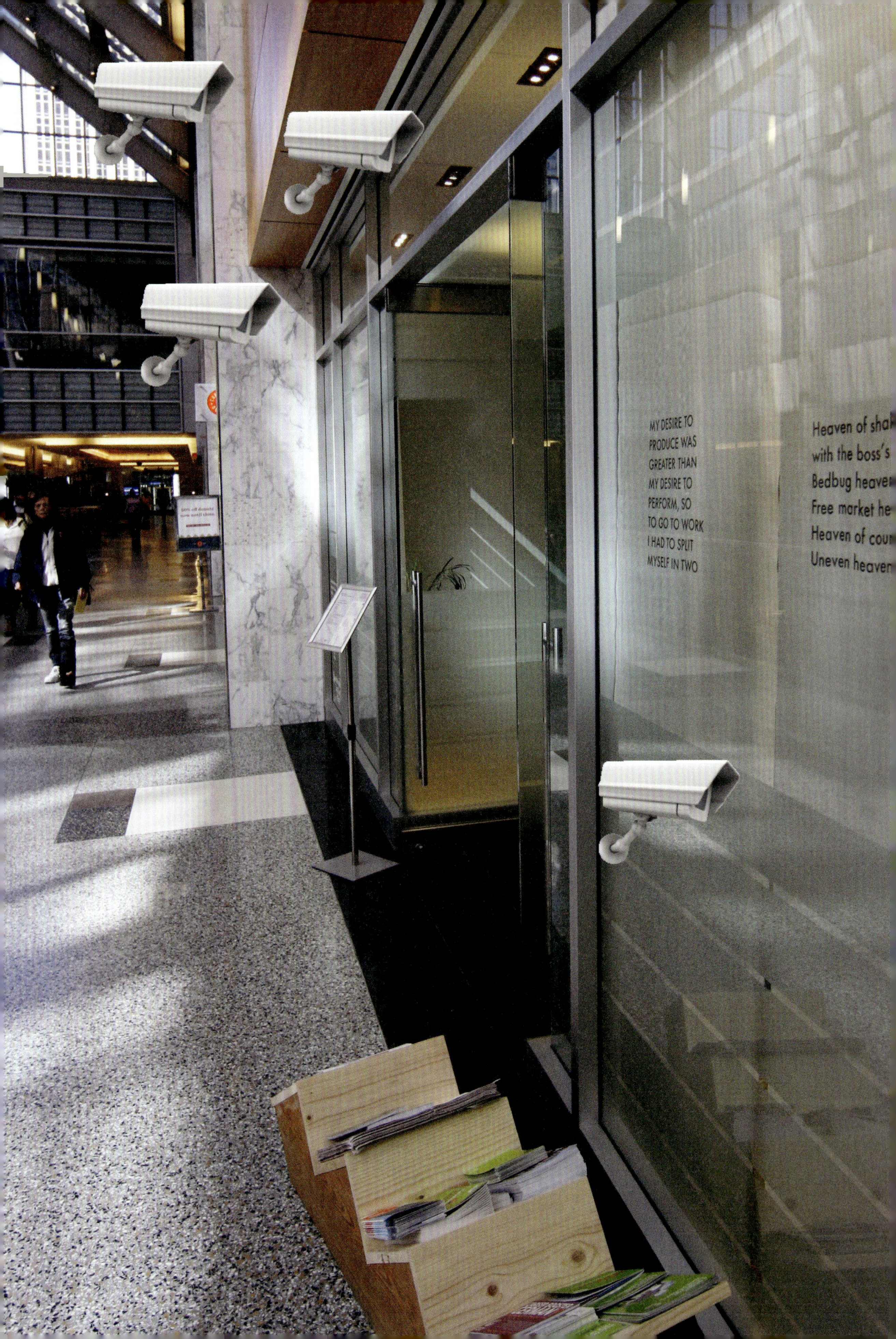
MY DESIRE TO
PRODUCE WAS
GREATER THAN
MY DESIRE TO
PERFORM, SO
TO GO TO WORK
I HAD TO SPLIT
MYSELF IN TWO

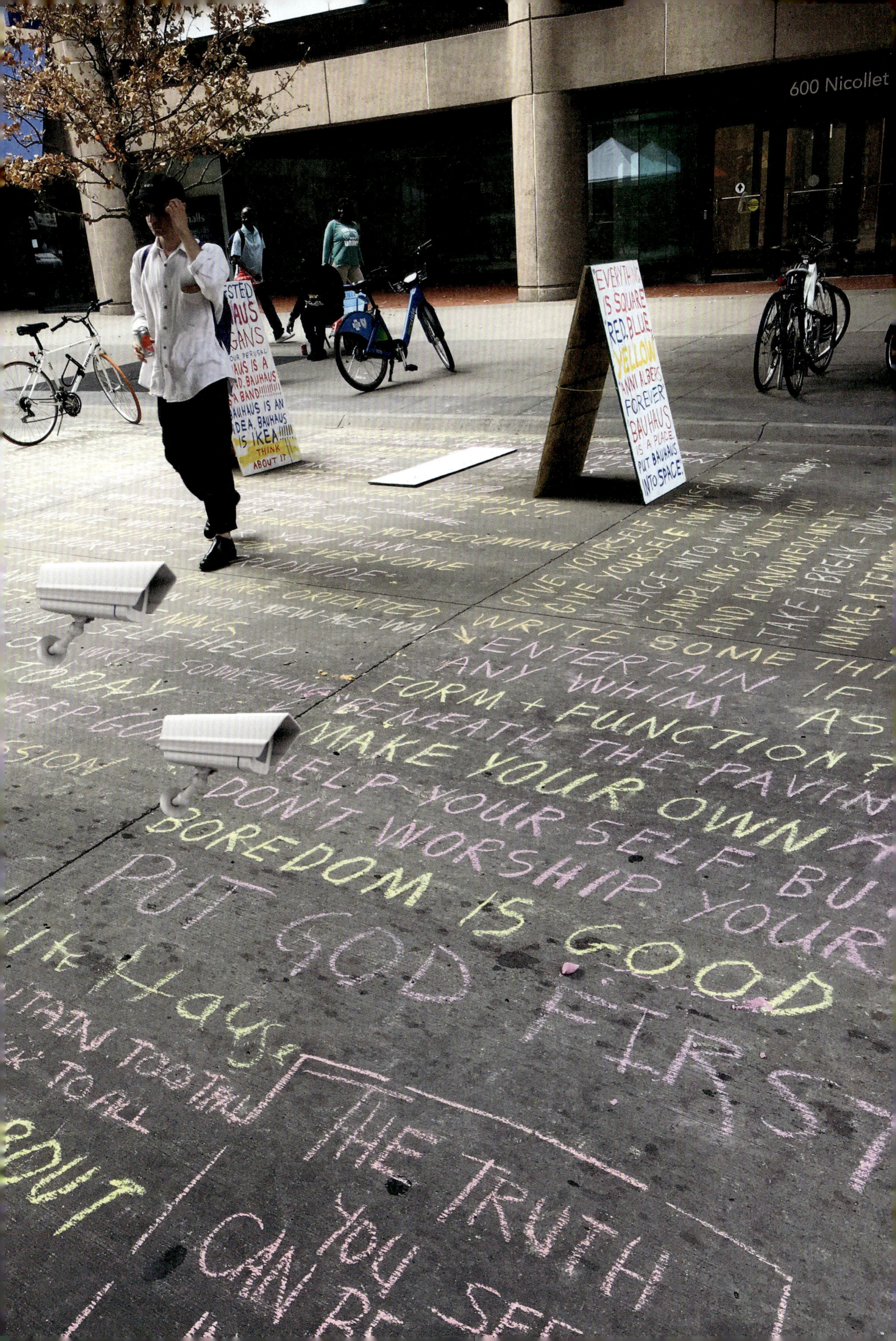
600 Nicollet
IS SQUARE
RED, BLUE,
YELLOW
ANNI ALBERS
FOREVER
BAUHAUS
IS A PLACE
PUT BAUHAUS
INTO SPACE!
BAUHAUS IS AN
IDEA. BAUHAUS
IS IKEA!!!!
THINK
ABOUT IT
GIVE YOURSELF PERMISSION
GIVE YOURSELF AWAY
SAMPLING IS MUTATION
TAKE A BREAK
FORM + FUNCTION?
MAKE YOUR OWN
BOREDOM IS GOOD
PUT GOD FIRST
THE TRUTH
YOU

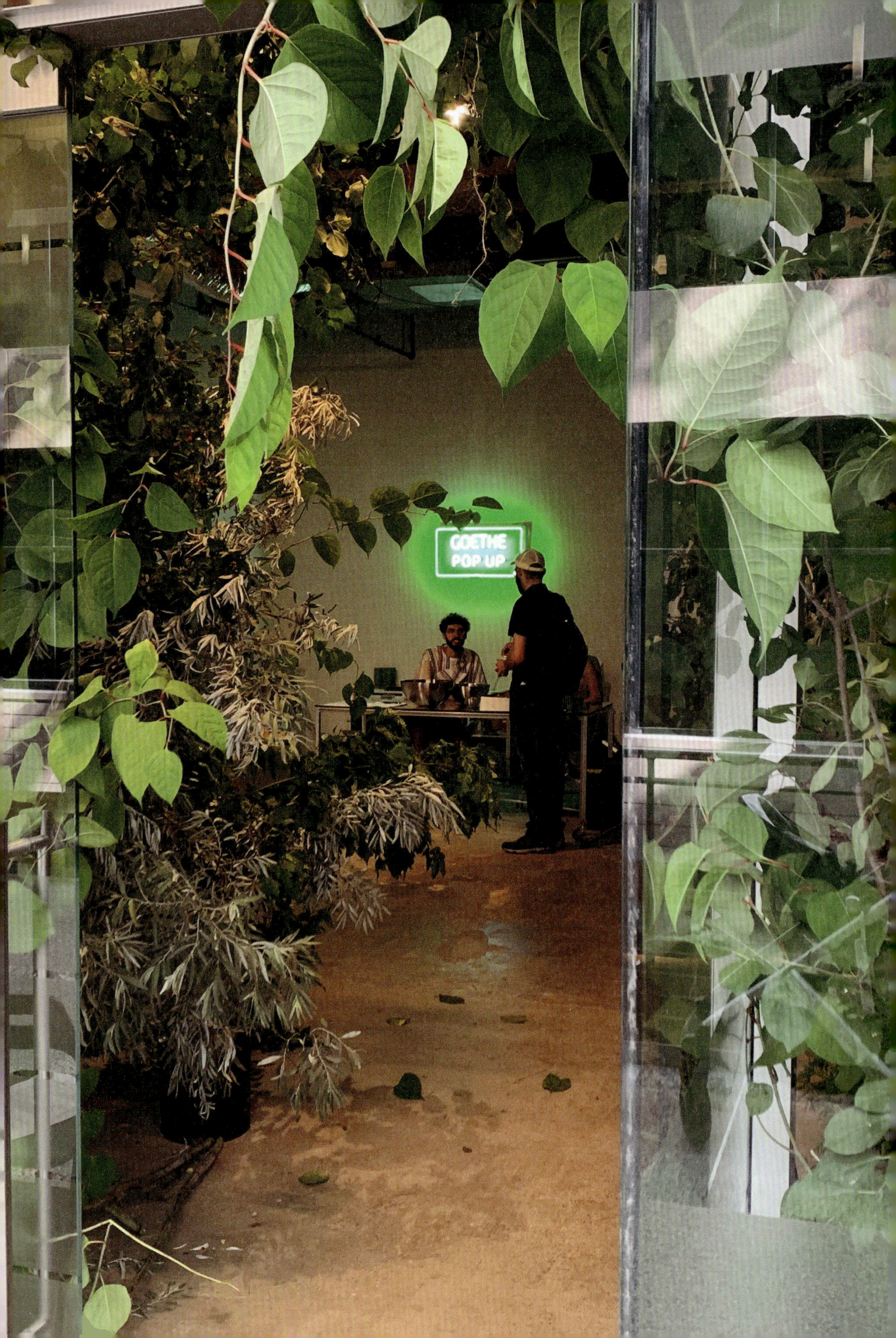
GOETHE
POP UP

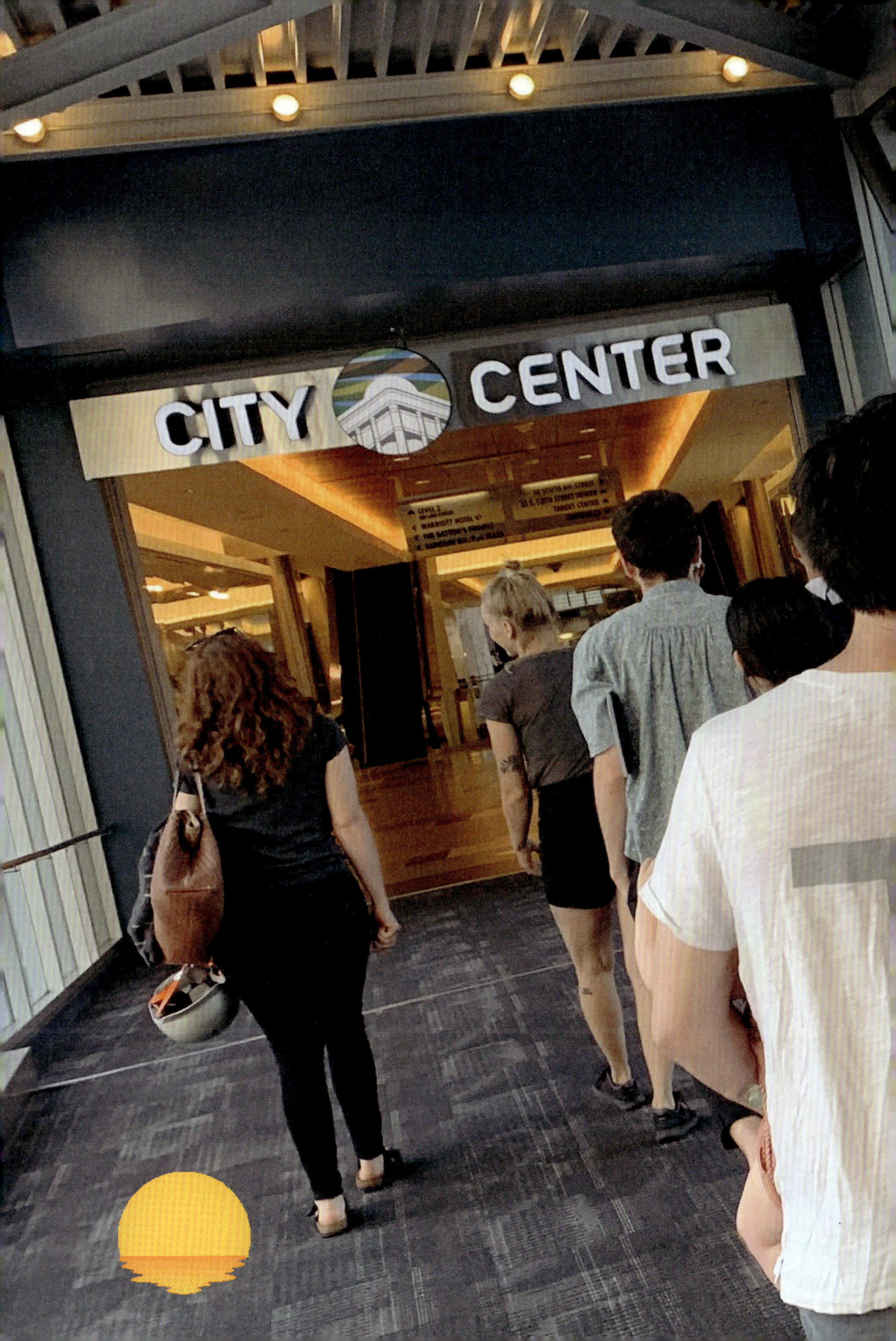
CITY CENTER

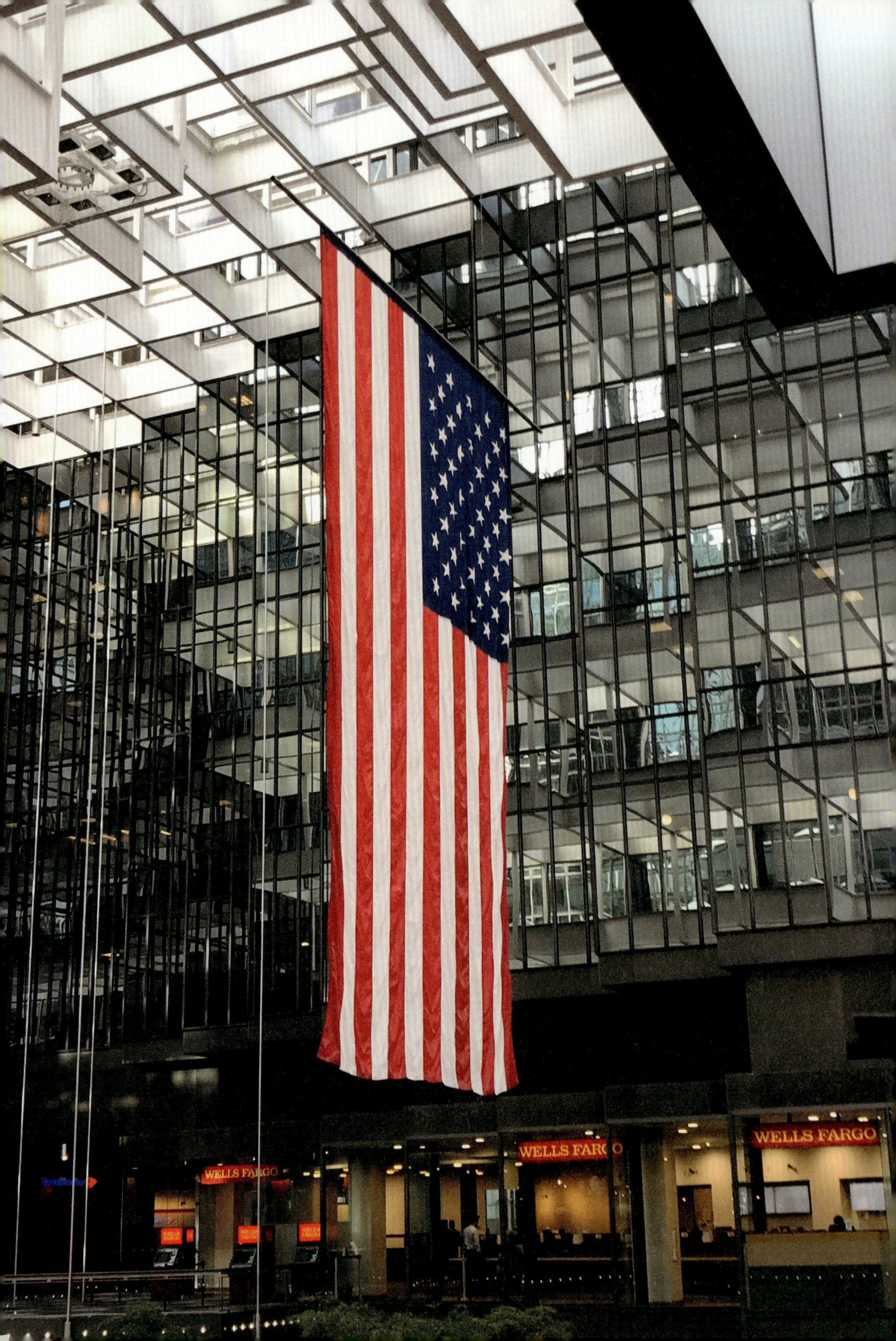
WELLS FARGO
WELLS FARGO
WELLS FARGO

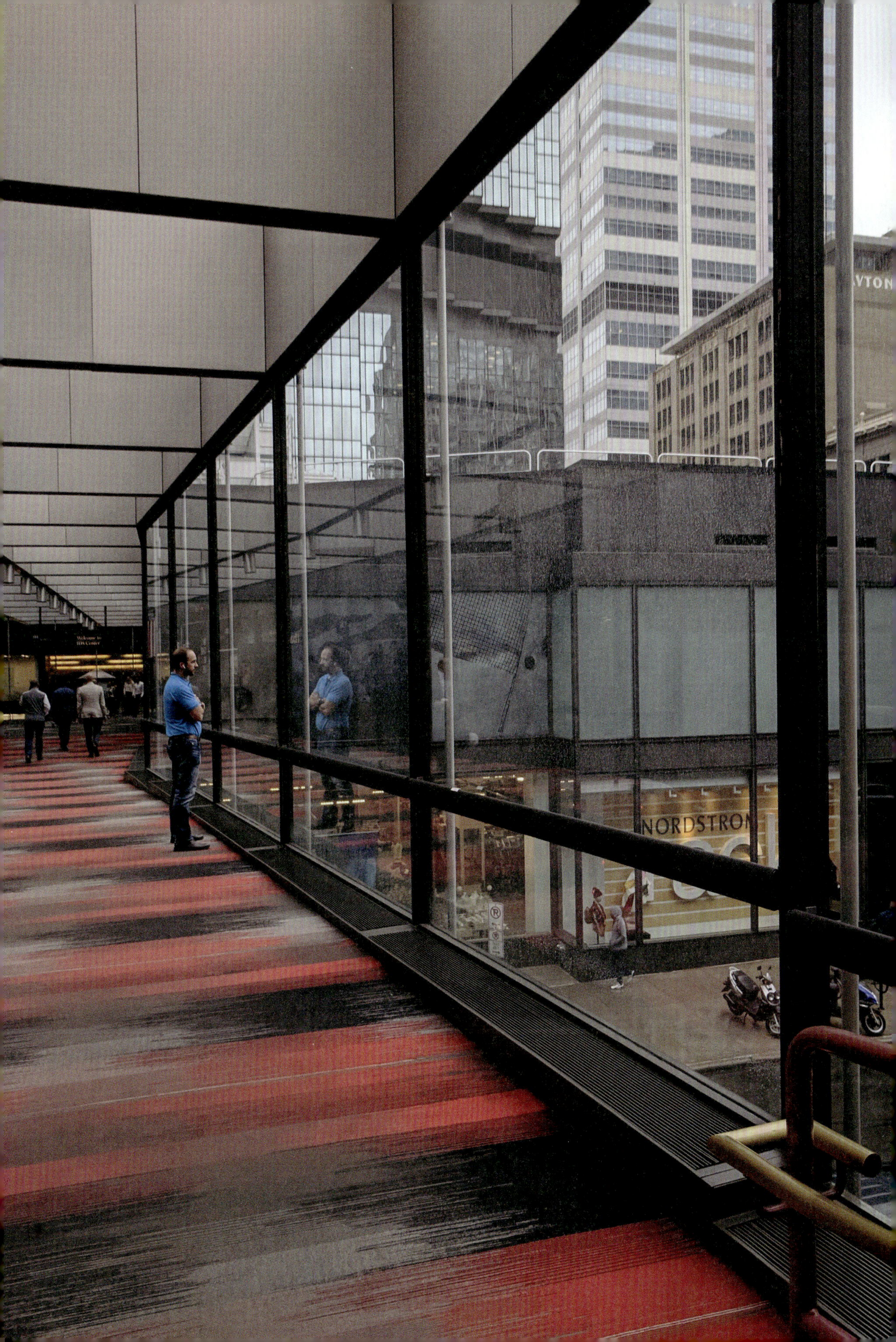
NORDSTROM

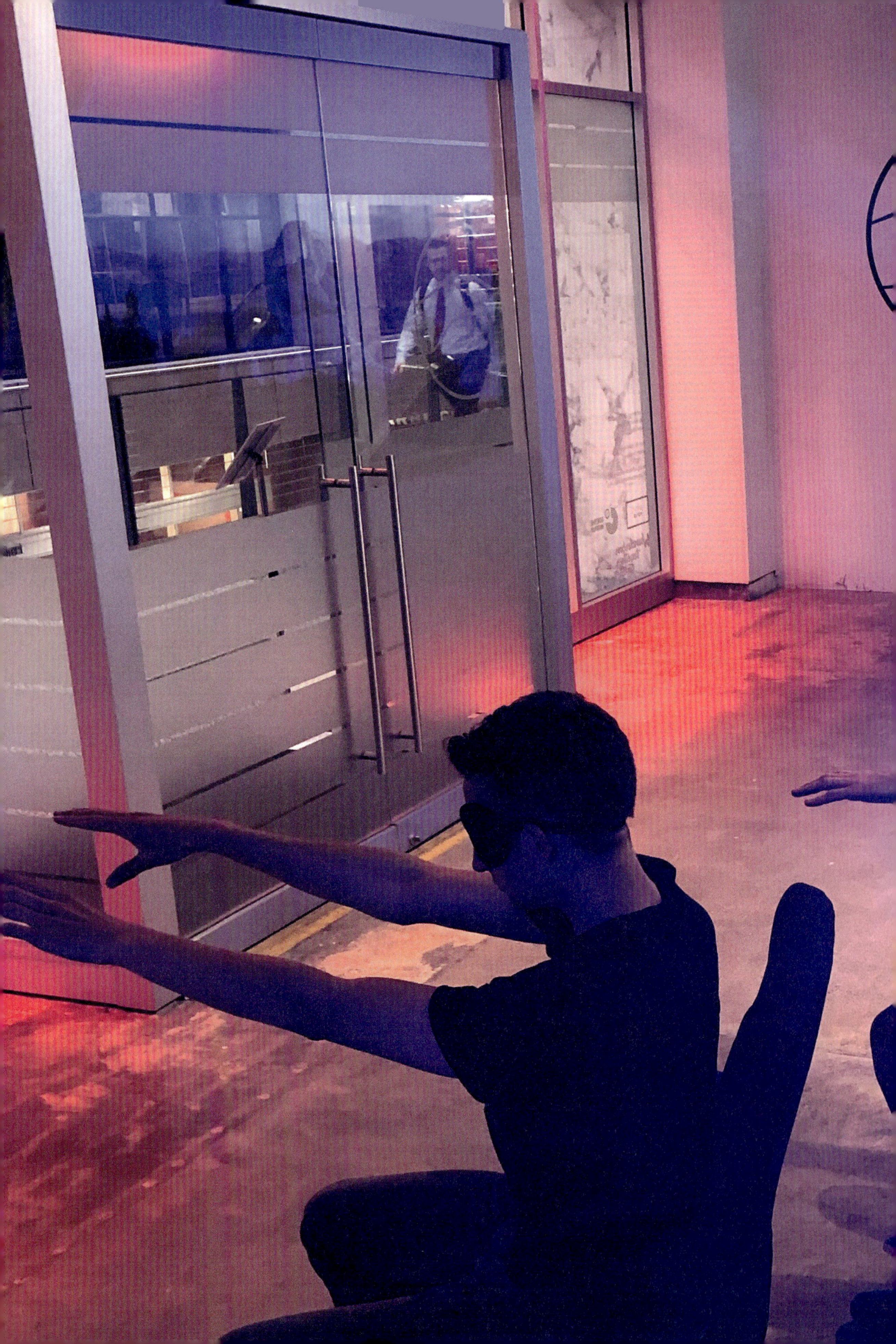

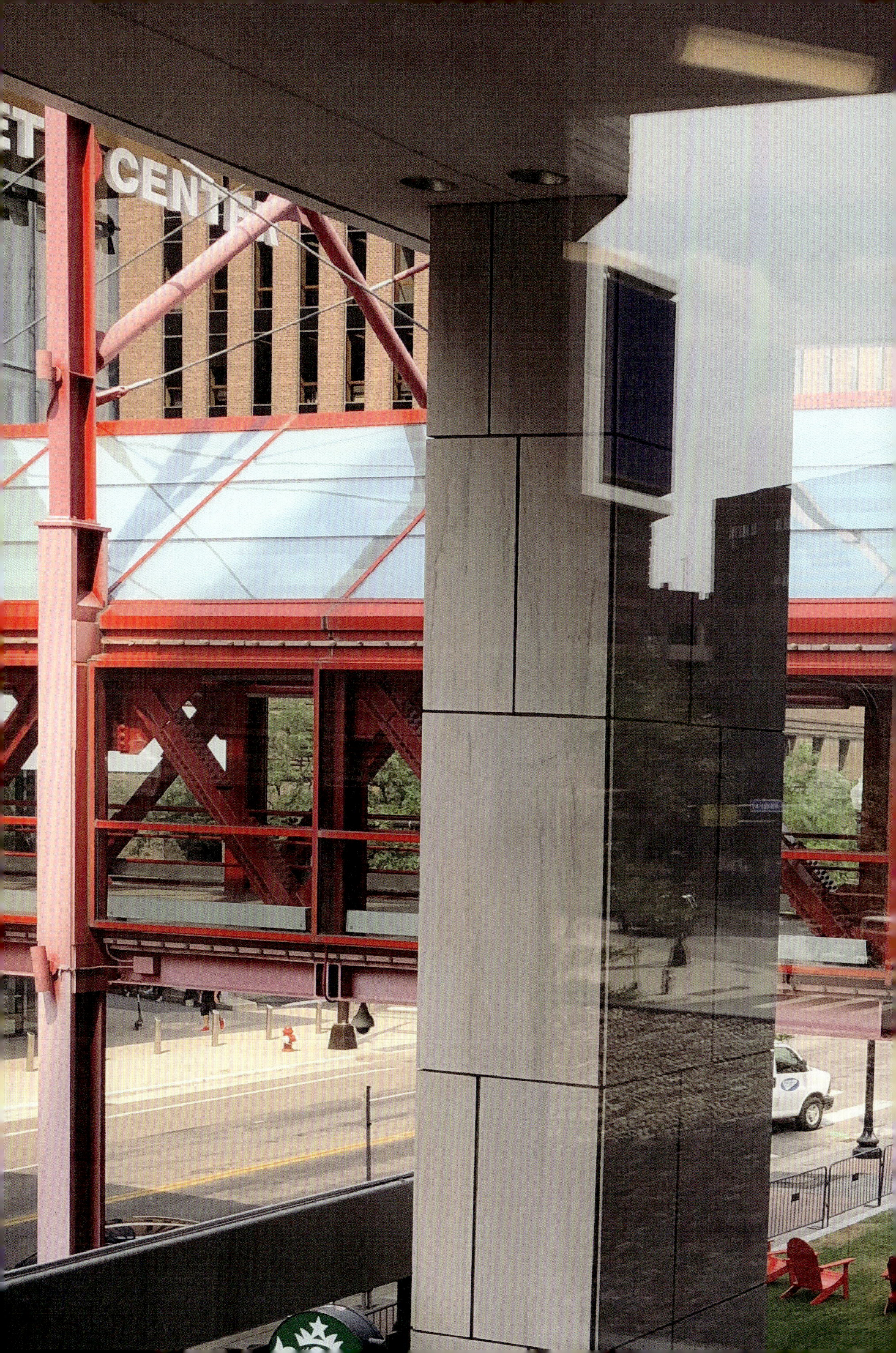
CENTER

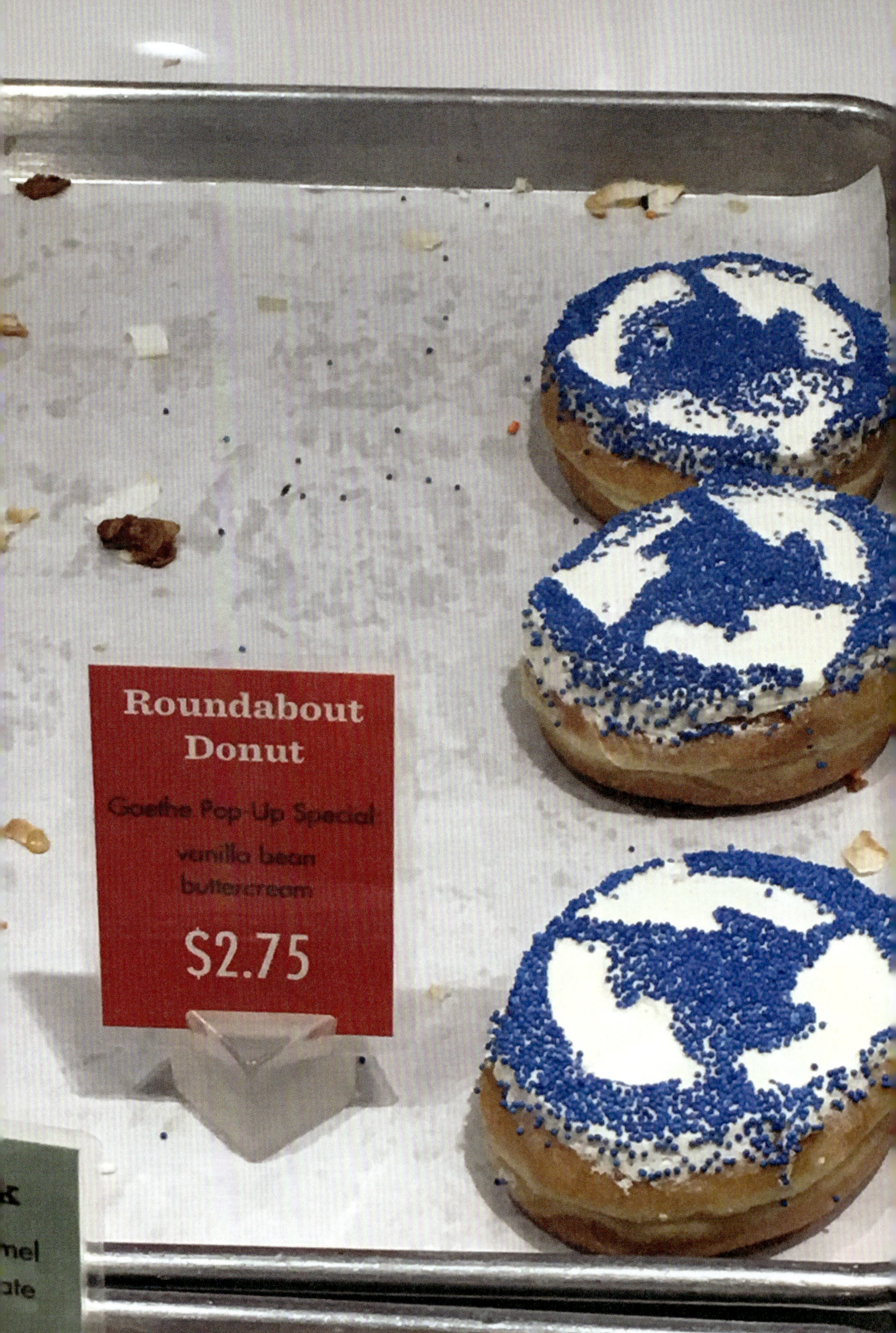
Roundabout
Donut
Goethe Pop Up Special
vanilla bean
buttercream
$2.75

Content

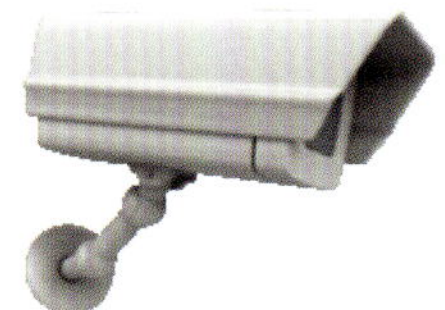

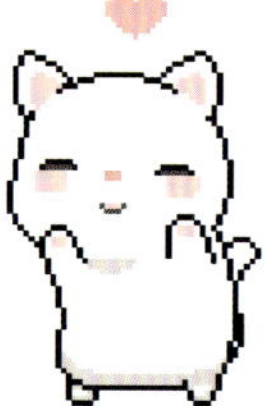

Foreword

Sandra Teitge

<u>Polar vortex 2019: eight dead as Arctic air spreads across midwest</u>

In a rare move, the US Postal Service appeared to temporarily set aside its credo that "neither snow nor rain … nor gloom of night" would stop its work: it halted deliveries from parts of the Dakotas through Ohio.

Andrew Orrison, a meteorologist with the service, said that some of the coldest wind chills were recorded in International Falls, Minnesota, at –55F (–48C). Even the south pole was warmer, with an expected low of –24F (–31C) with wind chill.

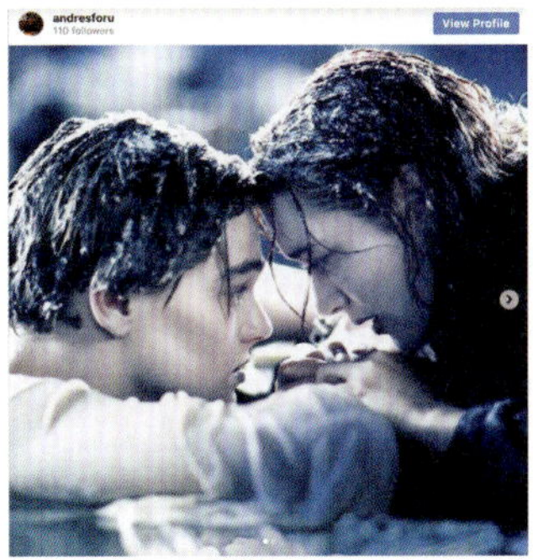

Some people shared pictures of their pet's multi-layered winter outfits, and reminded people to bring pets inside.[1]

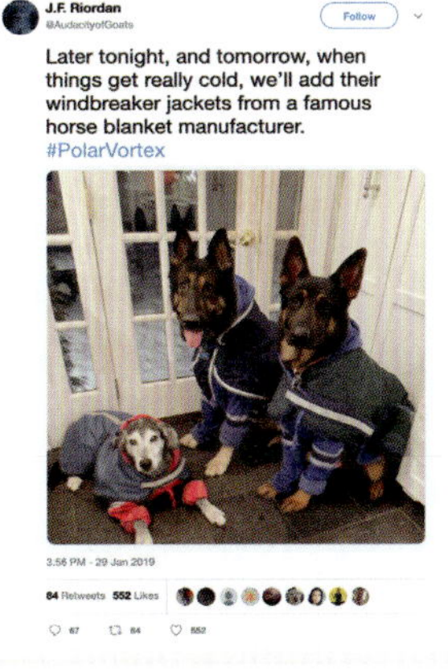

Welcome to Minneapolis.

1. Jessica Glenza,"Polar vortex 2019: eight dead as Arctic air spreads across midwest," *The Guardian*, 30 January 2019, retrieved from https://www.theguardian.com/us-news/2019/jan/30/polar-vortex-us-weather-latest-temperatures-midwest-east (photos added by author).

Thank God for the skyways.[2]

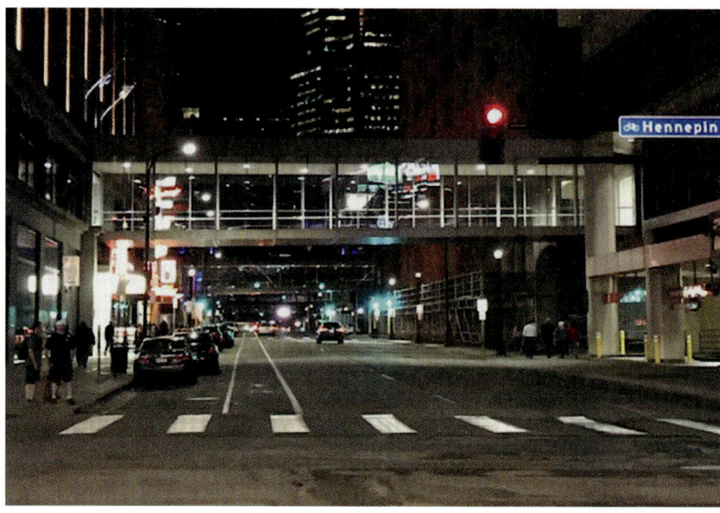

When tasked with finding a space for the Goethe Pop Up Minneapolis I wanted it to be in the skyways for different reasons: its central location; its corporate environment, which would attract a different public than the obvious artistic-cultural scene; its ambiguous nature between public and private. Perceived and used as public space but completely in private hands, the skyways embody so-called public life in the U.S., both within politics and economics, as well as within sports and culture. In the midst of this hybrid skyway situation, I wanted to create a platform for a critical consideration of the current culturally and politically contentious situation in the United States and in Europe, and to examine and discuss in light of the 30th anniversary of the fall of the Berlin Wall, a renewed rise of the New Right on both sides of the Atlantic, as well as recent global migration movements.

Of course, I was also intrigued by the urbanist aspect of the skyway system within a global movement towards "parallel cities" in the 1950s and '60s. In London, the Southbank Centre, a complex of cultural projects interconnected by elevated walkways, was incrementally constructed; the final master plan for the Barbican (Estate) was completed in 1954; and the Pedway, an elevated walkway project for central London, was planned and partially built. In the U.S. and Canada, architects and city planners like Victor Gruen and Vincent Ponte experimented with above ground and underground plans for "parallel downtowns" initially promoting pedestrian separation to create more active and socially-oriented urban centers. Atlanta, Cincinnati, Dallas, Calgary, and Montreal were all equipped with parallel walkway systems in subsequent years. In the following decades, these ideas would spread to Asia, particularly Hong Kong and Singapore, and other parts of the world.[3]

2. The Minneapolis Skyway System is an 18-km long indoor artificial gangway and pedestrian bridge network constructed in the 1960s, essentially designed to avoid the bitter cold of Minnesotan winters.
3. Vincent James and Jennifer Yoos, *Parallel Cities: The Multilevel Metropolis*, ed. Andrew Bauvelt (Minneapolis: Walker Art Center, 2016), pp. 63–65.

I had first discovered the Minneapolis Skyway System in the fall of 2015 when I was living in Minneapolis / St. Paul for the first time and running the artist residency FD13. The artist in residency, Julia Kouneski, and I were intrigued by the skyways and decided to organize her performance in one of them. Subsequently, we spent hours in the skyway system trying to find one that would work for her performance, getting lost, getting confused, becoming more and more obsessed (only me). Coincidentally, the one we ended up choosing was the one belonging to the Churchill apartment building where I would live three years later and, as their slogan goes, "where the river meets the skyway." [4]

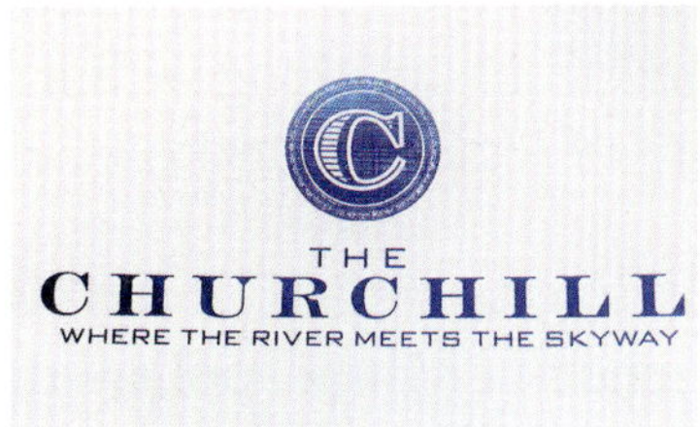

Through the performance, I also met my future colleague, Sarah Petersen, who performed with Julia Kouneski that day.

Do you believe in fate? [5]

Three years later, on October 8th, 2018, the Goethe Pop Up Minneapolis *Goethe in the Skyways* opened.

> "...from now on, it is allowed to dance at demonstrations."
> —Heiner Müller, 4 November 1989

The general approach of the program was to create cultural exchange between mostly Berlin and Minneapolis-based artists, musicians, poets, et al. Because a public in a city like Minneapolis is generated via personal relationships rather than (anonymous) curiosity I selected artists or artist projects that call for collaborators or participants, either within the research or as an inherent part of the project. This broader network of Goethe "agents" naturally attracted a larger and more diverse public that was radically different from one event to the next, primarily due to the shifting nature of the artistic projects.

Most projects involved a considerable number of local protagonists. Franziska Pierwoss filmed three Minnesotan families over the length of several days, one extremely liberal mother-daughter duo, one typically progressive Minnesotan St. Paul family, and one conservative Christian family with five children living

4. When you ask one of the many Indians stranded in Minneapolis who live at the Churchill why it seems they are all living in this building, every single one will tell you that it is because it is connected to the skyway system, that in winter you never have to go outside.
5. Although I was born in East Berlin into what was then a socialist regime hostile to practicing any kind of religion or faith that would challenge the state doctrine, I do believe in fate.

in Wisconsin. Anton Kats developed musical scores over three open studio and recording sessions with three Minneapolis-based musicians, all departing from Kats's research into ham radio. Albrecht Pischel commissioned five artists, three of whom were Minneapolis-based, to make miniature "roundabout sculptures" and pair them with a record of their choice. The sculptures were made to spin on the selected records, to, among other aspects of the project, explore the presence or absence of circular thinking in the United States. Hanne Lippard asked four Minneapolis-based artists/poets to write and also publicly read poems about the skyways on the escalators of the City Center atrium. For the symposium *Passages*, organized by Pétunia, we invited numerous Minneapolis-based designers, architects, and thinkers along with a selection of French theoreticians to discuss notions of legacy, transitions, and, of course, the skyways.

On a personal level, these relationships enabled the visiting artists to also have their own independent experience of Minneapolis—the city of Prince and First Ave, where "Purple Rain" was filmed; the city of the oldest fully enclosed, climate-controlled shopping mall (Southdale Center) and also for many years the largest mall in the U.S. (the Mall of America); the city of Al's Breakfast, where Bob Dylan used to start his day; and the city of U.S. Representative Ilhan Omar, the first non-white woman elected from Minnesota, and one of the first two Muslim women (along with Rashida Tlaib of Michigan) to serve in Congress.

> "I would like to see a blue shrub, or a pink tree, or a green sky … something out of order, a coconut tree, the Northern lights, sun in the middle of the night."
>
> —Brigitte Reimann, *Franziska Linkerhand*

Another main focus of the program was on language and communication, in a time when truth has become hyper-subjective and, in fact, almost entirely irrelevant. As Rudy Giuliani, the former mayor of New York and now President Trump's lawyer, simply puts it: "Truth isn't truth"—anymore, one could add.

The invited artists responded in different ways to this seemingly elastic truth, which characterizes the socio-political drama that has dominated U.S. and European politics and therefore public life since the last elections using spoken-word formats like reality TV, sound works, concerts, readings, performances, walks, workshops, and posters. With Christine Sun Kim, we created a billboard for outside and an equivalent banner for the skyway space that calls for more visibility for those who are deaf; Liz Magic Laser, Cori Kresge, and Hanna Novak offered workshops around our relationship to the screen; FRZNTE and DJ Kebap Benzin invited the public to a *Hyper Hyper Helium Karaoke* party; Kinga Kielczynska led a walking tour through the skyways coating the existing architecture with a fictitious layer of nature; Elske Rosenfeld presented her research on what she calls "revolutionary gestures"; and Roseline Rannoch adopted the figure of the zombie and the extremely popular phenomenon of the Zombie Pub Crawl for her performance *Dark Ride II: They are us revisited*, our last farewell to the skyways.

This range between high and low culture, popular media, and discursive panels, was of utmost importance, not only because it aligns with the mission of the Goethe-Institut and the broader context of this Goethe Pop Up, but also because I wanted to attract the masses and not the cultivated elite, addressing a separation that is even more pronounced in the U.S. than it is in Europe.

I'm extremely grateful to the people who made this year possible, first and foremost to Petra Roggel, the Director of the Goethe-Institut Chicago and my boss, who trusted me with the program and always defended my ideas; to Thomas Rupprecht who kept the numbers organized, day and night; to Sarah Petersen and Daniel Shinbaum who accompanied and supported me through this year making everything happen one way or the other, often ad hoc because of the nature of the artistic projects and my frequent spontaneity; to Valérie Chartrain for consistently and elegantly lightening the path and structuring my organized chaos; to our public who curiously attended and participated in our extremely active schedule of events and helped us to create an impact and hopefully leave a trace; and to Wiley Hoard and Rio A. Teitge Hoard for everything else.

What follows is a publication that brings together a series of commissioned essays intermingled with a full compilation of all projects that make up the Goethe Pop Up Minneapolis *Goethe in the Skyways*, keeping to a strict chronological timeline of events. The programming details, including dates and specific times, further express the temporality of the grand scheme of events. To help readers gain an understanding of the context of each project, short introductory texts outline the works' origins and my thinking around each piece of the year-long program in and around the skyways.[6]

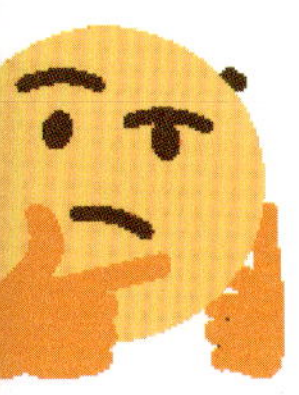

6. If you would like to know more about the artist projects, listen to the podcasts, which are in some instances conversations with the artists and in other instances an essential part of the artistic project, such as the audio for a guided walk: www.goetheintheskyways.org/podcast/.

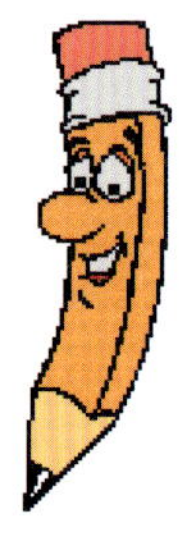
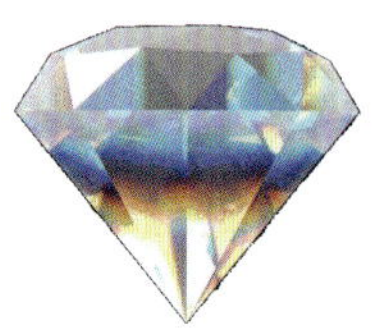
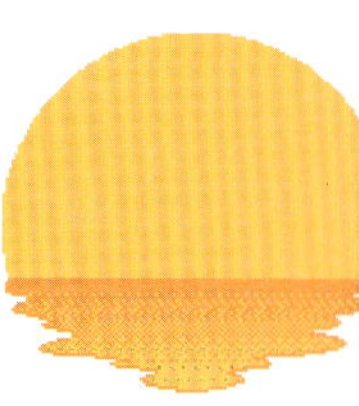
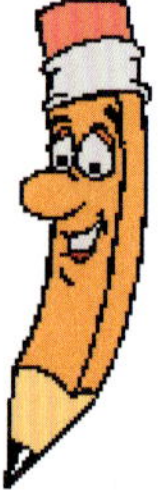
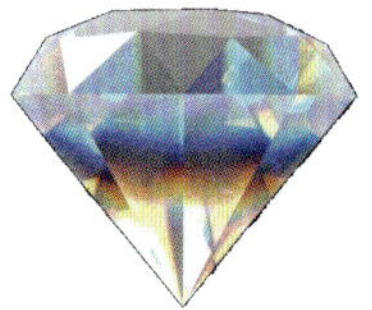
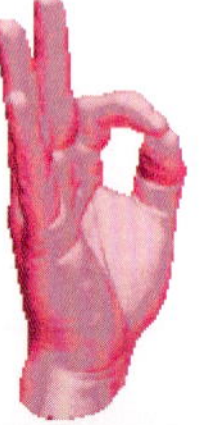

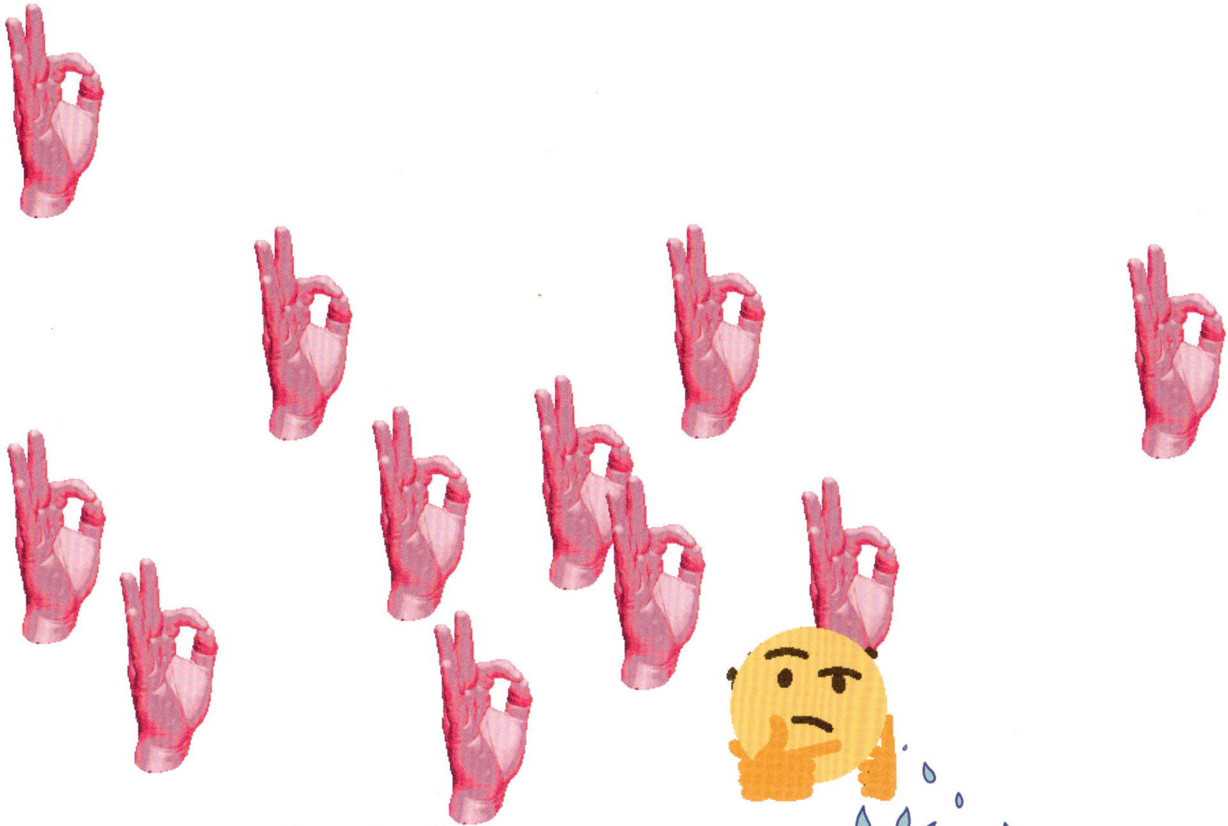

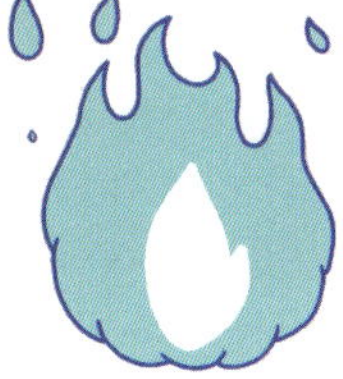

Jonas Lund
How To

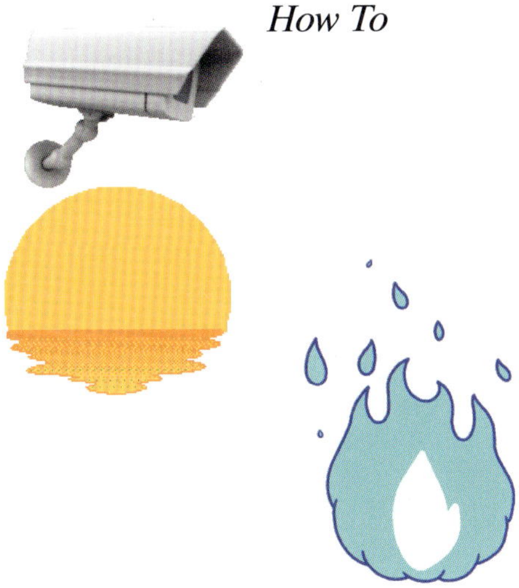

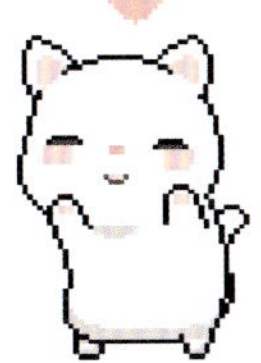

Jonas Lund

How To

October 2018 – October 2019

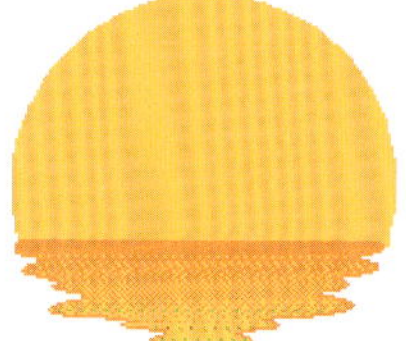

How to {Act Natural | Feel Together Alone | Confuse Someone Clearly | Choose the only Choice | Share an Open Secret | Behave Clearly Confused | Grow Smaller | Find Affordable Caviar | Have a Minor Crisis | Nearly Miss | Find Comfortable Misery | Make an Exact Estimate | Have an Unbiased Opinion | Work on Vacation | Fall Upwards | Find an Impossible Solution | Whisper Loudly | Conquest Peacefully | Be Seriously Funny}

"It is not enough to dislike a government; you need to know that others do, too."[1]

How To is an ongoing intervention on the *Goethe in the Skyways* website for the duration of the program in Minneapolis. The intervention operates on the site as an external agent, interfering with the typical flow of the visitor and presenting him/her/them with a range of interruptions—from simple questions to more intricate time-based actions—and inviting him/her/them to take a position before being able to continue. The intervention changes over the duration of the program, responds to the current, most pressing, ongoing socio-cultural developments and events, and posts targeted questions to the informed public of the website. The response and collected user behavioral data is analyzed, measured, and quantified into an ongoing analytical feedback dashboard that connects the desires and fears of the audience and guides the continuation of the intervention itself by responding to the user engagement.

"To know something is one thing, but to know it with others, know that others know it, and know that they know that you know it, … and all the way up to the top, is another thing altogether. In cognitive science it is described as common knowledge: to know that the other person knows that you know."[2]

The concept is critical in politics, as cooperation and team-building requires common knowledge. Online common knowledge, on the other hand, is difficult to create as we can't look each other in the eyes and agree to our shared common field. With social media it is even harder to tell the motivation behind people's actions. Are they state-sponsored agents, trolls, bots, or all together completely fabricated?

Taking the concept of common knowledge as a starting point, the *How To* intervention creates an ongoing feedback loop, where answers and responses from other audience members are fed back into the system and revealed to the current viewer, to make visible the divide in the potential for a shared understanding. Game mechanisms are further incorporated to encourage user participation, for example by rewarding repeat visits to the website or visits to the physical location in Minneapolis.

Drawing from previous work, such as *Critical Mass*, in which Lund converted an exhibition into a speculative space controlled by the visitors of the project's website, and *Fair Warning*, in which he created a never-ending synchronized and distributed set of probing questions directed at the audience, *How To* aims to bring together and connect the visitors of *Goethe in the Skyways* by means of disrupting the website.

1. Simon DeDeo. "The Bitcoin Paradox," *Nautilus*. Retrieved and adapted from https://getpocket.com/explore/item/the-bitcoin-paradox
2. Id.

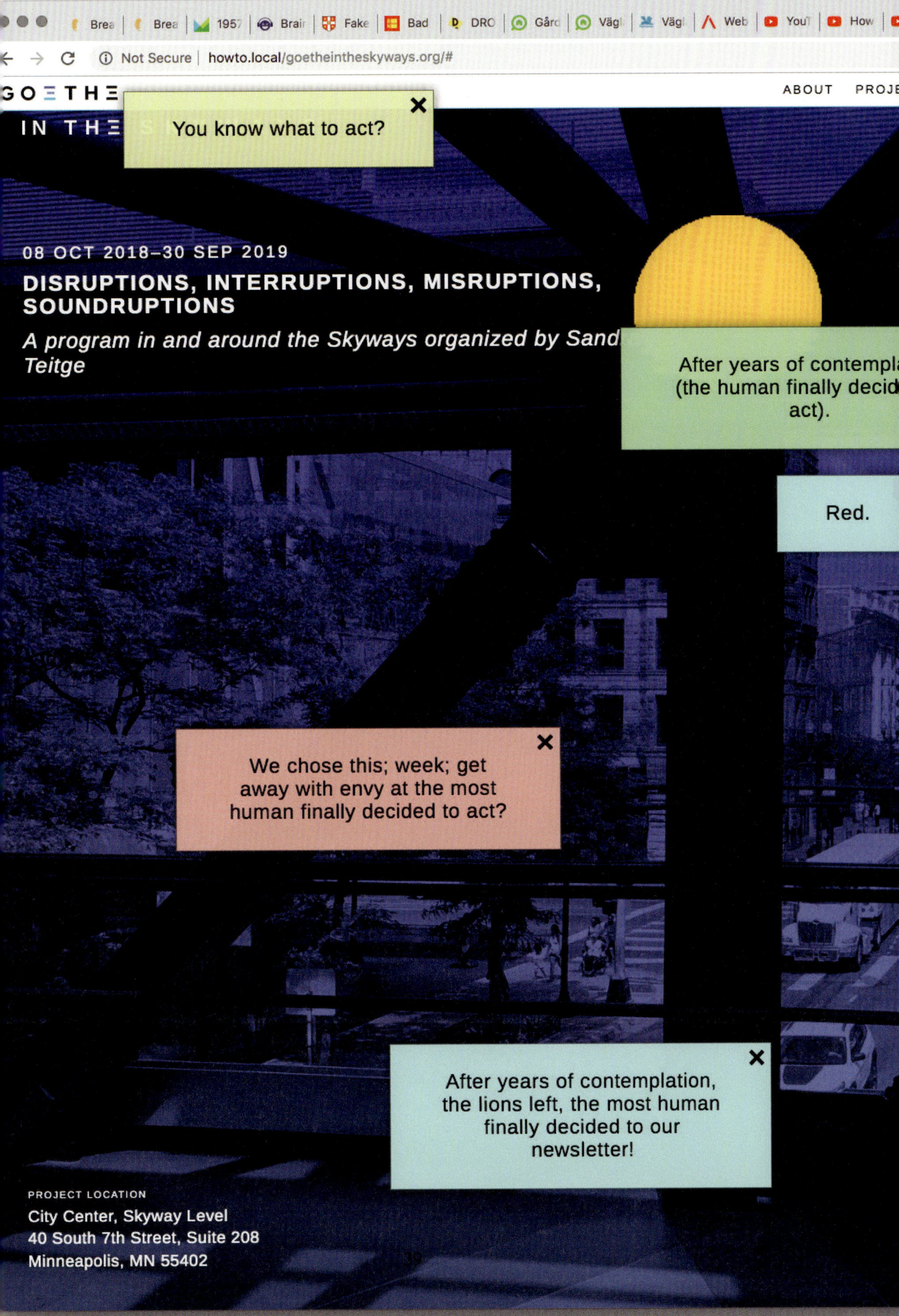

Not Secure howto.local/goetheintheskyways.org/#
GOETHE
IN THE
ABOUT
You know what to act?
08 OCT 2018–30 SEP 2019
DISRUPTIONS, INTERRUPTIONS, MISRUPTIONS, SOUNDRUPTIONS
A program in and around the Skyways organized by Sand Teitge
After years of contempl (the human finally decid act).
Red.
We chose this; week; get away with envy at the most human finally decided to act?
After years of contemplation, the lions left, the most human finally decided to our newsletter!
PROJECT LOCATION
City Center, Skyway Level
40 South 7th Street, Suite 208
Minneapolis, MN 55402

Philipp Rupp
Skyway Uniforms

Philipp Rupp

Skyway Uniforms

October 2018 – October 2019

Philipp Rupp designs outfits for the *Goethe in the Skyways* team inspired by signs and logos of surrounding skyway shops and food stands, including a map of the Minneapolis Skyway System—in case one gets lost.

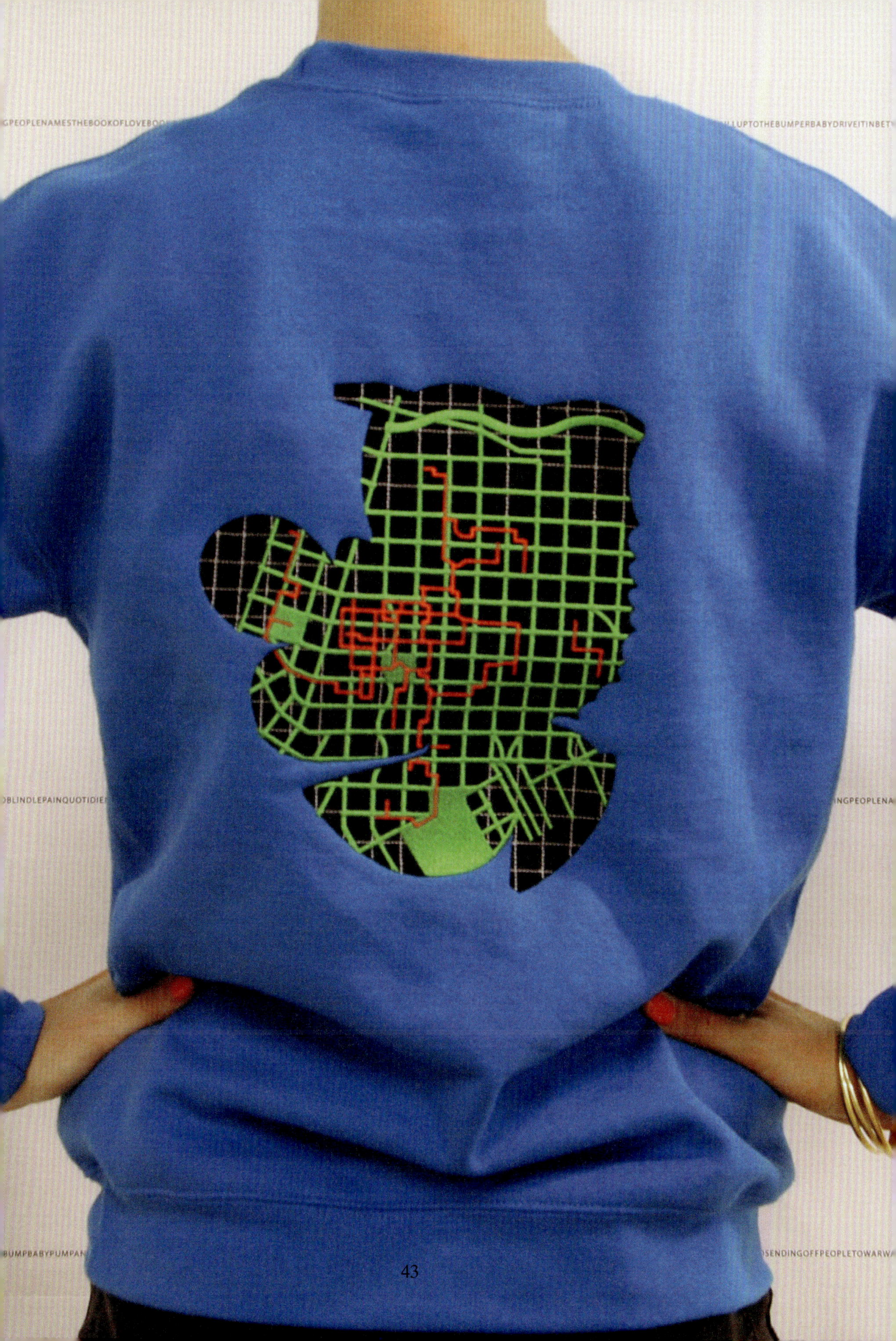

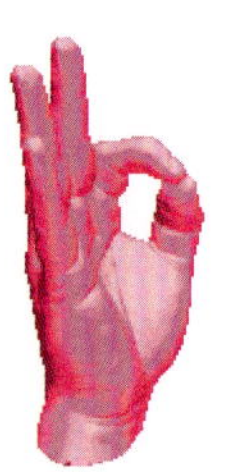

OOIEE
Skyway Furniture

OOIEE

Skyway Furniture

October 2018 – October 2019

The Minneapolis-based multi-faceted studio OOIEE designs and builds furniture for the *Goethe in the Skyways* space.

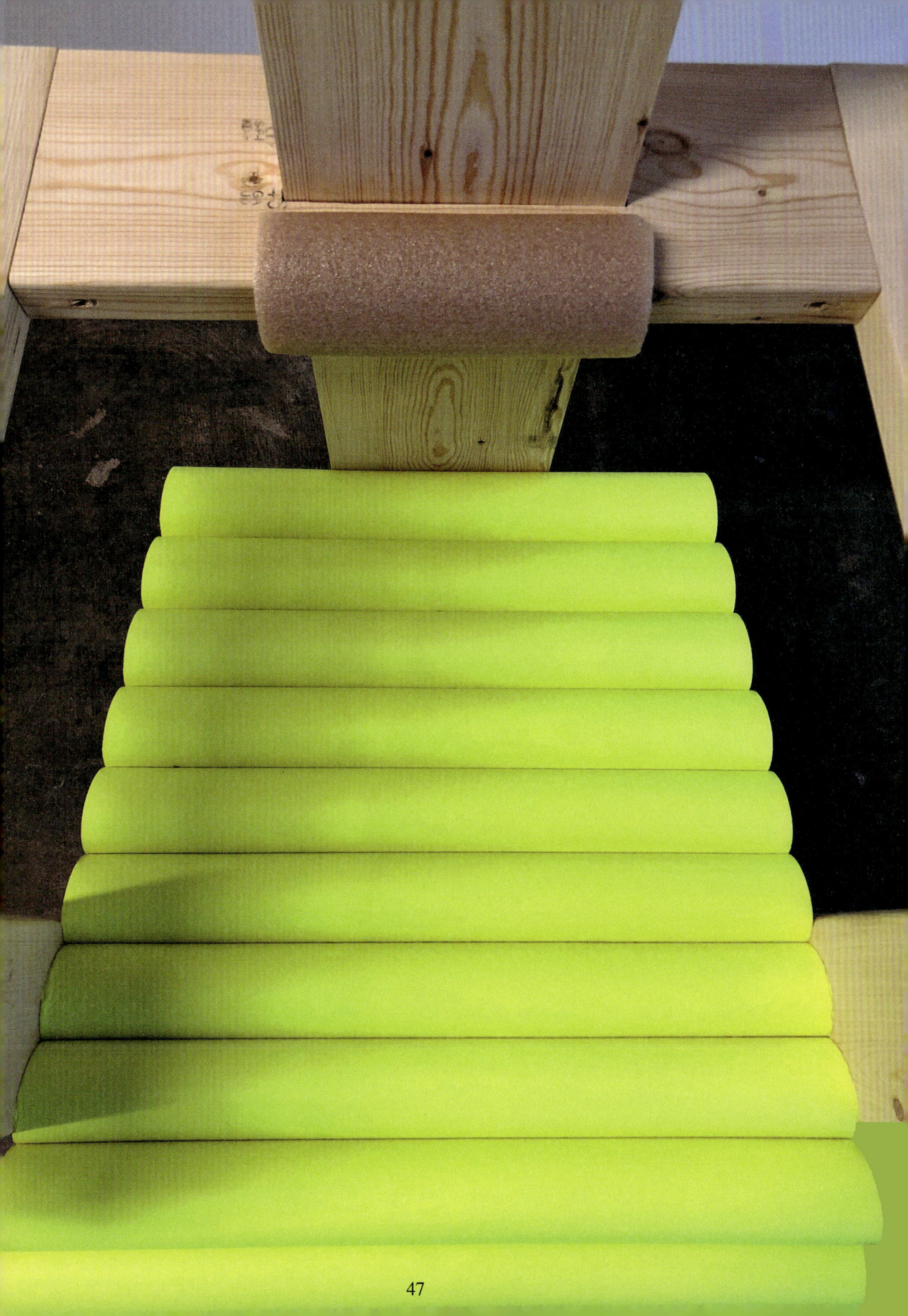

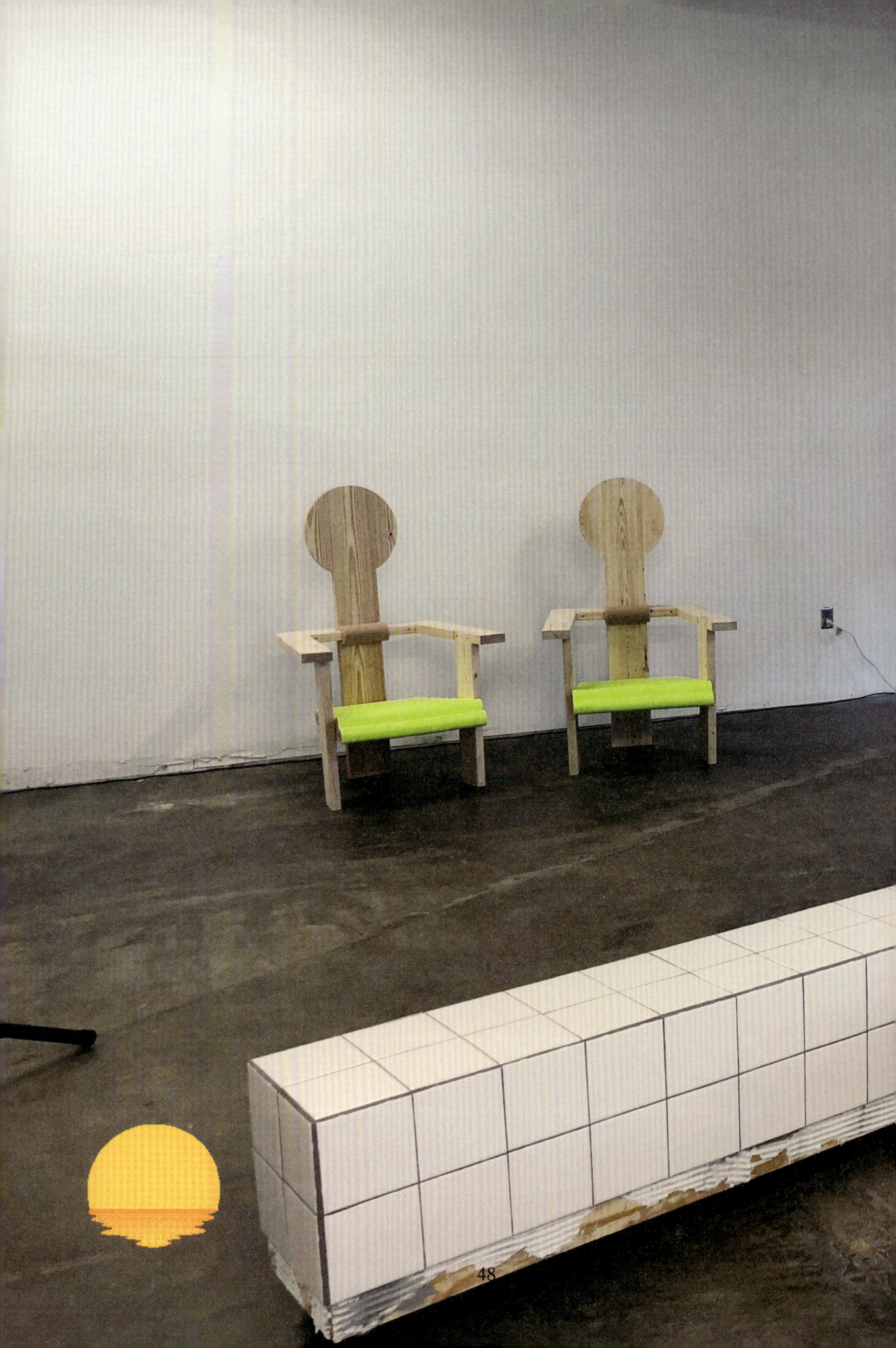

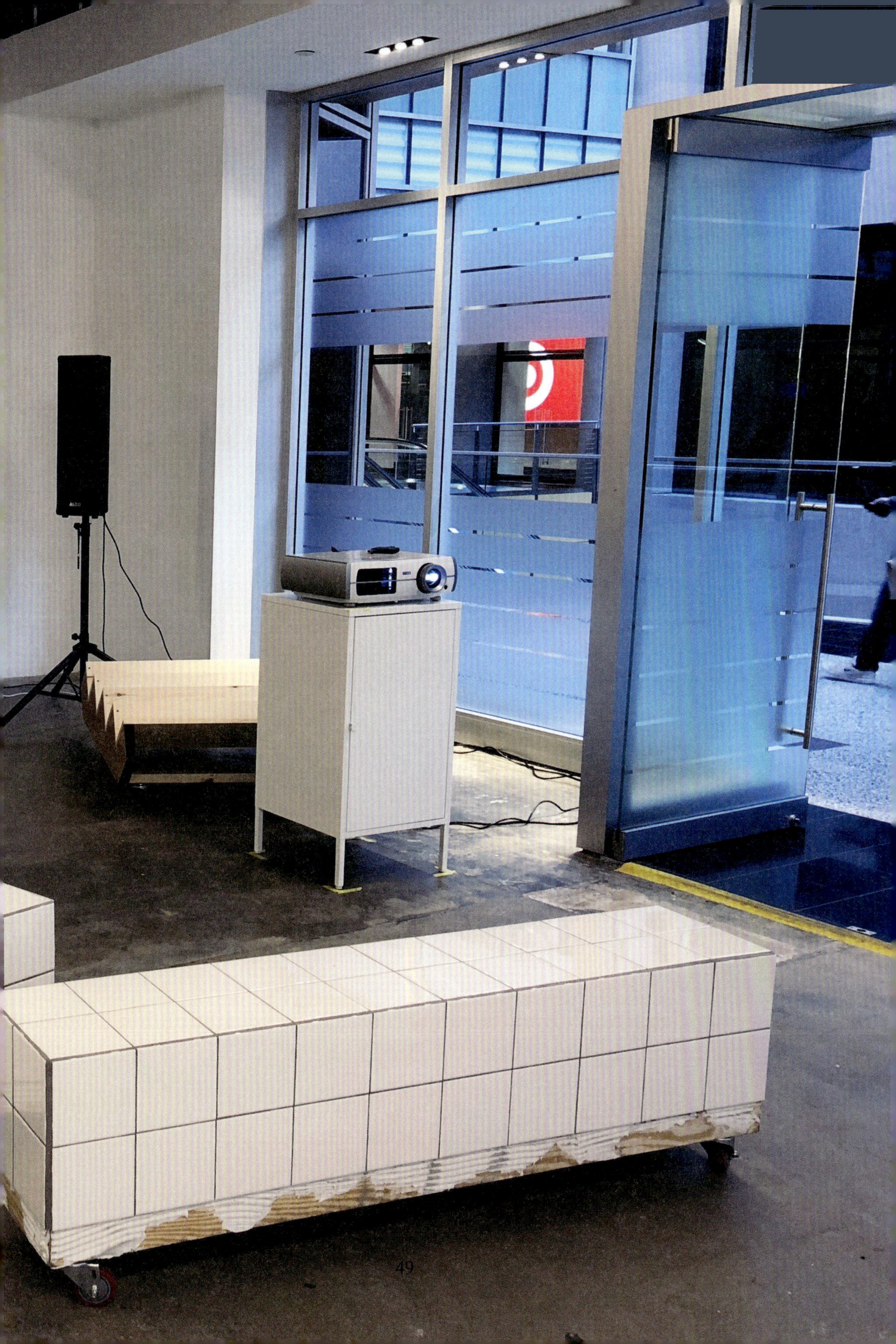

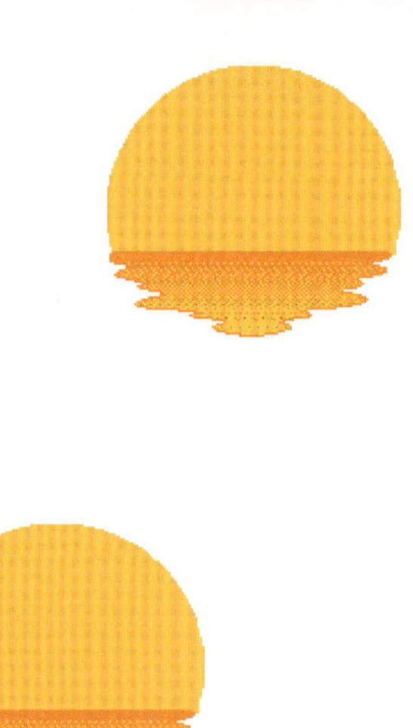

Aaron Van Dyke & Kelsey Olson
Untitled Wall Project

Aaron Van Dyke & Kelsey Olson

Untitled Wall Project

October 2018 – October 2019

"We have been interested in building something 'from the ground up', something 'before' the artwork that is also an artwork. A related appeal for us is the simultaneous creation of the artwork and its support. There is something interesting and absurd to us in building everyday materials (drywall, in this case) ourselves. This ubiquitous material, always hidden under layers of paint, is made by the acre in factories around the world (cheap and uniform), yet we labor over custom mixes of various powders to make a 'substandard' (nonuniform) version. Of course, even this is done all the time by people making various 'bespoke' products.

This wall is meant to support other artwork, and to some extent, the program itself. In this way it can seem to sink into the background. The wall is caught between rising up—being built as an artwork from raw materials—and sinking, retreating into the background as support for another work or a boundary within the space."

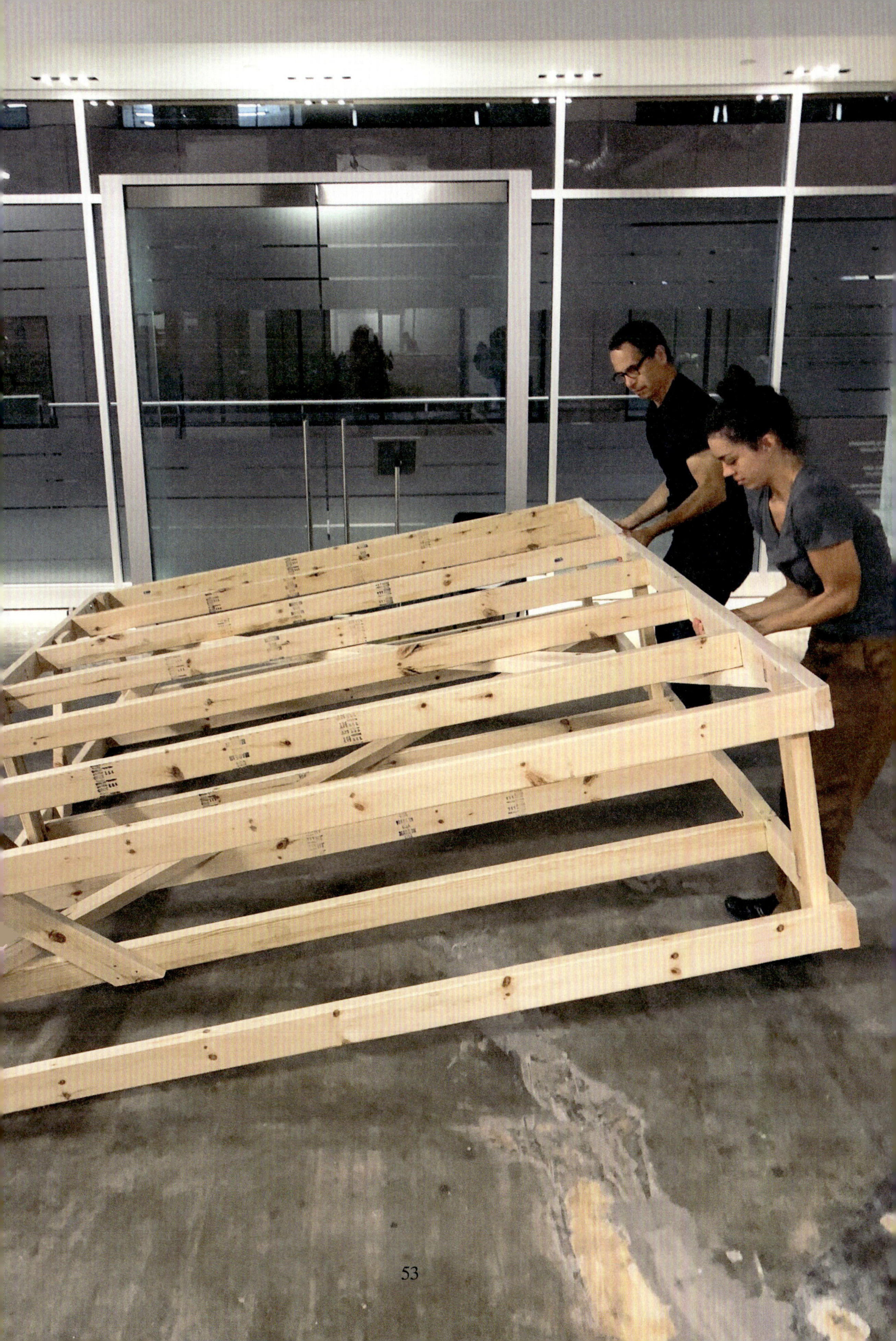

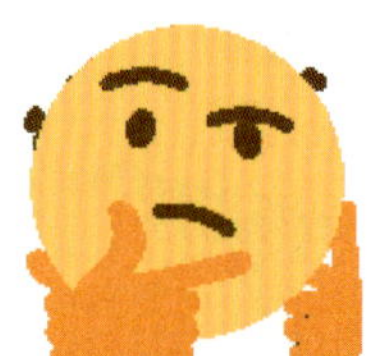

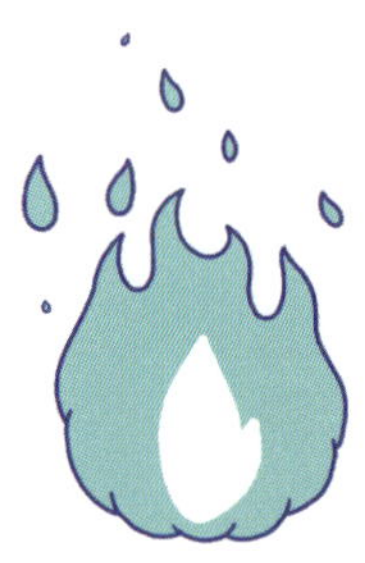

Skyways

Bill Lindeke

Years ago, in the thrall of my obsession with the Twin Cities skyway system, one of my favorite bizarre details was the existence of "skyways to nowhere" in both of the Twin Cities. What fun! In each of the downtowns, you could find a skyway that lingered over the street linking buildings that didn't exist, skyways built earlier to connect with a building that had since been torn down. Instead, without their connective tissue, these remnant skyways were urban appendices dangling uselessly and tempting gravity.

The two one-sided skyways—over Marquette Avenue in Minneapolis and over Wabasha Street in St. Paul—reminded me of nothing so much as the "escalator to nowhere" from *The Simpsons*, the coda to the famous monorail episode, a boondoggle civic project composed of a 20-story escalator that simply dropped its passengers into the air to plummet to their fates. I liked to imagine downtown skyway strollers walking placidly through the Minneapolis or St. Paul systems only to fall twenty feet when the skyway abruptly ended. Perhaps, they would land on a well-placed trampoline and hop lightly onto the sidewalk, free at last to wander the surface plane of the city sidewalks.

The twin amputated skyways symbolized the structural autonomy of the skyway systems themselves. These two useless skyways were the material incarnation of architectural agency, the way that our buildings shape us through time.

They are both gone now. The Minneapolis skyway was finally re-connected to a building when a new apartment tower was built at the corner of Marquette and 5th Street. Meanwhile, the St. Paul skyway was removed altogether when the former Dayton's store (now the Treasure Island Center) was remodeled. And yet, the overarching systems themselves remain, and, at least in downtown Minneapolis, continue to grow, seemingly of their own accord and despite the best advice of urban planning experts.

The Minneapolis Skyway System dates back fifty-seven years to August 26th, 1962. That was the day that, inside a small glass and steel structure bridging Marquette Avenue, a ribbon was snipped by a small group of people. That particular skyway no longer exists, but like a hydra, dozens more have taken its place, creating a network of passageways fifteen feet in the air. If you ask a Minneapolis visitor what they think of the downtown, chances are they'll mention the skyways. While most locals take these second-story building bridges for granted, the Minneapolis "skyway system" is the largest such network of infrastructure in the world. For better and for worse, this infrastructural oddity has transformed the downtown into a kind of urban space that's notably different from other cities.

For its part, the Minneapolis Skyway System offers counterintuitive lessons on urbanism, everything from its distinctions between public and private space, to its affect on the local economy, to illustrating how the human brain (fails to) navigate space. For decades, architects and designers have pointed out their negative effects, tourists and visitors have routinely gotten lost, and preservationists have bemoaned their effects on Minneapolis's historic buildings. Meanwhile, building owners and convention planners seem to love them, and businesspeople often declare skyways to be the one thing that "saved downtown" from economic obsolescence. And no matter how you come down on skyways as infrastructure, they stand in nicely for Minnesota's fraught relationship with its relatively extreme climate.

But to really wrap your fingers around the birth of the skyway system, you have to understand the history of American downtowns. A century ago, downtown business and property owners throughout the country were starting to panic about the rise of the automobile. Before that point, the majority of people traveled through the city on streetcars and bus lines that all intersected in the centers of cities. These downtowns had large shopping districts with huge department stores. For a while, the conventional wisdom was that the coming of the automobile was going to improve everything for downtown businesses. That is, if only city officials could figure out a way to make it easier to travel faster to and from the core.

But over the next few decades, increasing numbers of cars began clogging downtown streets, honking constantly, getting in the way of streetcars, looking fruitlessly for parking, and posing grave dangers for the people in cities used to walking in and playing on streets without an excess of caution. This was the era when the term "jaywalking" was coined, and this was the moment when the car-dominated future of American cities took firm root.

Supported by the various business interests, city officials in these days brainstormed ways to increase traffic flow, reduce congestion, and figure out how to park all these cars that kept coming downtown. Notable infrastructures that were born in this era included the stoplight, the limited-access freeway, the one-hour parking zone, and the parking meter. The point of all these new technologies was to attempt to seamlessly incorporate thousands of new drivers into the congested downtown streets, which had to accommodate not only increasing numbers of space-hogging cars, but clunky streetcars, stinky-sweet horse carts, and the kind of pedestrian throngs found today only at the State Fair.

The initial idea for skyways came out of this hectic downtown heyday, part of utopian fantasies about multi-level streets. There are lots of great turn-of-the-century illustrations of this dirigible-era vision of future cities, and most of them have a healthy dose of bridges stretched across the sky. Sky bridges even existed back in 1882, as urban historian Robert M. Fogelson described in his 2003 book *Downtown: Its Rise and Fall, 1880–1950.*

He writes:
"Elevated sidewalks were [...] a combined sidewalk and overpass, they were designed to expedite vehicular traffic by removing pedestrians from the streets. Pedestrian 'walks,' bridges that ran over the streets from rooftop to rooftop, were another."

Although this scheme "is hardly practicable yet," New York City's Real Estate Record and Builders' Guide wrote in 1882, "it may be worth thinking about seriously a few years from now."

In a similar vein, drawings of sky bridges kicked around the dartboards of city leaders and sci-fi novelists for decades during the early twentieth century, along with slightly more practical fantasies of subways, elevated freeways, and flying cars.

Almost all of these ideas turned out to be wildly expensive, and anyone who actually tried to build actual sky bridges quickly discovered the politics of bureaucratic gridlock. At this point, city governments hadn't figured out how to pay for very much except by hugely unpopular taxes and individual assessments. It wasn't until people like public official Robert Moses in New York City began to put together the modern freeway-industrial complex that anything much happened to change downtowns. By the time the Federal government began footing the bill for big infrastructure projects following World War II, the focus was on freeways, "slum clearance," and more parking lots.

Meanwhile, in post-war Minneapolis, things weren't going all that swimmingly for downtown business interests. By the time the 1950s had rolled around, an unfortunate series of events had taken place, the first of which was the exodus of some of the city's largest employers out of downtown and onto grassy corporate campuses. In 1956, General Mills, practically synonymous with the city's industrial glory, decamped for a sprawling new campus in Golden Valley. A few years later, agriculture giant Cargill leapfrogged them, ejecting themselves all the way out along Lake Minnetonka. A host of other offices and companies followed suit, part of a suburbanization trend all over the country that put fear into the folks who wanted to keep downtown a business center.

The second big change, also in 1956, was the Dayton's Company debut of the Southdale Center, the first indoor, climate-controlled mall anywhere in the world.

Designed by famed Austrian designer Victor Gruen, Southdale opened to pomp and dazzle. The new complex, surrounded on every side by massive parking lots, haunted the downtown retailers.

Faced with the twin exoduses of office space and retail, downtown leaders began to panic about the future of the city. There were emergency meetings at the Minneapolis Club, the old boy's network where Minneapolis's business decisions were made. Soon afterward, also in 1956, the Downtown Council was born. The new private group was a politically-involved downtown business association that—then and now—set the tone for discussion about urban design, business climate, and politics in downtown Minneapolis.

The first act of the Downtown Council was to demand that the city government form a Planning Department, and the first job of the new department was to figure out how to keep the city's downtown from becoming irrelevant. A few years later, as ordered, the Planning Department produced a plan for preserving the future of downtown. In 1959, the first draft of the big downtown plan arrived, a comprehensive study with many chapters on problems and potential solutions. Tucked into that plan, towards the end of the chapter on transportation, is the first mention of what would become the Minneapolis Skyway System.

Granted, the 1959 plan is full of suggestions about improving transportation, streetscapes, and reducing congestion, many of which are good ideas focused on improving the downtown sidewalks. For example, there are discussions of the importance of street furniture and street trees, and no shortage of thoughts about how to improve transit efficiency and user experience. But at the very end of the section, the idea of "second-level walks" appears as one solution for downtown congestion. These proto-skyways were defined in the plan as "any connecting walkway built one or more floors above the ground level," and they were seen to have many advantages over traditional sidewalks. For example:

"[Second-level walks] can be built without interfering with vehicular movement, can be easily enclosed and air conditioned […] they could be designed to include sales space and conveniences which would make them function as an integral part of the buildings which they connect. The impression could be given that the structures which are linked together are all a part of one huge whole rather than being separate buildings between which one must travel […]. Interesting and dramatic views could be obtained from upper level walks. […] They could increase the variety and interest of street scenes by limiting and framing views [… and, finally] some pedestrian traffic would be removed from surface streets thus reducing conflict with vehicular movement and thus reducing congestion."

On the other hand, the plan points out disadvantages like their expense and the difficulty of negotiating the complexities of property ownership. But overall, the 1959 plan is sanguine about skyways. Not only would pedestrians move faster, they'd lead healthier lives. As the plan states:

"Persons in the central area will gain a more relaxed attitude which will presumably add to their efficiency and improve their general well-being and attitude toward life. Since there are so many of them, this could have a salutary effect on the whole city."

In other words, second-level walks were to be the urban equivalent of Prozac.

It was in these fertile circumstances that the skyway was conceived, and the father of the skyway system appeared. He was a downtown property owner named Leslie "Les" Park, and, according to Kaufman's short history of the Minneapolis skyways[1], he rather personified Minneapolis's WASP moralistic business class. A devout Methodist who owned some key downtown properties, Park famously claimed to have donated all of his hotel-based liquor profits to charity because he believed them impure.

In the early 1960s, Park had just completed a new downtown office and retail building on the corner of Marquette Avenue and 6th Street called the Northstar Center, and he'd been for some time pitching an idea of bridging his building with the one on the other side of Marquette. The more the suburbs gained economic and social traction, the more people listened to Park. Eventually, he received agreements from the city and his neighbors and created his first second-level walkway. On August 26th, 1962, the first skyway was born.

Park's first skyway across Marquette Avenue proved to be popular, and the next year he followed it up with another one across 6th Street a half a block away, bridging the Northstar Center with its neighbor on the other side. This one is still there, the oldest extant skyway, and when you walk across it, it's worth noting the differences between this fifty-year-old skyway and the newer versions elsewhere in the system. The original skyways were much smaller, simpler, low-ceilinged, and less adorned than their current incarnations.

Slowly, through the 1960s, other building owners followed suit elsewhere downtown. Bit by bit, office buildings began docking with each other like a science-fiction space station, and the skyway system kept expanding outward.

But the burgeoning network of bridges did not truly reach a critical mass and become a bona fide "skyway system" until the IDS Center was constructed on the corner of 7th Street and Nicollet Avenue in 1971. With its massive central atrium,

1. Sam H. Kaufman, *The Skyway Cities*. Minneapolis: CSPI, 1985.

five-story fountain, and wide modernist skyway bridges, the building's Crystal Court truly knit together the ground floor and the skyway level. When it was completed, the IDS building joined all the skyways together and immediately became the definitive center of the Minneapolis skyways. From that point on, the skyway system took on a life of its own.

During the subsequent building booms, just about every new downtown office building was designed to feature the skyway system, often with central atria and minimal access points between the sidewalk and the building's interior. The new skyway-centered, internally-focused buildings were joined by dozens of smaller links in the system, parking lots linked with skyways, or older buildings where skyways were retrofit into narrow second-floor hallways.

Eventually, the elaborate complexity, fragmented regulation, and maze-like quality of the system emerged. In response, the city of Minneapolis began officially regulating the skyways in the late 1980s. They put in place some broad, and sometimes-ignored regulations, such as mandating hours of operation, installing consistent way-finding signage, and setting some vague principles about how the skyways fit legally into the category of public or private space.

Still, the fundamental challenge of keeping one's bearings in a series of often windowless, narrow passages full of right angles, lacking focal points or landmarks, meant that the skyways have always been a confusing maze to anyone who didn't work downtown every day. The plans and documents focused on downtown Minneapolis from this era display recurring concern about how to improve and fix the skyways, particularly around issues of accessibility, navigability, and legibility, especially for tourists and convention goers.

In that same vein, for decades, the skyway system has been seen as a negative drag on downtown Minneapolis by some urbanists, architects, and designers. Back in 1986, a consultant from New York City's Project for Public Spaces told a roomful of downtown leaders that they needed to tear down the skyways, for the sake of downtown street life and economic vitality. And almost like clockwork, every few years, as Minneapolis leaders invite consultants to visit and help revitalize downtown, they suggest simplifying or reducing the skyway system. By the time the twenty-first century came around, the skyways had become a key issue of disagreement in urban policy circles, one where local leaders both defend and castigate the infrastructure, creating an almost schizophrenic tension.

So, have skyways "saved downtown," as many business people and politicians suggest? Or, as others argue, are they one of the main things casting a dark shadow on a potential urban renaissance, holding Minneapolis back from being a world-class downtown?

It's complicated, but I side with the latter camp. My personal criticism of the skyways comes down to three main things. First, there's the architecture. With few exceptions, skyway-centered buildings tend to lack windows, doors, shops, or anything interesting along their sidewalk façades. In practice, buildings with skyways have the effect of treating the public sidewalks with blank-walled disdain, lacking either detail or interest and leaving the street vacant and uninviting. This has a detrimental effect on the walkability of downtown, to say the least.

Second, and more importantly, because they are difficult to access and privately controlled, skyways stratify the downtown into two groups. On the one hand, you have the second-story office workers who mostly drive into downtown. Below them, on the other hand, you have the first-story *hoi polloi* who walk or take the bus. Because skyways are so confusing and unwelcoming to those who are not members of the office class, these two groups do not often rub elbows.

This is the nice way to say it. The more pointed critique is that the skyway system segregates downtown Minneapolis. Any passing glance at these two groups of people will tell you a lot about the city's persistent racial and class divides, as these two groups stand in nicely for the city's inequality.

This split is one reason why, for so long, the skyway has lacked straightforward, easy-to-navigate connections between the second-story landscape and the sidewalks below. There is no grand public entrance to the skyways off Nicollet Mall, no city-owned park connection, and no link between the skyways and the Central Library.

Instead, in many ways, skyways are implicitly designed to be exclusionary and to send architectural and visual signals that these are more private spaces. In practice, they are welcoming to the majority-white office workers, but tend to keep out anyone who is not downtown earning or spending money. Even at their best, the skyways function like a suburban shopping mall, complete with occasional problems around racial profiling and unjust policing. In a way, the downtown skyway system is the perfect symbol of Minnesota's passive-aggressive racism, allowing suburban downtown workers to conveniently ignore the realities of visible poverty and racial segregation, and then blame it on the weather to boot.

Third, this de facto segregation makes the city as a whole worse off, because skyway and sidewalk businesses are forced to cater to only one of these two distinct populations. As shopkeepers are forced to choose between the skyway office workers and the general public, the economic vitality of downtown as a whole is worse off. Anyone passing through the system can see this at a glance, when almost all skyway businesses close each afternoon, and the skyways empty like a ballpark after the game is over. Meanwhile, sidewalk-focused businesses have to deal with the opposite patterns of traffic, most of them focused on evening or after-work crowds.

Imagine how many more businesses, shops, and bustling street activity might thrive in Minneapolis if all the city's passers-by were on the same level? The density and diversity of a downtown sidewalk is pretty much what defines a city, and I believe that Minneapolis is missing out, ending up less than the sum of its parts.

In short, the skyway city is a segregated and stratified one, where walkability and street life are marginalized, where racial and class inequalities are perpetuated, and where the aggregation and agglomeration potential of the downtown is minimized, to the detriment of both the local economy and civic life.

And yet, there are always the cold winters. If you ask anyone about why they like the skyways, that's what they'll talk about, and downtown workers and residents love to walk around in January without puffy coats. This is a mixed blessing, and as urbanist Gil Penalosa argued when he visited the Twin Cities a few years ago, you should design cities for the 250 good days of the year, not the few weeks or months of inclement weather.

That said, like them nor not, the skyways are literally embedded in the urban fabric of the urban core. It's clear they're not going anywhere. Instead, downtown denizens have to make an uneasy peace with the skyway system, hopefully escaping them during the majority of months when the weather is lovely, and retreating into them when convenience beckons.

It's for this reason that many of the twenty-first-century buildings in downtown Minneapolis attempt to bridge the divide between the second-level skyway city and the world of sidewalks and public street life. Meanwhile, the skyway-laden office core sits uncomfortably alongside and atop the increasingly popular, skyway-free hot spots like the North Loop, the Warehouse District, and the Mill District. In a way, these two downtowns are overlaid alongside each other, each with their own populations and patterns, rarely interacting.

In the end, the skyway system certainly makes downtown Minneapolis a unique place. The challenge of the next fifty years will be to figure out how to mitigate their fundamental flaws, bring the disparate parts of the city closer together, and once more create a vibrant, thriving downtown.

Wermke / Leinkauf, Korpys / Löffler
Disruptions, Interruptions, Misruptions

*I wanted to start the program with work that could be seen simultaneously from the outside as well as inside, work that is easily accessible and doesn't demand context, work that draws people in, the way the donut shop next door—Cardigan Donuts—incites the nostrils and lures an appetite to the front counter. The themes of the works touch upon the themes of the upcoming program, the 30th anniversary of the fall of the Berlin wall, the notion of artistic interventions in private-public space, and the current socio-political climate in Europe and the United States.

Wermke / Leinkauf
Korpys / Löffler

Disruptions, Interruptions, Misruptions

8–26 October 2018

23 October 2018, 7pm

Screening Korpys / Löffler, *The Nuclear Football* and *Reflecting Absence*

"You may think that history is elliptical, but it's a heap."
—Thomas Heise

The film series *Disruptions, Interruptions, Misruptions* launches the program of the Goethe Pop Up Minneapolis *Goethe in the Skyways*. It presents four films by both East and West German artists and filmmakers that all reflect the program's approach and thematic interests alluding to the upcoming artistic actions, interventions, and performances that will take place from November 2018 through October 2019 in and around the *Goethe in the Skyways* space within the City Center.

Wermke / Leinkauf's *Grenzgänger* (2006) documents the early morning crossing from the Eastern to the Western bank of the Spree river by a person at the exact spot where, until 1989, the inner-German border existed.

Korpys / Löffler's trilogy *World Trade Center, United Nations*, and *Pentagon* (1996/2018) shows the everyday comings and goings of the employees of three New York City sites, in which the strings of political, financial, and military power are being pulled on a global scale. Two of these three locations became the target of serious terrorist attacks only a few years later.

The Nuclear Football (2004) documents George W. Bush's arrival at Tegel Airport in Berlin, a state reception at Bellevue Palace, and the President's departure from the same airport the next day. Although such visits are a kind of choreographed ritual that the media film like an extended photo shoot, Korpys / Löffler found opportunities to deviate from the guidelines. They simply took a slightly different look, pointed the camera in the other direction, or lingered on seemingly insignificant details. *The Nuclear Football* makes it clear how trivial this whole fuss is in the end—beyond the symbolic handshake, ceremonial and honorary formation. Brian Eno's minimalist album *Ambient 1: Music for Airports* (1978) can be heard in the background. A rhythmic, strangely choppy, whispering male voice comments on the whole film, revealing details of the behind-the-scenes security measures. These confidential revelations provide insights into what's happening behind the scenes of political power, or right before our eyes.

Following on closely from older films (*World Trade Center, United Nations, Pentagon*) Korpys / Löffler use Super-8 film recordings in *Reflecting Absence* (2016), the name borrowed from the memorial to victims of the terror attacks in New York on September 11th, 2001. Places and buildings relating also to tourism are shown in cinematic moments of convergence, places located in the immediate surrounding area of the former World Trade Center. These images are accompanied not only by the piece of music "Two Emotions" by Helmut Lachenmann (1992) but also by soundtracks recorded on the spot, each of which is processed digitally by Korpys / Löffler.

(Adapted from Cara Schroeder, *Reflecting Absence*)

Images:
1. Installation view, Wermke / Leinkauf, *Grenzgänger*
2. Installation view, Korpys / Löffler, *World Trade Center, United Nations*, and *Pentagon*

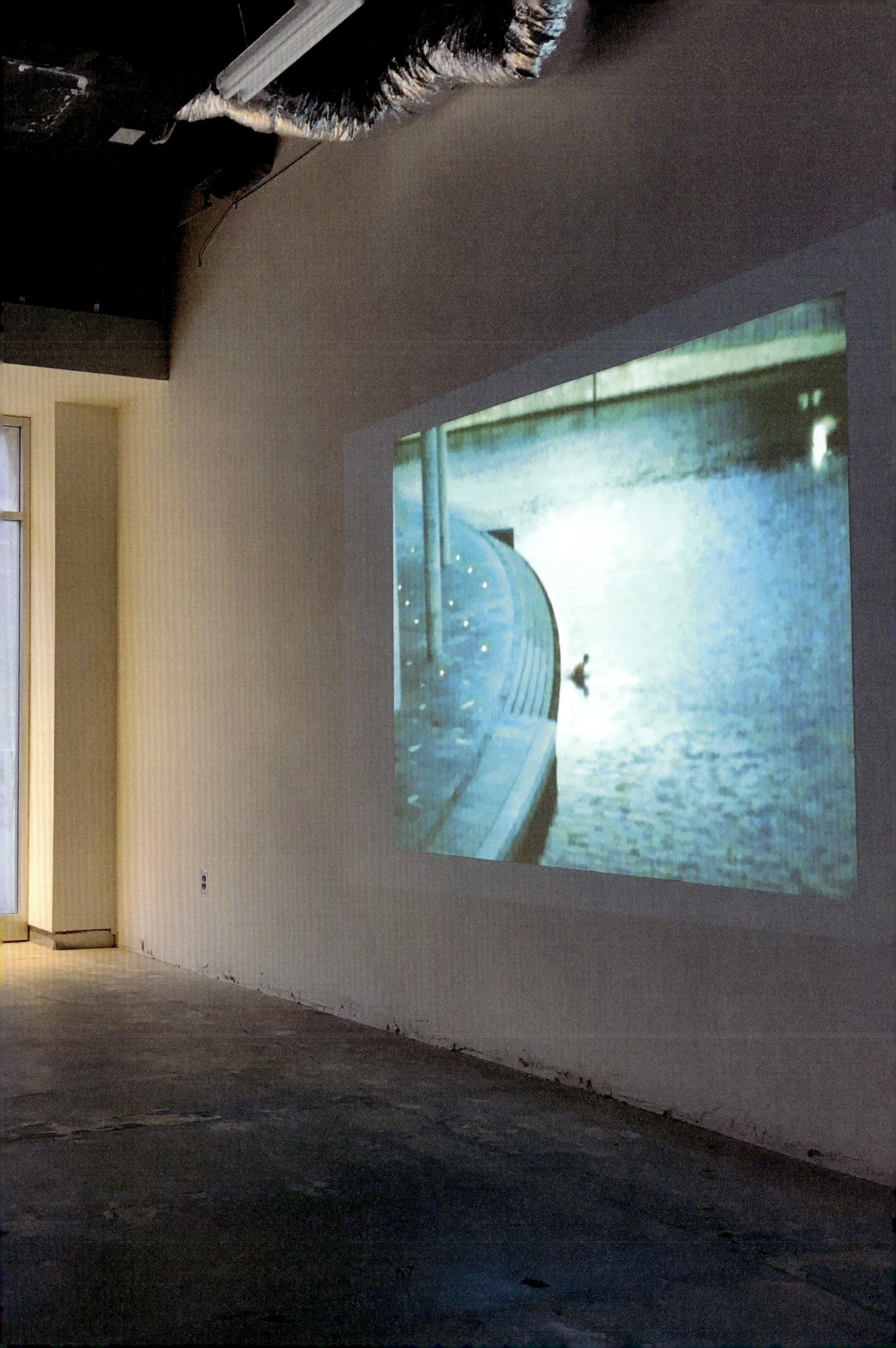

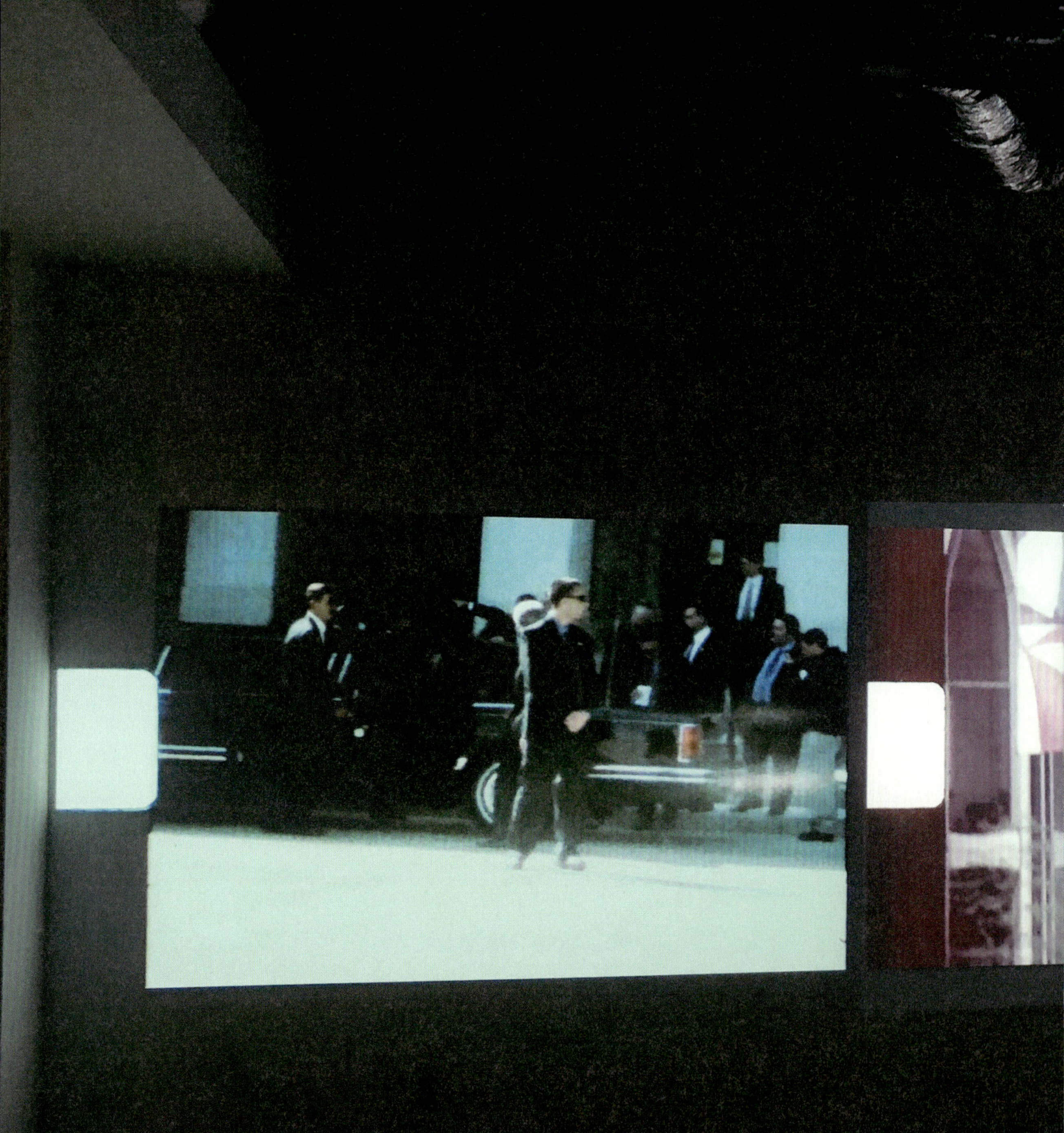

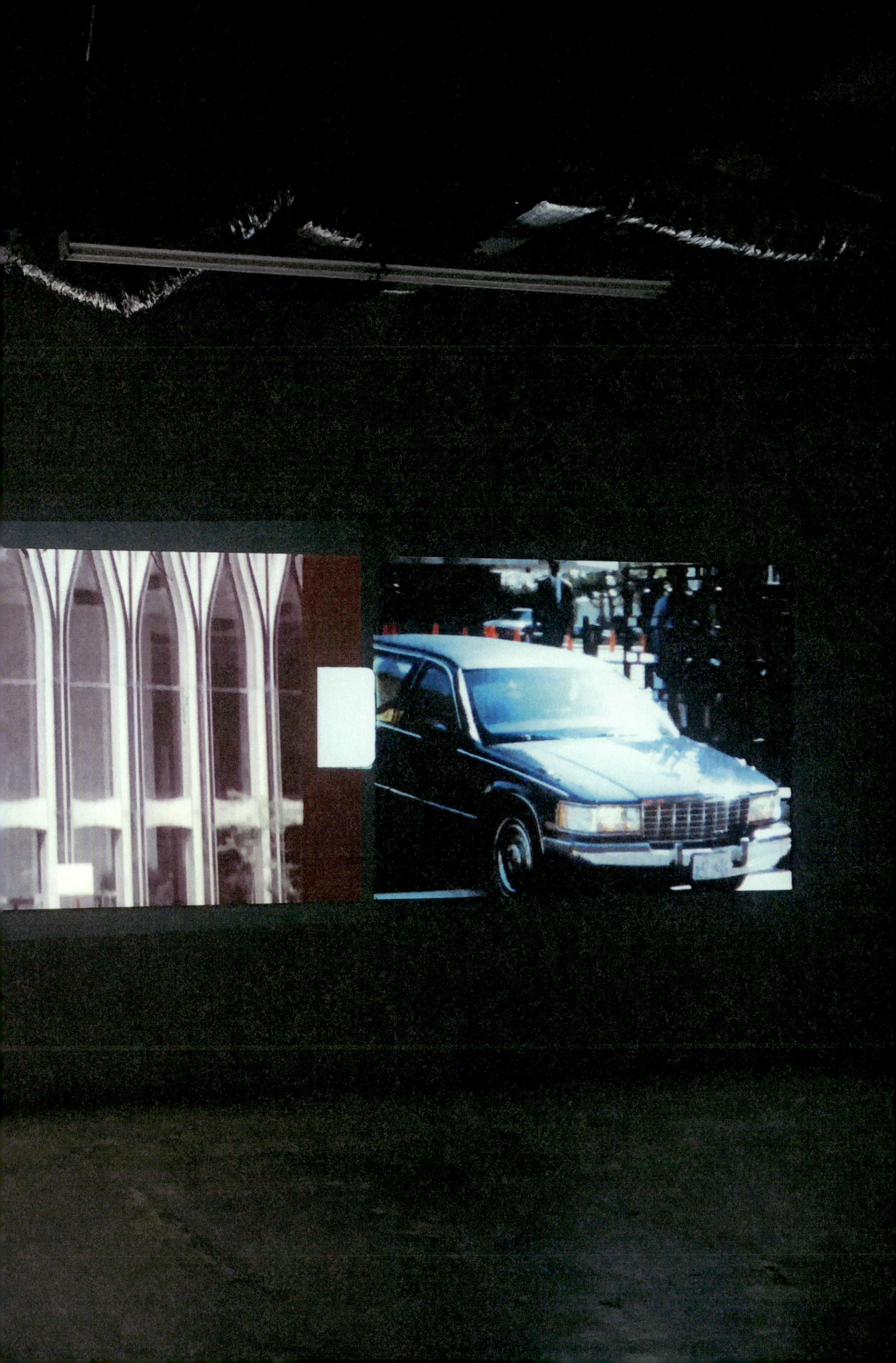

Sam Gould, Drew Peterson, Jenny Schmid,
The People's Library
Pre-Election Poster Action "Early & Often"

*Surrounding the U.S. midterm elections, the space became a platform and safe zone for discussions around the current state of the country, about possible future actions or initiatives, thoughts, joy, anger... We invited a few Minneapolis-based artists and printmakers to activate these sentiments through their works. A series of posters where created live during the opening hours of the Pop Up and were distributed to the steady stream of pedestrians that made their way to and from their offices in the skyways.

Sam Gould
Drew Peterson
Jenny Schmid
The People's Library

Pre-Election Poster Action "Early & Often"

3–12 November 2018

Inspired by Wolfgang Tillman's pro-EU campaign utilizing his signature images as the basis for a series of posters and related print ads, as well as a second campaign encouraging fellow Germans to participate in their country's Federal elections (a vote held September 24th, 2017, that resulted in the far-right Alternative für Deutschland party winning seats in the Bundestag), *Goethe in the Skyways* invited Minneapolis-based artists and printmakers to use the skyway space as a platform for distributing posters and other ephemera printed with regard to elections and broader political processes in the United States.

The posters filled the walls of the *Goethe in the Skyways* space a few days before and after the year's midterm elections.

1. The People's Library, *We*, screen print, 2018
2. Jenny Schmid & Drew Peterson, *"I Float(ed)"*, screen print & wall stickers, 2018
3. Sam Gould, *Queer Democracy bricks (from Roberts Shoes building)*, 2018

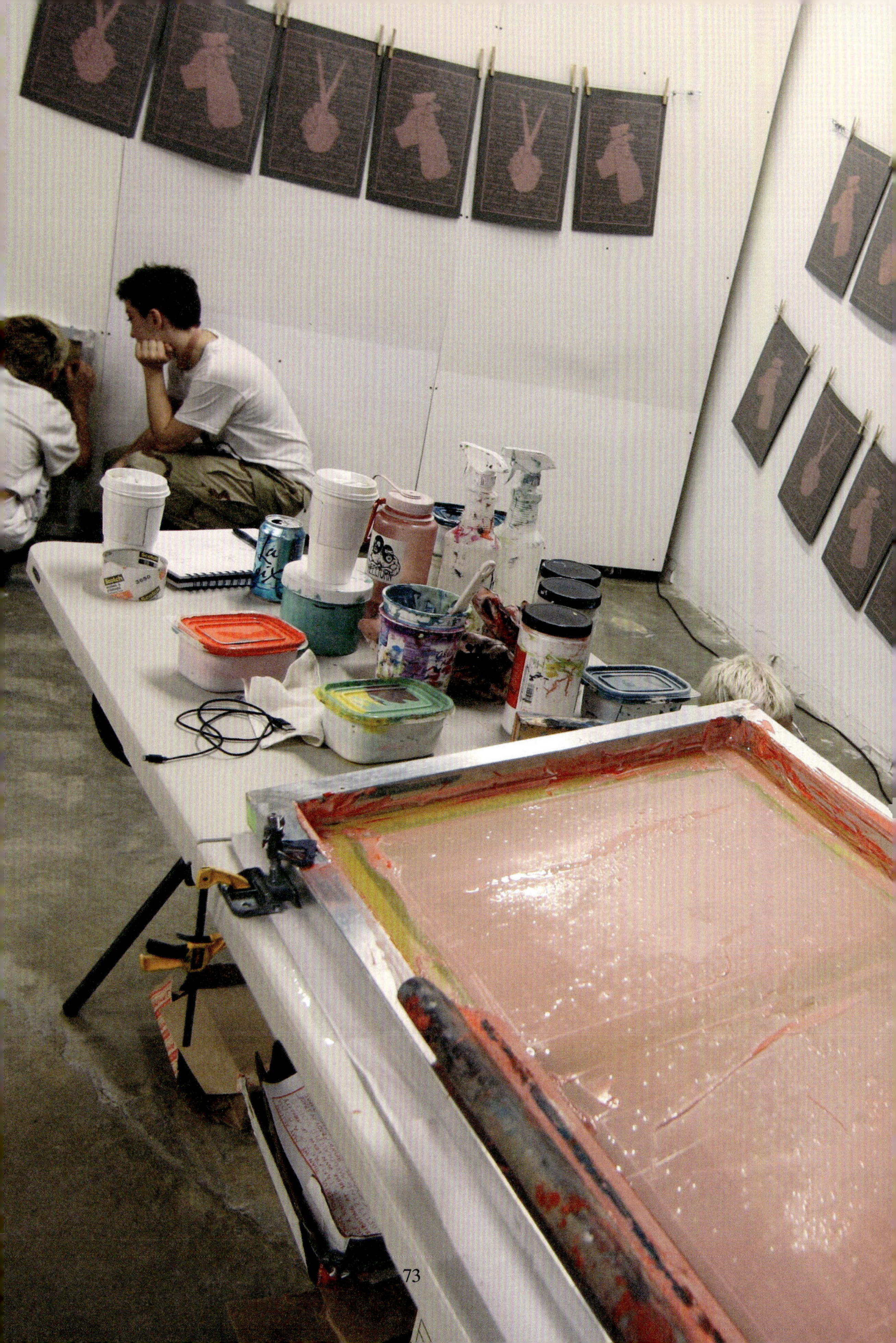

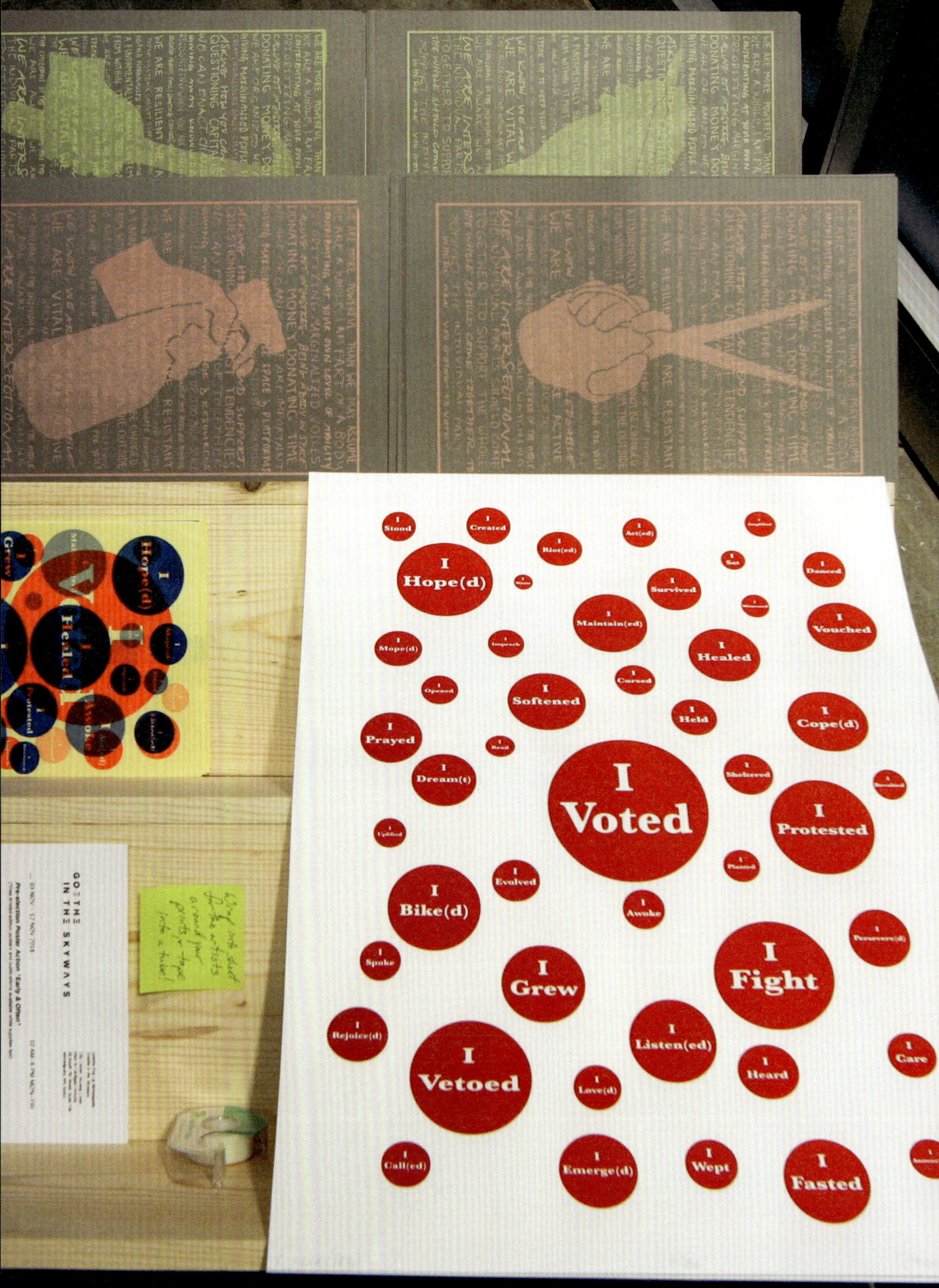

I Stood
I Created
I Riot(ed)
I Act(ed)
I Sat
I Hope(d)
I Danced
I Survived
I Maintain(ed)
I Vouched
I Mope(d)
I Impeach
I Healed
I Opened
I Softened
I Cursed
I Held
I Cope(d)
I Prayed
I Read
I Dream(t)
I Voted
I Sheltered
I Protested
I Uplifted
I Planned
I Evolved
I Bike(d)
I Awoke
I Spoke
I Grew
I Fight
I Rejoice(d)
I Vetoed
I Listen(ed)
I Heard
I Care
I Love(d)
I Call(ed)
I Emerge(d)
I Wept
I Fasted
I Hope(d)
I Healed
GOETHE IN THE SKYWAYS

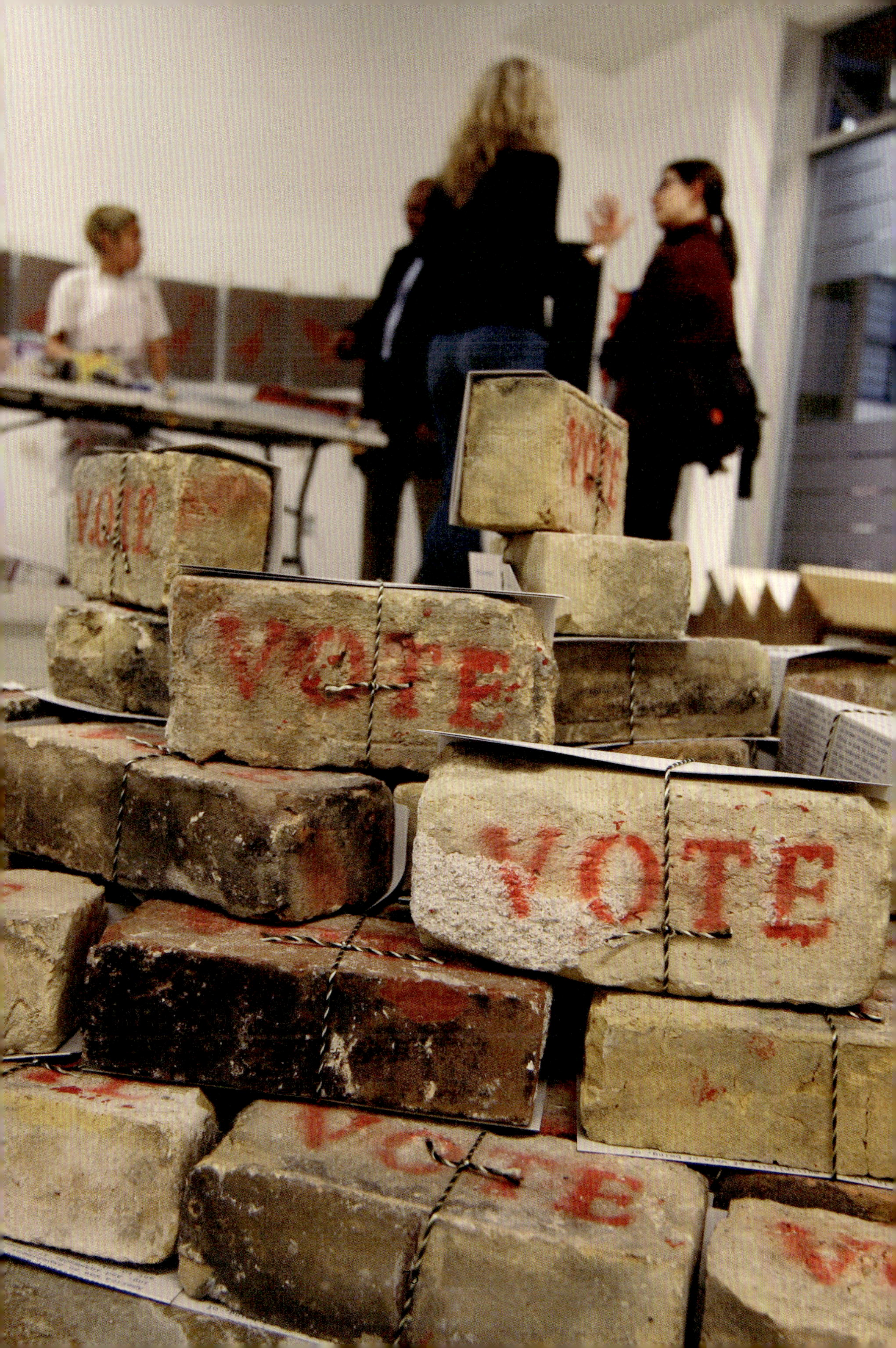
VOTE
VOTE
VOTE
VOTE
VOTE

Franziska Pierwoss
The Art of the Deal

*Franziska Pierwoss has been fascinated by the reality TV format for a long time and is a frequent watcher herself. Years ago, while living in New York, I had come across workshops that were being offered to young New Yorkers on how to deal with your family over Thanksgiving in the event they voted on the more conservative side—this was the 2016 presidential election. I mentioned these workshops to Franziska and they became the starting point for her work in the frame of *Goethe in the Skyways*, which was just after Thanksgiving and the 2018 midterm elections. The title of Franziska's project refers to a book of the same name, *Trump: The Art of the Deal*, that journalist Tony Schwartz wrote in 1987 based on interviews with Donald Trump. It is part memoir, part business-advice book. Another reference was different, partially documentary, reality television programs: *An American Family*, the first reality series on U.S.-American television; *The Apprentice*, featuring Donald Trump as host, which sets out to judge the business skills of a group of contestants whilst conducting a job talent search for a person to head one of Trump's companies; and, of course, *Keeping up with the Kardashians*.

Franziska Pierwoss

The Art of the Deal

12–29 November 2018

The Art of the Deal was filmed over the holidays in November 2018 and a rough cut of the first episode was presented at the Goethe Pop Up space followed by a discussion with the artist and some of the featured family members in November 2018. After many months of post-production, four episodes were presented at the Goethe Pop Up Minneapolis in September 2019 during a Binge-Watching Week.

Inspired by reality TV, *The Art of the Deal* stars three Minnesotan families who openly discuss family politics during the holiday season.

Forty years after its birth, reality TV seems to have become an integral part of people's life, no matter which country or continent, whether in the United States, in Germany, or elsewhere. And more than a decade of *Keeping up with the Kardashians* has certainly shaped the way realities are being performed all over the world.

Following a docu-style aesthetic, *The Art of the Deal* depicts the private sphere of three families that serve as a platform to debate and stage questions of individual behavioral patterns but also collective dynamics. During holidays, unlike any other time of the year, the discrepancy between personal expectations and the actual reality of a family gathering frequently results in some kind of drama.

8 November 2018, 6:30 pm

Screening & Talk with Katy Anderson, Laurie Ouellette, and Franziska Pierwoss

Franziska Pierwoss collaborated with three families that had no prior experience with TV series production in order to test their very *real*ities as potential footage for broadcast.

Pivotal, universally valid questions emerged in this process. How do families communicate today? What verbal and body language is at play? How does the public sphere of politics interfere with the private sphere of family? Who speaks at the table and who talks behind someone's back and instead at the camera?

The episodes are available on www.goetheintheskyways.org

Images:
1. Interviews with the featured families
2. Installation view, Binge-Watching Week *The Art of the Deal*
3. Screening *The Art of the Deal*
4. Stills from *The Art of the Deal*

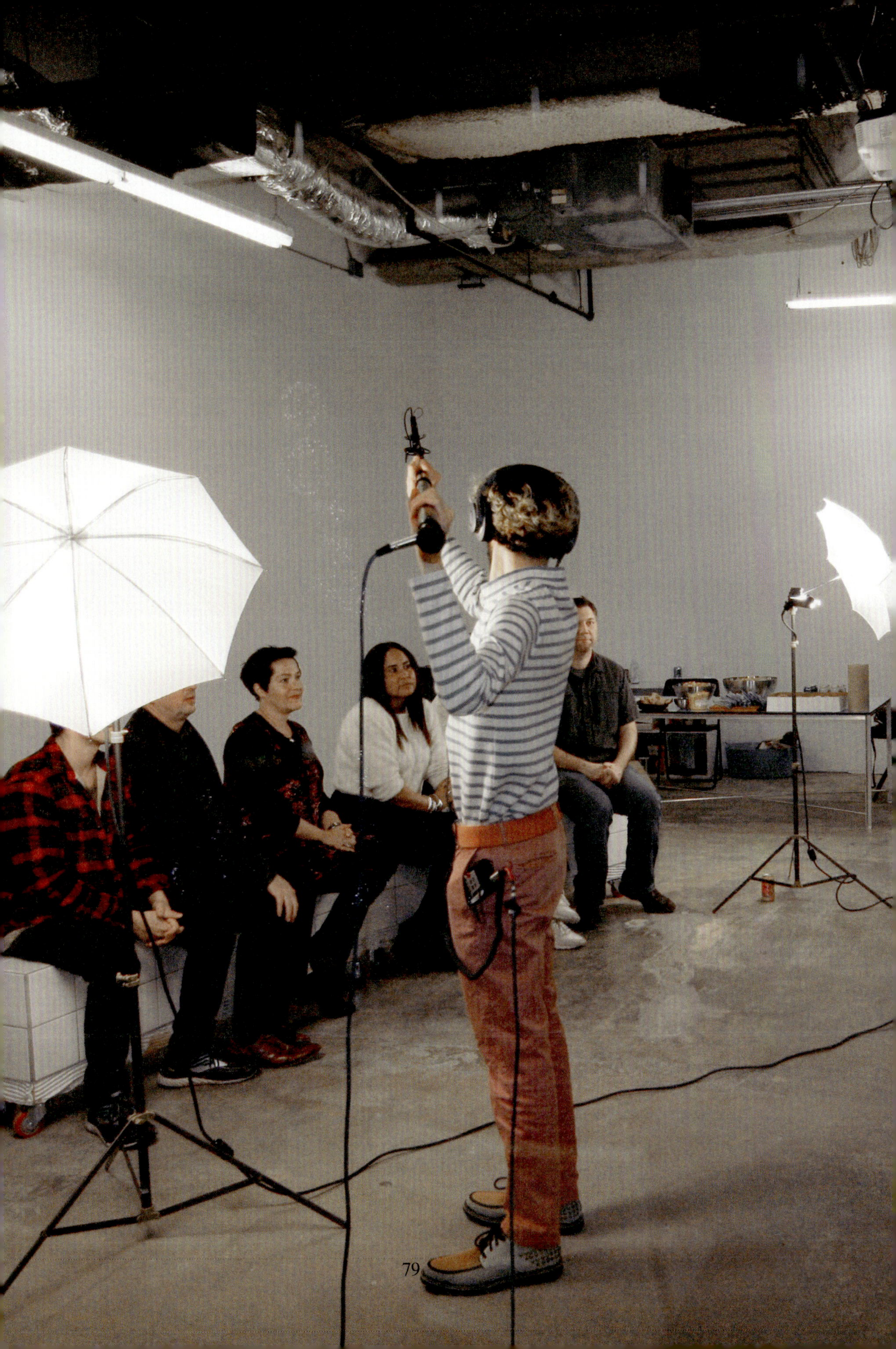

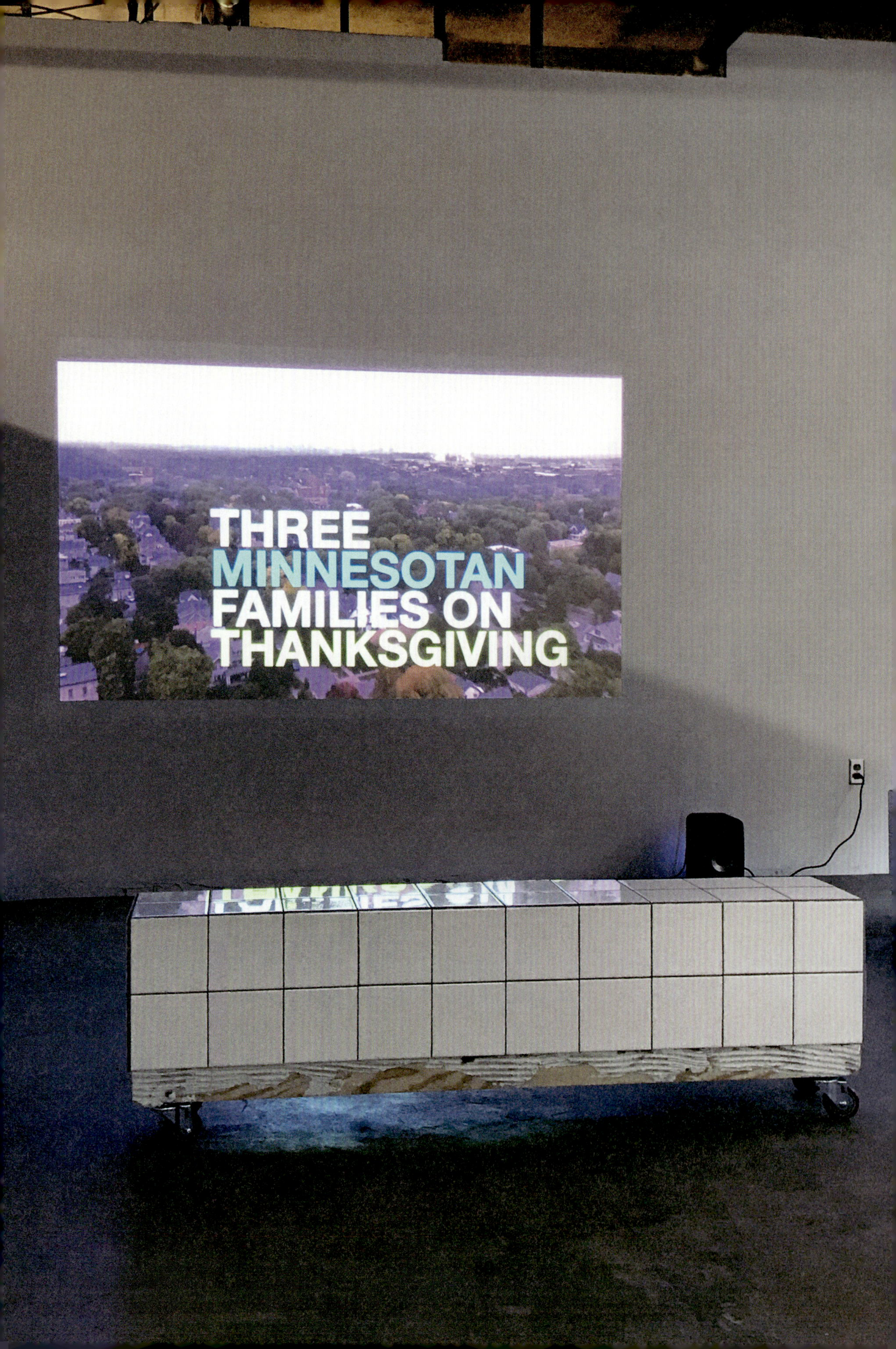

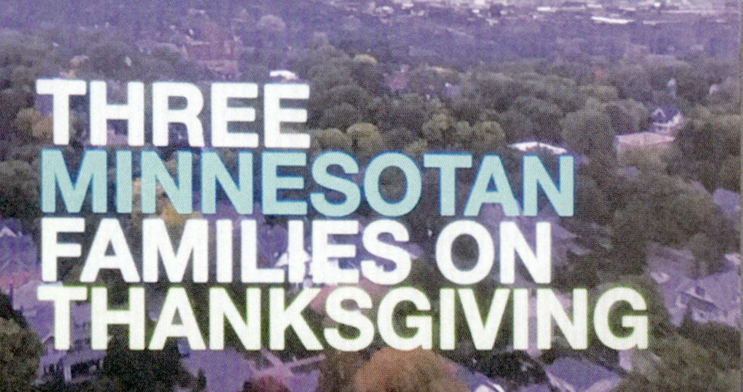
THREE
MINNESOTAN
FAMILIES ON
THANKSGIVING

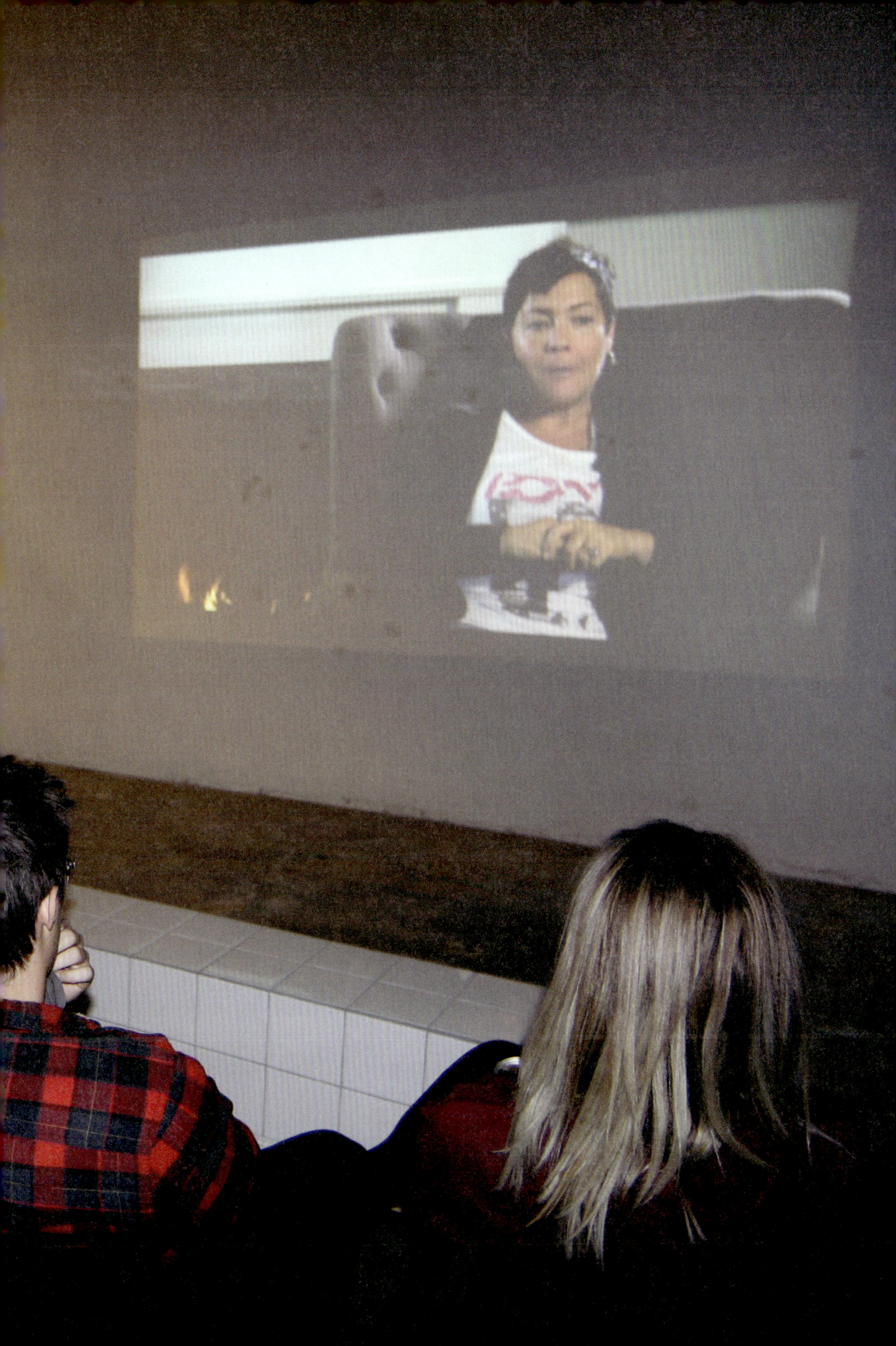

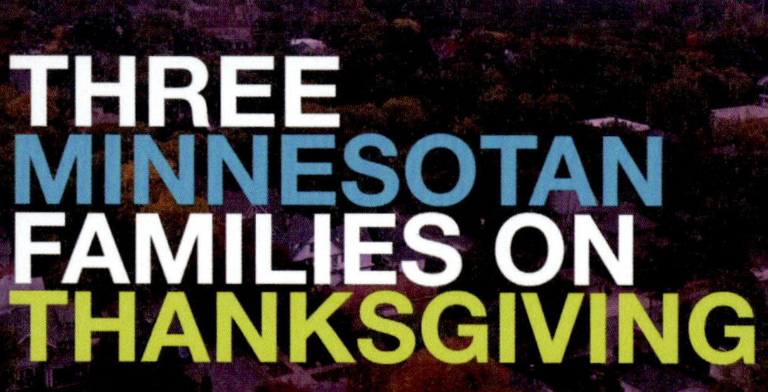

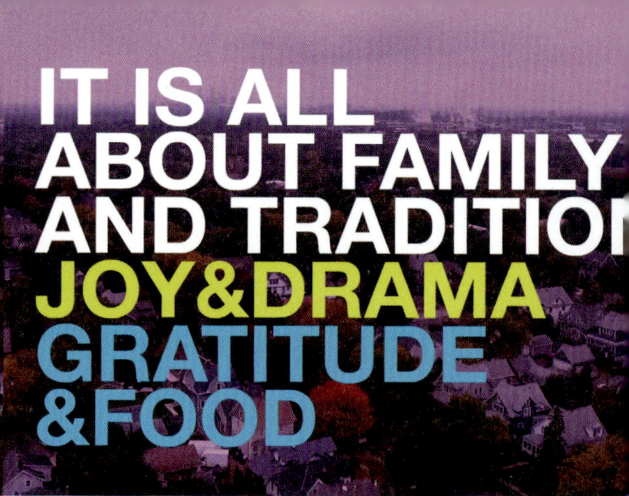

IT IS ALL
ABOUT FAMILY
AND TRADITIO
JOY&DRAMA
GRATITUDE
&FOOD

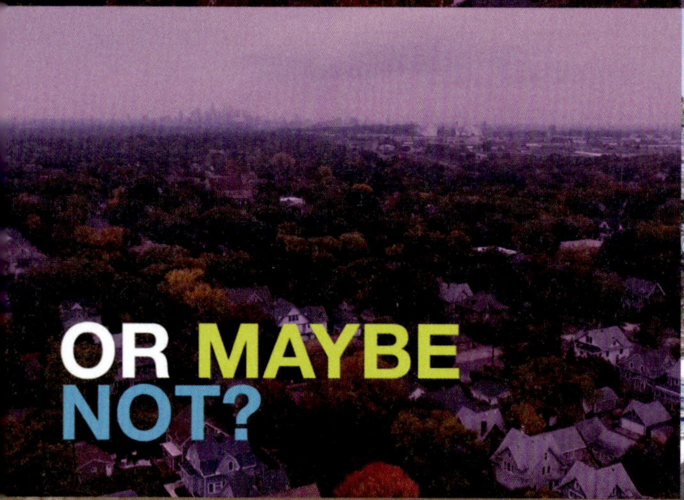

OR MAYBE
NOT?

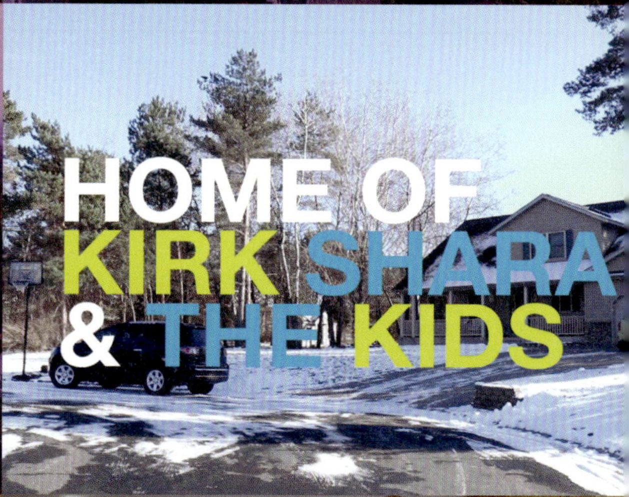

HOME OF
KIRK SHARA
& THE KIDS

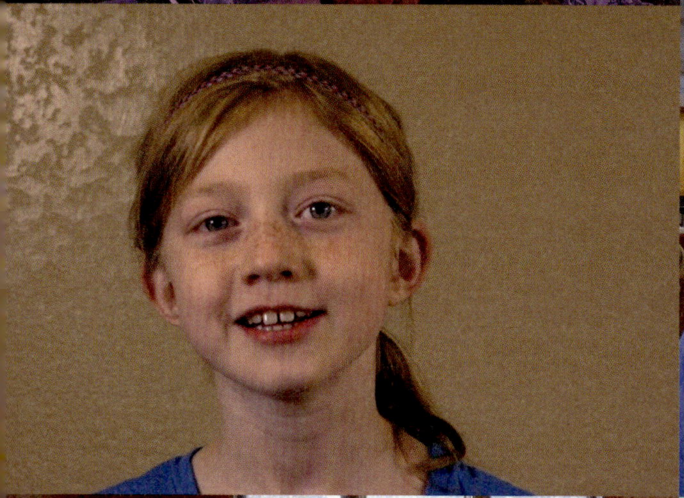

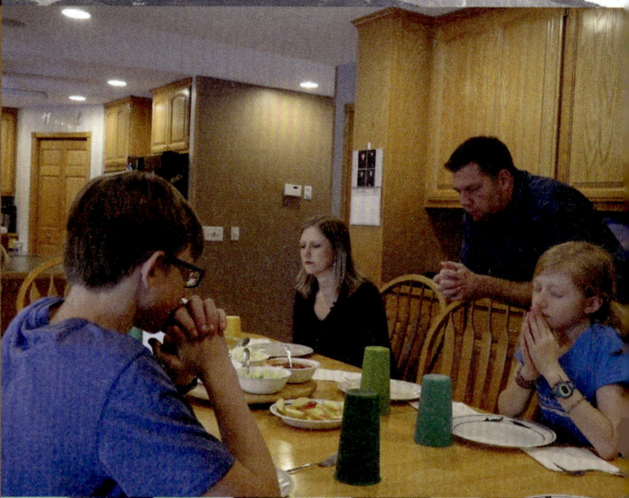

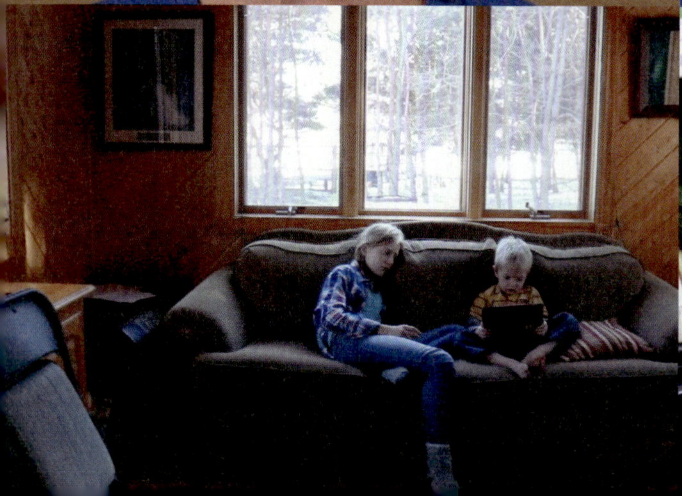

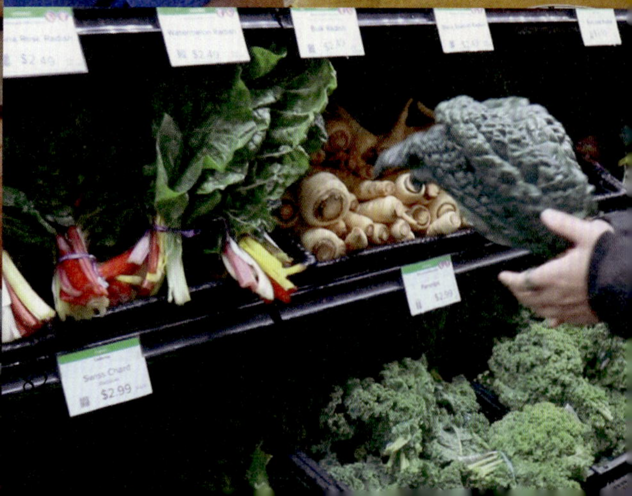

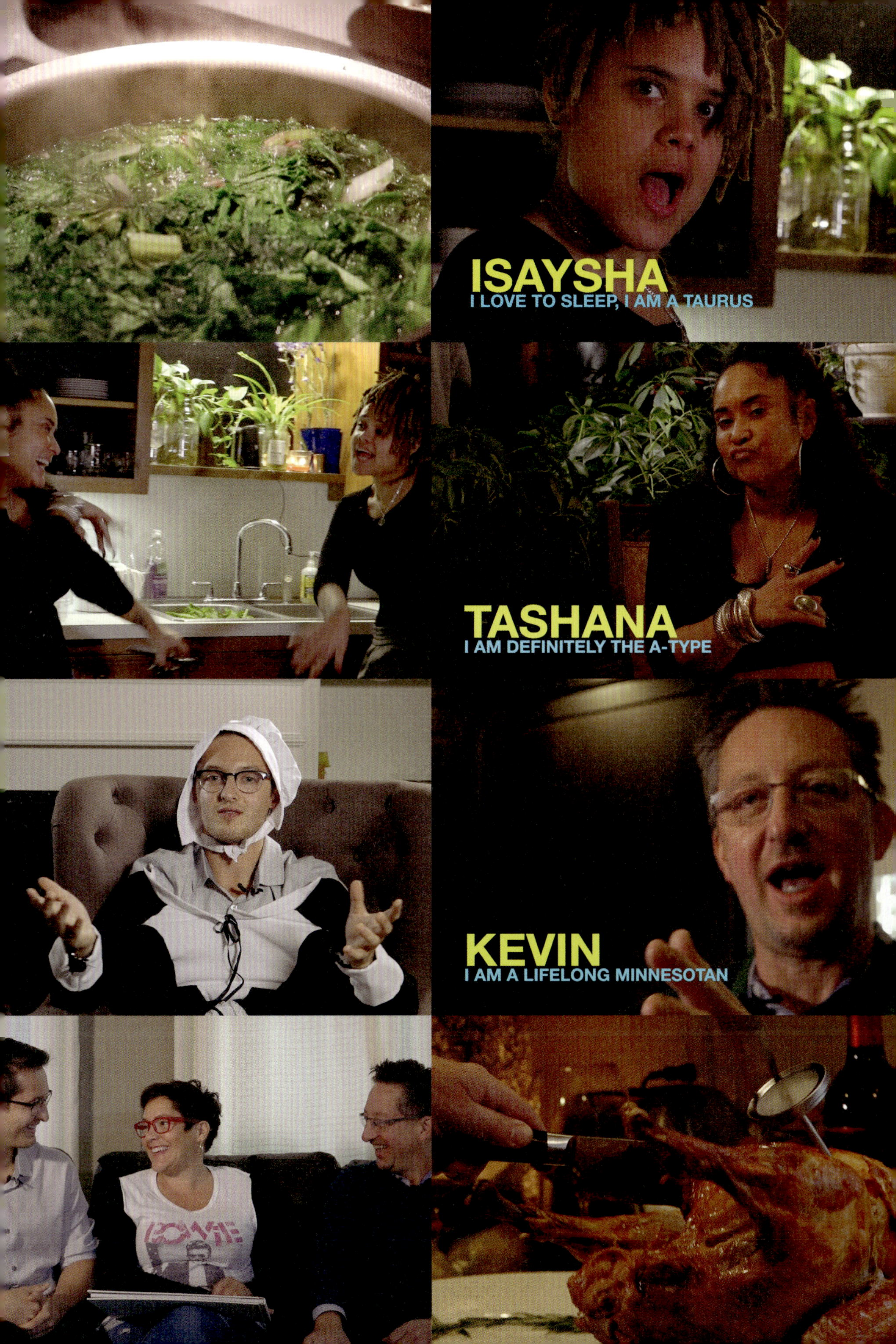
ISAYSHA
I LOVE TO SLEEP, I AM A TAURUS
TASHANA
I AM DEFINITELY THE A-TYPE
KEVIN
I AM A LIFELONG MINNESOTAN

Constant Dullaart, Karl Holmqvist, Hanne Lippard, Laure Prouvost, and Ruth Wolf-Rehfeldt
Collusion, Collision, Illusion

*For the month of December, I wanted to create a group show that involved a few events but wasn't such a high production. As one of the themes of the program is language and its inevitable medium of communication, I gathered artists whose work uses, questions, and challenges language on the most diverse level and is motivated by different cultural, generational, and socio-political contexts: Ruth Wolf-Rehfeldt's typeset writings, which subtly evoke the general spirit prevalent in 1970s East Germany amongst the artistic community; Hanne Lippard's *The Ssecret of SsucceSs iSs in the Ss-eSs* (2014), a playful salute to the corporate nature of the skyway system; Constant Dullaart's "Phantom Love" (2018), a work of hacker poetry existing within a public-private Minneapolis entity's Instagram account displayed on an iPhone showing each line in the form of a comment of one of many imaginary Instagram personae reflecting on the ambiguous nature of private-public space; Karl Holmqvist's wallpaper *Untitled* (2018), a personal note on the current state of the United States. *Collusion, Collision, Illusion* was probably the most classic visual art exhibition that happened in the space throughout the whole year. For this show, we tried for the first time the concept of the *Happy Hour*, which starts at 4:30pm, coinciding with one of the pedestrian "rush hours" of the skyways as employees head home from their office jobs, and runs until 7pm, attracting the outside public that doesn't work in the skyways. We read Constant Dullaart's poems "Phantom Love" collectively in the framework of this show following a strict choreography devised of by the artist. The *Happy Hour* format continued throughout the whole year, mainly to adapt to the skyway environment and to attract another public to our space, the office workers.

Constant Dullaart
Karl Holmqvist
Hanne Lippard
Laure Prouvost
Ruth Wolf-Rehfeldt

Collusion, Collision, Illusion

3–21 December 2018

Mondays in December, 4:30pm

(Holiday) Happy Hour
with a reading of Constant Dullaart's
Phantom Love

Elfriede Jelinek: Why do you so rarely tell the truth?
Heiner Müller: Because you need a lot of imagination to tell the truth.

—Interview with Heiner Müller, 1987

Rudy Giuliani: When you tell me that, you know, he should testify because he's going to tell the truth and he shouldn't worry, well, that's so silly because it's somebody's version of the truth. Not the truth…
Chuck Todd: Truth is truth.
Giuliani: No, no, it isn't truth. Truth isn't truth.

—Rudy Giuliani and NBC's Chuck Todd on "Meet The Press," quoted in: Caroline Kenny, "Rudy Giuliani says 'truth isn't truth,'" CNN, 19 August 2018

Die Wörter schlafen nicht in den Wörterbüchern.
Sie ziehen um den Block, ziellos, spielen mit Munition
Wie Kinder, die Krieg in sich tragen lang nach dem Krieg.
So hatten wir nicht gewettet, Herr Nobel, dass Dynamit
Alles austauschbar macht in Materie, Moral, Malerei.
Partikel, die wild durcheinanderwirbeln, Artikel
In allen Fachzeitschriften, für jedes Fach Abertausende –
Eine Wüstenpiste des Wissens. Und die riesigen Löcher
Zwischen der und jener Bedeutung von „Devotion",
Die Satellitenbilder von „Delirium" oder „Demokratie".

—Durs Grünbein, "Vom Erlernen alter Vokabeln," *Zündkerzen*

Images:
1. Ruth Wolf-Rehfeldt, *Aufbruchstimmung*, 1970s; Karl Holmqvist, *Wallpaper*, 2018
2. Hanne Lippard, *The Ssecret to SsucceSs iSs in the Ss-es*, 2014
3. Installation view

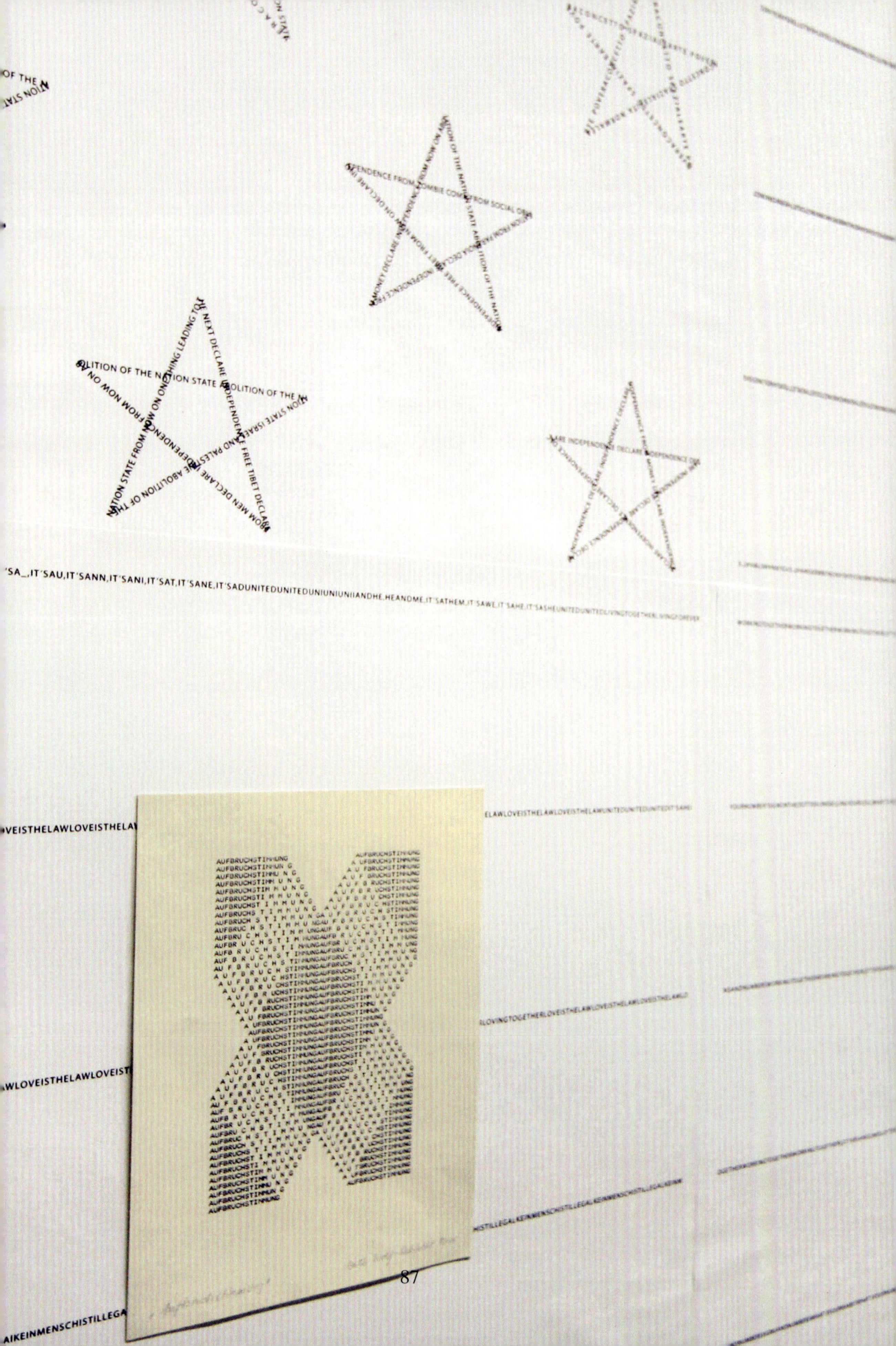

'SA_,IT'SAU,IT'SANN,IT'SANI,IT'SAT,IT'SANE,IT'SADUNITEDUNITEDUNIUNIUNIIANDHE,HEANDME,IT'SATHEM,IT'SAWE,IT'SAHE
VEISTHELAWLOVEISTHELAV
WLOVEISTHELAWLOVEISTI
AIKEINMENSCHISTILLEGA
AUFBRUCHSTIMMUNG

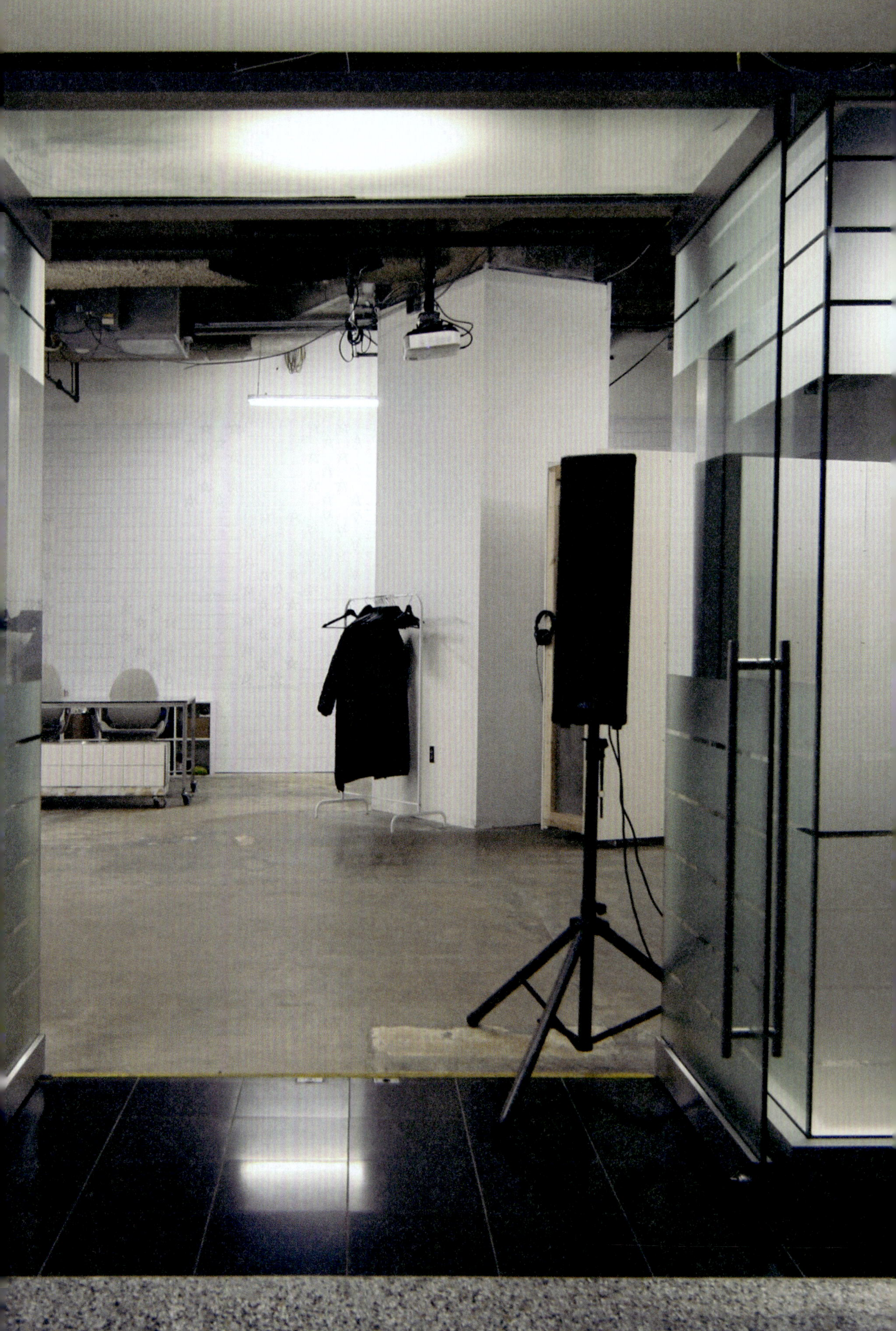

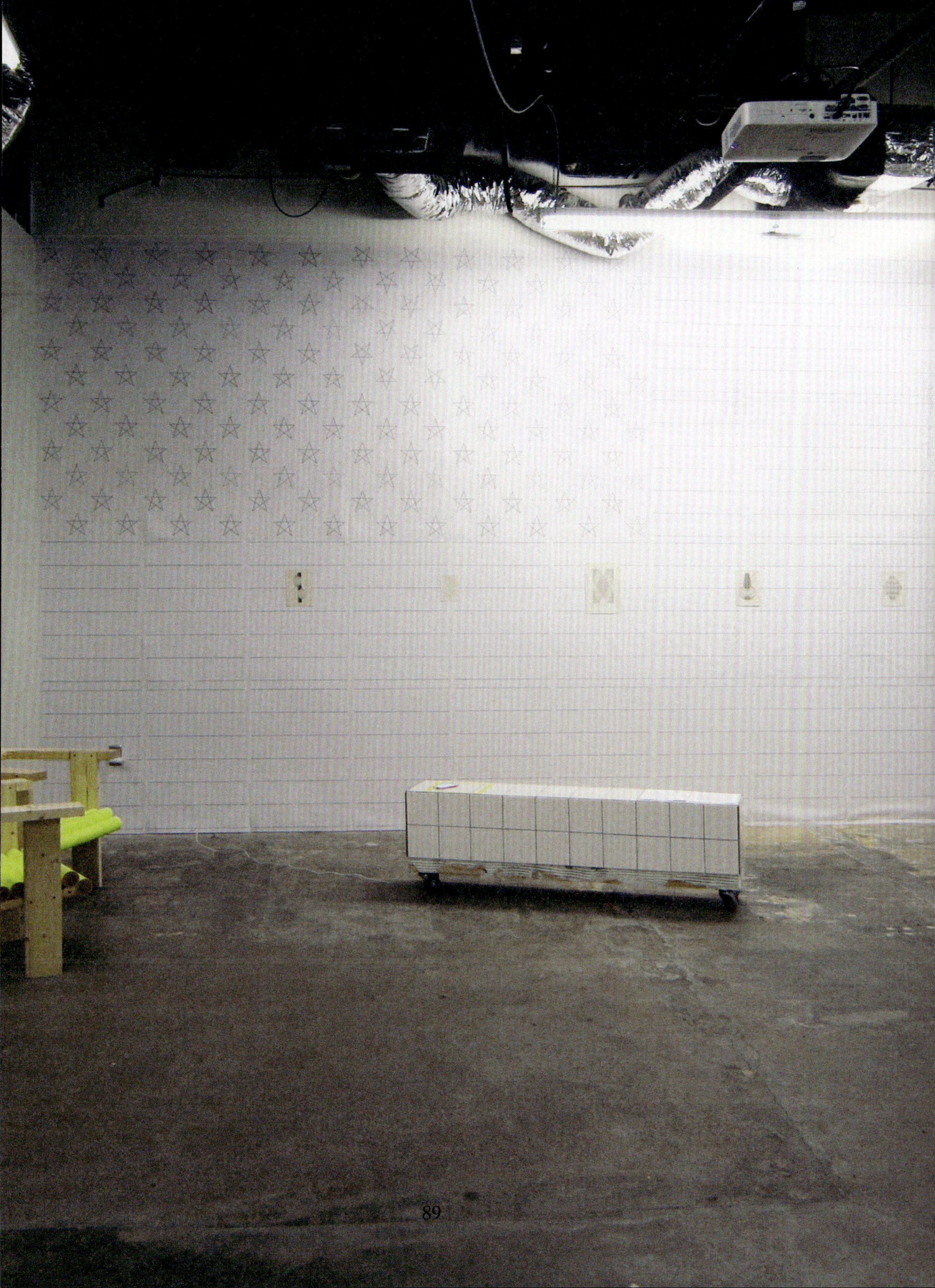

Let's Go Outside…

Bartholomew Ryan

I know you say this doesn't matter, but I fucking hate the skyways. I remember all the writers I like in today's art, how fluid they are and how the personal and the theoretical flow in and through each other. And I don't think I can bring that because I can never remember the theory, and I've really just learned to connect to the personal, and it's still mine.

Walking across a gray skyway with back-lit advertisements for a local financial firm on the wall. They feature the husband of a Walker Art Center board member, the institution I work for at the time.

Waiting for the dentist Downtown, looking up an escalator to a Caribou, and running up to sip on some coffee. Shocked by the hordes of professionals I find marching through their day. All up here.

Seeing an army of Target employees descending to the streets. It's Target Day, a friend tells me. They wear tan pants and those red shirts with white bull's-eyes. Having that feeling of absolute panic that that might be me someday. Thank fucking God I'm gay, I whisper for the millionth time, (not that Gayness is reprieve, but it does increase one's chances to evade).

Late at night in a skyway trying to figure out how to get out. Every exit is locked, walkways are dark and sinister, I feel exposed and visible on glass bridges.

Lost in the skyway trying to read my GPS, which does not distinguish heights. A bored guard points me in the right direction. The way-finding is non-existent. Complete opacity. The skyways are for the workers, not the casual visitor. "If you're hopelessly lost," states a peppy local article, "just ask someone who appears to be walking confidently for help. Skyway mastery is a point of pride for many Minneapolitans."

Skyway mastery, as if anything so banal could be capable of submission.

Realizing that they are not public, public streets accommodate the unwanted, the homeless and listless. The skyways seem free of such inconvenience. In Minneapolis they are completely private, with closing times and security guards, and codes of conduct.

Thinking about how Minnesotans feign this toughness when it comes to their merciless winters, but most of them leave their warm houses, into their warm cars, to their warm workplaces, and if in downtown walk around their warm skyways.

The skyways as an interior strip mall delivering the suburbs to the suburbanites who work in the city but have figured out a way to largely forget that fact.

Watching a video released by the Minneapolis Police Department, it shows a preppy white dude in shorts holding a giant cell phone. It's nighttime. He is approached and talked to by a number of young black men, who circle and retreat and ultimately grab for his cellphone. He puts up a fight, but is thrown to the ground and kicked in the head a number of times.

"I wouldn't want to work downtown," a manager says. "Yeah? I wouldn't care I'd just bring my gun," says another.

A friend says that while they are for criminal justice reform in general these kids who cross the line into violence should be locked up forever. My friend is trans and tells me they feel vulnerable and afraid.

A friend's grandmother, who is comforted by Fox News, tells him that she worries about him all the time because he works downtown.

"What about the criminals in the buildings?" says a pop music professor named Elliot that I meet in a bar. He's responding to this argument I have heard about how if the skyways didn't exist the civilized people would be on the streets thereby warding off crime.

A lot of kids hang out downtown because there is nowhere else for them to hang out. This is their suburb, and it is often safer here than their own neighborhoods.

Skyways as disease but not symptom. The streets as symptom but not disease.

Nicollet Mall, which runs through the heart of downtown and was refurbished just in time for the Super Bowl, is kind of nice. During the day they put out freestanding, fun-colored chairs—some kind of social practice project—and people sit in them. Not everyone who sits in them is homeless. Late at night after work on the way to play pool I will take a seat and eat a chopped salad with chicken. Sometimes I sit under this skyway that pumps out disco pop tracks or soft melodious Jazz late into the night. Sometimes people dance underneath it. I am genuinely surprised that the city provides something that increases the quality of life for its homeless population. So I assume the chairs will go soon.

It's evening and a man is trying to get out of a skyway. He pushes at the door, and then the next, but nothing gives. My friend knocks on the window and gets his attention. Over there, my friend points to a side door. The man tries it and escapes. "Thanks, bro, I appreciate that," he says shaking his head. Out onto the street. Free at last.

A short drunk man approaches us at the bus stop. The skyways loom overhead and into the distance. His jeans are sagging and most of his pale moonlike bottom is visible. He is perhaps fifty, but who the fuck knows? For some reason he wants to talk about horses. It's hard to follow, but he used to ride horses and he misses them. It's hard to believe this guy ever did anything. Our bus approaches and the man goes out onto the road in front of it. His pants are around his thighs now, he is gripping them above his crotch at front. The bus driver honks gently. My friend and I persuade the man to come back onto the pavement. He doesn't really understand anything. He shuffles back to the edge of the pavement but can't get his foot up the five or six inches he needs. Reluctantly I take his hand and help him up. We get on the bus and drive away with the man standing there talking to no one.

Residents of the skyways in downtown St. Paul, which are publicly and privately owned, are concerned about the people congregating in groups that can be loud and disruptive. They want to know what the city is going to do about it? One couple retired there are shocked by the slow creep of unwanted bodies into their spaces. In St. Paul the city owns the skyways, and the companies own the buildings. The city treats the skyways as public, therefore open to anyone. Some apartment communities have armed themselves with pool cues, baseball bats, or whatever they can get their hands on. They step outside and act as protectors of fellow residents as they make their way home after dark.

I'm listening to Spotify walking on Nicollet. It's 1am or so and this man is coming across the road towards me too fast for my liking. He trips, keeps his footing, but stumbles towards me even faster. "Sir, Sir," he shouts, but I *run* twenty feet then turn and ask him what he wants? "I hurt my eye, Sir, I need help." I look at his left eye, which is scarred and distended. I can't tell if the wound is fresh. Okay, I take out my phone, "I'll call you an ambulance." "I don't want no fucking ambulance!" He marches off his hand covering his eye.

Three years ago yesterday I tied myself to a suitcase and jumped off the Stone Arch Bridge. When I hit the Mississippi I broke four vertebrae. I spent a long time trying to drown and then was rescued by a handsome fireman who broke a lot of rules. Since then I've learnt a lot about my two main issues, mental health and addiction. I've met many many people who are still in pain, are dead, or are recovering like me. My first six years in Minneapolis was my museum, art studios, travel, and art events, philanthropic interiors, and interiors of philanthropists. Of course there was also drinking spaces, and later meth and sex and all that comes with that. The last three years Minneapolis has been hospitals, treatment centers, recovery meetings, therapists, busses, and streets largely populated by the dispossessed. Paradoxically, I am much more at home in this Minneapolis.

I write to a friend in Berlin. When I arrived in Minneapolis ten years ago he worked in Visitor's Services for the Walker. This experience had given him an ambient contemporary art education and also a deep distrust for the institution of art. He and I were both pretty depressed, we would walk around the lake and talk about how terrible the world was and this would cheer us up a little. "What do the skyways mean to you?" I ask via WhatsApp. "I always thought of them as gerbil tubes," he responds. For a while there I couldn't step into one without meeting some guy I had wanked off at the "Y".

Gerbil tubes. I am a little disturbed by the ease with which I welcome this description. The employee as gerbil, mindlessly shuffling through their day then eating large salads with chopsticks on their lunch break while discussing their upcoming wedding plans.

I know that we are all animals because when I was drowning or trying to drown my animal would not let me go. It fought for life not because that is all it knows how to do but because it had not said goodbye yet to the other animals it loves, like my mammy animal, my daddy animal, and my sister animal. If I, at my most alone, drowning in the Mississippi, am an animal, then aren't these gerbils also animals? With other animals that they love and desire to be beside, breath beside, and smell beside?

My friend recommends some literature, and I buy a few books. The first one I pick up is *Last Days at Hot Slit*, the collected writings of radical feminist and anti-porn polemicist Andrea Dworkin. I am drawn to a suicide letter she wrote in Paris in 1999. (Dworkin died of natural causes). "I was old and tired," she writes, "and I was taking myself out of the rape pool." Something that as a woman could only be achieved by death because the potential for rape was everywhere all the time. Reflecting on life, she writes, "Fuck and lie is the name of the game. Fuck and lie."

I don't think animals lie, gerbils are not so into intrigue. I don't think my animal lies, but I do. My becoming animal is about scraping away layers of personhood to become something more complex and true and base. The problem with the skyways is that they are lies of omission, they literally make themselves through exclusion of the messiness of the everyday, and therefore they have further sublimated the inner animal of their occupants. They demand conformity of movement and behavior at an even greater level than the streets below. Calling them gerbil tubes is not fair on gerbils. They are human tubes, full of nice snacks.

The skyways represent what many people wish was happening; the streets with their messy civic-ness reveal something else. Imagine an elderly man on the streets below. He's sitting back on a Nicollet chair relaxing in the sun on an otherwise cold fall day. Several years ago his addiction caused him to lose his job as a trucker, his wife left him, he was sent to treatment, but recovery didn't take. When they foreclosed on his house they took away whatever hope he had left of a retirement, a legacy, of his children having an inheritance. Across the U.S., across Europe and the Globe, he was blamed for the financial crisis despite the fact that he never should have qualified for the ridiculous loans he received from his mortgage broker. The people who own his loan and traded it for profit are bailed out by the taxpayer. Some of them are looking at him right now. Hands in pockets, far far above. They shake their heads disapprovingly. Fuck and lie is the name of the game. Fuck and lie.

The latest addition to the skyways network will be the Public Services Center set for completion in the fall of 2020. The building will preserve two existing skyways but also have a new suspended bridge reaching into the two-story ground floor. A number of the cities prevailing ideologies swirl and contest within the context of this project. The architect Michael Sørensen of Henning Larsen insists that they will open the skyways to the street, by bringing them into the building in " a very extroverted way." An open planned "social stairway" and various other devices will make it seem present and connected to a ground "street" level.

Many prominent figures in Minneapolis society have turned against the skyways as a damaging legacy of the past, which have starved the streets of life and traffic. They want the streets to live again, to thrive with commerce. Planning commissioner Sam Rockwell sees the retention of skyways in the new building as a mistake. "This is an opportunity to break part of the spine here, and to start to make it a little less convenient." In defense of the skyways, many point out that its fucking cold as hell out there, and also that disabled people find it difficult to navigate the icy streets in winter. Eric Dayton, a local businessman and scion of one of Minnesota's primary philanthropic families, urges disabled activists, "Let's look at what other cold-climate cities around the world are doing to keep their sidewalks clear and safe for wheelchairs." As someone who has navigated this city without a car for the last decade, I can say the idea that Minneapolis is going to clear its pavements of ice and snow any time soon should be treated with a strong degree of skepticism.

I'm kind of torn here, I don't love the skyways, but the fact that so many dignitaries also dislike them makes me want to like them again. If all these neoliberal urbanites want to get rid of them, what am I missing?

"Why are people against the skyways?" my roommate's sister asks. She is Somali and a scientist. "Don't they know it's freezing outside?"

Google the word "civic" and see what you get.

The city just voted unanimously to approve a giant hanging sculpture for the two-story atrium of the public services building. The work will have, "a mesmerizing visual effect," says city arts administrator Mary Altman, and will change along with shifts in temperature outside. "I thought it was a big fish net," says Joe Tamburino of the Downtown Minneapolis Neighborhood Association. Joe is lobbying for a higher police presence downtown. Joe wants the city to commission a painting or sculpture by some young local artist and save the 700k price tag for cops. In response to the sculpture's kinetic qualities he declares on local television, "Unnecessary! You want to see the changes in the city? Look outside." In the local television report, Joe turns and looks at his office window, which has a mostly closed dark venetian blind. The screensaver on his PC shows the Colosseum, monument to a fallen empire. The colors are deeply saturated, almost painterly.

Joe looks outside to see the changes in the city; we go outside to feel the changes in the city.

A few weeks back the President was in town for a rally. In the late afternoon I left the deserted skyways and descended to the streets. It was gray and starting to rain but the air was literally alive with the moment—supporters and protestors swarmed to the Target Center arena. Whistles, placards, arguments. A tense civic quality.

A homeless dude, mid-twenties, sits beside me in the coffee shop. He is enjoying his overpriced pastry and coffee. He smells pretty bad. He asks me for money, and I give him some. I ask him if he's an addict, and he tells me no that he doesn't do drugs. We talk for a few minutes. I realize that he was in the psych ward with me three years ago at Hennepin County Medical Center. I spent a month there in a giant neck brace watching CNN. This guy was there for at least a week of that. At the time he was clean and much better dressed. He sat in the corner most days and cried with his hands over his face. I ask what he thinks of the skyways? "I really like them," he says, "they make me feel peaceful. I wrote a song about them once."

The year is 2040. The Great Thaw explodes the banks of the Mississippi, flooding the plains and cities. In Minneapolis the survivors are downtown, saved by the heights of the skyways buildings. Floors of office space are turned over, scavenged, repurposed. Having fended off the drowning streets, the remaining humans fight for true mastery of the skyways—the arteries to resources and survival. Apartment complex leisure centers become communal dining halls. Pool tables once used in casual games between groups of drinking straight people become ritualistic sites of arbitration between alpha males who otherwise would resolve their differences with a baseball bat. Gyms are training centers for a new warrior class, some machines repurposed for use in medieval torture chambers.

Ever loyal to the corporate cultures that gave their lives meaning, the humans align into familiar gangs. For instance, following a civil war between its diverse and optimistic retail types and the powerful (quietly conservative) managerial class, the Target company evolved into the Targs. To broker peace and resolve internal strife, the Targs gather around a ritual that operates to successfully fudge the differences between its progressive and conservative wings. Namely, gay marriage.

This stealthy and creative gang elevates its faggots to deities in golden handcuffs. Homo visibility can be touted by staff as progressive victory, while the managers can revel in the absorption of homo doctrine into old school family values. The gang is sustained by elaborate gay wedding rituals where managers make affirming dinner toasts about love and tolerance. Fed and protected, when the homos are not getting married they are passed around amongst the straight couples to arbitrate between them and give friendly advice on performing fellatio.

Anton Kats
Radio Amateur Ensemble

*Anton Kats calls his radio community projects "narrowcast" or "listening stations," which are accessible to the public and enable direct exchange and creation of musical scores with the locally created community. I felt the open nature of this project, how the content produced is open to contributions as opposed to the one-way direction of a broadcast, aligned itself nicely with the overall approach of *Goethe in the Skyways* and the alternative micro radio scene of Minneapolis—St. Paul. On site, Anton investigated the ham and amateur radio community, as well as the city's music scene, all of which are quite vibrant. We made our entry into this community by getting in touch with the owners of the most important radio equipment store in the Midwest, Radio City, and were introduced to the mature and very charming ham radio community through them, some of whom attended one or more of the Open Studios surrounding Anton's *Radio Amateur Ensemble*.

Anton Kats

Radio Amateur Ensemble

9 January – 15 February 2019

Radio Amateur Ensemble explores Minneapolis's ham radio enthusiast community, taking the sonic, social, and technological aspects of ham radio communication as scores and notations for improvisation and the sharing of new sound compositions. Considering listening as a generative act, *Radio Amateur Ensemble* transforms the Goethe Pop Up space in Minneapolis's skyways into a walkable audio-visual score featuring musical performances / open studios, recording sessions, set design, and an accompanying podcast. The ensemble, developed in collaboration with Patrick Marschke, Cole Pulice, and Noah Ophoven-Baldwin invites the wider audience to take part in the ongoing dialogue exploring amateur radio as a tool manifesting new social constellations, networks, and organisms.

Kats's project is developed in respect to Bertolt Brecht's critique of radio as an instrument that standardizes individuals into passive listeners. Translating research findings sonically and rhythmically during the duration of the project, the compositions developed by the *Radio Amateur Ensemble* are performed and recorded during several public events at the Goethe Pop Up Minneapolis and released on a limited edition 7-inch vinyl.

22 January 2019, 4:30–6:30 pm

Open Studio
with Anton Kats, Patrick Marschke, Noah Ophoven-Baldwin, and Cole Pulice

29 January 2019, 4:30–6:30 pm

Open Studio & Recording Session
with Anton Kats, Patrick Marschke, Noah Ophoven-Baldwin, and Cole Pulice

5 February 2019, 4:30–6:30 pm

Opening & Podcast Panel
with Anton Kats, Patrick Marschke, Noah Ophoven-Baldwin, and Cole Pulice, moderated by Daniel Shinbaum

Images:
1. Installation view
2. Mobile Sound System
3. Open Studio & Recording Session

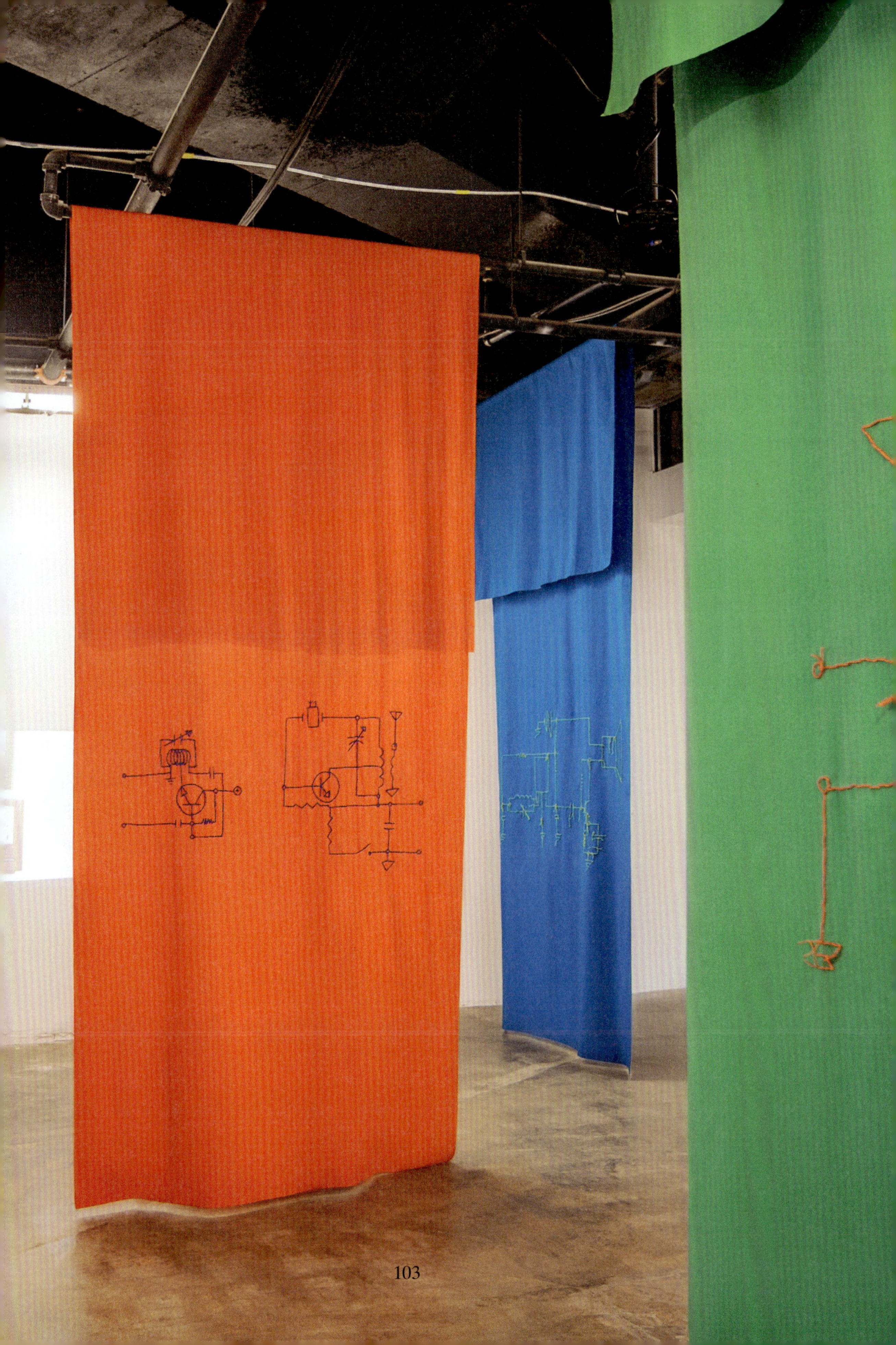

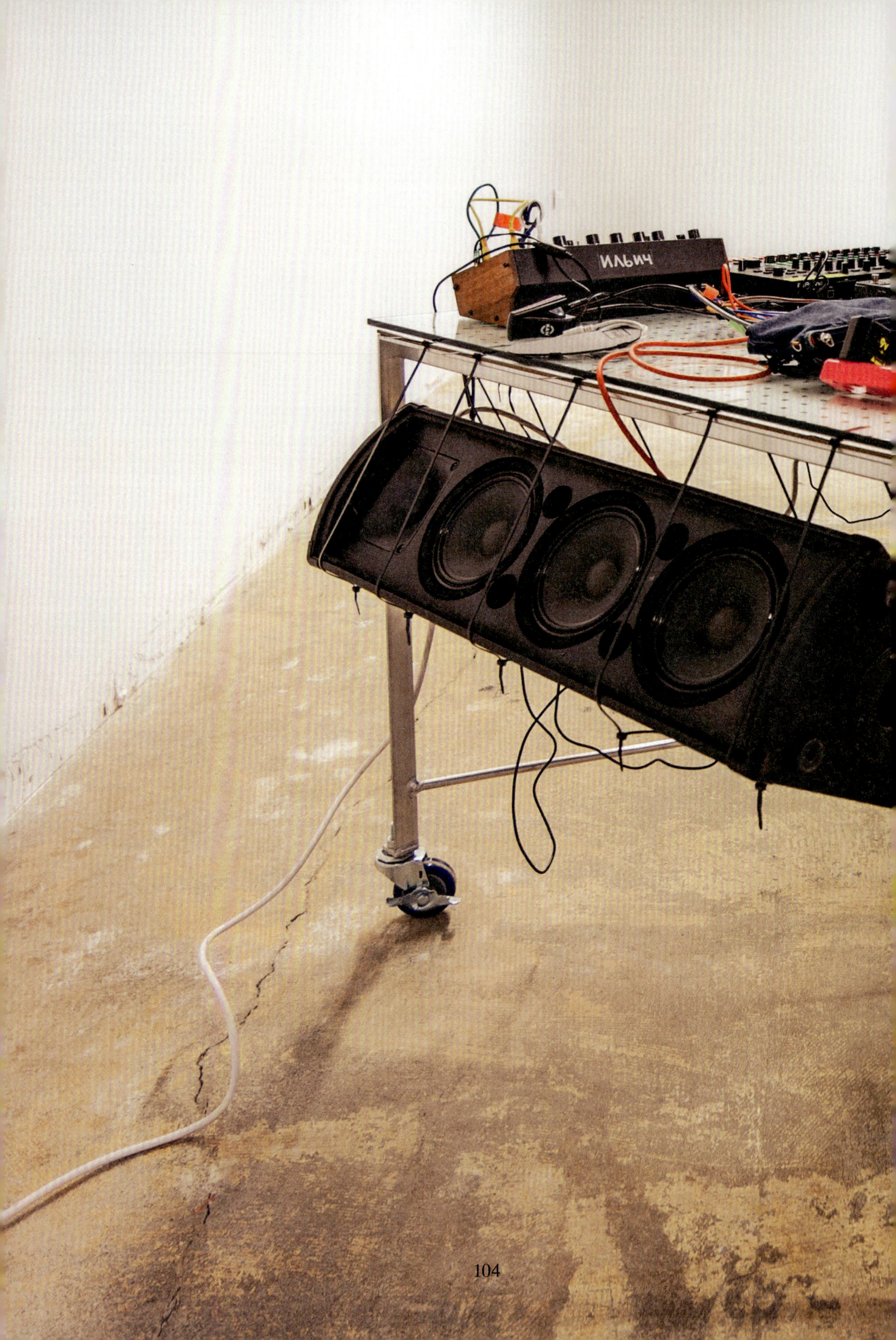
ИЛЬИЧ

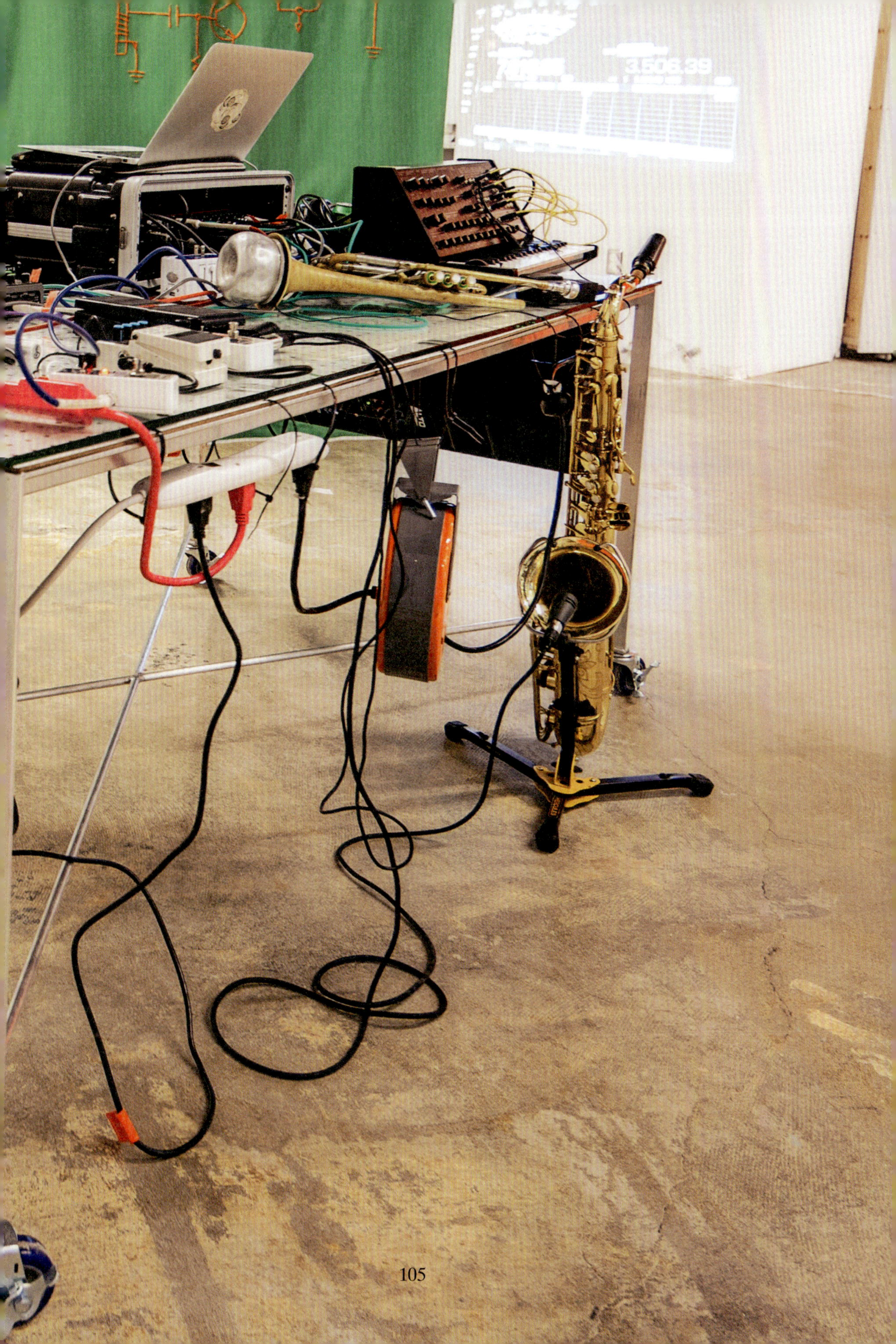

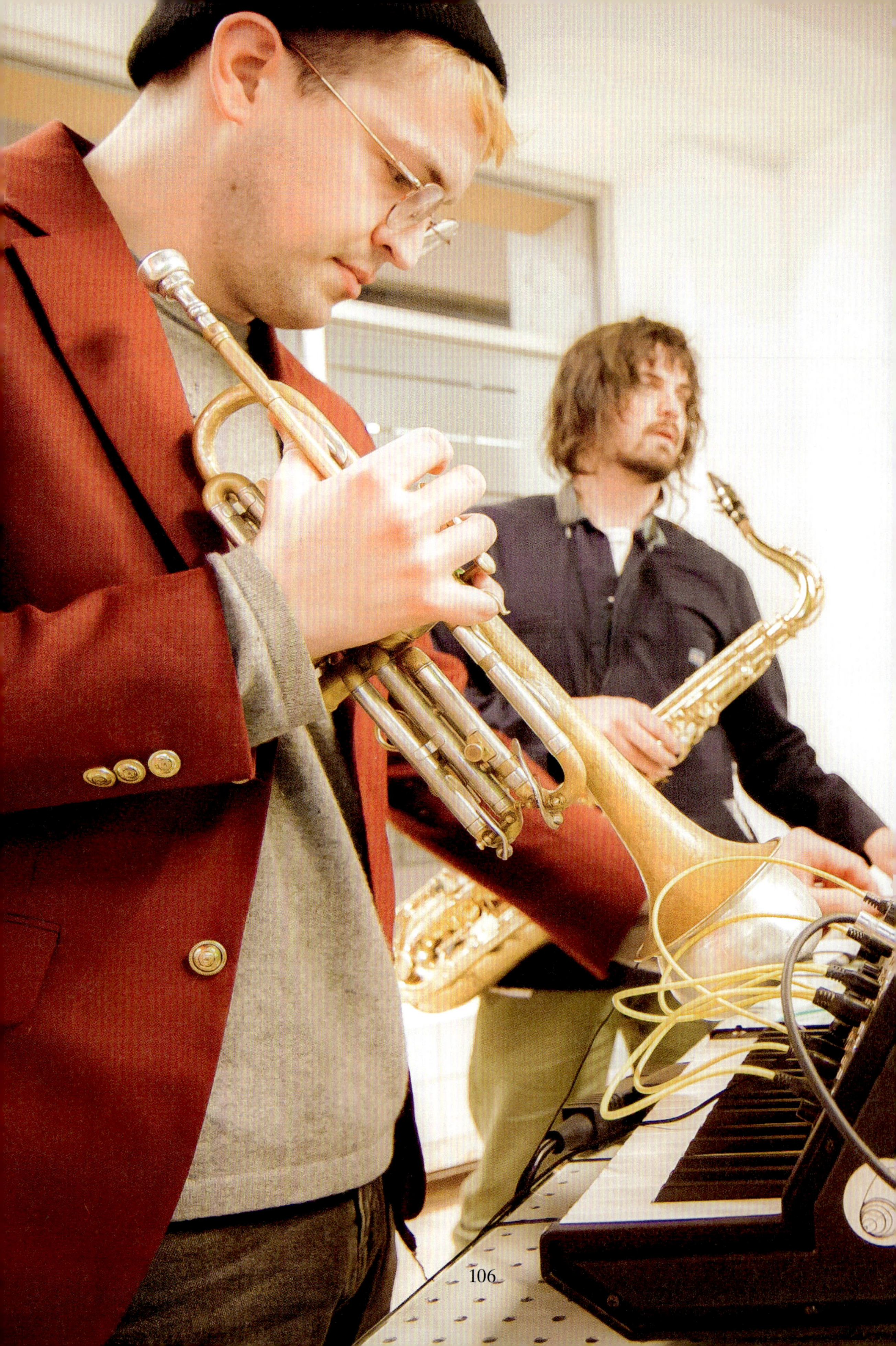

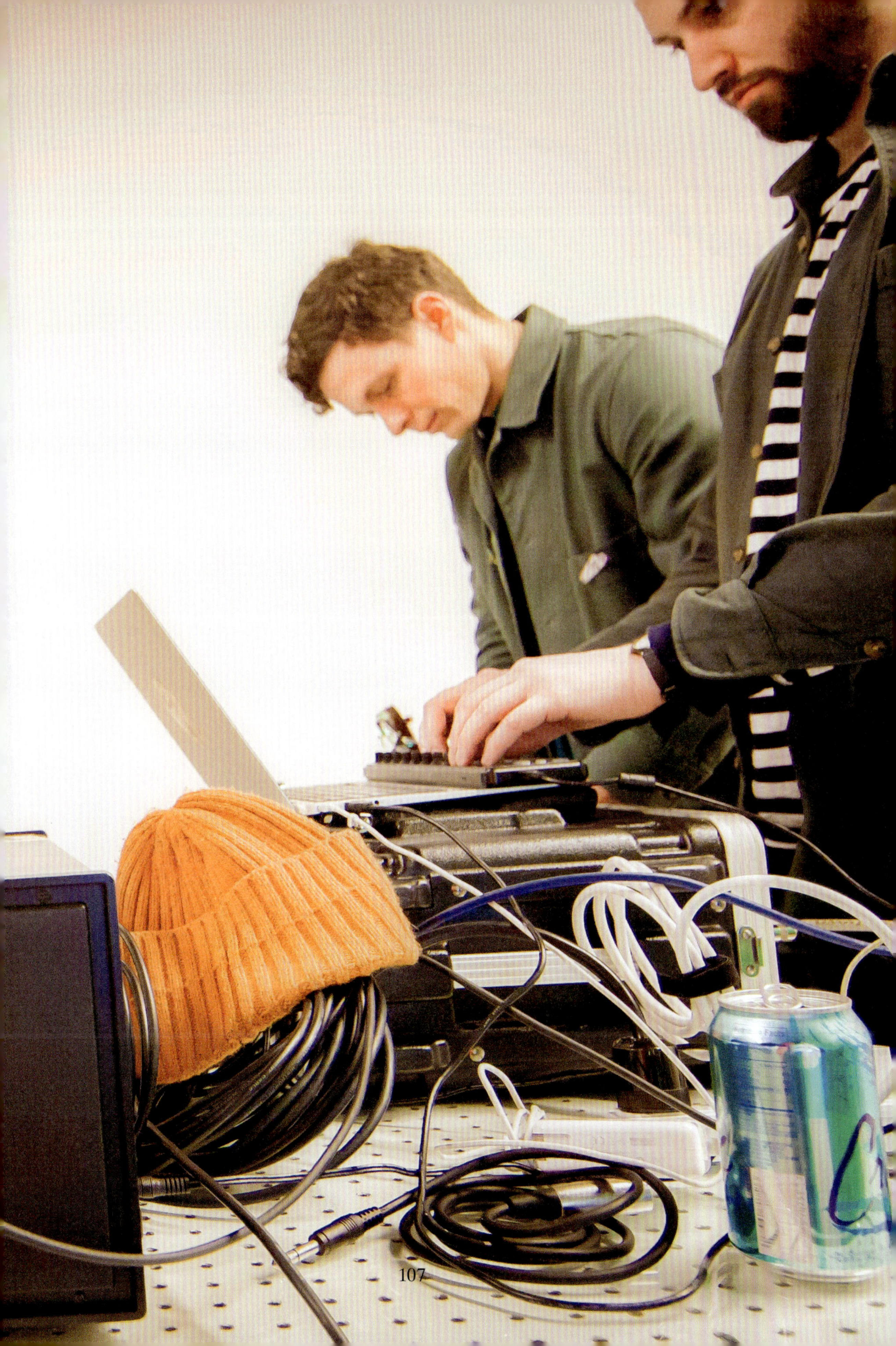

Albrecht Pischel
Commission Roundabout

*As I read about protests in northern Minnesota against newly installed traffic roundabouts, I immediately thought of Albrecht Pischel's project *Commission Roundabout*. Its musical component and collaborative nature of inviting fellow artists to contribute new sculptures for the project made it even more appealing. Albrecht talked about the work in this context in terms of "cultural dispositions that favor the cross(ing) over the circle," because the U.S. seems to prefer the intersection to the roundabout. I think of the project as an illustration of different mindsets, one in which people have to engage, negotiate, and co-habitat with each other and their surroundings, and the other as more individualist and definitive. In order to connect this artistic interpretation of the roundabout to the reality of traffic roundabouts, we invited the responsible engineer at the Minnesota Department of Transportation (MnDot) to come to the Pop Up and promote the idea of the roundabout to the public. I'm always interested in connecting the often abstract and sometimes cryptic realm of visual art with the "real" world.

Albrecht Pischel

Commission Roundabout

26 February – 22 March 2019

26 February 2019, 4:30 pm

Opening & Launch of New Roundabout Sculptures by Andy Delany, Katelyn Farstad, David Flaugher, Chris Larson, and Setareh Shahbazi

7 March 2019, 7 pm

Concert at Palmer's *Heavy Metal*

11 March, 6 pm

Panel discussion with Matylda Krzykowski, 2019 Mitchell Visiting Professor at SAIC, and Ken Johnson, traffic engineer (MnDOT/ Minnesota Department of Transportation)

For *Commission Roundabout* Albrecht Pischel transforms the Goethe Pop Up Minneapolis into a temporary agency for roundabout sculptures. The corporate identity conceived for the occasion blends the appearance of the venue with its surrounding—the mall-like labyrinthine skyway system of Minneapolis.

Commission Roundabout—Pischel's ongoing edition project—invites artists to produce a sculpture for an imaginary roundabout. This time around Andy Delany (Minneapolis), Katelyn Farstad (Minneapolis), David Flaugher (Detroit), Chris Larson (Minneapolis), and Setareh Shahbazi (Berlin/Tehran) contribute miniature sculptures that are on spinning display in the center of accompanying LPs and their players.

Traffic roundabouts as relevant synapses of modern civil infrastructure have recently been highlighted as such by occupations of the "yellow vests" in France during the so-called "roundabout protests." In the United States, roundabouts in their most rudimentary form emerged as early as 1907 and modern versions were built from the 1990s—decades after they became ubiquitous in Europe and other parts of the world, particularly the Middle East. In Minnesota, roundabouts have recently gained ground as a safer, quicker, and more harmonious way for vehicles to pass through intersections. Despite this development and their popularity abroad, they remain highly controversial in the automotive U.S. at large.

Pischel takes the seeming banality of the roundabout as a starting point for speculations on underlying cultural dispositions that favor the cross(ing) over the circle.

Images:
1. Chris Larson, *Little Nemo (in Slumberland)*, 2019 (spinning on Hüsker Dü LP)
2. David Flaugher, *Untitled*, 2019 (front); Setareh Shahbazi, *Presenting the Spectacle*, 2019
3. New roundabout sculptures with accompanying records
4. Panel discussion with Matylda Krzykowski and Ken Johnson
5. Albrecht Pischel, *Heavy Metal*

Andy Delany, *Floaters*, 2019
Aluminum, glass, contact lenses
LP: *Solitudes. Environmental Sound Experiences*

Don't get too close I'm sorry but everything might fall apart it's a little silly but it's the only way to have things stay together I'm sorry it's what's around and it's shiny and light and rigid and it looks nice like my macbook and a mall and it's what's around and I can see through it you just can't get too close it's a little silly but when you're up you just try to forget what you can't help and grasp what you can see and I try I guess not to look down or too close around and be happy and free

Katelyn Farstad, *The Best Way to Get Rid of the First Version is to Not be Sure What You Can Find in This One*, 2019
Found objects, ceramic
LP: Edith Piaf, *I Regret Nothing*

I made five totally different sculptures for this edition: one is a vase with dried flowers, one is a vase with a hat on, one is two pineapples made of different materials stacked on top of one another, one is a salt shaker in a snow storm, and the last one is a proposal for a trophy for a sport event, or award that is of an undetermined nature.

David Flaugher, *Untitled*, 2019
Found salt shaker
LP: DJ Assault, *Where the Hoes*

DJ Assault is one of the many local seasonings that makes Detroit a city worth living in.

Chris Larson, *Little Nemo (in Slumberland)*, 2019
Miniature bed
LP: Hüsker Dü, *Land Speed Record*

The album used in this sculpture is a recording of an exact replica of the drum track featured on Hüsker Dü's 1981 live record under the same title. My version of the album was recorded live in the 7th Street Entry on April 14th, 2016 and played by death metal drummer Yousif Del Valle. The drums are the same that Grant Hart played on the original Hüsker Dü album that was recorded live in the 7th Street Entry in 1981. The title of this sculpture comes from a character created by American cartoonist Winsor McCay and is the title of a song by Grant Hart from his 1999 *Good News From Modern Man* album. Slumberland is also the location of my studio in St. Paul.

Setareh Shahbazi, *Presenting the Spectacle*, 2019
Car tire, cement, wood, plastic, iPhone, video
LP: Fearless Iranians From Hell, *Foolish Americans*

Fearless Iranians from Hell were a 1980s hardcore/punk band from San Antonio, Texas whose lyrics criticize U.S.-American politics of the time through an alleged Iranian lens. None of its members were actually Iranian. Shahbazi's miniature sculpture is inspired by the phenomenon of accidental street sculptures prevalent in—from a Western perspective—dysfunctional Middle Eastern countries. Such sculptures informally mark holes in the road or reserve temporary parking spots, often consisting of tires and other debris.

Previous roundabout commissions include: Christiane Blattmann, FORT, Kathi Hofer, Alexi Kukuljevic, Veit Laurent Kurz, Matt Mullican, Dan Peterman, Paul Sochacki, Raphaela Vogel, Rolf Walz, and B. Wurtz.

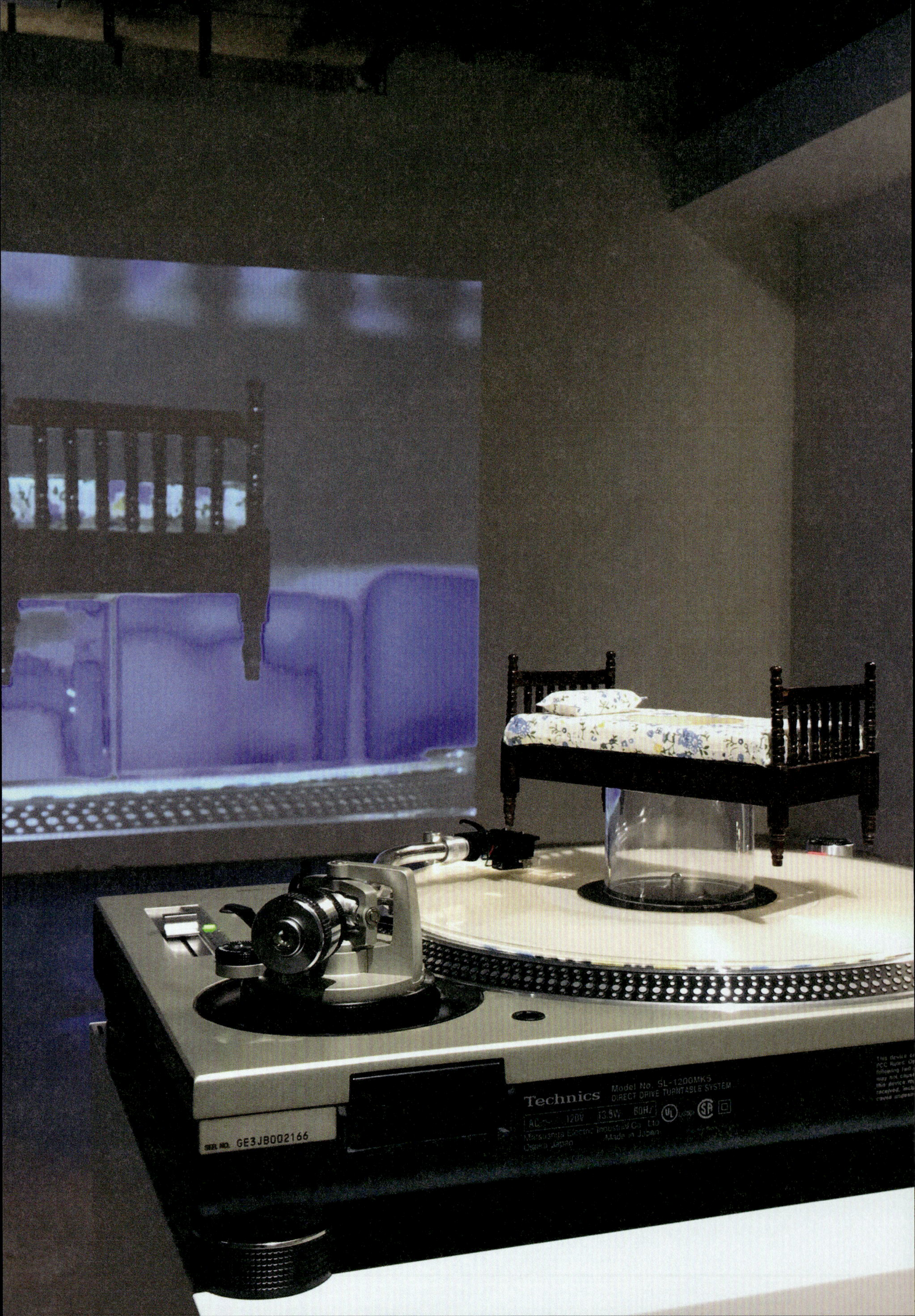
Technics
Model No. SL-1200MK5
DIRECT DRIVE TURNTABLE SYSTEM
120V 13.5W 60Hz
Made in Japan
GE3JB002166

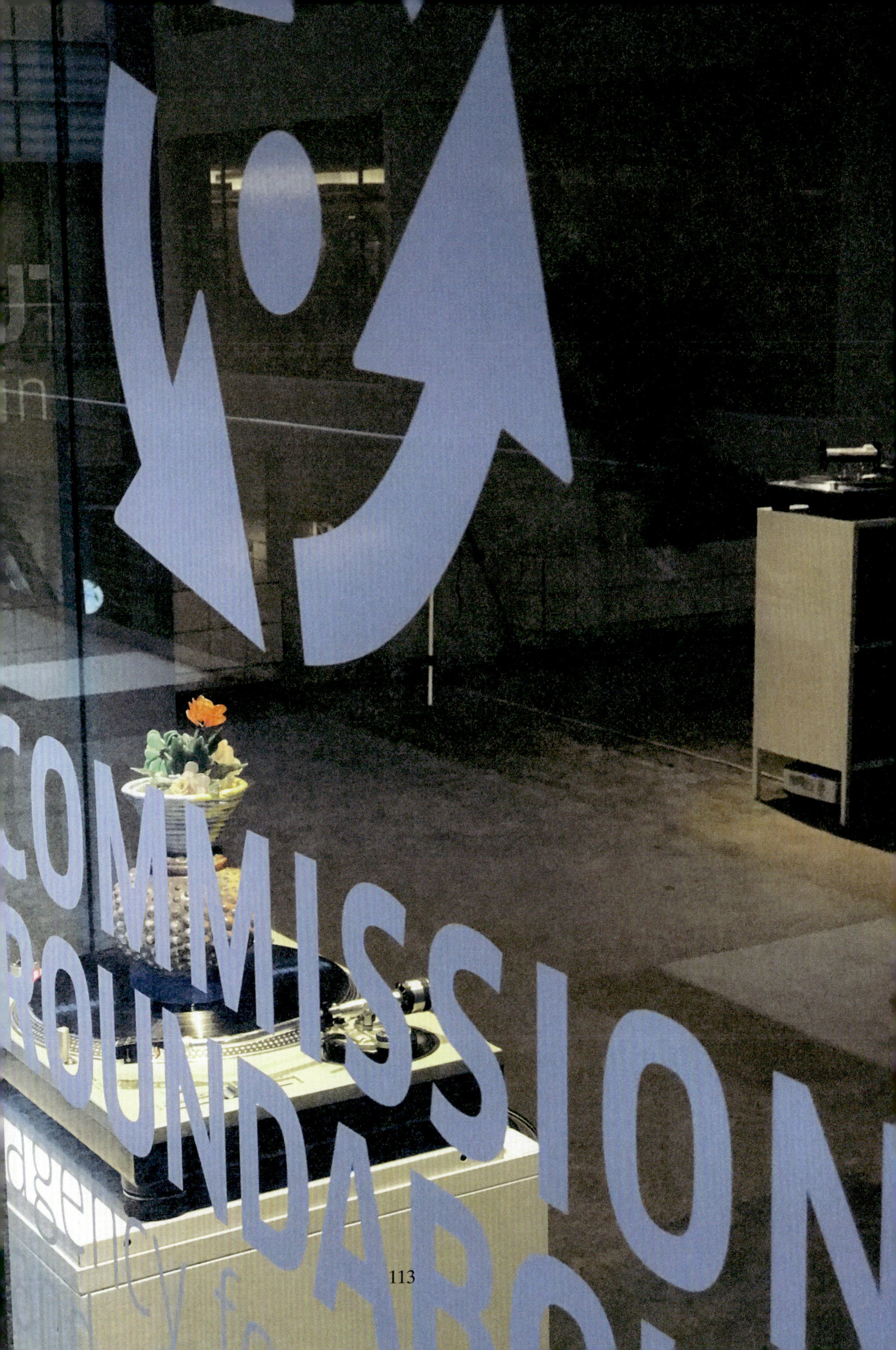
COMMISSION

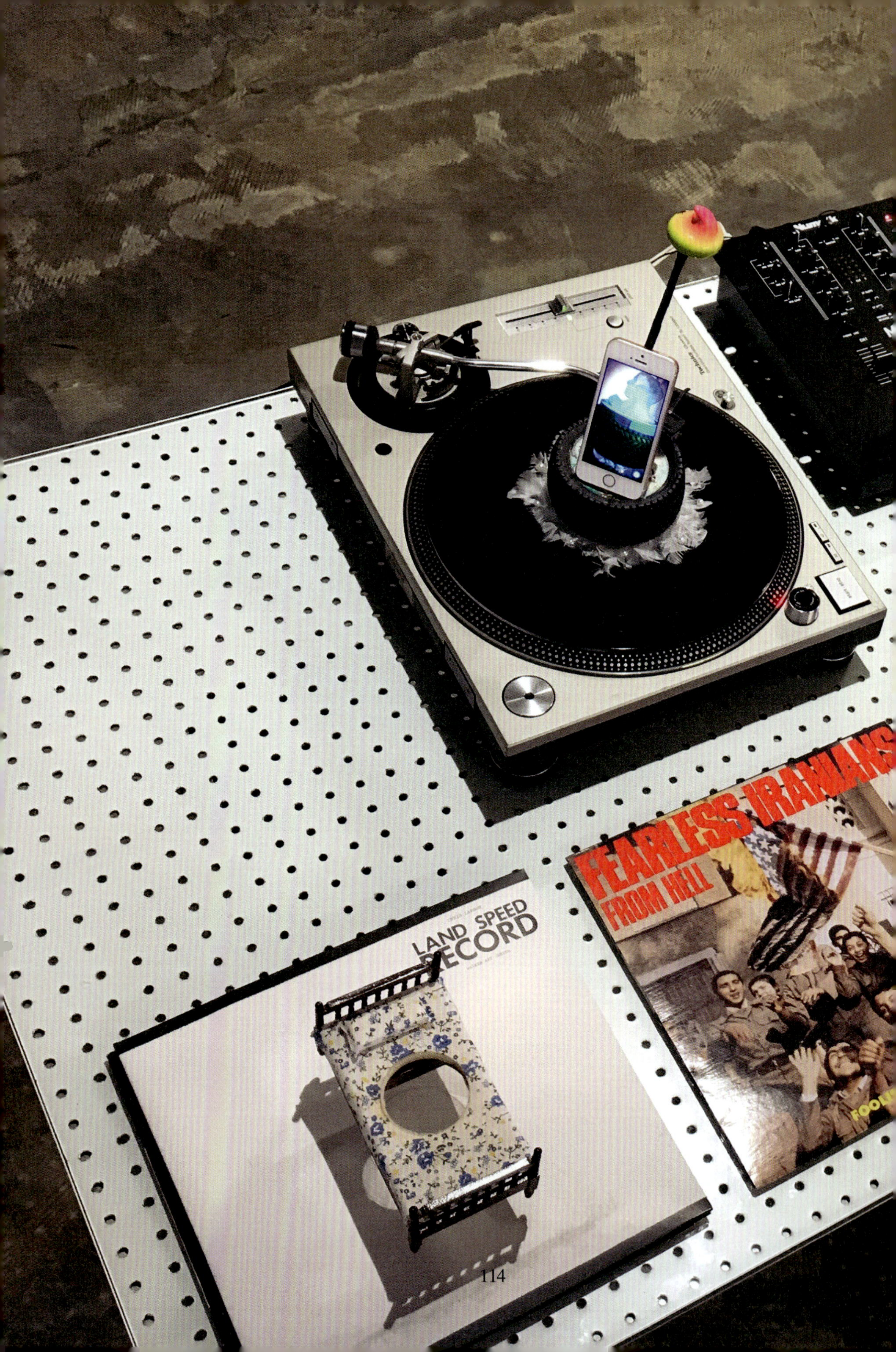
LAND SPEED RECORD
FEARLESS IRANIANS FROM HELL

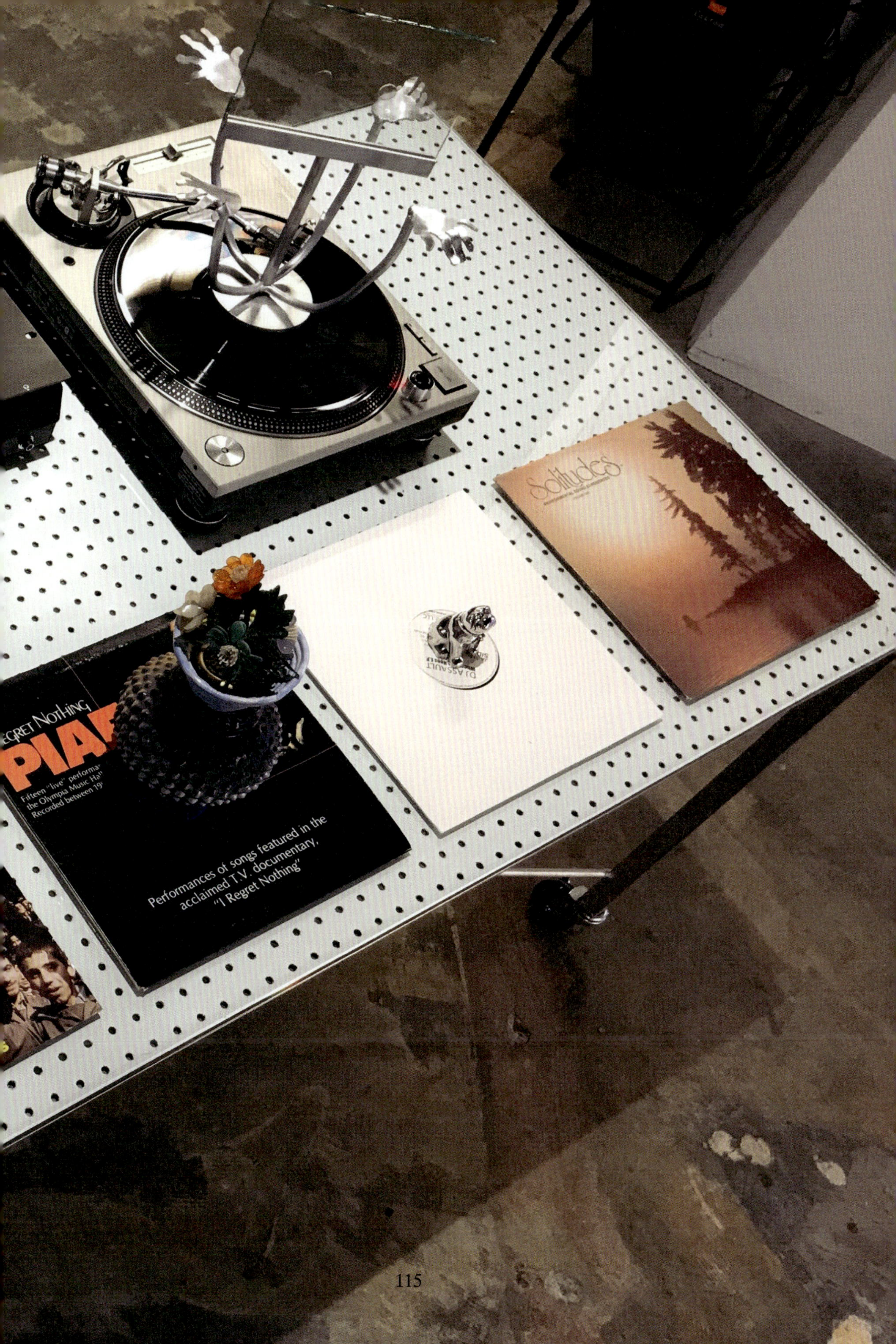
Solitudes
Performances of songs featured in the
acclaimed T.V. documentary,
"I Regret Nothing"

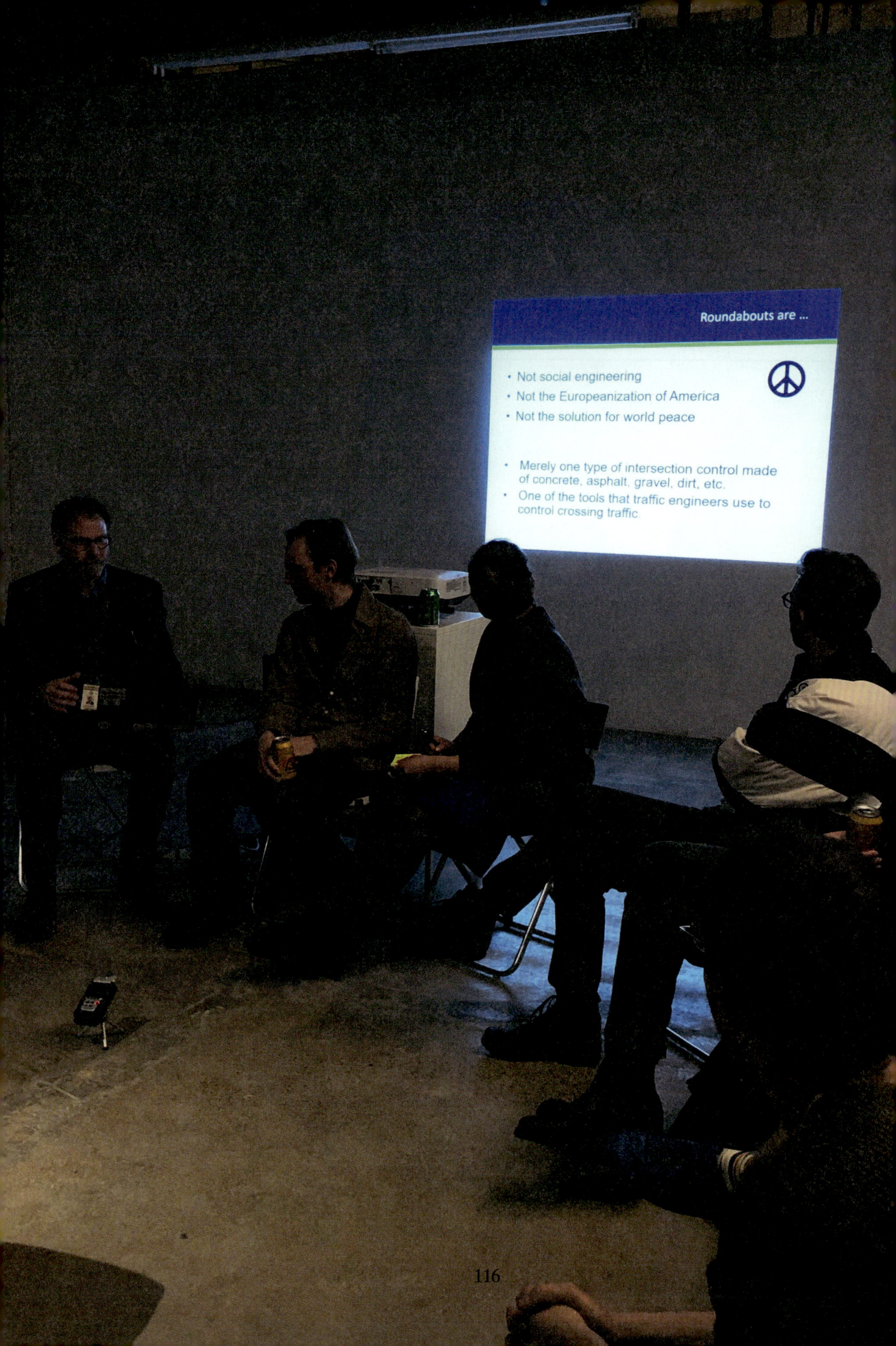
Roundabouts are ...
Not social engineering
Not the Europeanization of America
Not the solution for world peace
Merely one type of intersection control made of concrete, asphalt, gravel, dirt, etc.
One of the tools that traffic engineers use to control crossing traffic

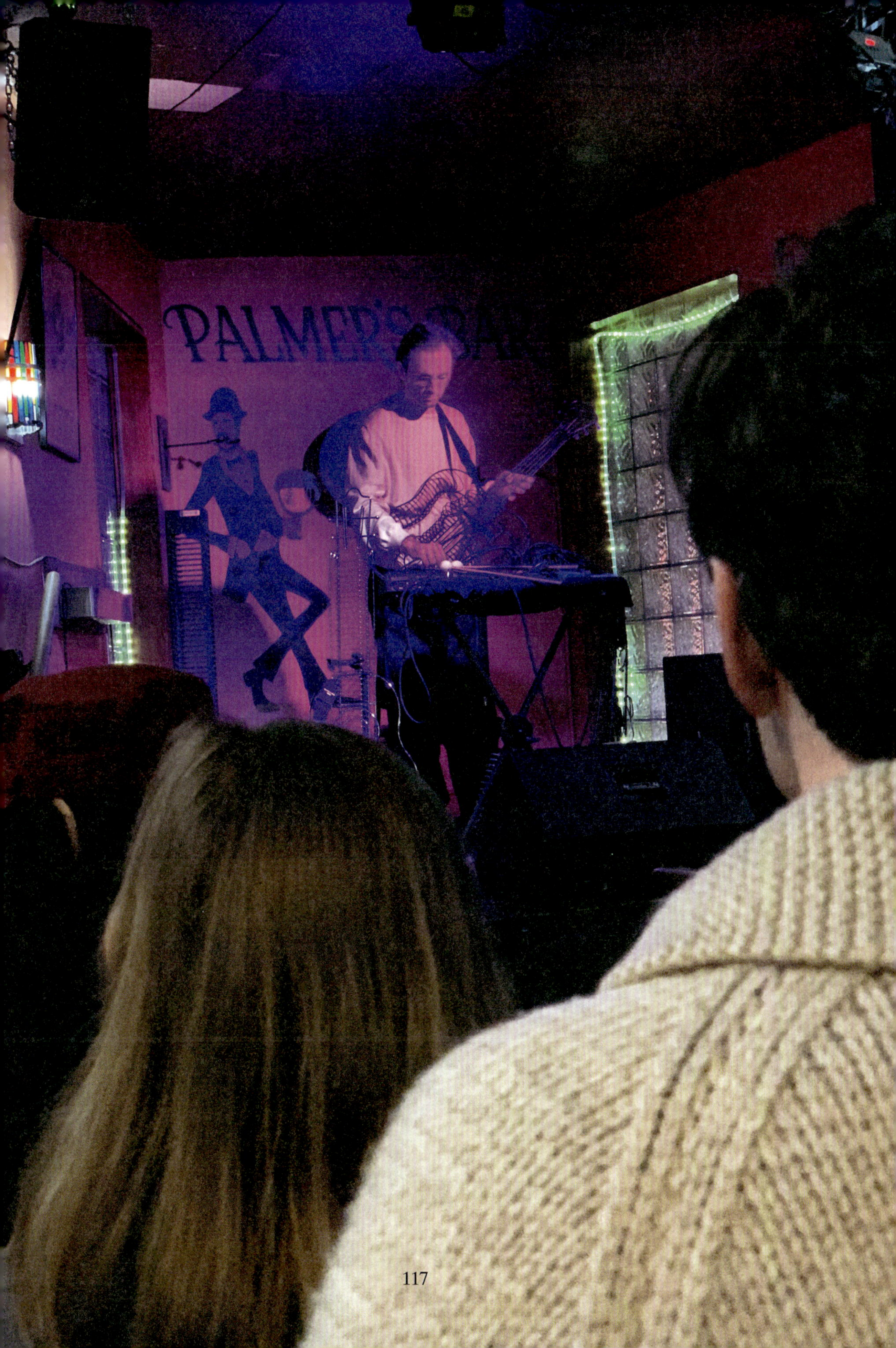
PALMER'S

The Possibilities of Negative Space

Kimberly Bradley

My initial thoughts were of politics. When I was asked to write this essay on *Goethe in the Skyways*, my initial thoughts were of politics. What could a yearlong celebration of German-American friendship—in the Minneapolis iteration of a Goethe Pop Up venue with an ongoing series of exhibitions, actions, performances, and on-site collaborations between Germany-based artists and local ones from Minneapolis / St. Paul—mean at this fraught point in transatlantic history? Can a temporary art space truly foster such a thing? *Should* it, at a time in which art and culture are so often instrumentalized for diplomacy?

Then came the requisite art-nerd considerations. How can the cultural or artistic scenes of two western localities, the Twin Cities and Germany (with a focus on Berlin), interact in a meaningful way? What does the "local" still represent in a globalized, intricately networked art system? And why did curator Sandra Teitge choose a former retail space within passages frequented by office workers, shoppers, and non-art-inclined passersby, just off Minneapolis's elevated skyway system—a unique, patch-worked infrastructure linking commercial buildings over 80 city blocks with a labyrinth of elevated corridors over the streets (see essay on TK)—in which to exhibit visual art and orchestrate happenings, talks, screenings, and other events?

Last, I perhaps selfishly considered and questioned my own diffuse identity. I grew up in Minnesota. I have lived most of my adult life in Germany. Maybe because I first experienced the skyways in downtown Minneapolis as a child, I still possess an almost childlike fascination with them (my age was in the single digits when I first saw people walking through the glassy halls, suspended between buildings, in the 1970s). My tastes and references in contemporary art have certainly been shaped by the two decades I have spent in Germany, most of which time I've worked as an art professional. What happened to the skyways, and Minnesota's art scene, since I left my home state in 1986, lost my Minnesota Nice [1] and adopted a more direct, critical Central European stance? I am a privileged, first-world, voluntary migrant, but I had never before witnessed the two regions that have most profoundly shaped my sensibilities coming together

1. A regional way of being—exceedingly pleasant, cordial, humble, and unassuming, which makes for lots of smiling in public. Minnesota Nice is also nonconfrontational, which at its worst morphs into passive-aggression. Minnesota Nice is the opposite of how most northern Germans think and behave—they are direct, dispassionate, and don't always smile at strangers. I now lie somewhere in between: Germans think I'm too friendly and often misinterpret it. Minnesotans, especially the members of my immediate family, are horrified at my perceived brusqueness.

in the institutional art field. So why, when I first learned of *Goethe in the Skyways*, did this pairing, or juxtaposition, seem more like a collision than an opportunity at reciprocal generosity?

Several decades after World War II, the United States' long military occupation of Germany, and the Marshall Plan, the notion of German-American friendship feels almost innocent,[2] like the American Baby Boomer dream of big houses and cars; eternal expansion with no environmental consequence. Or conversely, the German security and postwar *Wirtschaftswunder*, with both sides ignoring troublesome issues like the Cold War and walls on a logistical level; and American hegemony on the abstract one. Economic as well as less tangible, soft-power links between the two countries remain, although as time passes, they are often forgotten—Germans began immigrating to what would later become the United States in the late 1600s with a large influx occurring in the mid- to late-1800s. Thirty-nine percent of Minnesotans claim some German heritage, myself included.

Goethe in the Skyways organizers were well aware of these regional links, but these became merely the most obvious points of departure to bridge German and Minneapolitan cultures, the latter of which leans more toward music and theatrical performance than on nonperformative visual arts—the acclaimed Walker Art Center, MCAD, MIA, some excellent galleries, and an active community of visual artists notwithstanding. Teitge's strategy to insert a dose of contemporary Germany/Berlin into a unique urban infrastructure in the American midwest, and in turn to insert local artists into a commercial space quite foreign to them,[3] was part of the strategy to challenge both sides and create unexpected synergies.

Goethe in the Skyways's programming played with the tensions and potentialities of bringing together two localities and their idiosyncrasies and then linking them to more universal issues, like language (*Collusion, Collision, Illusion* was an exhibition featuring Laure Prouvost, Constant Dullaart and other Berlin-based artists in the skyway space, playing with written and spoken language in surprising ways), alternative communication (*Z and be seen*, a series of outdoor billboards by Berlin-based Christine Sun Kim, who exposes the vocabulary of American Sign Language), and knowledge production with a dose of urbanism (a symposium called *Passages* reflected on liminal spaces, including the skyways

2. *Goethe in the Skyways* is part of *Wunderbar together*, a larger project initiated by several bodies within the German government (Goethe-Institut, IFA, and BDI) to underscore and promote the two countries' longstanding economic and cultural cross-relationship to roughly coincide with the commemoration in November 2019 of the fall of the Berlin Wall thirty years before. The Minneapolis project was one of four pop ups around the United States.
3. Minneapolis's Northeast district has emerged since the 1990s as a primary hub for art galleries and artist studios, most of them in reclaimed warehouses—downtown's skyscrapers and skyways are a world apart and unlikely venues for artistic interventions.

themselves,[4] as well the importance of the commitment to the local), to name just a few. There were poster campaigns, happy hour readings, radio jam sessions, performances, poems, specially-made uniforms, and even locally designed exhibition furniture. Some Germany-based artists came to spend three weeks or more in the Twin Cities. But was there anything particularly German about the artwork from abroad, or anything particularly Minneapolitan about the artwork coming from within the local scene?[5] Can one even still speak of the local in terms of cultural production?

Cultural theorist Irit Rogoff and others have long grappled with questions of geographies and how important local zones might be in the wake of globalism and its accompanying human mobility:[6] a sweeping topic beyond the scope of this essay and usually coming from a postcolonial-studies stance and not one that considers two affluent localities from the Global North/western world. But it's interesting to consider the curatorial challenges in sensitively intermeshing local scenes at the same time as addressing global topics. Zooming out and taking into account the methods used by artists and curators since art dematerialized in the last decades of the twentieth century, Teitge's intervention-, sound-, and performance-heavy approach followed a familiar and successful curatorial trajectory. In researching what's gone on in Minneapolis in the many years since I left—I don't get back nearly often enough—I also ran across a show that the Walker Art Center mounted in 2003 called *When Latitudes Become Forms, Art in the Global Age*, in which the focus on "location-based art" turned to process-based work. Curators have espoused exactly this, to a greater or lesser extent, since Harald Szeeman mounted his seminal exhibition *When Attitude Becomes Form* in the late 1960s.

For good reason, it seems. Locational definitions can be artificially rigid. Teitge followed a fluid, flexible approach to joining practices and the people practicing them to each other and to their audiences (both voluntary and involuntary: most Minneapolis skyway-goers are not generally people who frequent contemporary art galleries; people who go to contemporary art galleries are not those who normally spend time in the skyways). The fluidity was also temporal—pop ups are by definition temporary—and thus inherently unstable. But from that instability, fruitful connections can form, and conceptual seeds can be planted that have reverberations.

Still, while the curatorial practices of the past few decades have tended to follow globalization's threads of networking, ephemerality, and process, local conditions

4. See: Walter Benjamin's *The Arcades Project* (German: *Passagen-Werk*) in which he collaged impressions of the glass-roofed shopping arcades in Paris in the early twentieth century. The unfinished work is seen by some as his masterpiece of literary criticism. The texts were written from 1927 until he fled the Nazi occupation in the early 1940s. Harvard University Press only managed to publish the work in English in 1999, after a long editing process.
5. Many of the Berlin-based artists are neither from Berlin nor German: Karl Holmqvist is Swedish, Christine Sun Kim is American, Hanne Lippard is Norwegian, Kinga Kielszynska is Polish, and so on.
6. See Irit Rogoff, "Liminalities: Discussions on the Local and Global," *ArtJournal* (Winter 1998).

remain unique and important. Berlin and Beirut-based artist Franziska Pierwoss's project *Art of the Deal,*[7] in which she filmed the dynamics of four Minneapolis families reality-TV style (the films were screened in the skyway space near the end of the yearlong project and are now online), underscores such regional and local behavioral codes and nuances. *Goethe in the Skyways*' many projects seemed to gently plumb and probe into the dialectic between macro and micro, the zoomed-out and zoomed-in—but also, how specific conditions in geographically far-flung places can still share a certain spirit.

On a certain level, even the unusual venue—a vacant storefront in a nondescript, escalatored atrium near a skyway passage—connects to Germany in general and Berlin in particular. Minneapolis's skyway system has expanded organically since 1962 with glitches, stops and starts, and lately, given the issues retail faces with regards to online shopping, are filled with negative spaces, so to speak, with unclear ownership (the Minneapolis skyways are perceived as public space, but are in fact privately owned). Berlin, too, has grappled with negative space the past thirty years, some of which played a key role in birthing its much-hyped post-wall creative scene. Abruptly erected in 1961, the Berlin Wall was breached on November 9th, 1989. The period immediately following this was one in which Berlin's then-art world, along with musicians and clubbers, took advantage of a good deal of governmental chaos—including profoundly unclear real-estate ownership—and squatted or temporarily used commercial spaces for galleries, studios, illegal bars, clubs, and more. The condition of the in-between or liminal, and how to creatively occupy (or, as the *Goethe in the Skyways* materials states: "*disrupt, interrupt, and misrupt*") a time and space is an approach, an attitude, that the two zones might share. Liminal spaces, which seem to be disappearing in our late-capitalist era, allow for experimentation and unexpected results.

What of my initial emotional reaction to the project? I've since analyzed it somewhat. As hybrid as my personal identity now is, I realize it's rooted to time as much as place. Which strangely dovetails with *Goethe in the Skyways*' mission—a nudge to remember that the Berlin Wall fell thirty years ago but, although we're older and history has marched or even raced on, we (Germany and the United States) are still friends.

As a child I often visited the Twin Cities and found myself either observing the busy people in the skyways from the street or, once indoor shopping malls began moving from the suburbs[8] and replacing department stores in the downtown streetscape in the 1980s, venturing into the labyrinthine system myself to go shopping, or just to see how far the upper-story maze would take me (I regularly

7. The same title as Donald Trump's 1987 memoir, perhaps an ironic nod to current politics.
8. The world's first indoor mall was conceived by an Austrian but planted in Minnesota in the late 1950s. See the essay by Bill Lindeke in this publication, p. 55.

got lost). Then, the skyways retained their veneer of modernist optimism, even if the beginnings of a demographic segregation were certainly well underway. By the time I could drive, the seedy zones on Hennepin Avenue were already less seedy than they'd been a decade before; after a wild summer of dancing in 1st Avenue and Seventh Street Entry in 1990 (the club in which much of "Purple Rain" was shot, and some of Prince's circle, like Morris Day, were still regulars) I moved to a Germany in transition. Berlin's art and clubbing scene was just beginning to venture into the empty spaces and tread on the metaphorical ripped seams that geopolitics has roughly left behind. No one quite knew how to put the city, the two Germanies back together. Helmut Kohl was chancellor; East Berlin languished under a cloud of coal smoke,[9] and the country's art world was still focused in Cologne, not the forthcoming capital.

With this in mind, viewing the work of so many Berlin-based artists I know[10] next to a doughnut shop in a multistory atrium near a passageway in Minneapolis's City Center complex became less about local artistic exchange or predominant curatorial methodology—and more about the passage of time and history. The fall of the Berlin Wall began redrafting the only geopolitical map my generation—at the time not yet named Generation X—had known. In the thirty years that have passed since the Cold War thawed and western hegemony began to wobble; since experiencing the profound shifts in the global financial structures, in the production and distribution of consumer goods; in the amplitude of various inequalities, a spike in human (hyper)mobility (not to mention forced migration) and contemporary visual art's increasing and sometimes confusing plurality, only now do I understand, only maybe, what German-American friendship in the cultural field might be.

I, in middle age, stand looking back at one of the most rapidly transformative and interconnected periods in human history, at the same time as looking forward and bracing myself for more with a mix of profound skepticism and cautious hope. Many of the artists who showed at *Goethe in the Skyways*—from both sides of the pond—address many of the same issues. *Goethe in the Skyways*' initial mission was part of a much larger, government-funded one of fostering international artistic exchange in the name of diplomacy. But in the end, the questions it put forth were perhaps less about friendships between nation-states (the nation-state increasingly a dated notion in itself) than one of celebrating the plurality of our global interconnections, the common problems so many of us face, and new ways to think of how to overcome them individually and collectively.

9. Central heating was rare, most Eastern Germans heated by burning coal in tiled ovens. Nowadays I can only sometimes smell coal smoke in the air in Berlin; it has become an olfactory memory.
10. I visited *Goethe in the Skyways* on my way home from Germany to the northland in Christmas 2018; works by familiar European artists were on view. But there was of course a hyperlocal connection, too: a childhood friend wrote to me in advance and told me to especially greet Sarah Petersen, *Goethe in the Skyways* director, during my visit.

Hanne Lippard
Inefficiencies

*Hanne Lippard works exclusively with language and uses it in a very playful yet pointed, often impudent fashion. This audacity and mischievousness makes her work "applicable" for non-art settings and therefore suitable for the skyways. For her solo project in Minneapolis, Hanne worked for the first time with other poets and choreographed their movements and readings within the City Center atrium. We asked four Minneapolis-based poets to write a poem that on some level reflects their relationship to the peculiar atmosphere of the skyways. For the performative part (and the name of the featured poem and project), Hanne referred to a reading performance she had done in 2016 in the elevator of a hotel in the tourist resort Sunny Beach by the Black Sea called *C U L8tr Elevator.* The reading performance in the skyways, *C U L8tr Escalator*, was a sort of adaptation of the 2016 performance. The poet performers used the two escalators that frame the atrium of City Center. Whenever they rode up or down the escalator, they read their poems out loud. The public was invited to follow the poets, switch from one to another, as they pleased, for the duration of the performance, which lasted roughly 20 minutes.

Hanne Lippard

Inefficiencies

5–25 April 2019

5 April 2019, 5:30pm
C U L8tr Escalator
Readings in the skyways
with Miriam Karraker, Chris Martin,
Lara Mimosa Montes, and Mary Moore Easter

Inefficiencies

Efficiencies
are often found
within offices
and
Inefficiencies
are mostly found
outside
The donut circumscribes a hole without content
Once it is devoured, both its nontent and form
cease to exist
Adjacent to the space
Is an option of *descent* and ascent
A slow move
In the wrong direction
Will get you into trouble
Welcome to the City Center!
Please follow these rules to ensure your own
and everyone else's safety, health and comfort:
Don't
Don't!
Don't!!
Don't!!!
Dont!!!!
Dont!!!!!
Dont!!!!!!
Dont!!!!!!
Dont!!!!!!!
Donut.

Images:
1.–2. Installation views
3. *Inefficiencies*
4. *C U L8tr Escalator* readings

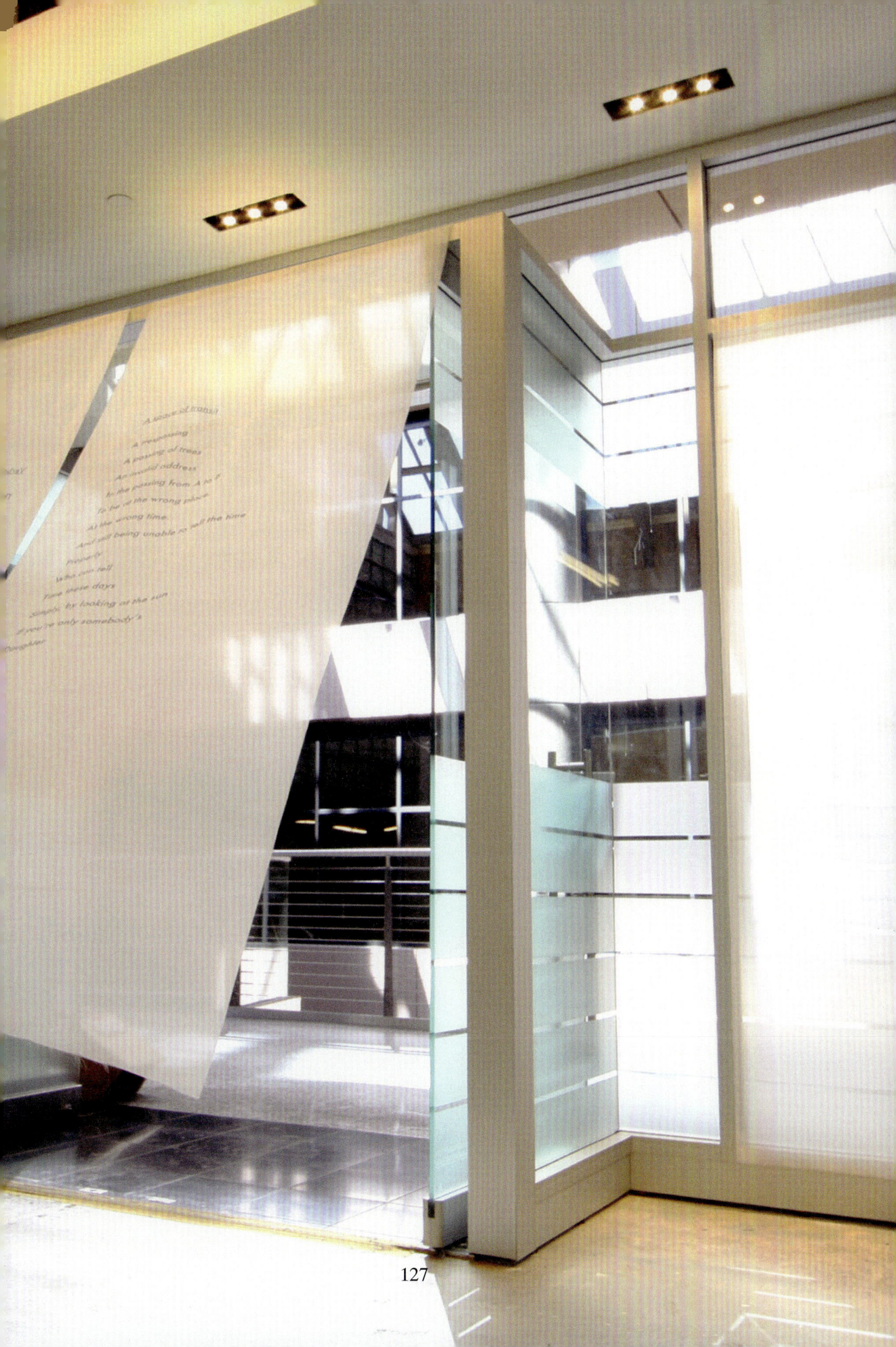
A passing of trees
An invalid address
At the wrong time
Time these days
by looking at the sun
only somebody's

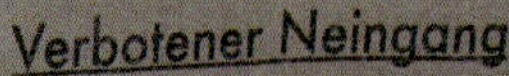
A space of transit
A trespassing
A passing of trees
An invalid address
In the passing from A to B
To be at the wrong place,
At the wrong time.
And still being unable to
Properly
Who can tell
Time these days
Simply, by looking at the sun
If you're only somebody's
Daughter
Verbotener Neingang
This door is locked
This door is also locked
Now you are locked in between two locke
All you can do is
Sit down
Silently
And wait for someone to lock you out again
It might take
Days
Weeks
Months
Years
Who knows
When
Nobody knows
You are here
Seated
Silently
Between two locked doors
Waiting

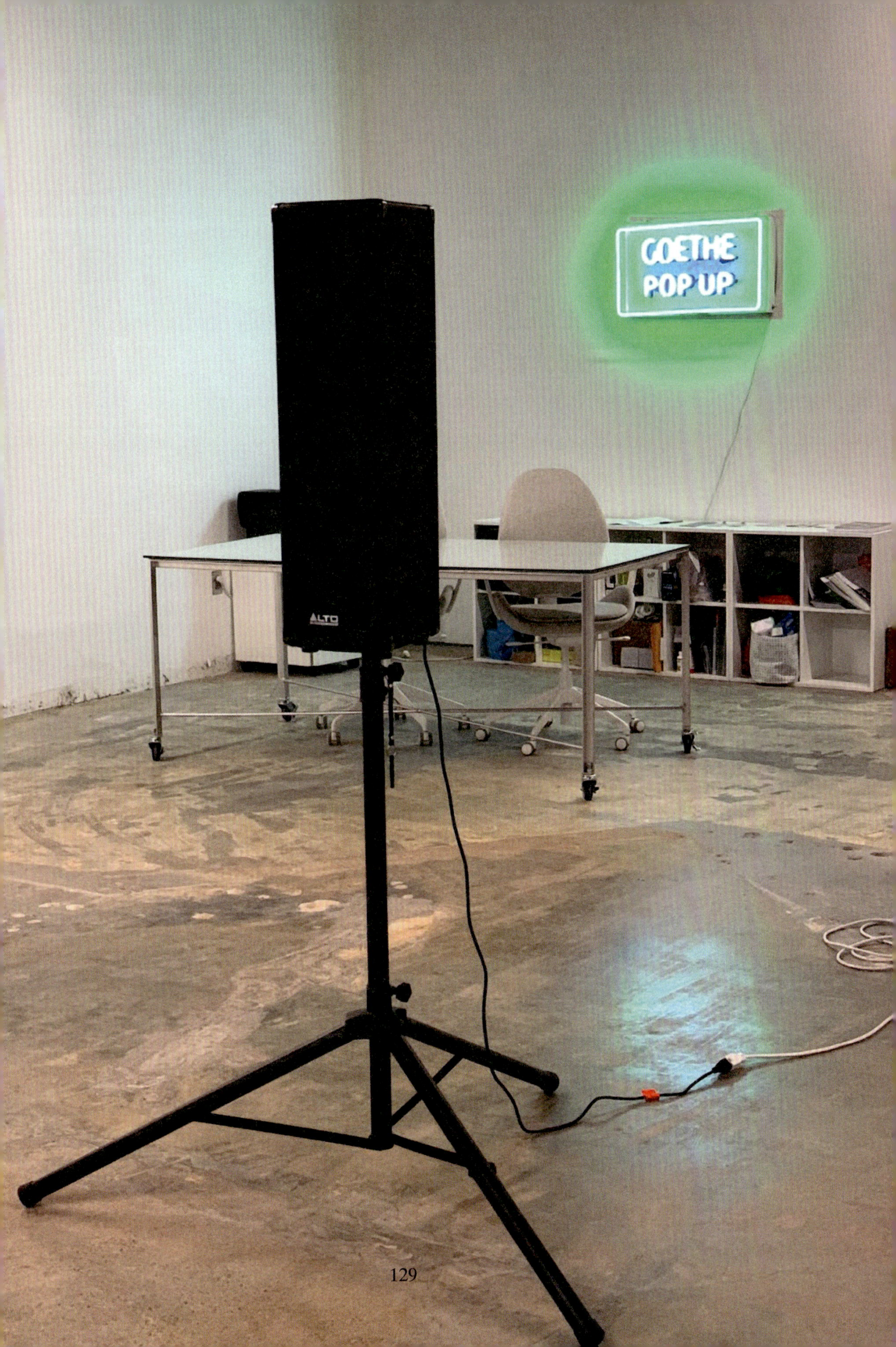
COETHE
POP UP
ALTO

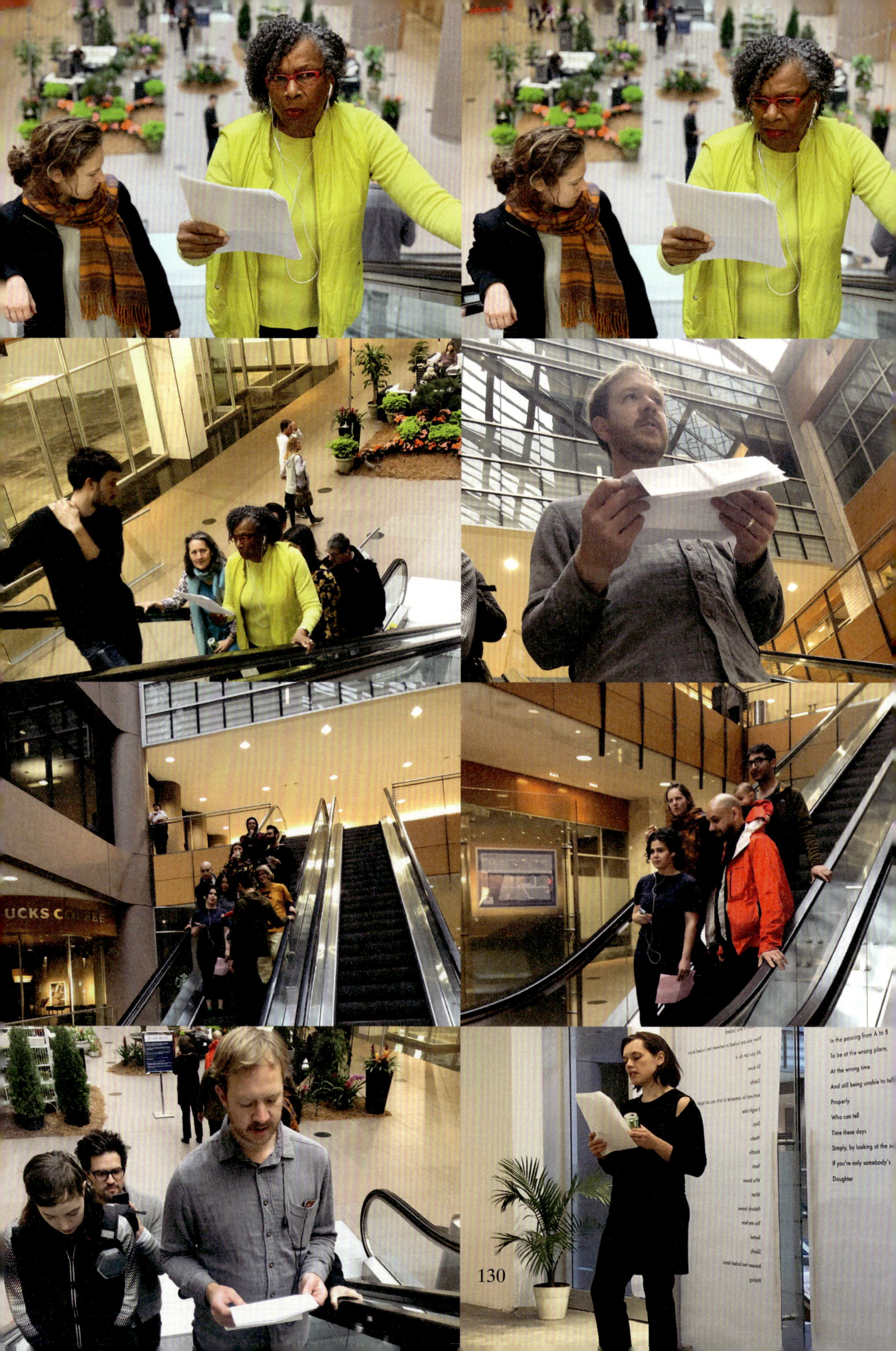
UCKS COFFEE
In the passing from A to B
To be at the wrong place,
At the wrong time
And still being unable to
Properly
Who can tell
Time these days
Simply, by looking at the
If you're only somebody's
Daughter

FORT
The Calling

*This project broke the format of what had taken place up to this point a bit, which is always healthy. FORT showed *The Calling*, a sort of antithesis to the skyways' hyperactivity. The image of *The Calling* projected on the mobile wall extended into the space with office chairs and carpet that emulated an indifferent office environment. The entire installation could be viewed in an equally detached manner, through the windows of the space that otherwise divide the inside from the outside. As I heard later on from my colleagues, the work was received extremely well. The skyway's public seemed to understand the message; they felt recognized.

FORT

The Calling

29 April – 15 May 2019

In the bustling, corporate climate of the skyways mostly frequented by workers on their way to the office, to meetings, or lunch, FORT's *The Calling* shows a contrasting environment, that of employees fast asleep at their workplaces. While sleep has historically been considered a time and space to rest and regenerate the body, to evoke dreaming, perhaps even fantasizing, in our late capitalist society sleep is often a reaction to an overdose of work… or life, and seen as a dysfunction. Wide-spread phenomena in capitalist societies like exhaustion, burn out, or depression manifest themselves in sometimes day-long sleep.

The employees in *The Calling* all seem to have collapsed into a very deep sleep, possibly triggered by exhaustion. While the technical devices around them continue to work, the human bodies are out, completely dysfunctional for the work context and a mirror to the busy dynamics of the skyways.

Images:
1.–3. Installation views

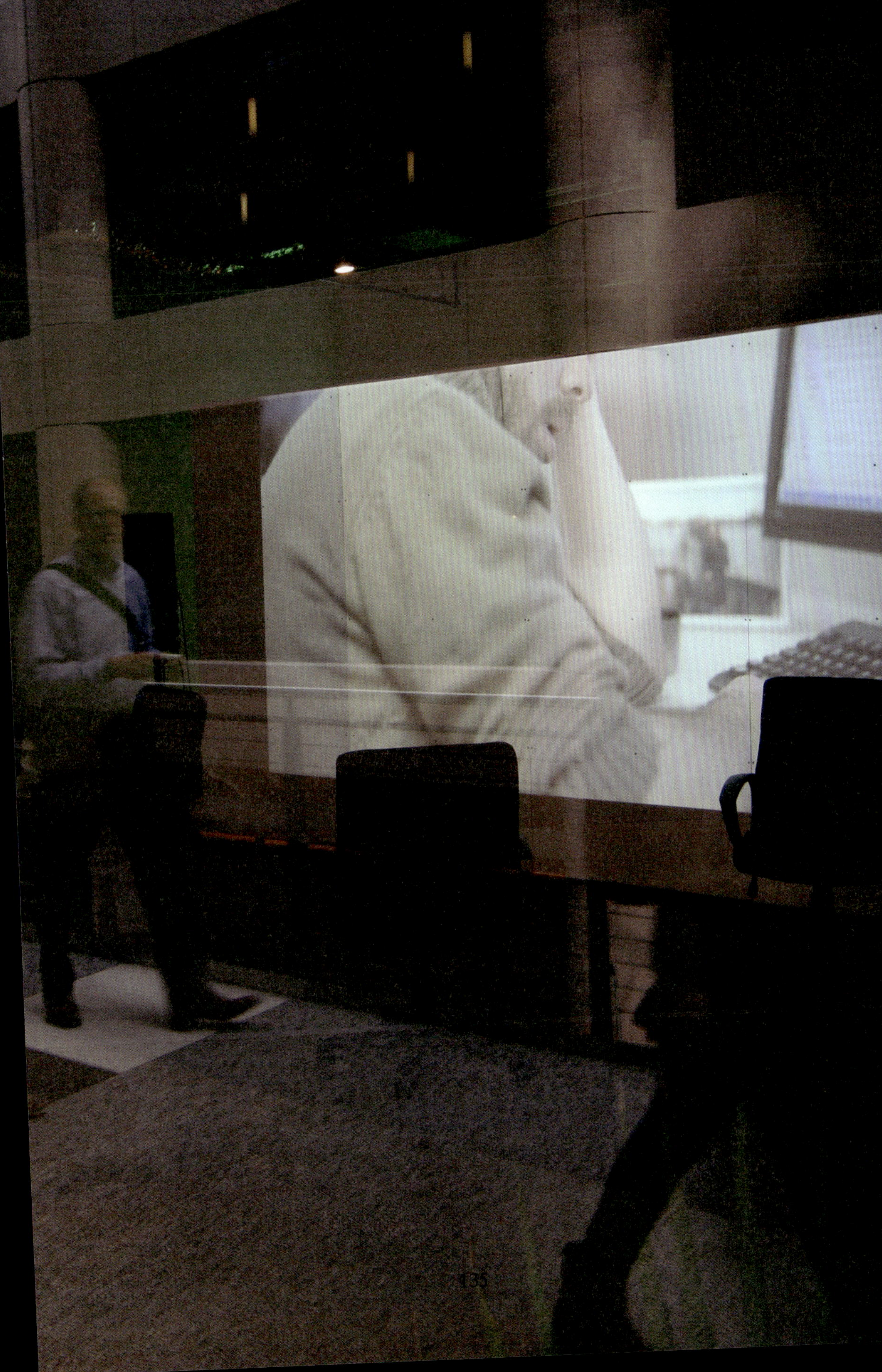

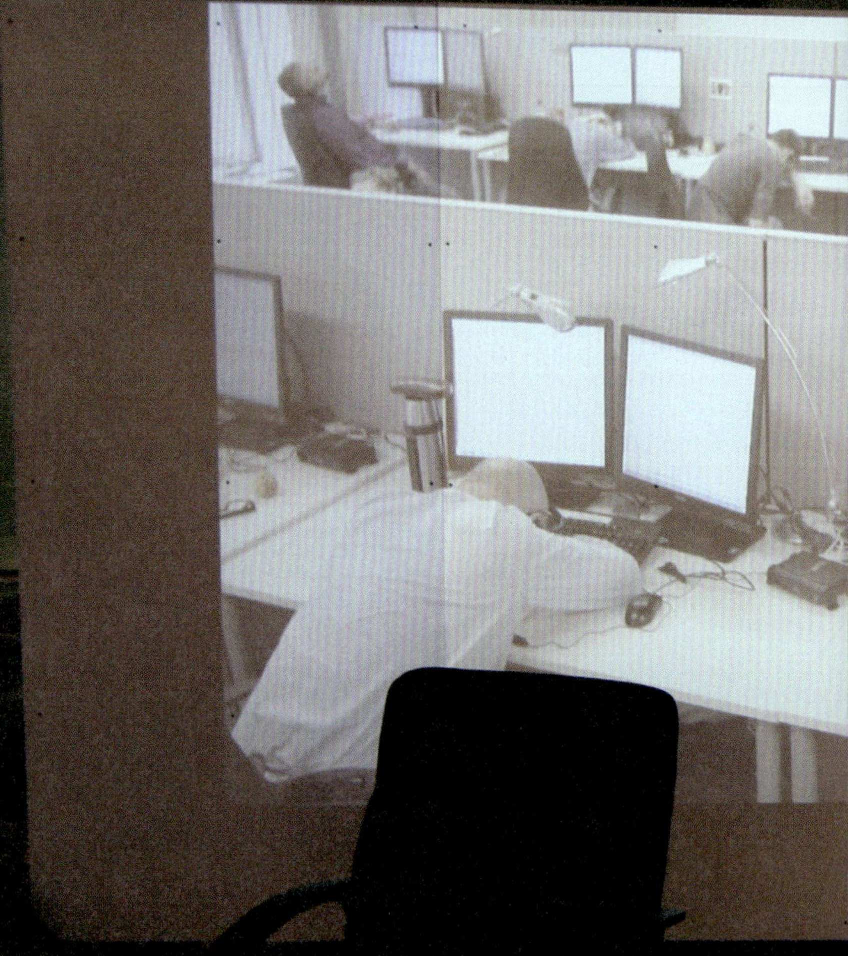

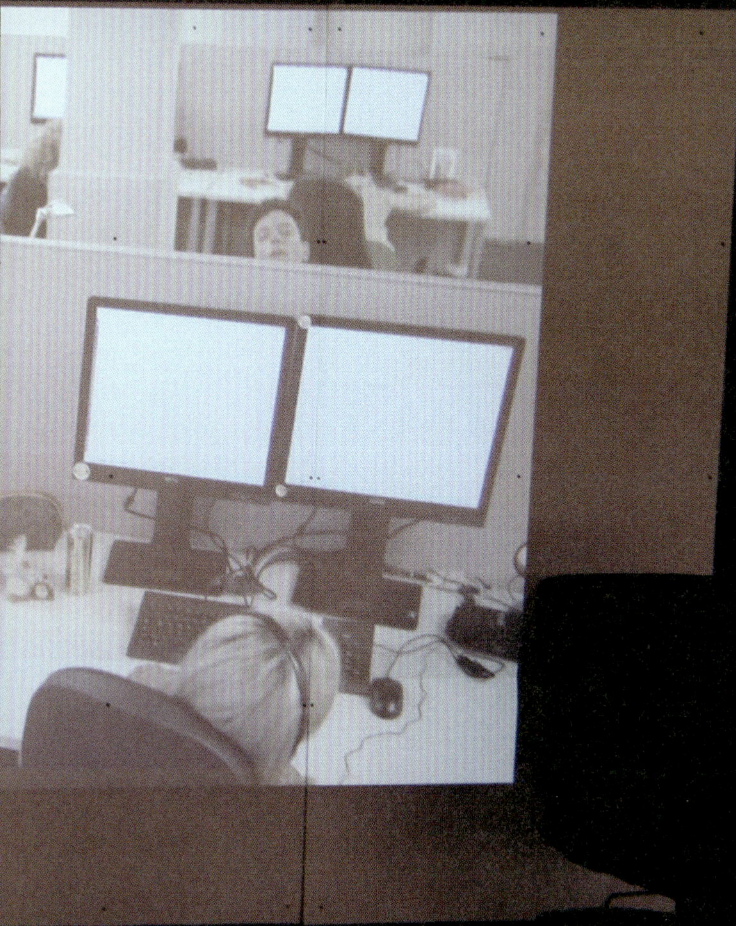

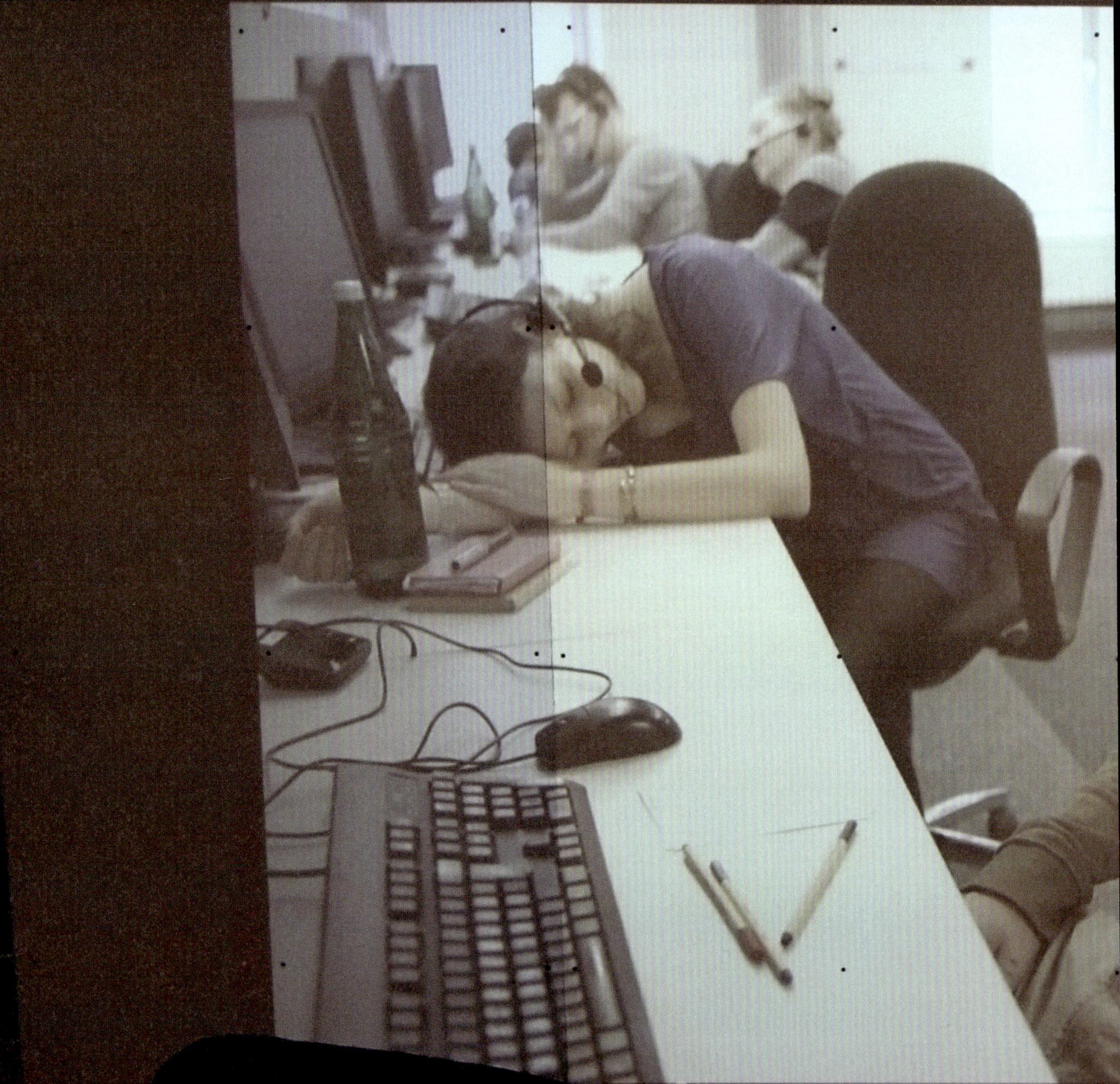

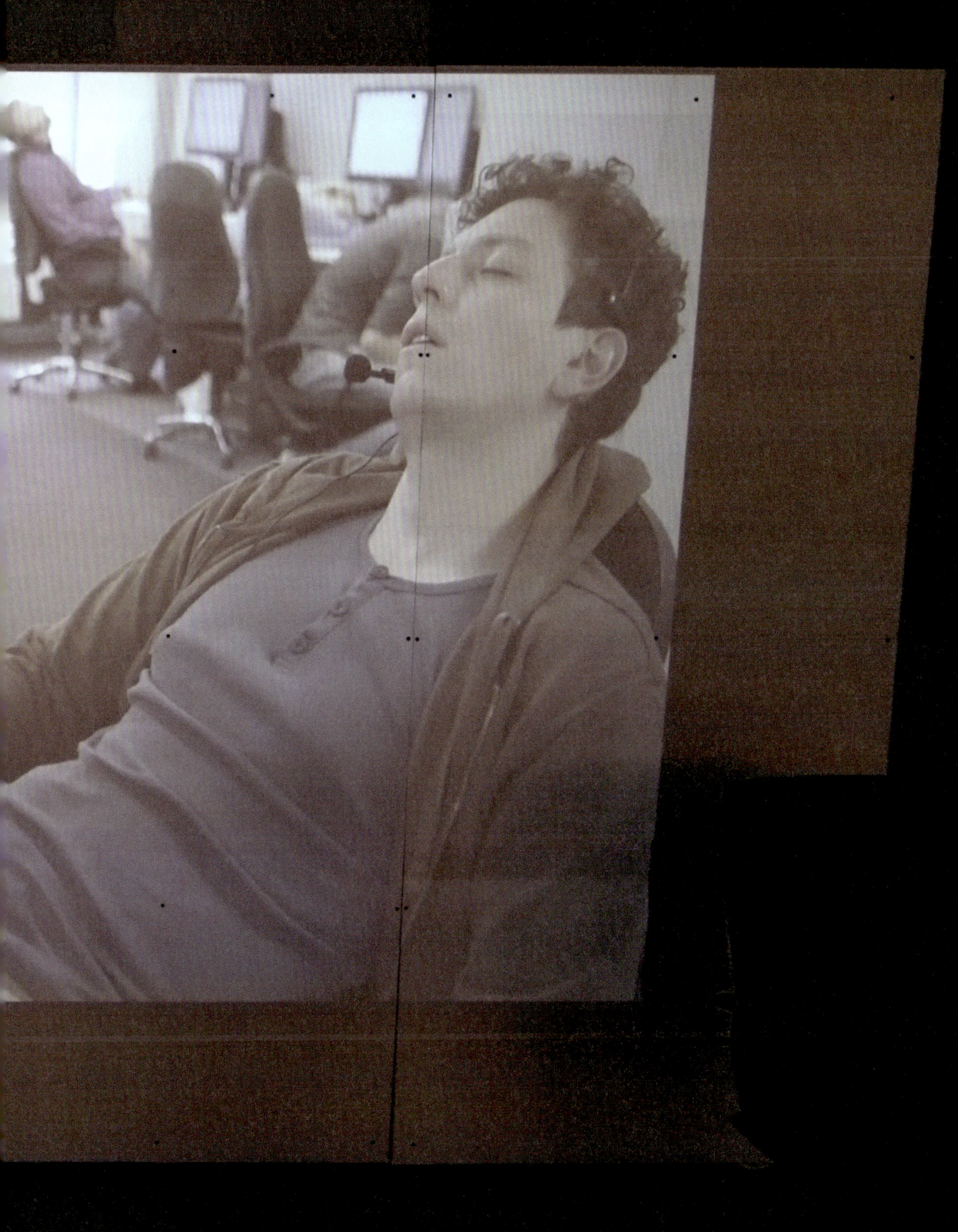

On Parallel Cities

Sandra Teitge in conversation with Jennifer Yoos and Vincent James

Sandra Teitge: How and when did you become interested in the skyways?

Jennifer Yoos: I believe it was in 1997 or '98. There were a couple of things that we were seeing, some of the same ideas in contemporary architecture that heightened the awareness of our own system. In 1999, we saw Constant's *New Babylon* at the Drawing Center in New York, and in 2003, the World Trade Center competition.

Vincent James: Yes, these are the main things that pushed us to do serious research. Because we live here, we were aware of the informal history of how the skyway systems developed. We were also aware that the Walker Art Center had been part of the process of developing and promoting the idea as well as bringing current urban strategies to Minneapolis in the 1950s and '60s. They brought in Reyner Banham to speak about informal implementation and had an exhibition of Victor Gruen. Later, after the system was well-established in the late 1980s, they hosted a symposium with David Dillon from Dallas and Trevor Boddy, who were strong opponents of the multi-level city.

JY: David Dillon criticized the social segregation that such systems created in cities like Dallas and Trevor Boddy critiqued their informality—he called it the Analogous City. There was also Colin Rowe who advocated for place-making in the skyways, which in the post-modern period led to a range of eclectic proposals, varying in quality. A common response by outside advisors is to take down the skyways.

At the time we started researching we were frustrated by the limited awareness of where these ideas came from and what their potential was. You hear similar stories in a lot of these cities—there's often the story of some great man who came up with the idea. It's usually a developer or somebody in the city. And then it just happened. There isn't really any acknowledgement of the migration of these ideas or an understanding of what they were originally intended for and why people were introducing them in the first place. So, we set out to trace back to the origins of these systems with an interest in how they were spreading. We found they were actually coming out of avant-garde artistic movements in Europe with their more utopian and experimental strains originating in turn-of-the-century France and Russia; they then developed into their current form in the U.K. Through the influence of CIAM and Team 10 they proliferated in North America and Asia.

ST: Do you think that the developers in the U.S. were aware of these origins and theories?

JY: Well, some people did pass between the worlds, so to say. A good example is Victor Gruen. Coming from Vienna at that period of time, he had in mind a very different kind of shopping culture and a related city center familiar in historic cities. He was also aware of CIAM 8, entitled *The Heart of the City*, that promoted the modern versions of these ideas. Gruen was interested in a lot of the work being done that was more experimental and essentially about social equity, and in creating a pedestrian city. So, it wasn't purely about shopping. And if you look at some of the early ideas he brought in to Southdale, the first indoor regional shopping mall in the U.S. in the suburbs of Minneapolis, and some of the strategies he proposed, it becomes clear that he aimed to make a new kind of a city center that was for everyone. His plans had dentist offices and banks and grocery stores, all of the things that would make it urban, even though it was interiorized.

VJ: That was a kind of idealistic movement. But there were many key figures that were technocrats who were less idealistic and worked against some of these principles. The general motivation was to move the car to the perimeter of the city.

JY: Which included moving parking to the perimeter of the city, keeping cars out. These ideas migrated and developed. To us, they were socially utopian ideas proposing to open up the city, free the city, make people interact more, and create more communal space. But then the way they were deployed came through people like Gruen, who appeared and proposed things and then just disappeared leaving incomplete proposals. A lot of these cities came up with methods to allow the skyways to develop informally on their own without design. Nobody ever properly designed a system, except arguably in Calgary. They designed a way of implementation, as in, here's how air rights happen; here is how they are sized. So, they founded regulatory methods without really thinking about all the implications. It all just happened automatically from there.

ST: Do you think that Les Parker, or Ed Baker, the businessmen who initiated the skyway system in Minneapolis, were aware of these developments? Were they aware of Victor Gruen?

JY: Gruen was just one of the proponents, but he did build the first skyway bridge in Minneapolis and promote them among downtown developers. Athelstan Spilhaus is also credited with inventing the skyway system. He did the Minnesota Experimental City project at the University of Minnesota with Buckminster Fuller that was promoting multi-level city concepts. We think the most significant influence was by Gruen. He had an office here in Minneapolis in 1952. He did a Minneapolis decentralization study, then Southdale, which was concurrent with his plan for Fort Worth and which really resembles our St. Paul skyway systems in many ways. In 1956, he started working with the city of St. Paul and between 1957 and 1961 created a 12-block plan for downtown. St. Paul had access to public money for its system, federal money that caused the system to be slower to implement. So even though it was proposed in St. Paul before Minneapolis because Minneapolis was private it happened faster here. Many of the same people working in both cities had property, or businesses, or other connections. So it is obvious that someone said they're doing this in St. Paul, let's do this in Minneapolis. There were shared interests in the two downtowns to be competitive with Southdale. The 1959 plan for Minneapolis also looked similar to the plans that were being presented by Gruen and others. So, they were all picking up on this work and spreading the ideas, but not really acknowledging where it originated, and, in doing this, they leave behind all of the ambitions that were more social or were more holistic in their design.

VJ: You have this fall away in the process as it takes on its own life, because once you start businesses that do connect, they benefit from the flow of people; it helps their businesses and food venues and whatever else. In a climate like that of Minneapolis or St. Paul, there are a lot of advantages when it's 20° below for people to go out to lunch and just walk within the system.

JY: But they're never really assessing how this is functioning. Alternatively, you look at cities like Hong Kong where planners are tracking complex data from many sources, surveying neighborhood people, looking at crime incidents, traffic accidents, pollution, and very localized economic indicators. They try to look at all of these layers of information to understand where they need to intervene and what the problems are. So it's a more complex problem, and they're acknowledging a range of factors.
Many things were interesting within your symposium. The navigation and way-finding discussion was one in particular that made me think. It seemed to highlight how those "designing" these systems are only asking the businesses about their needs and not really talking to those using it or to the public. Even if the Mpls Downtown Council sees the tenants as their clients, it would obviously be in their interest to be more aware of user experience.

ST: It always seems like the skyway system is meant to get lost in. There isn't a regulated signage system; it's as if it's meant to be confusing. So you keep shopping, or you keep eating, or I don't know what. It just seems strange because, especially from the eyes of a European, American cities are so organized, they are grids, and everyone talks about North, South West, whatever. It's so rational. And then you enter the skyway system and It's so irrational. It seems so strange that people let that happen.

JY: But it's because of the negotiations between a few entities…

ST: …between individual landlords and businesses that each have their own agendas, their existing conditions. It's all negotiation. Some systems tried a little harder to make a coherent pattern, right?

VJ: Like Montreal. I think the origin of Montreal and *La Ville Souterraine*, the underground system by Vincent Ponte, started with the train and commercial development, but there are connections to the street. It feels coherent, at least to some degree. And then as you move out, it gets more and more ad hoc.

JY: But it started also with that underground train line. It had an infrastructure to attach to. In Minneapolis, they tried to do that with Nicollet Mall. There was a spine that they were connecting in this downtown core. And in St. Paul, they did that with that urban renewal area of the twelve blocks around what is now Macy's, which was Gruen's project. I haven't seen the drawings that made it seem like it was going to cover the whole city. Whereas in Calgary, there was a city planner who, right after he graduated from MIT, went to Calgary and basically employed his thesis. He developed this whole infrastructure based on a quick napkin sketch that the city actually followed.

VJ: It integrates all the major kinds of transportation. So, overall, it was very coherent. It did become more ad hoc later on. But they're still following the basic plan. To a large extent, it's orthogonal. It follows the logic of the street, but it still has a lot of problems in being, for the most part, separated from the street.

ST: Do you think the protagonists were interested in this separation?

VJ: It was a bifurcation between the "megastructure" concepts that Europeans Reyner Banham and Cedric Price promoted as well as the non-plan concepts that grew out of their respective work. Frei Otto was doing his research on urban and non-plan settlements, which was concurrent to that line of thinking. You have that and then you have megastructures, these master structures that could also be changeable. That's what Constant was doing too. He was creating megastructures that could be occupied and creatively changed.

We were interested in the organic nature of the growth of these systems, the ad hoc aspects. Even going back in history, the Vasari corridor in Florence is the Medici's skyways to connect their buildings. It winds its way. They had to negotiate with some of the other noble people to do it. That was ad hoc. So when you go into a city and introduce a whole new system, the logic is different.

City Center, where the Goethe Pop Up Minneapolis is located, is a good design, in my opinion. Because it's open space, it's understandable. You can see the street. It makes an effort to make a connection between levels. But many of them are just about, “Hey, I can get a quarter here. I don’t have to move that tenant over there.” And then people can find their way through like rats in a maze. And that’s more typical and very problematic, I think.

ST: Yes. There are all these utopian ideas at play in the development. It’s such a shame that people don’t really like to come downtown nowadays, or maybe it’s the whole package of downtown. Everyone is so anti downtown and anti skyways, except for researchers like you… or Europeans like me. I as well as the artists I invite are fascinated and also see this utopian connection, but people here in Minneapolis are rather disinterested, I found.

JY: I must admit that we have a bias toward designers. They are not seeing the design potential of an urban space being exciting and attractive. So people who are looking at civic space aren’t thinking about what is going to draw people here. The programing of Nicollet Mall is a good example of successful activation of civic space. Why couldn’t they do something similar in the skyways? Some of these atriums could have some of those same kinds of activities and have connections between inside and outside. Then you could start to activate the system.

VJ: But very few of the building owners are that committed to a shared system.

ST: Not at all. This has been our experience because we had a space in City Center, and we’ve tried multiple times to exchange ideas, to propose something. There’s always a very strange, very vague excuse. They don’t really want to have a conversation.
They seem to feel very uncomfortable about things that they may not exactly understand or can fully envision. I think it’s actually impossible. We started to just do things without asking for permission.

We were stopped during the performance of Emilie Pitoiset that happened in the frame of the symposium *Passages* in one of the skyways on the edge of the skyway system. Five performers dressed in white with white helmets were stopped by private security and asked to leave. Concurrently, the police passed and allowed them to stay. So there was this interesting interplay of this private and public body or entity. The superior of the private security guard made the decision that we should leave. And so we had to leave, though the police had allowed us to be there. I think that’s the issue in the skyways in the end. The private owners don’t allow anything “other.”

VJ: There is a historical aspect to this because during the 1950s and ’60s all of the movement to the suburbs based on fears of the city made businesses concerned that they were going to be marooned on an island with no one around, so the skyways were intended to bring people back to the city. How would it do that? Would it do that by segregating them from the dangerous stream? So everyone goes up and then you feel comfortable because you're all roughly the same social and economic class, and it feels like the suburbs.

ST: So you think that there was definitely this intention to create segregation?

VJ: Yeah. It wasn't articulated. But it was very real. It's still real.

JY: It doesn't seem planned, but it happened. It's interesting to me, though, what is targeted by the property owners and what is allowed to happen.
The Somali president was speaking at the Target Center a while ago and I walked in the skyways and there were all of these people marching with Somali flags, all different colors, hundreds of people marching through the skyways, all the way through the whole system. It was really fantastic.
Also, there were anti-foreclosure protests during the recession around Wells Fargo in the skyways and those were allowed to happen. But individual people who are spending too much time in one spot or students who are there in a group and taking photos are not allowed. It's odd what they will allow and what not.

VC: St. Paul is a public system, but there was the case of a black father who was waiting for his daughter and was taken away by the police. You always hear that public is better than private. But there is something about the private owners where they don't have the same amount of overarching control. But basically, the skyway police, the skyway security, even though they're publicly employed, they really work for the business owners. So they work for very few people. They don't work for the general public. It's much easier to have that kind of abuse in a system like St. Paul, where it is a kind of symbol of control. Andrew Blauvelt, who worked with us on our book, suggested that the Minneapolis system is more open because the fragmentation of all of the business owners makes it harder to control.

JY: The skyway regulations of St. Paul are pretty funny because they're so intrusive. They're about chewing gum. They're about the volume of your voice. They're about skateboards. They just go on and on and on about what you're not allowed to do in the skyways.

VJ: One of the points we're getting to, and one of the major fascinations for us, was the sociology that surrounds these multi-level urban conditions and their lengthy history around the world. The fact that in many cases the utopian version is about connecting people.
When you connect people, who are you connecting? You're often excluding someone at the same time. Even the most radical proposals like Fourier and the Phalenstere from the nineteenth century always exclude someone. So the

question is, what is public space? And this is as old as urbanism. How do you manage public space? Who gets to use it? How can you make people feel safe being together?

JY: Minneapolis has been called a hub and spoke system, where it has these atriums that are deep in the center of the building. To get outside, you have to know where to go. There are no visible connections. Only when you're on a bridge, you can look out and you can orient yourself. But generally the Minneapolis system prevents this kind of interconnected inside/outside that some cities do really well.

VJ: Ultimately the people passing through are, in a sense, a commodity; they're captured market for businesses. There's no point in giving someone a chair unless they're paying money to buy some food. This architecture or design exacerbates a transactional social relationship logic. You don't have people wandering or sitting or bringing a guitar or just playing. It eliminates much of what actually creates real urban life, diversity, and texture. This is one of the things that we were really intrigued by.

VJ: But going back to the beginning, we started out talking about the World Trade Center competition and the High Line opening and examples of a good multi-level urban space. The High Line may be about gentrification, and that's a legitimate critique. But nevertheless, people use it. People like to go and wander through the city when they don't have to stop at every street. It also has landscape. It has some very positive characteristics that attract people.

There are other good examples of multi-level urbanism. Steven Holl does buildings with skyways that are pretty interesting. For the World Trade Center competition, most of the schemes had some kind of interconnected buildings above ground. We realized that architects keep proposing these ideas over and over again. Yet there has never been a real assessment of the concepts underlying these ideas' pros and cons. So that really spurred us on to take the book seriously.

JY: We were also interested in just how radical they are. The idea that you could do something on a city scale and have it be completely invisible. Somebody comes into a city, drops an idea down, and the idea just grows over time. Then twenty years later the system exists. It just seemed like dropping a spore in very different contexts that happen in very different ways. That idea versus the way architects think about design as in you have a singular client to present something that's complete, it gets built, and you go away… It was such a different way of thinking of urban form.

VJ: We also got into some of the psychological issues of this kind of space and thinking about the continuous interior, John Portman's work, how these interior

spaces work on your psychology. You commented earlier about the skyway system as a maze, it can be scary. Then there are other perspectives like Portman and his huge atria, which are part of his networked urban conditions like Atlanta. These are spaces that are spectacularly scaled. They're huge. You're kind of mesmerized when you go into them. But it's debated as to whether or not they're alienating people who are attracted to them because of the 'wow' factor.
We call it charismatic. So, we were trying to understand the psychological differences between being inside the urban city or being too close or too far from other people.

JY: There's also the vertiginous. The higher up you go in cities like Hong Kong the more parks there are. Chongqing in China for example has this extreme topography. The city was started in the 1970s with urban systems that include an elevated train twenty storeys up and bridges. Because they're starting high, they just stay up high and it's exciting and thrilling. But you don't get that here. You're just one storey up, and it is entirely horizontal.

VJ: One of the reasons that these systems did take off and succeed is, even though they don't fulfill that vertiginous experience all the time, they are exciting places to be, the top of a building or on a train crossing. People came up with the idea of flying bridges in the early 1920s in New York City for instance. Being up high is a very seductive idea of urban space, and it attracts people. It's just like the vessel by Thomas Heatherwick recently built in Hudson Yards adjacent to the High Line. You pay a fee to climb up the stairs and you do it just for the excitement of going up. It's kind of a perverse piece because you pay to do something that you normally would not want to do, you climb through a parking ramp, so to say.
This vertiginous aspect is something that drove a lot of our interest.

ST: You do think that there are cities where the systems work better than here? You mentioned Calgary?

JY: I think Hong Kong works better. I think the cities that have more diversity, more parts, whether they're looking at connections down or trying to connect interiors to exteriors in a different way. You walk through Hong Kong and in one part of the system you go through this aviary. You are high up and you come out into a park and it connects to the public library. They are connecting urban amenities and experiences. You move fluidly between inside and outside.
It is not just pure single-minded shopping.

VJ: But you're also on a hill, a very steep hillside. So you often come in contact with the original terrain and then you go up. You are always being re-connected to the ground plane as you use the various systems, which makes it fragmentary.

It's done incrementally for different reasons, to solve different problems.
They have a lot of podium-concept modern buildings that create a plinth that ties to the hillside and then it has connections out from that. So it's more organically tied to the earth.

JY: The other part of that is also how much density you have downtown. In larger cities, like Mumbai, parallel urban systems can reduce congestion and so on; they≈can be very helpful.
I think Minneapolis tips back and forth between the two, of whether it's dense enough. I don't think St. Paul has the population density, and I think it harms St. Paul more than Minneapolis.

VJ: As we worked on the book, we realized that multi-level urbanism will continue. So it's really important that architects and planners start to think about the 3D city.
It's going to be used for different reasons and it will be highly segregating.
But hopefully it will sometimes actually bring people together.

JY: However, when Herzog & de Meuron did the Walker Art Center extension, they said that the skyways should be taken down.

ST: Did they really?

JY: Yes. Also Jan Gehl and Clement Greenberg. They also claimed that it's ruining the city and called for the skyway system to be taken down. But you can't take it down.

VJ: That's one of the reasons we did the book, because that kind of perspective is absolutely closed. We saw the ideas and proposals for these systems at Harvard. We discovered them when walking through the gallery, all these urban city proposals that were multi-level. And yet no one actually talks about their history or the very banal systems that presently exist in many cities.

ST: If you could be a part of developing Minneapolis's skyway system, how would you do it? What do you think would help?

JY: I think having more diversity in terms of kinds of typologies of urban spaces. Hong Kong is so interesting in that context. You have a bridge and stairs coming up from multiple points on the street; you have a circular bridge that goes over the intersection and that connection goes into a building. They're much more formally complex, like circuit relation diagrams.
The studio that we're teaching at Cooper Union is called Stair Ramp Bridge Corridor. It's basically trying to look at these basic components that have the potential to make a multi-level city more exciting.

ST: There would have to be some sort of overarching organization or someone that pushes for this kind of thinking and building.

JY: Well, that is what I think is interesting about these different forums, the fact that they happened in the first place, through the Walker or through local architects advocating with the city to make something at that scale happen. But this kind of convening doesn't happen anymore. If you had a symposium and a public competition and people could show different interventions and how those could activate the city in different ways, it might create some interest. More public urban programs, like the ones on Nicollet Mall, are also very promising.

ST: Last time we talked you mentioned these bike races that used to happen in the skyways…

JY: The St. Paul skyway bike race was just wonderful; it was fantastic. The other one was Skyway Mini Golf. I noticed that they rebranded it. In the light rail, it said "Skyline Mini Golf sponsored by the Walker Art Center."

ST: There were also beauty pageants?

JY: Yes, in the 1950s and '60s, there were beauty pageants.

ST: So the skyways used to be more accessible and more "public"?

JY: When there was a lot of shopping downtown, they used to have a holiday parade, which would go up and down Nicollet Mall, and people would go into the skyways and watch the parade from above. There were a lot of those ideas about making the city more social and equitable.

ST: During your research was there anything surprising that came up?

JY: Yes, all the time. That kept us interested. I think one of the things that shocked us, is that you start to gather and collect things and so much is relevant. How do you start to sort that information? At some point we did a timeline of the skyway projects that are high design and low design. What are the kind of everyday designs in the city of Minneapolis or some of the Gruen material that is more popular and just kind of happened and seems less designed? You start to put them together and you realize that they're actually in dialog with each other, that they're influencing back and forth. Another surprise appeared as we were trying to map where the idea came from. You have the French utopians, the socialists utopians; then you have the migration to the Russian constructivists and the Bauhaus. And you start to see that kind of coalescing in London. So we did this diagram looking at all of the London County Council bureaucrats promoting their systems, developing these kinds of multi-level projects. They proposed a 20-mile system for London in the 1950s, way before ours was developed. These ideas were being conceived of in secret influenced by the French and the Russians. It was both in academia and within the city. They were many crossovers. Archigram, for instance, was working for the London City Council. Off hours, they did really radical experimental work and during the day, they were either working for shopping mall developers or the government. These strange connections made you understand how such radical ideas were being experimented with for public space.

ST: Vince mentioned earlier that what kept the research interesting was the conviction that Parallel Cities will continue. For which reasons?

JY: Well. When we started the research I was at the AA in London and my studio was across from Cedric Price's. He was always working on ideas, starting with the Fun Palace. The Dutch architect Winy Mass from MVRDV who I worked with was really obsessed with multi-level urbanisms. It just seemed to be everywhere. We kept seeing more examples of it. Every single entry of the World Trade Center competition presented a multi-level system though not connected to the street and high up, more like a gated community. But it just seemed to be constantly coming back.

ST: Why do you think that is? Do you think it's because people want to be separate from other people?

JY: I think it's due to some other kind of globalization. Architects were working in Asia and elsewhere and were influenced by some of the more spectacular systems, in Riyadh, Hong Kong, Singapore. There were a lot of Chinese systems that started to develop. The experimentation that was happening in Asia is very different from the U.S.-American banal, rule-generated approach. I think people don't connect the two systems. That was something we've heard over and over again, that "whatever happened in the U.S. is totally different from whatever happened in Asia." Yet it's not. It actually came from the same people in the same place. The same British people who influenced the Asian system influenced our U.S. system.

ST: Why are they doing it in Asia? Is it also because of traffic or congestion?

JY: Congestion. I think it was proposed as a way to make a new city that will solve all problems, just like it was done here in Minneapolis. You want to get people out of the suburbs. You want people to use downtown. Here's how to do it. Here's how to deal with traffic.
All of these cities have very different but also very similar problems.

ST: Is there anything when you look back on the book that you think is missing or that you would have added if you could?

JY: Because we started with our own city, Minneapolis, we never really completely documented that history. It started to feel provincial when we realized that the topic had a much larger global impact. So I would have liked to circle back to the city. Also, there are cities that we just didn't get the chance to explore. Singapore came really late in our research. I think Singapore is really a fascinating city just because of the spectacle of entertainment. Their housing policy has forced these skyway systems into the housing system. They're designing it for a lot of different reasons, in interesting, smart ways. I would have also liked to explore more of what's happening in China. There were things that would have required more travel and more research…

ST: Has the research made you see the Minneapolis system in a different way?

JY: I'm frustrated by the system here. Trying to do or change anything seems like an impossible task. The general attitude is against making the skyways into an interesting experience; some people want to take them down. But there are positive examples of creating well-functioning spaces for the public. The IDS Center [designed by Philip Johnson] does it successfully. Its Crystal Court is a fantastic space. Or Jean Nouvel's *Endless Bridge* in the Guthrie Theater, which overlooks the Mississippi river, resembles a skyway. Those are experimental designs that I'm excited about.

Christine Sun Kim
Z and be seen

*For *Goethe in the Skyways*, I was finally able to work with Christine Sun Kim with whom I have had numerous conversations over the years, incidentally and gratefully joining forces with the Walker Art Center, where Christine participated in a sound marathon. I suggested to her to come up with a billboard design keeping in mind the billboards Christine had created for the Whitney and *For Freedoms*, a collective of artists, institutions, and organizations across the U.S. that invites artists to create billboards in order to politically mobilize the population. We worked with Joan Vorderbruggen, a power house who heads the Hennepin Theatre Trust, to help secure a spot on five different Clear Channel billboard locations all over the city. Christine had the billboard's design and colors mirror that of her German identity card for the disabled. We brought this idea further to life and into the skyways by taking the same image that appeared on the billboards across the city and putting it on a massive banner that cut across the entire length of the Pop Up space.

Christine Sun Kim

Z and be seen

17–31 May 2019

19 May 2019, 2pm

Artist Talk

Berlin-based artist Christine Sun Kim explores the materiality of sound as well as the representation of spoken language, in relation to drawing, painting, and performance. Kim combines aspects of graphic and musical notation, body language, and ASL (American Sign Language), and uses these systems as a means to expand what each is able to communicate and to invent a new grammar and structure for her compositions.

For the Goethe Pop Up Minneapolis, Christine Sun Kim appropriates the ASL slogan "You true biz," which loosely means "You exist and I see you," for a banner and billboard as a means to provide broader visibility for ASL. ASL has several writing systems but none of them are considered an official equivalent to written English.

Installed as a billboard along downtown Minneapolis's central axis, Hennepin Avenue (and on four other Twin Cities billboard locations—see list), as well as in the city's corporate skyway system, Kim's message infiltrates the spaces otherwise reserved for advertising.

Billboard locations:
I-94 North of Broadway, facing north (visible when driving south on I-94)
I-94 North of Broadway, facing south
Hennepin Ave & 7th/8th Street (across from the Skyway Theatre)
I-35W & Hennepin Ave, facing south
I-94 & Chicago Ave, facing east

Images:
1. Billboard on I-94 North of Broadway; billboard on Hennepin Ave & 7th/8th Street
2. Artist talk
3. Banner *Z and be seen*

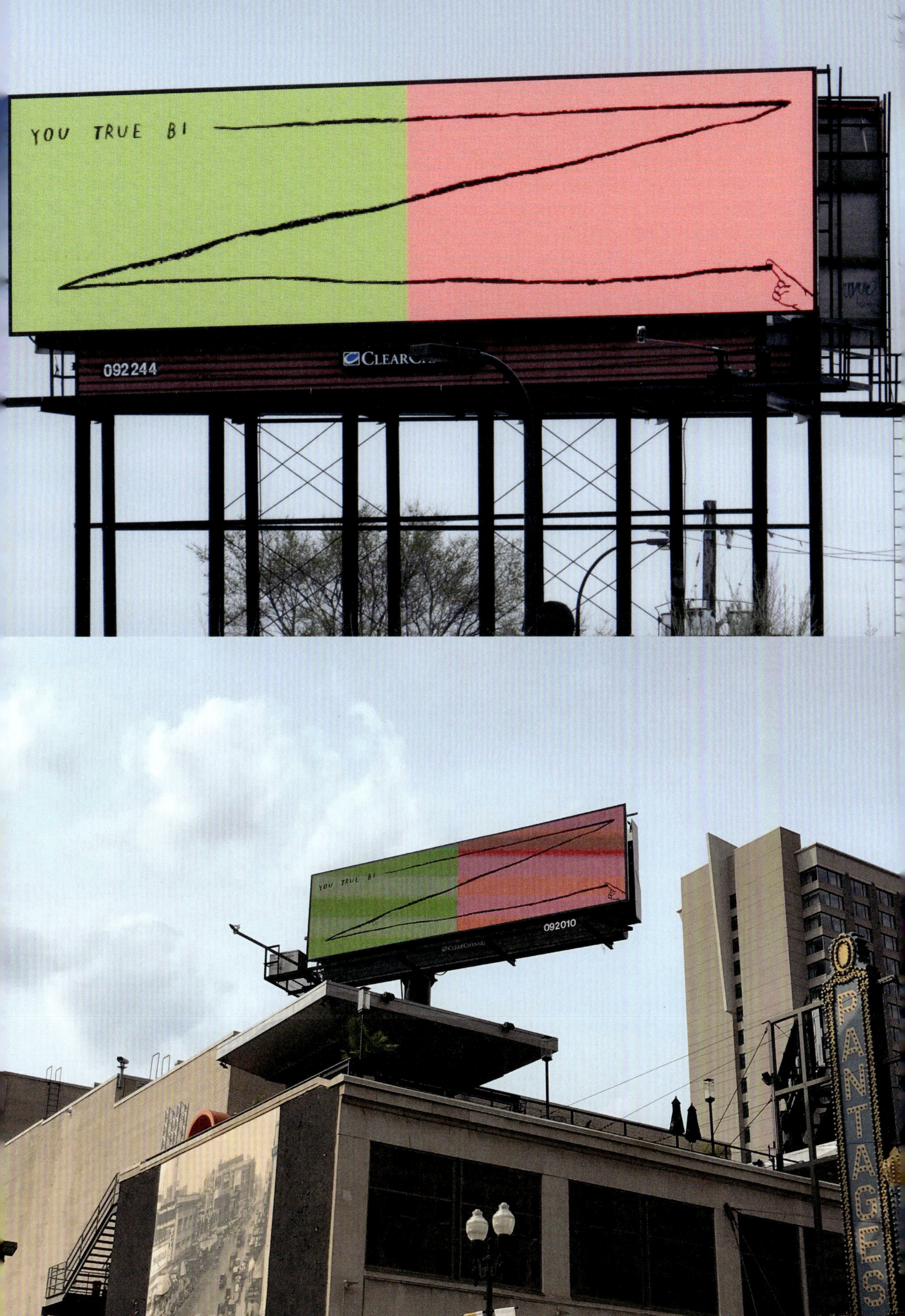
YOU TRUE BI
092244
CLEARCH
YOU TRUE BI
092010
PANTAGES

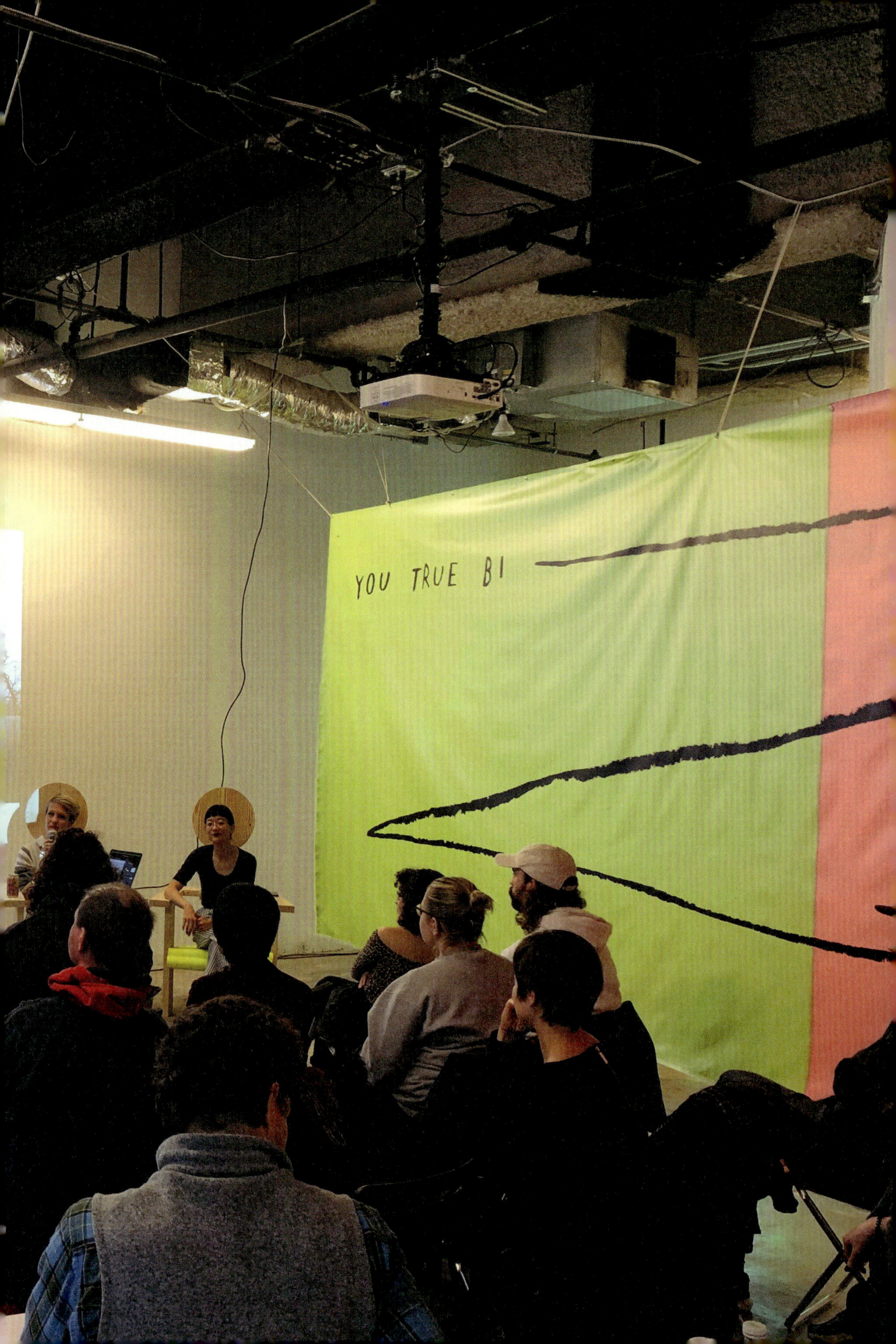
YOU TRUE BI

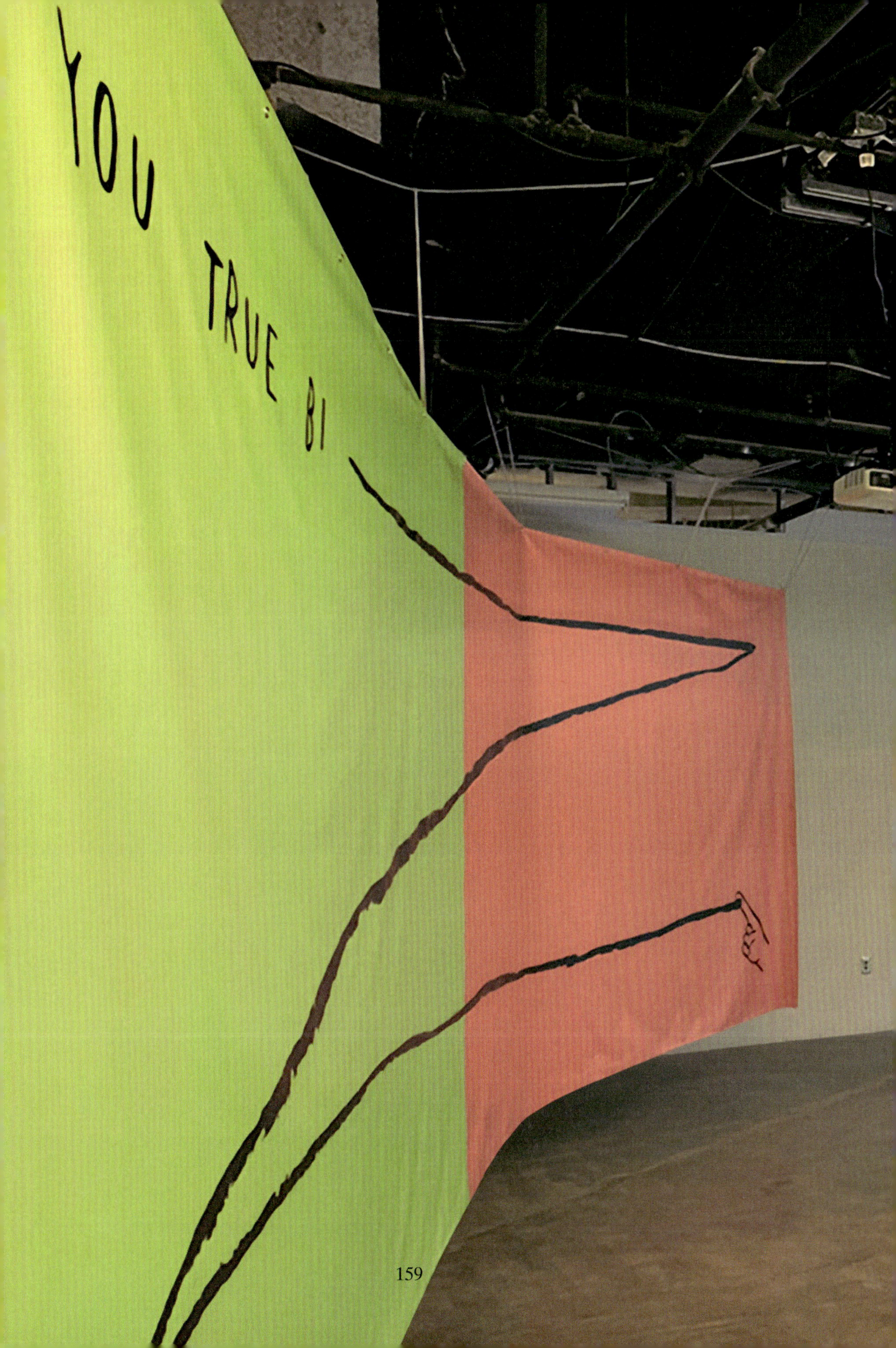
YOU TRUE BI

DJ Kebap Benzin & FRZNTE

Hyper Hyper Helium Karaoke & Dance Party

*I've attended many of FRZNTE's parties in Berlin, have danced away with her on different dancefloors, and was also aware of her relatively new collaboration with DJ Kebap Benzin, *Hyper Hyper.* I invited them to throw a karaoke & dance night in Minneapolis. This is the city of Prince after all and it seemed that at least one large party at some point during the year was necessary. The Skyway Theatre lent itself perfectly to this format. Minneapolitans know it from when downtown was a different place; it is close to the Goethe Pop Up and carries "Skyway" in its name. A dream team.

DJ Kebap Benzin & FRZNTE

31 May 2019

Hyper Hyper Helium Karaoke & Dance Party

Skyway Theatre on Hennepin Avenue

An unholy marriage of the greatest bangers and yourself, in the surgical spotlight of a most intimate Karaoke nightmare.
You are standing under a surgical UFO spotlight on an empty road to nowhere.
In front of you is the autobahn to the future along with a sign that says: "DJ Schlager Bangers."
Behind you is the obstacle course of your past. It is marked "Your wet Karaoke nightmare."
What will you do?

✘ Dream of a Future that will likely never happen
✘ Dwell on your glorious past
✔ Ride your hydraulic pogo stick to Valhalla at the HYPER HYPER

Part Submission, part Domination, absolute inhalation of noble gases.
The taboo art form of participatory performance has never been so accessible, never have the stakes been so low.
It's your party, your body, your pogo stick to ride to Valhalla at the Hyper Hyper.
"The only event in Berlin where helium is a performance enhancing drug"—A Veteran of the Italian Juggalo Scene

Accompanied by Well Trained Monkey, the Minneapolis-based one-person electro-funk Calypso band.

Images:
1. DJ Kebap Benzin dancing
2. *Hyper Hyper Helium Karaoke & Dance Party*

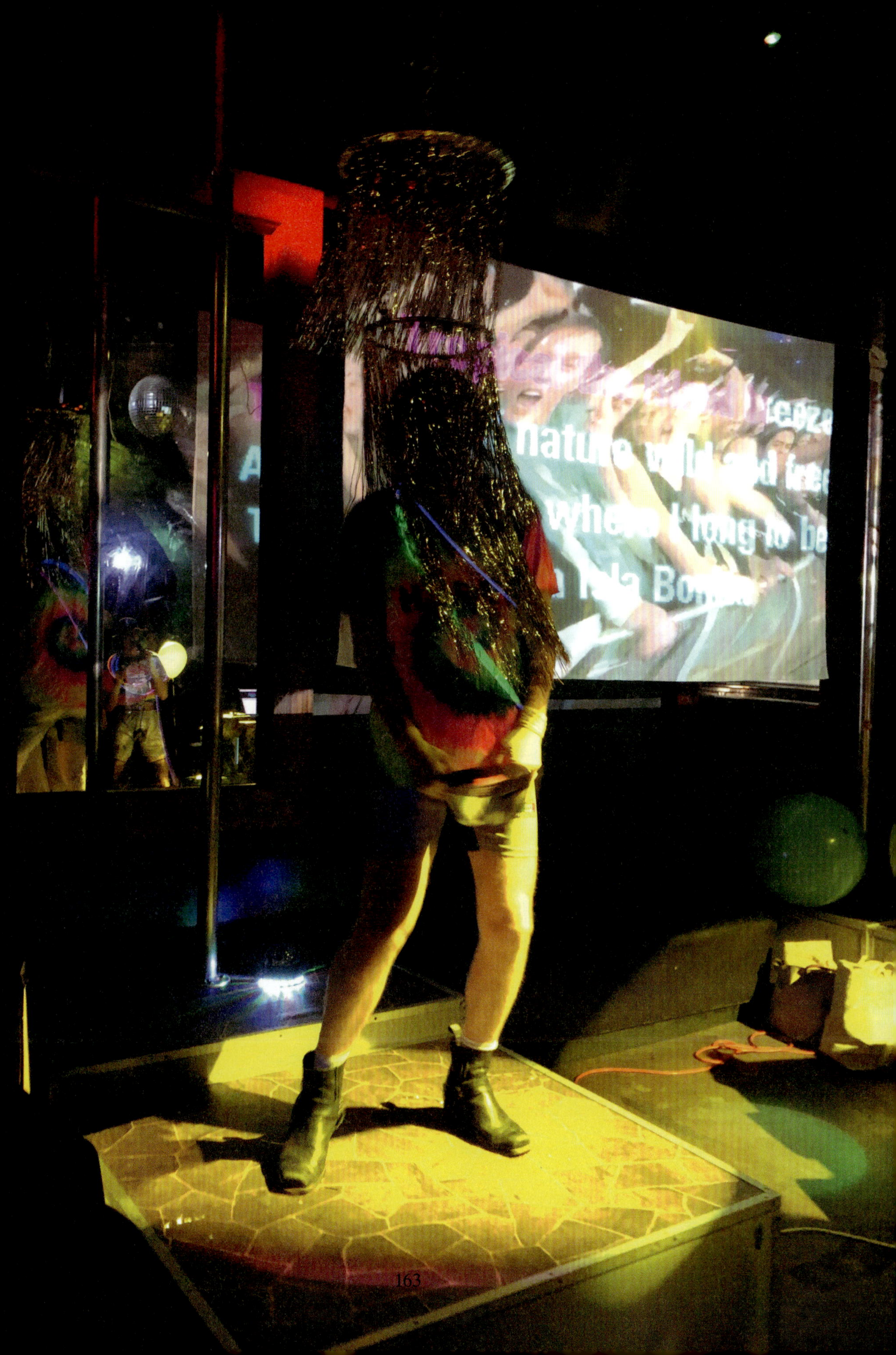

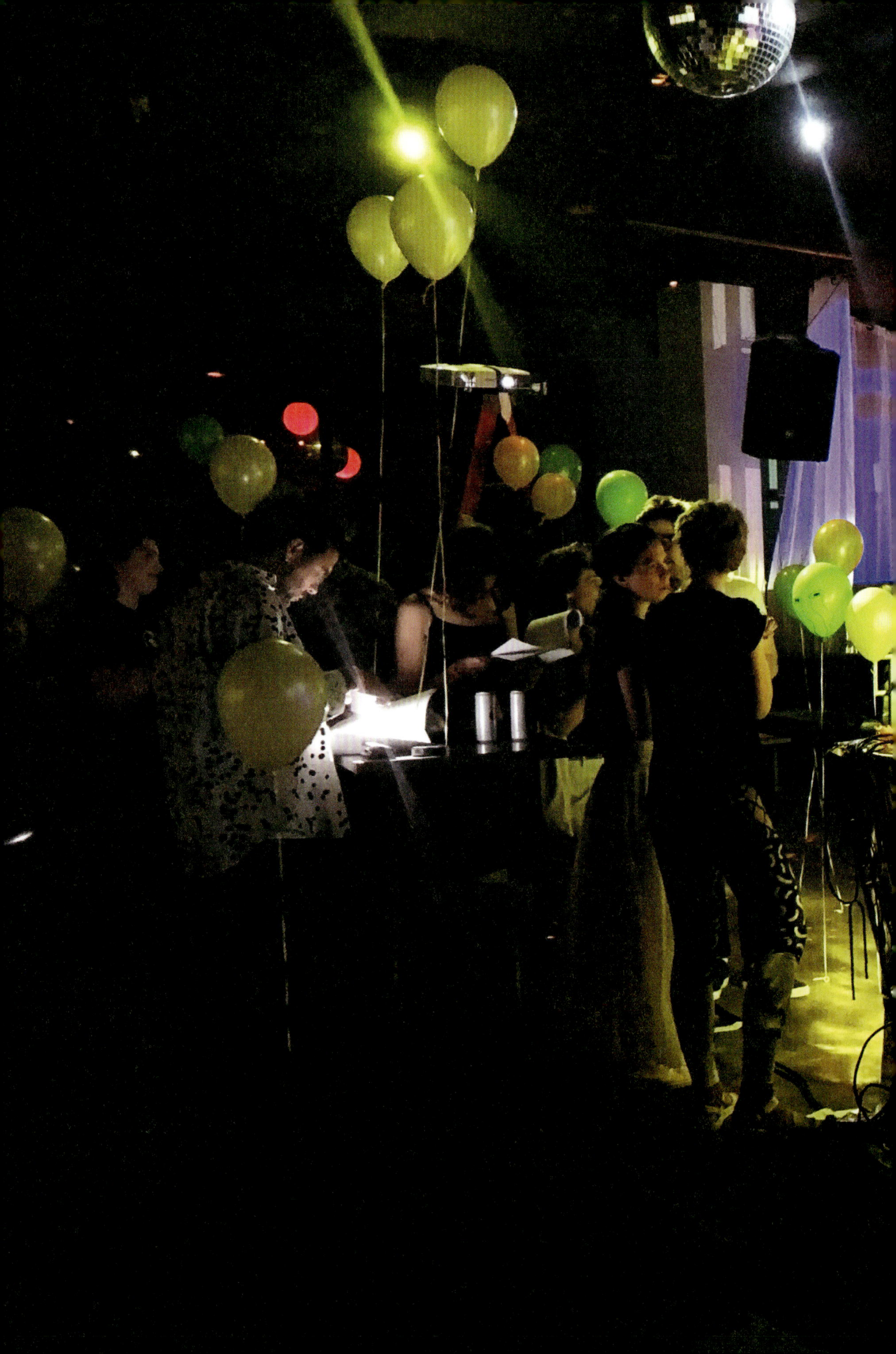

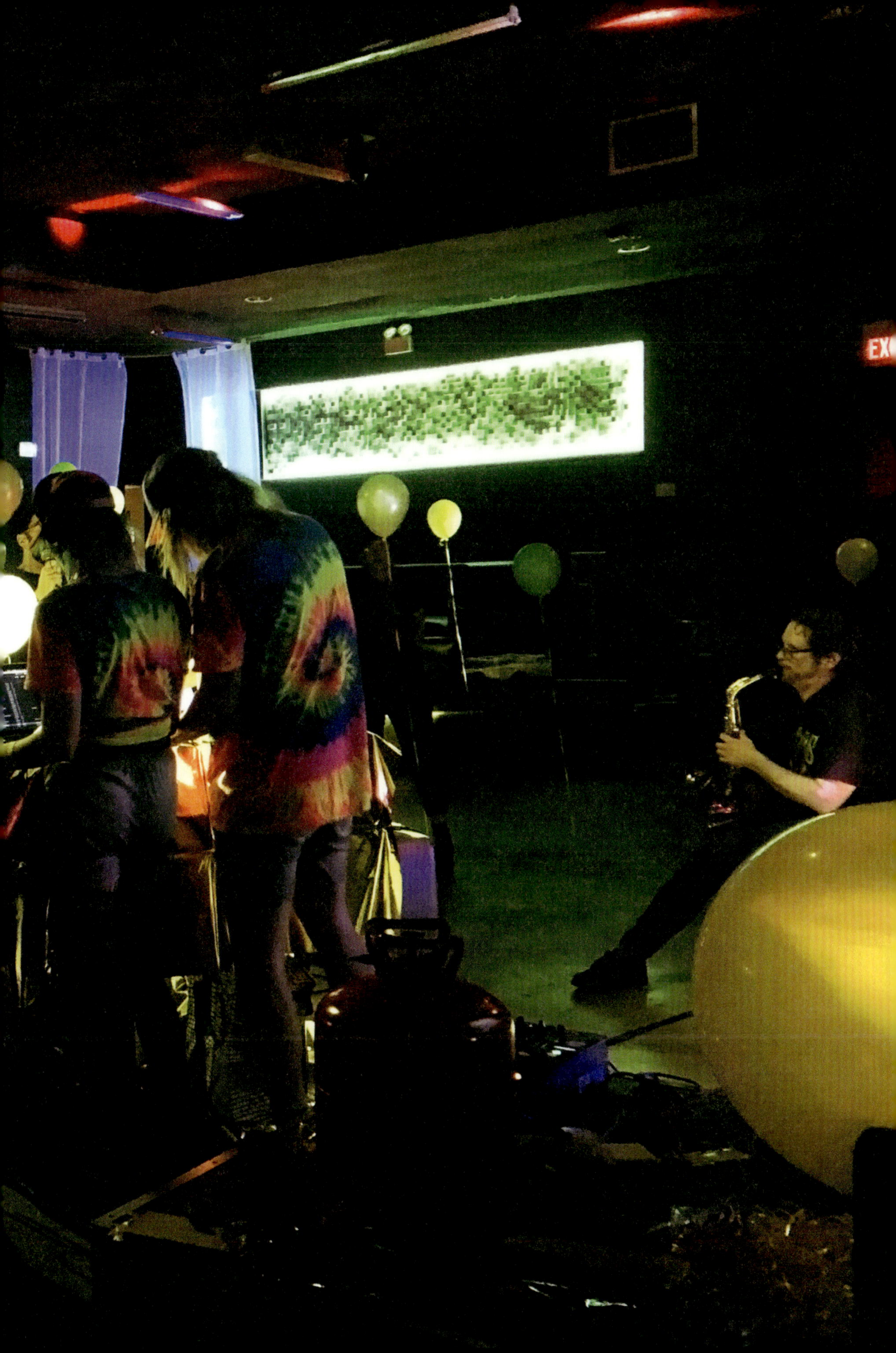

Liz Magic Laser, Cori Kresge, and Hanna Novak
User Friendly

*Liz Magic Laser and I had been in conversation for a long time about working together. I appreciate the depth and subtle political undertone of her projects, which all are developed over a long and extensive research phase. I envisioned workshop sessions for Liz in the skyways. At the time, she was working on an idea for a workshop-like performance for *Elevation 1049* in the mountains of Switzerland. The more we talked about it, the more it became clear that this project, which evolves around one's relationship to the screen, would also work very well in the skyway environment, replacing the mountain vistas with corporate skyway vistas. Cori and Hanna were an essential part of the project, Liz's collaborators, so they came to Minneapolis, as well. It was the first time that the three of them were able to stage this work together in person.

Liz Magic Laser, Cori Kresge, and Hanna Novak

User Friendly

4–28 June 2019

4 June 2019, 4:30 pm, 5:30 pm, 6:30 pm

A performative workshop (three sessions)

In an exclusive guided experience, performer and healing practitioner Cori Kresge leads participants through a dynamic exploration of breath, sight, and touch to radically reimagine our relationship to the screen.

User Friendly draws on the artists' research into current practices of "biohacking," ecstatic movement, and mind-expanding corporate retreats. Participants are led through hand-and-eye conditioning exercises, breathwork, and meditative visualizations, which draws on the corporate mall-like vistas of the skyways.

Images:
1. Display (equipment for workshop)
2. Cori Kresge leading a workshop session
3. View from outside
4. Hanna Novak assisting Cori Kresge

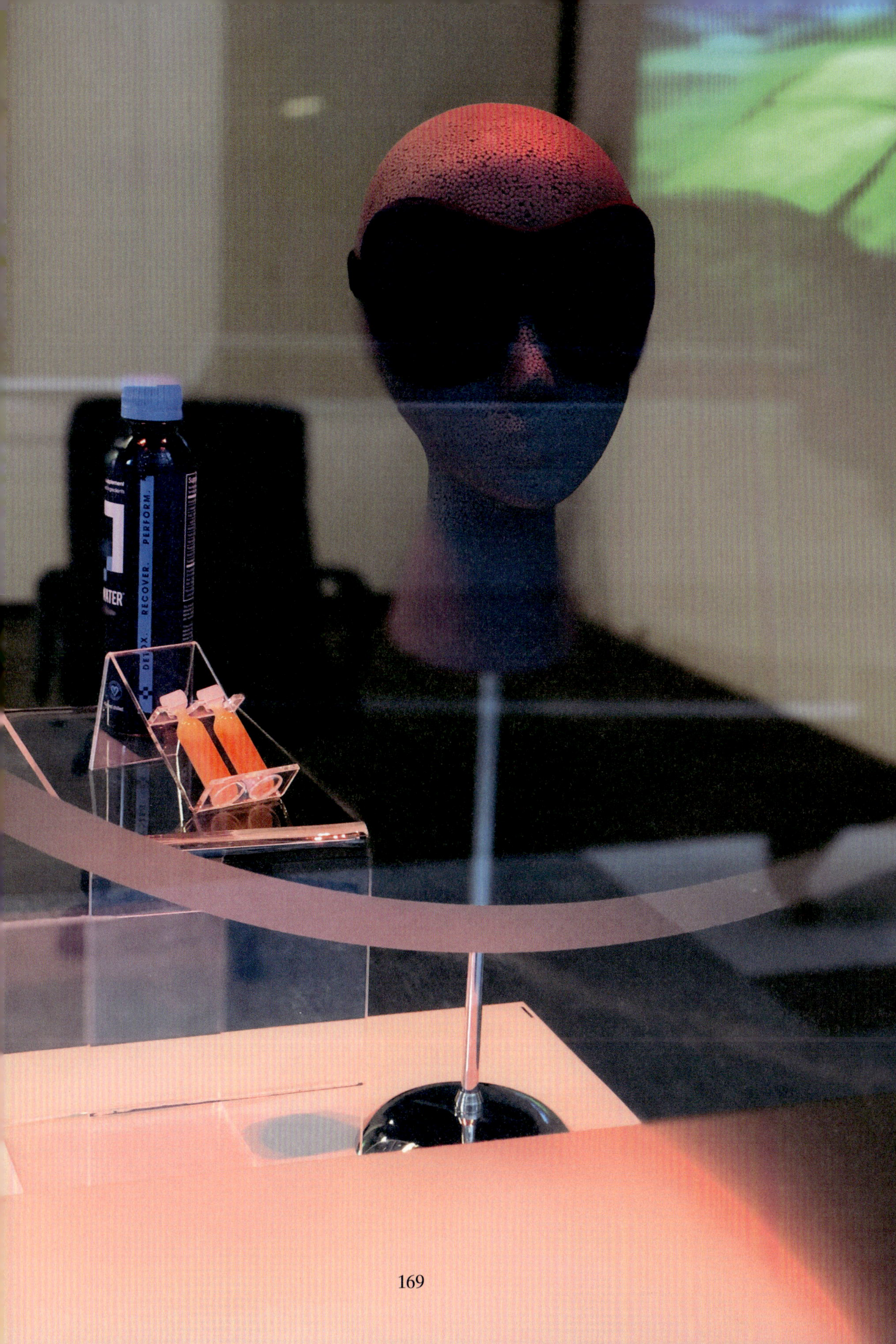
RECOVER.
PERFORM.

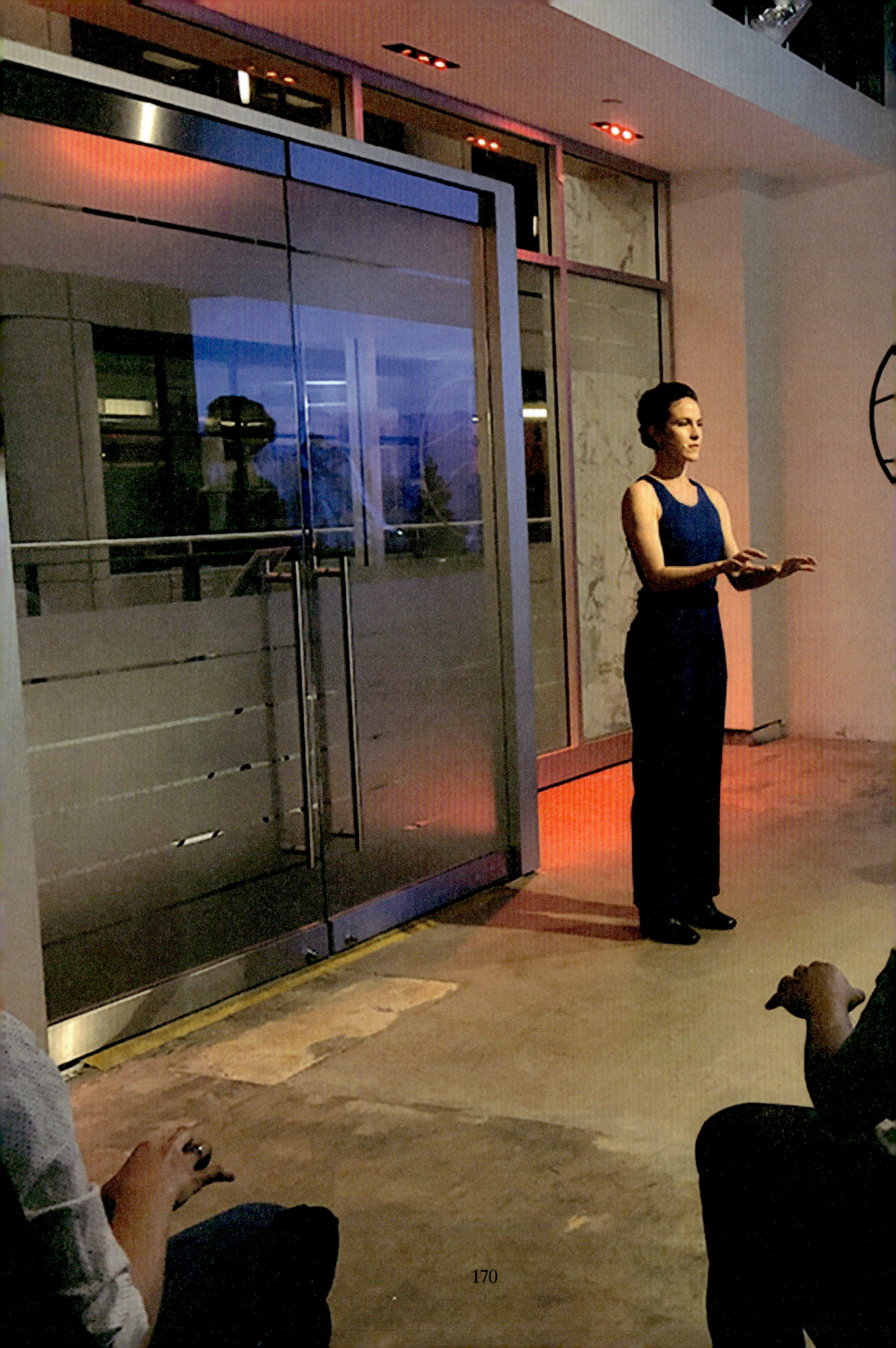

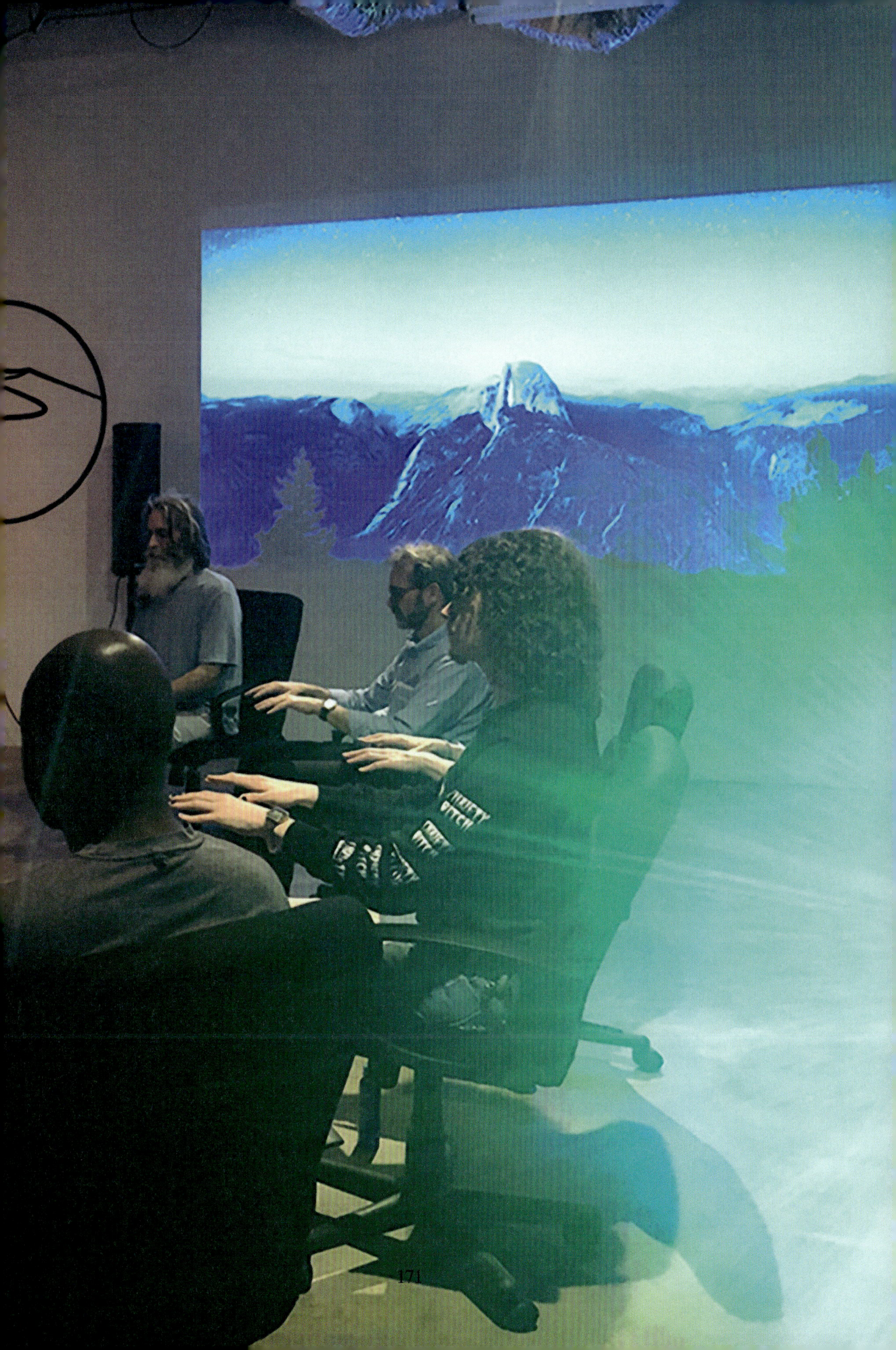

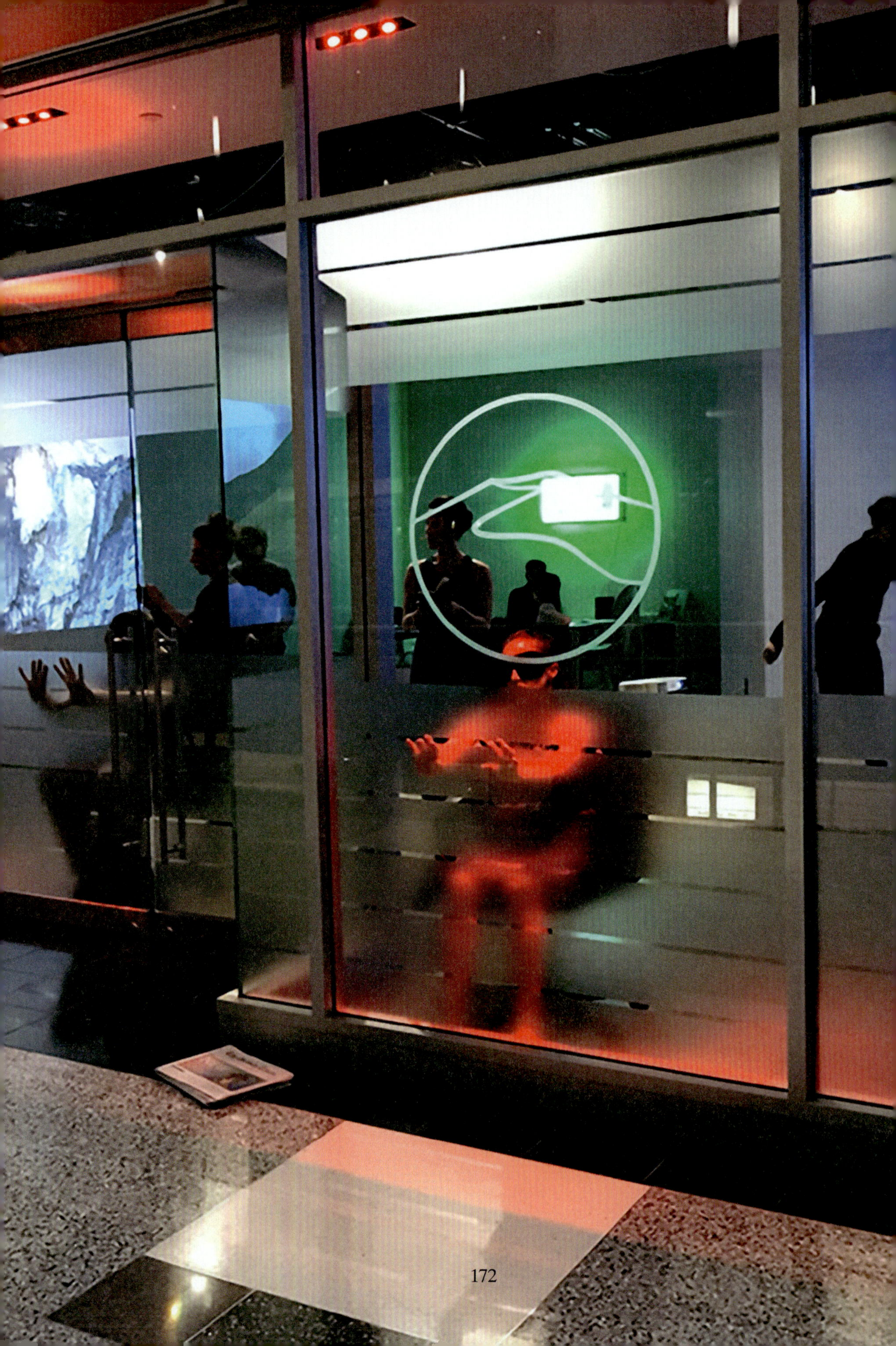

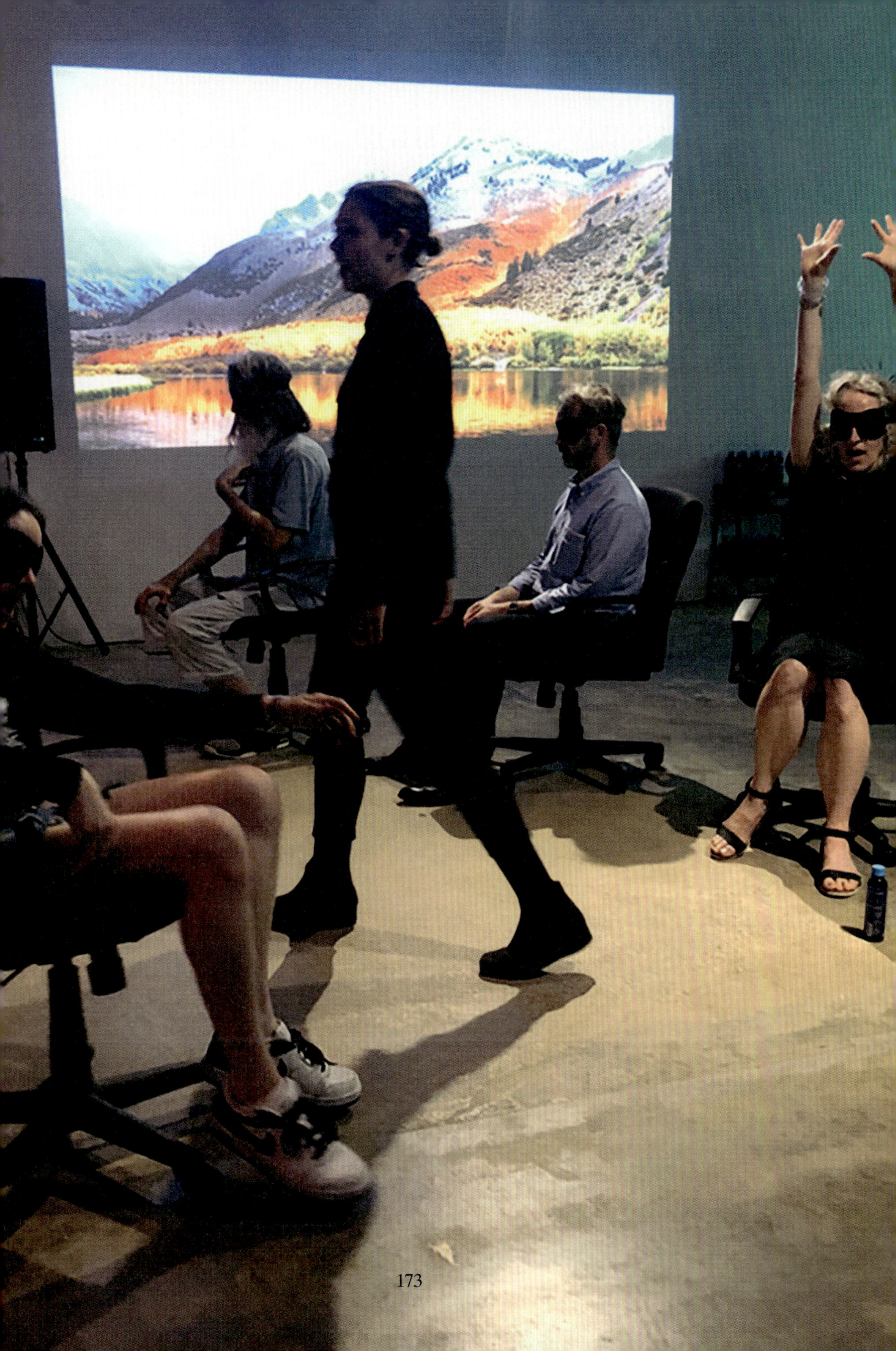

User Friendly
A performative workshop and audio installation

By Liz Magic Laser, Cori Kresge, and Hanna Novak
Performed by Cori Kresge

WELCOME

[TRACK: Ambient Low Energy]

Welcome. Please find yourself a chair and take a seat. Hanging on the arm of your chair, you'll find a pouch that contains a supplement that enhances brain function, as well as a hydrating beverage to support your mind and body in this practice. You'll also find an eye-mask to be used later. I'll direct you when it's time to put it on.
We'll get started in a moment so please silence your device and put it in the pouch.
Feel free to consume the supplement ampule now.

INTRODUCTION

What we're going to be doing today is a practice of mindful engagement with the screen. We have designed it to help you optimize your screen-time and maximize the quality of your daily experience.
I'd like to start by asking you to take a moment to consider the value of your screen-time. Can you reflect on today? Even within the last hour how did you handle your device? What was the quality of your engagement? Were you distracted? Bored or fully present? Disappointed or fulfilled?
Have you received or sent an important message today?

This is a method of radically reimagining our relationship to the screen. In some form, everyone here today has chosen to participate in alternative culture. Why, then, would you let yourself succumb to the stereotypical pathology of our times? You've got to believe there's something more than the draining paralyzing effects of screen time as *we* know it. We have these powerful machines at our disposal. They put so much within our reach. You are like the conductor of your own life, orchestrating other people and things with the simplest of gestures, the tap of a finger. Somewhere inside yourself you know that you have not reached your potential before the screen.

WARM-UPS

[TRACK: Ambient Medium Energy]

1) Hovering hands and tingle

   The first thing we're going to do is just a couple of warm-up exercises. Start by getting comfortable in your chair. Make sure you don't have anything in your hands. Find both feet on the floor, nice and grounded and relaxed. You're going to lift your hands and assume your typing position with your fingers on an imaginary keyboard.

   Let your hands and forearms hover in space, palms down. And just hold here. Note any sensations, change in temperature, slight tingle in the fingers. I'll ask you to bring 100% of your attention to the tips of your fingers. Just noticing any micro-movements that want to occur, any twitching, any energy moving, and just keep reiterating that attention 100% into your fingertips. Hold here.

   And hold. Hold. Hold.

2) Eye movement / spine

   Now, bring your fingertips to the back of your neck, lightly resting your fingers just below the ridge of your occipital bones to that soft, concave, area there. Ahhh. And we're going to feel for any movement as we move our eyes. Left and right. Left and right. Repeat. Just noticing any small, subtle sensation. The optic nerves and optic muscles are braided into the back of the neck at the base of the skull. So let's just wake up that sensation here. Moving the eyes side to side, or in a circle, keeping your touch light and receptive.

3) Nerve-flossing

   With your dominant hand, make a fist. Like this [demo]. Open your hand and extend your fingers up. Hyperextend your hand back, and point your thumb towards you. Rotate your hand and forearm in a gesture of offering, your palm skyward. With the index finger of your other hand, reach around and stretch your thumb back. Let's try it all together. Fist. Hyperextend. Rotate. Reach around. Pull the thumb back. Repeat. First. Hyperextend. Rotate. Reach around. Pull the thumb back.

   Shake it out.

[TRACK: Ambient High Energy]

4) Finger walking

   This next one is a more advanced exercise, but let's give it a try. Think of it as a tongue twister or brain-teaser, but for your dexterity. Bring the index fingertip of your right hand to the thumb-tip of your left hand. (*Demonstrates*) Allow this to be a pivoting point. Now, pivot the thumb of your right hand up to the index finger of your left hand. Release the first index finger of your right hand and pivot until the middle finger of your right hand touches the thumb of your left hand. Pivot and repeat with the middle finger of your left hand and thumb of your right hand. Repeat this with your ring fingers and pinkies, like this (*demonstrates*). Now, we'll reverse. Like this. You'll get there.

5) Fingers/mountain through holding imaginary device

OK now let's bring your hands in front of your face, just softly holding them like this (*demonstrates*). I want you to focus your perception on your fingers. Now look past your fingers to the window glass. Focus on the glass surface of the window. Let your fingers blur. Now, shift your focus beyond the glass. Everything else softens. Bring your focus back to your fingers. We're going to practice this in intervals. I'll count us down. Focus on your fingers for 5, 4, 3, 2, 1. Glass for 5, 4, 3, 2, 1. Beyond 5, 4, 3, 2, 1. Fingers for 4, 3, 2, 1. Glass 4, 3, 2, 1. Beyond 4, 3, 2, 1. Fingers 3, 2, 1. Glass 3, 2, 1. Beyond 3, 2, 1. Fingers 2, 1. Glass 2, 1. Beyond 2, 1. Fingers. Glass. Beyond. Fingers. Glass. Beyond. Fingers. Glass. Beyond.

And rest.

6) Rest

You can close your eyes for a moment, just really allowing your hands and eyes to rest. You just did a lot of work.

OK. Let's come back. You can open your eyes. We're going to start the next phase.

BREATHWORK

This work is a development and modification from holiotropic breathwork. Breath is the most effective way of releasing any tensions, any anxious impulses out of the body. All the demands of our daily lives can easily feel overwhelming. In your everyday communications, do you always find yourself responding to the needs of others? Are you burdened by the onslaught of messages from the outside world? This is work is about reconnecting with your own internal compass, to pursue your own searches and drives. I'll ask you in this next phase to follow whatever comes up for you. Whatever it is, pursue it for yourself. Go deeper into it. This is a modality of active response. You may experience some uncomfortable feelings or sensations during this work. Your fingers may become tingly, frozen or claw-like. You might feel dizzy. You might even drool. All this is actually good. It's part of the process. It means that tension that's been accumulating in you for years or decades is finally ready to be let go. It's counterintuitive, but the body needs to maximize tension in order to get the best release. Now, it is time to turn off your dominant sensor. Please put on your eye mask. Allow your screen to go black. It's time to power down.I'm going to demonstrate a few different postural options for you. Firstly, find a comfortable, upright seated position. A slight tuck of the chin. Place your hands either hovering in front of you over the imaginary keyboard, grasping a device in front of you or with your hands reaching out, like this (*demonstrates*). Or, reach your arms out in front of you. Go with whichever feels best for you. Whatever it is, pursue it.

[TRACK: Hand Drums and Hums]

Navigate the terrain of your mind. You know where you're going. You know what you're searching for. No one is going to throw you off course.
Breathe in and out.
I want you to imagine that you are a climber, scaling a mountain. With each inhale, you are climbing upwards. And as you exhale, you descend. Breathe in, ascend, breathe out,

descend… (*repeat 3 times*). Enjoy the peaks and valleys of your breath.
Breathe in and out (*demonstrates*). Increase the tension in your fingers ever so slightly, notice them vibrating just a little. Now, check in with the rest of your body. Notice the points of contact between you and the chair. Explore them with movement, rocking back and forth or finding a vibration.
Feel the chair supporting your posture. Holding your body's weight. Feel the chair move as you move. Maybe rocking or swaying or swiveling in your chair. You're free to move your arms now, in whatever way feels best for you.
Breathe in and out. With each inhale, you are climbing upwards. And as you exhale, you descend.
Breathe.
Breathe.
Breathe.
Let's begin breathing faster and deeper: faster, deeper, faster, deeper. In and out through your mouth, like this (*demonstrates*). I'm going to guide you through some connected breathing. A moment before the exhale is complete, inhale again. Before the inhale is complete, begin to exhale so that the breath becomes circular with no gaps.
(*Breathes audibly*)
Let your breath be audible. (*Breathes louder*) Make sound. Let it out. Now let me hear you. Let your breath make sound, let your breath speak, let your body speak, let the chair speak. Breathe in, and "ahhhhh."

[TRACK: ADHD High Energy]

Now again. Breathing in. Let it out, "ahhhhh."
Deeper. Faster. Deeper. Faster.
Scale up and descend.
Allow your consciousness to open up to the fact that we are human beings from around the world breathing together. Anytime people breathe together, there is always this energetic net of support.
Whatever you're feeling, feel it more. Fear, rage, joy, boredom, skepticism, physical discomfort, the urge to move. So move! Trust it. Feel it more. Go with your breath.
Breathing deeper, faster. Deeper, faster.
Keep going.

[TRACK: Alpha Low Energy]

Gradually, let your breath begin to return to its natural rhythm. The peaks and valleys of your breathing are going to elongate.

(*Attendants roll blindfolded participants towards window*)

MEDITATION

Bring your attention to your physical and emotional self. Notice what you're feeling, sensing. Look into yourself for a moment. Be curious about your emotional state.
Are you excited? Calm? Anxious? Frustrated? The important thing is not what state you're in, but just really start looking inward. Everything is OK.
Extend your hands forward until your fingers lightly graze the glass. Reach out.
Feel the coolness of the air on the other side of the screen. Feel the hard surface softening under your touch as the warmth of your fingertips presses upon the cold, smooth barrier. Beyond the glass, a mountain vista appears. Trace the mountain's form

with your fingertips as they glide across the screen. Sense its seamless texture. Feel the smoothness of the sky. Let your fingertips conjure the shadows and the light. Be curious. Explore. Glide. Tap. Trust your touch to lead you where you need to go.

For the tourist, the mountain is a site of beauty. But if you need to get somewhere, the mountain is an obstacle in your way. Every journey needs its obstacle: people, places, pressures, the demands of others. The magnitude of things in the way can seem overwhelming.

Through your practice here today, you honor this screen that serves as both barrier and portal between you and the outside.

Focus 100% of your energy on that interface where you end and the other begins.

In the screen there is only the screen.

I invite you to stay here for as long as you like. This time is yours. Whenever you are ready, let your fingers disconnect and remove your eye mask.

CONCLUSION

To conclude our session today I invite you all to take out your device.

[Pause]

Do you have an important message?

[TRACK: Neuro Space]

Ten Things to Take to the Sky, which Unintentionally Start with the Letter S, Except for One, and Why Again?

Paula Hildebrandt

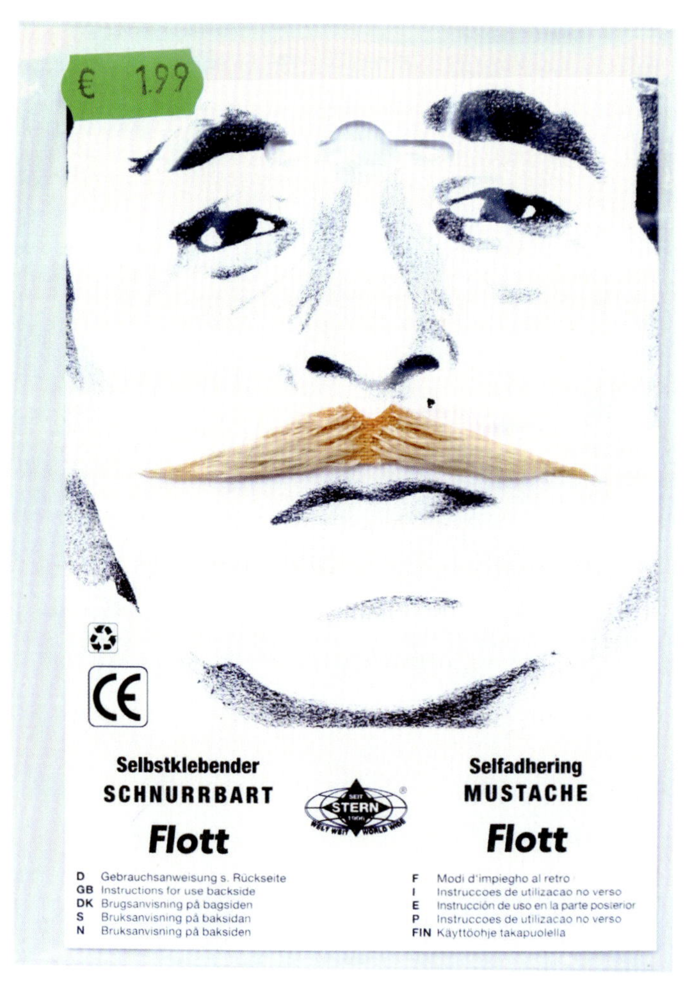
€ 1.99
Selbstklebender
SCHNURRBART
Flott
STERN
Selfadhering
MUSTACHE
Flott
D Gebrauchsanweisung s. Rückseite
GB Instructions for use backside
DK Brugsanvisning på bagsiden
S Bruksanvisning på baksidan
N Bruksanvisning på baksiden
F Modi d'impiegho al retro
I Instruccoes de utilizacao no verso
E Instrucción de uso en la parte posterior
P Instruccoes de utilizacao no verso
FIN Käyttöohje takapuolella

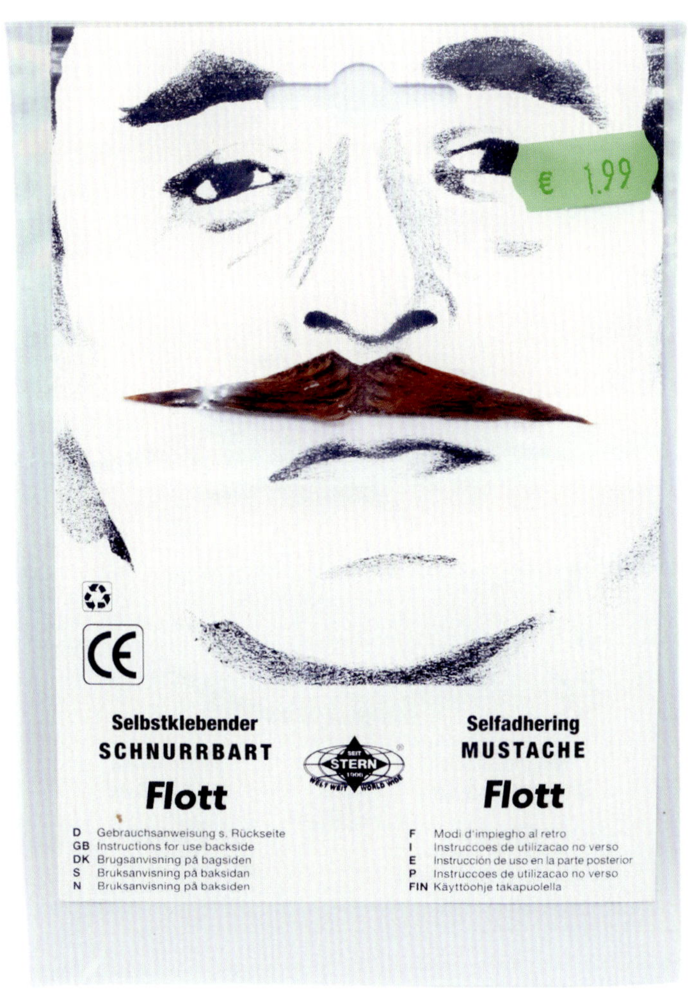
€ 1.99
CE
Selbstklebender
SCHNURRBART
Flott
SEIT
STERN
1906
WELT WEIT WORLD WIDE
Selfadhering
MUSTACHE
Flott
D Gebrauchsanweisung s. Rückseite
GB Instructions for use backside
DK Brugsanvisning på bagsiden
S Bruksanvisning på baksidan
N Bruksanvisning på baksiden
F Modi d'impiegho al retro
I Instruccoes de utilizacao no verso
E Instrucción de uso en la parte posterior
P Instruccoes de utilizacao no verso
FIN Käyttöohje takapuolella

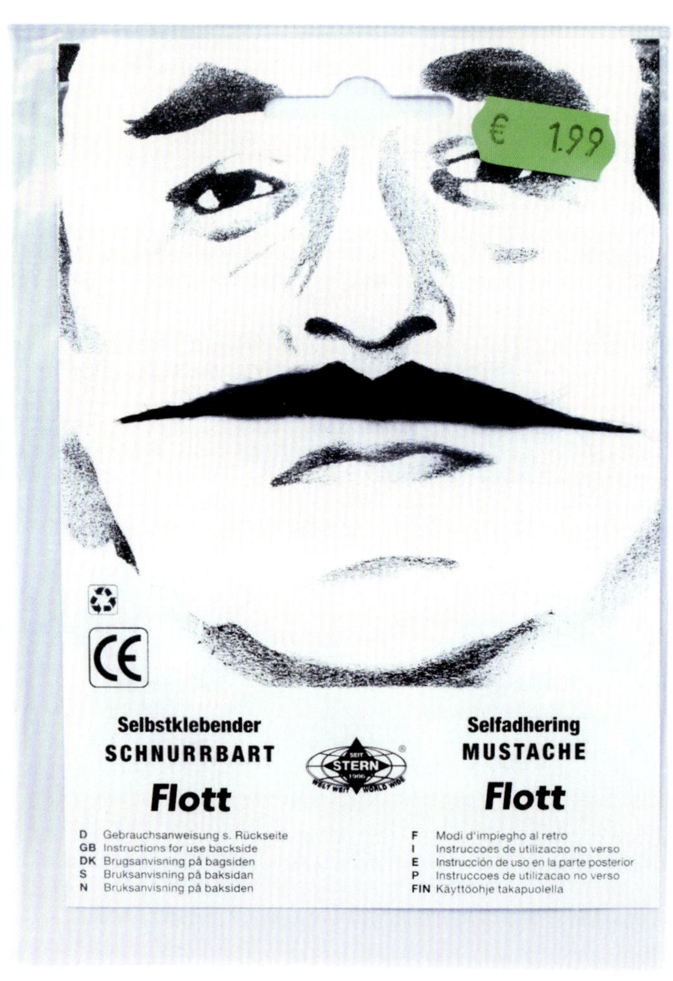
€ 1.99
CE
Selbstklebender
SCHNURRBART
Flott
SEIT
STERN
1906
WELT WEIT WORLD WIDE
Selfadhering
MUSTACHE
Flott
D Gebrauchsanweisung s. Rückseite
GB Instructions for use backside
DK Brugsanvisning på bagsiden
S Bruksanvisning på baksidan
N Bruksanvisning på baksiden
F Modi d'impiegho al retro
I Instruccoes de utilizacao no verso
E Instrucción de uso en la parte posterior
P Instruccoes de utilizacao no verso
FIN Käyttöohje takapuolella

1. Self-adhering mustache

Guy named Richard goes on a blind date with a woman named Linda. They set it up over the phone. This Linda says, "Meet me at the soda fountain." The guy Richard goes to the soda fountain and waits.

A young woman walks up to him. "Are you Richard?" she asks.

He says yes.

She looks him over. Says, "I'm *not* Linda."

Rachel Kushner, *The Mars Room*, London, 2018.

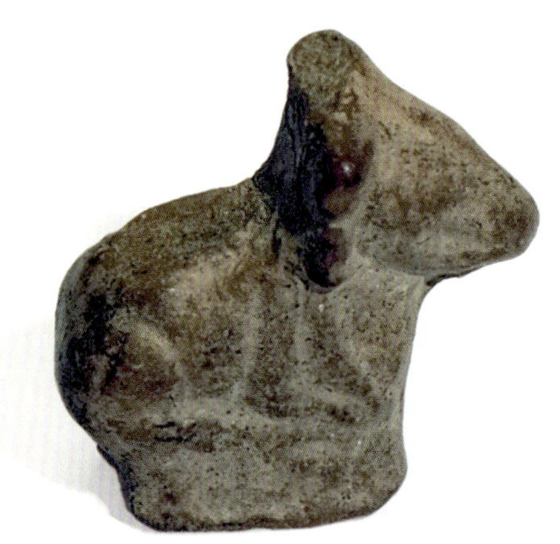

2. Sheep

Hand flattering (Handschmeichler) refers to objects which, when touched, create a pleasant feeling due to their smooth surface and rounded edges. They are small companions that fit into any pocket or purse. They are usually round and made of materials such as bronze or other metal, wood, stone, soapstone, minerals or semi-precious stones artificially manufactured.

But it can also be a natural object such as a walnut. Flatterers usually have no specific function and got their name because of their size, because they fit comfortably in each hand.

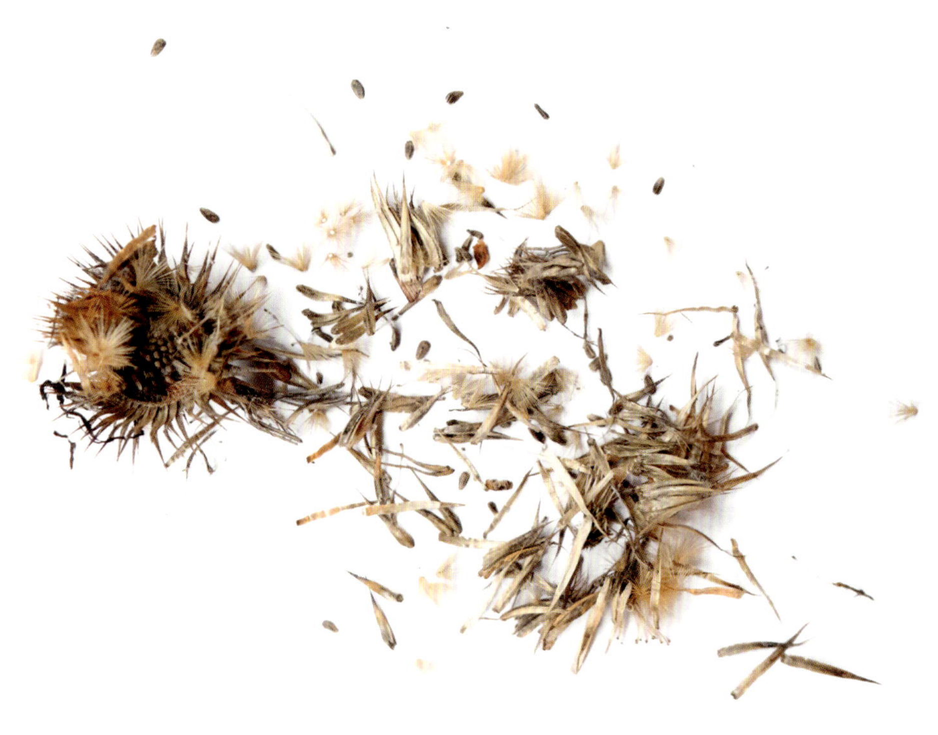

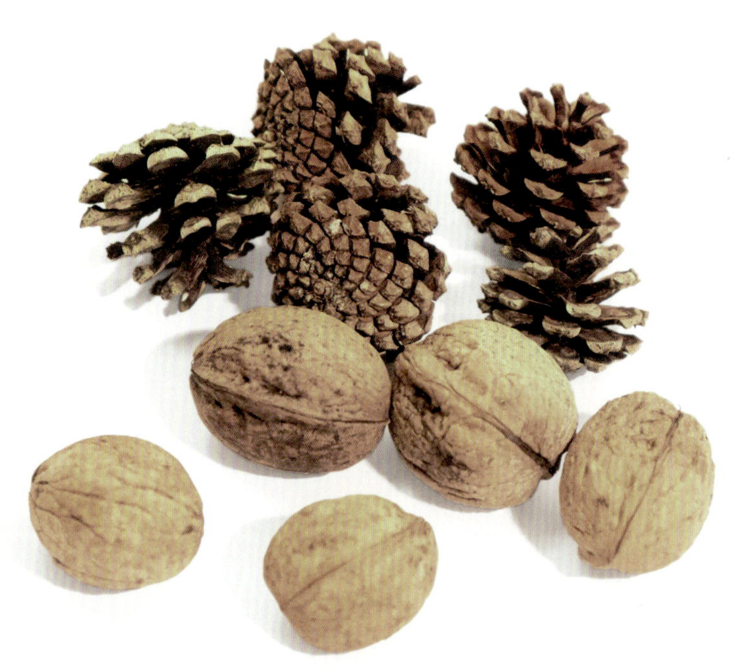

3. Seeds/Simulants

If humans are going to establish a base on the Moon or on Mars they will have to grow their own crops. An option is to use Lunar and Martian regolith. These regoliths are not available for plant growth experiments, therefore NASA has developed regolith simulants. The major goal of this project was to cultivate and harvest crops on these Mars and Moon simulants. The simulants were mixed with organic matter to mimic the addition of residues from earlier harvests. Ten different crops, garden cress, rocket, tomato, radish, rye, quinoa, spinach, chives, pea and leek were sown in random lines in trays. Nine of the ten species grew well with the exception of spinach. It was possible to harvest edible parts for nine out of ten crops. The total biomass production per tray was highest for the Earth control and Mars soil simulant and differed significantly from Moon soil simulant. The seeds produced by three species were tested for germination (radish, rye and cress). The germination on Moon soil simulant was significantly lower in radish than for the Earth control soil.

G.W.W. Wamelink, J.Y. Frissel, W.H.J. Krijnen, M.R. Verwoert, "Crop growth and viability of seeds on Mars and Moon soil simulants," *Open Agriculture 2019*, 4.

4. Sesame Oil

Here's a simple tip to help you stay warm in winter.

It doesn't take much time, or cost much; it is very sensual and enjoyable, it helps to ground you, and it has multiple health benefits. Oh, and it helps to maintain youthfulness and vitality too …

Why does sesame oil have such a powerful effect?

In Ayurvedic terms, sesame oil balances Vata dosha. Vata is the principle that governs "movement" in the body. It controls the nervous system and is quick, light, cold, rough and moving. When Vata is disturbed (as a result of lack of routine, travel, talking a lot, late nights, etc) we feel unsettled, jumpy, out of balance, and may suffer from disturbed sleep. Sesame oil has an immediate warming, calming and nourishing effect, and is a powerful means to balance Vata.

www.aromachat.com

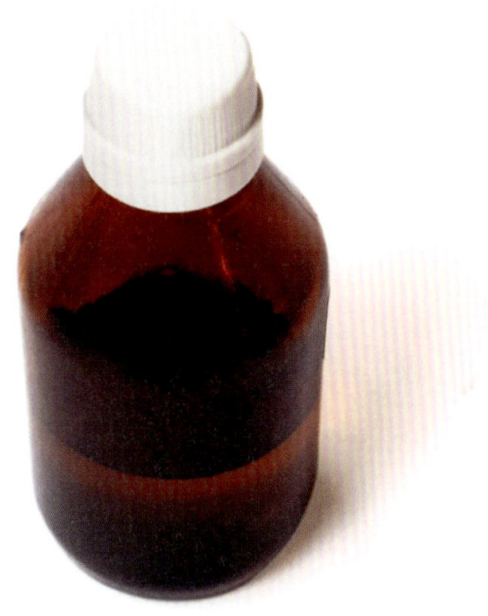

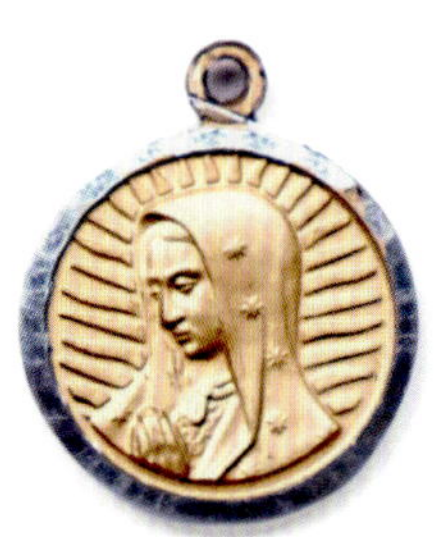

A nun is a woman who has very good reasons to enter the convent. She has had them ancestrally. When divorce was not allowed and a woman had to marry, the nun entered the convent fleeing from marriage. Today it is a flight from hunger in the family, in search of the abundant food in the convent.

The nun is a silent woman who cleans the floors, sweeps the courtyards, takes care of the flowers in the garden, cleans the altars, makes the hosts or goes around the neighborhood listening to the problems of people. She likes to put on those wide clothes and hide her body, because the nun is a woman who also flees from her own body. The bishops and priests think she is silly and continue their conversations in her presence, as if she was a piece of furniture, while they devour the *masitas* that the nun singing has prepared for the tea on Saturdays. She knows through which door the priest's lover enters his bedroom at night. She knows where he hides the whisky and washes his filthy underpants so many times loaded with semen, so many times loaded with urine. The nun knows that there is nothing about the vow of poverty that the Church proclaims. The priest has a four-by-four, trips to Rome, salary, donations that nobody controls and a life full of the well-being that the neighborhood lacks. She was the older sister of a family of eight siblings, and she dedicated herself to raising them. There was never enough in her house so she decided to go to the convent. Her decision was practical and her life in there is practical too; lower your head, obey and shut up, but your eyes see everything, your ears hear everything.

The nun has already helped to abort several women in the neighborhood. She has decided to do so because she learned the procedure from her mother who learned from her grandmother. When she saw that a woman died from abortion leaving three *wawas* orphaned, she decided to help anyone who asked, without sermons and out of a pure sense of justice. She thinks that the priest and the mother superior know nothing, and slips through the alleys without any pretext when it comes to performing an abortion, but the priest and the superior know it and shut up. They prefer silence because they are afraid of the meek nun. The parish priest does not forget the occasion when the nun helped in the abortion of a novice who was pregnant by the seminarian. The priest is afraid that it will be revealed that he also demanded that a catechist have an abortion.

The sexual life in the convent is full of threats, rapes, clandestine and compulsory abortions, of bastarded children, feelings of guilt and humiliation, and it is the need to cover that that takes the cure in the Sunday sermon. That is why he preaches shouting and condemning, because he can no longer be with his double standards, because he can no longer has his double life. The nun will never say it, she will never rebel, she will never run away from the convent, nor she will leave the tasks undone because she is one of those meek beings who go through life for fools in the eyes of the powerful. The hosts that Catholics eat in communion are made of a mass moistened with tears of nuns, catechists and parishioners raped, groped and humiliated. These hosts are kneaded with semen from a hypocritical priest, a seminarian who demands sex without a condom. The hot iron that flattens the hosts and cooks them is heated by the heat of the contained pain that is forbidden to be talked about.

The sharp scissors with which the hosts that Catholics eat in communion are cut off is the edge with which anyone inside the convent is threatened to tell the truth, and nothing but the truth. Your Church crucifies women every day, feminism resurrects them.

Original text by María Galindo, "A monja abortera/The Abortive Nun," *Pagina Siete*, March 29, 2017.
María Galindo is a member of Mujeres Creando, a Bolivian anarcha-feminist collective.

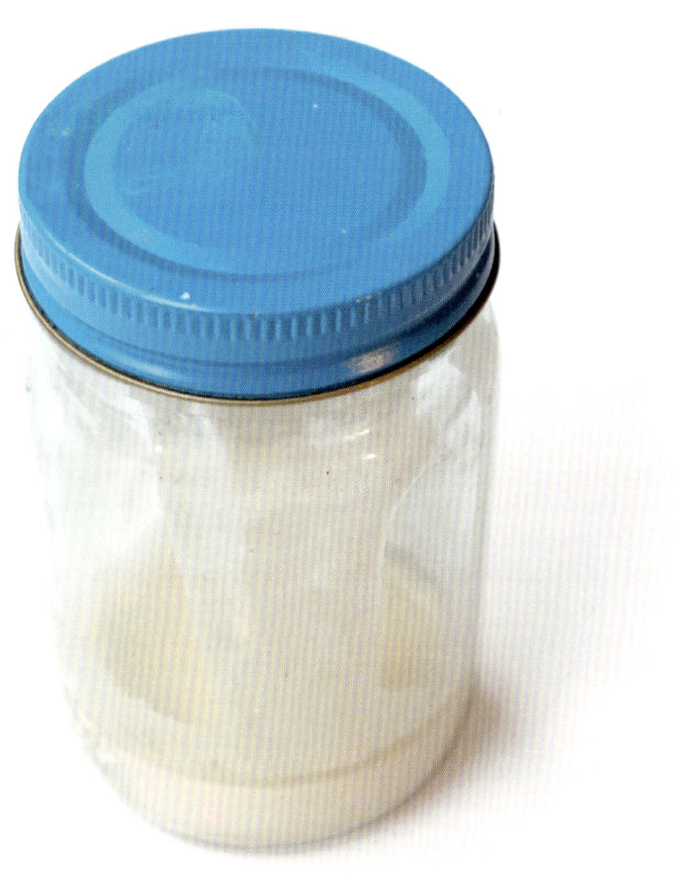

6. Sourdough

The Skyway My Burger is hiring an AM cashier!
My Burger—Minneapolis, MN
$11 an hour

The Skyway My Burger is looking for a cashier superstar! No nights! No weekends!
High volume!

Hours for this position are Mon–Fri, from 9am–3pm.

Job Responsibilities:
Must be able to give outstanding customer service, legendary hospitality, and be a team player!
Must be able to follow the direction of the Shift Supervisor, or Restaurant Manager including but not limited to; prep, cleaning tasks, closing duties, specs, and store organization.
Must be willing to do dishes, as everyone does their part!

This position is HIGH VOLUME! POS experience necessary, being calm under pressure is a must!

Starting pay from $11.00/hr–$13.00 depending on experience.

We are a family owned burger joint based out of Minneapolis. We have 7 locations and a food truck, but we aren't stopping there. We are looking to add quality talent that can grow with us. Nearly all of our managers have been promoted from an hourly position. No joke. We reward results and hard work! Are you the next one? Apply now!

https://www.indeed.com/viewjob?jk=9f92498afb0c834d&from=serp&mobRdr=1

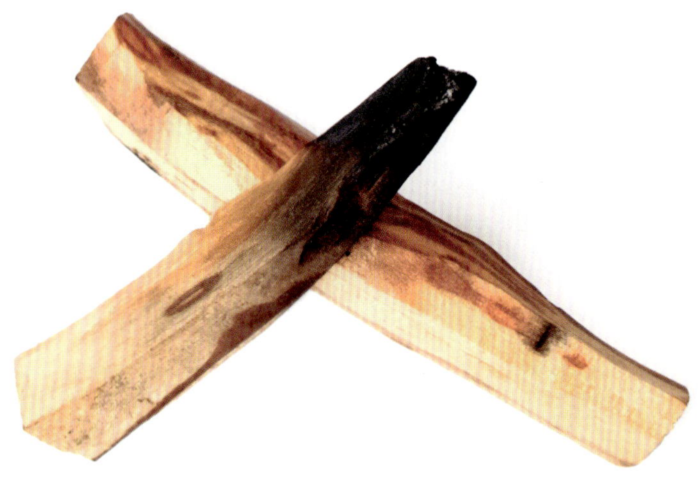

7. Smoke (to clear the energy after yet another Zombie Pub Crawl)

The zombie body is often seen in the public sphere: town squares, cemeteries, schools, streets, and even in malls—providing overt social critique. The fear that the public realm is being invaded by pure necessity, or pure consumption, is expressed through the drama of the inhuman, ever-consuming zombie.

Sarah Juliet Lauro and Karen Embry, *A Zombie Manifesto: The Nonhuman Condition in the Era of Advanced Capitalism*, boundary 2 35:1 (2008).

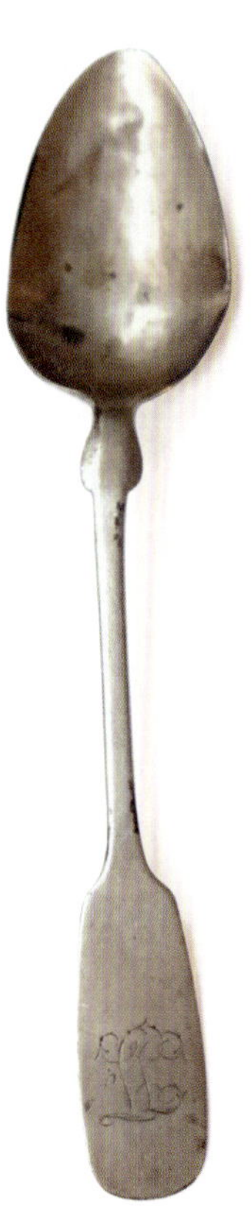

8. Spoon

UT: Baby-Löffel von Oma, 1867

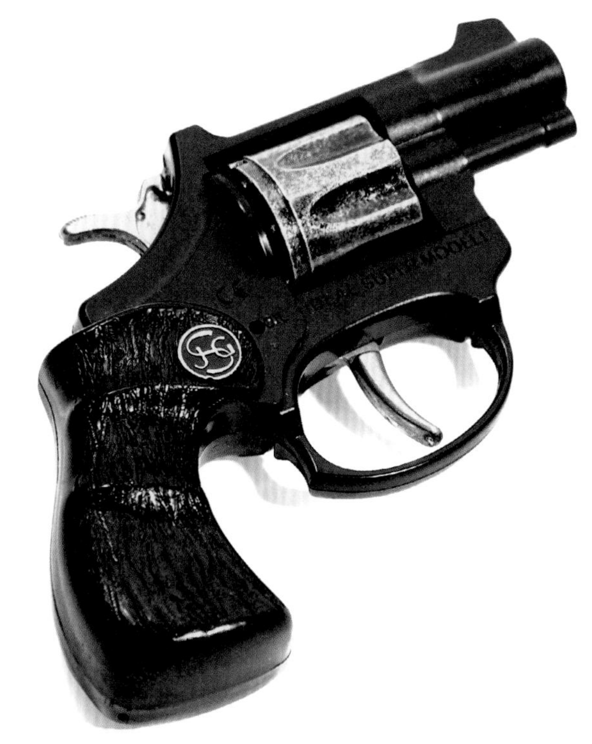

9. Stethoscope

And, of course, you want the days to add up to something more than you came in out of the sun and drank the potable water of your developed world—

yes, and because words hang in the air like pollen, the throat closes. You hack away.

That time and that time and that time the outside blistered the inside of you, words outmaneuvered years, had you in a chokehold, every part roughed up, the eyes dripping.

That's the bruise the ice in the heart was meant to ice.

To arrive like this every day for it to be like this to have so many memories and no other memory than these for as long as they can be remembered to remember this.

Though a share of all remembering, a measure of all memory, is breath and to breathe you have to create a truce—

a truce with the patience of a stethoscope.

Claudia Rankine: *CITIZEN, An American Lyric*, 2014: 156.

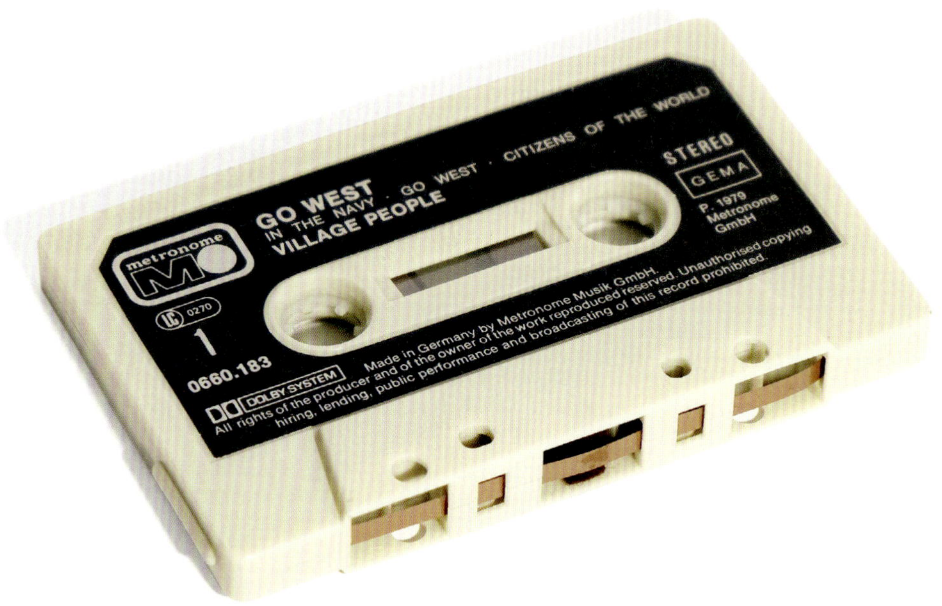
metronome
GO WEST
IN THE NAVY · GO WEST · CITIZENS OF THE WORLD
VILLAGE PEOPLE
STEREO
GEMA
P. 1979
Metronome
GmbH
0270
1
0660.183
DOLBY SYSTEM
Made in Germany by Metronome Musik GmbH.
All rights of the producer and of the owner of the work reproduced reserved. Unauthorised copying
hiring, lending, public performance and broadcasting of this record prohibited.

Creamcake
Euromall

*I had become aware of Creamcake in the summer of 2018 through their project *Europool* at Tropez, a space for art, which takes place inside a public pool in Berlin. I liked their mix of political discourse and music. I knew Creamcake's project would resonate in Minneapolis as there is actually a touch of Berlin already alive within the electronic community; one of Berghain's resident DJs, DVS1, was born and raised in Minneapolis and organizes semi-legal electro club nights in Minneapolis twice a year. So I invited Creamcake to adapt their *Europool* program to the U.S. for the following summer, as a sort of assessment from a European perspective of the relationship between Europe and the United States. With participants from both sides of the Atlantic, one day of discourse and one club night, *Europool* came to life within a new city in "The New World."

Creamcake

Euromall

15–16 June 2019

Discussions, Performances, DJ sets, and Video Games with: Alobhe (Berlin), Salim Bayri (Amsterdam), Bleak Roses (Mpls), Rana Farahani/Fauna (Vienna), Anna Hankings-Evans (Berlin), Steph Kretowicz (London/Los Angeles), Aleksandra Lakić (Berlin), Larry (Berlin), Surabhi Saraf (San Francisco), and Creamcake (Berlin)

15 June 2019, 3pm

Euromall Day Program

Goethe Pop Up Minneapolis

16 June 2019, 9pm

Euromall Night Program

honey mpls

Initiated by Berlin-based music and art platform Creamcake, *Euromall* creates space for conversation. The series of two day-and-night events aims to encourage exchange across disciplines and experiences, emerging from a belief in the possibilities of political organization and direct action and in creativity as the expression of a will to change social realities. While the main drive for Creamcake's original *Europool* project came as a response to the dramatic socio-political shifts in the European Union between 2017 and 2018, its concerns are certainly not limited to it.

The *Euromall* program in Minneapolis showcases and reflects upon the ties between Europe and the United States today by spotlighting grassroots initiatives, cultural collaborations, and artistic practices emerging across borders. Anna Hankings-Evans's lecture combines storytelling and legal methodology in discussing notions of empathy and law, while Steph Kretowicz's live reading explores the personal effects of fear, fake news, and new technology across continents. Salim Bayri's video game *Road to Schengen* follows the insurmountable bureaucracy of global movement, and Surabhi Saraf's sound performance questions the risks and possibilities of technological solutionism when applied to emotional labor and social relations. Moderator Aleksandra Lakić speaks on the EU parliamentary elections in her "How soon is the end of Europe as we know it?" lecture and Fauna presents on the right-wing populist movement of Austria's FPÖ party and the "Ibiza scandal," followed by participation in a night of music at honey mpls, along with Alobhe and DJ Larry.

It is within this framework that the *Euromall* discussions, performances, readings, DJ sets, video game, and dancing call for solidarity through exploring our differences. By urging active participation in a dialogue around multiple concepts, approaches, and political desires, it is possible to reverse, or at least repair unacceptable developments inside and outside of Europe.

Images:
1. *Euromall*, logo design by Riccardo Benassi, 2019
2. Rana Farahani and Anja Weigl, "Between satire and reality: Austria's Ibiza affair"
3. Anna Hankings-Evans, "The Law of Empathy"

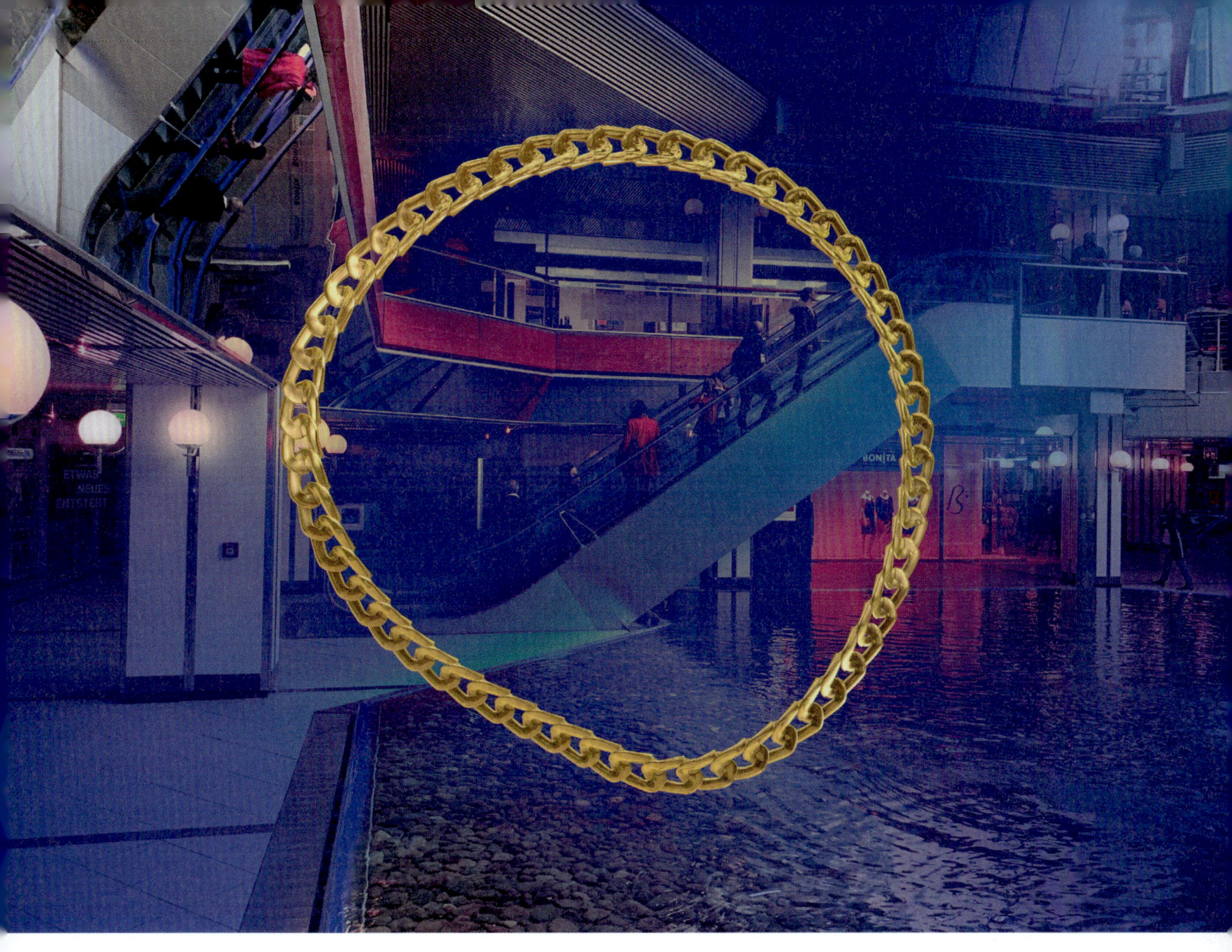

CREAMCAKE

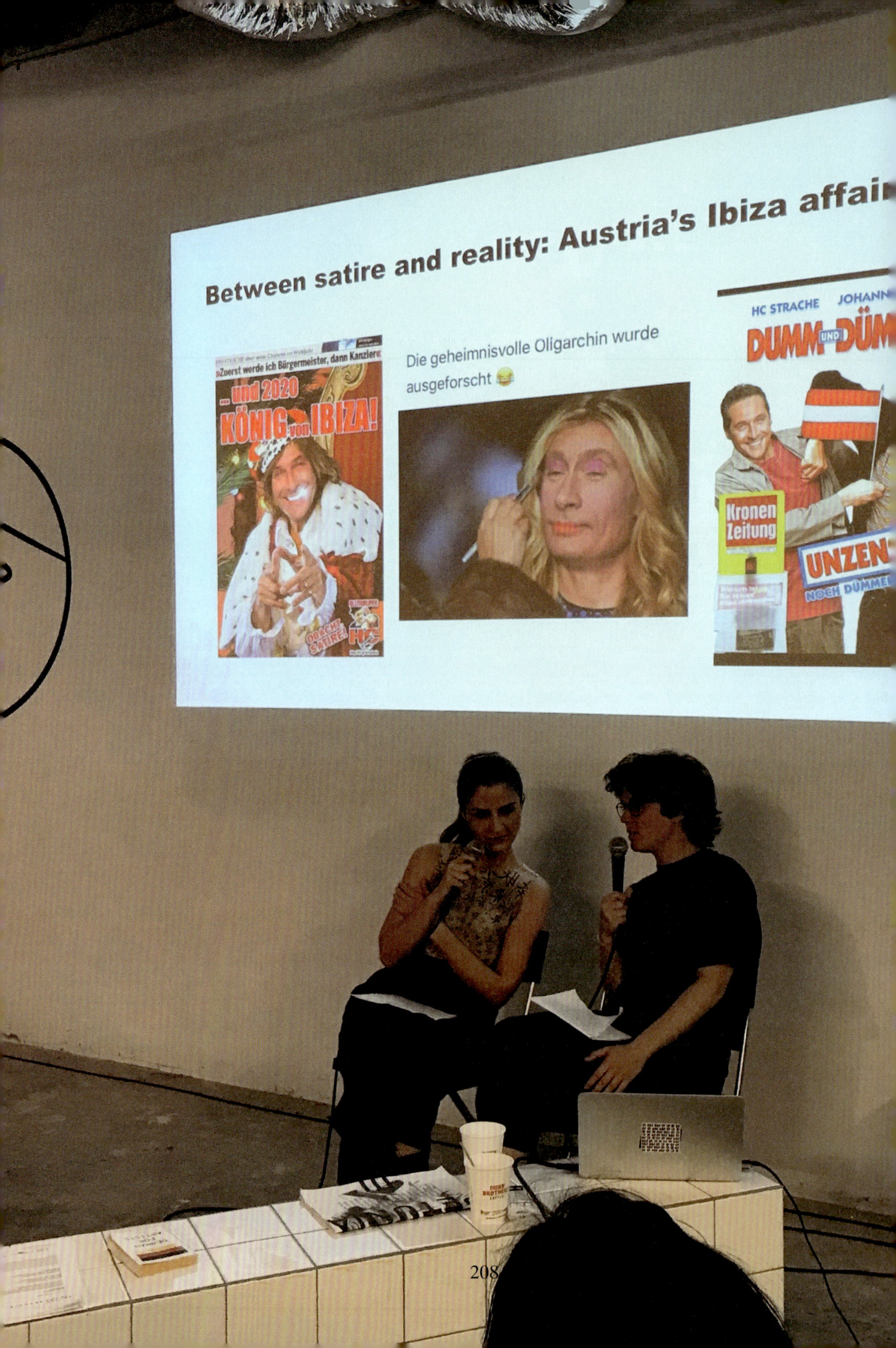

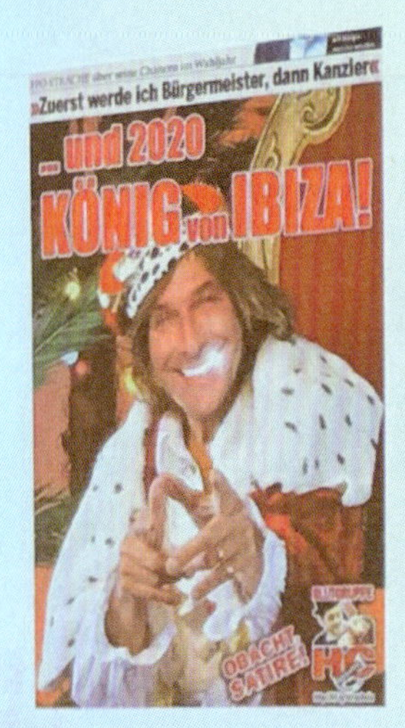
Between satire and reality: Austria's Ibiza affai
»Zuerst werde ich Bürgermeister, dann Kanzler«
... und 2020
KÖNIG von IBIZA!
OBACHT, SATIRE!

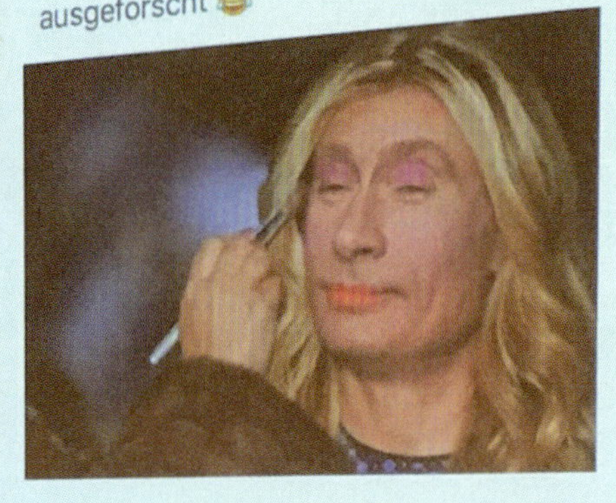
Die geheimnisvolle Oligarchin wurde
ausgeforscht

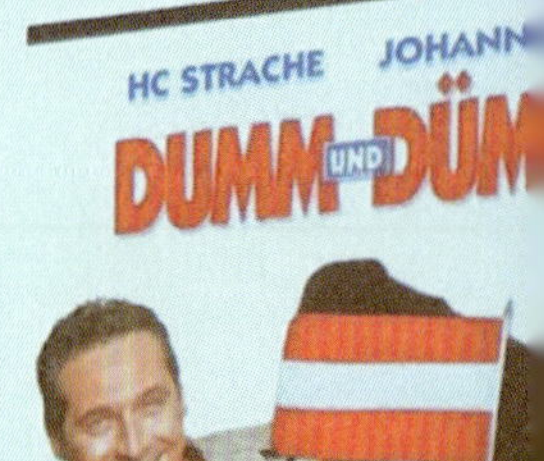
HC STRACHE JOHANN
DUMM UND DÜM

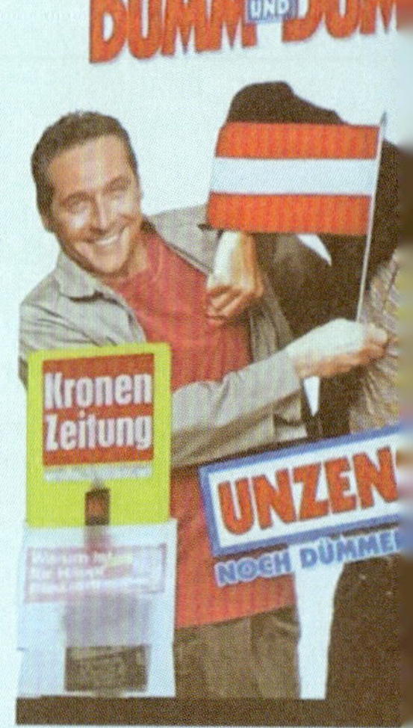
Kronen Zeitung
UNZEN
NOCH DÜMME

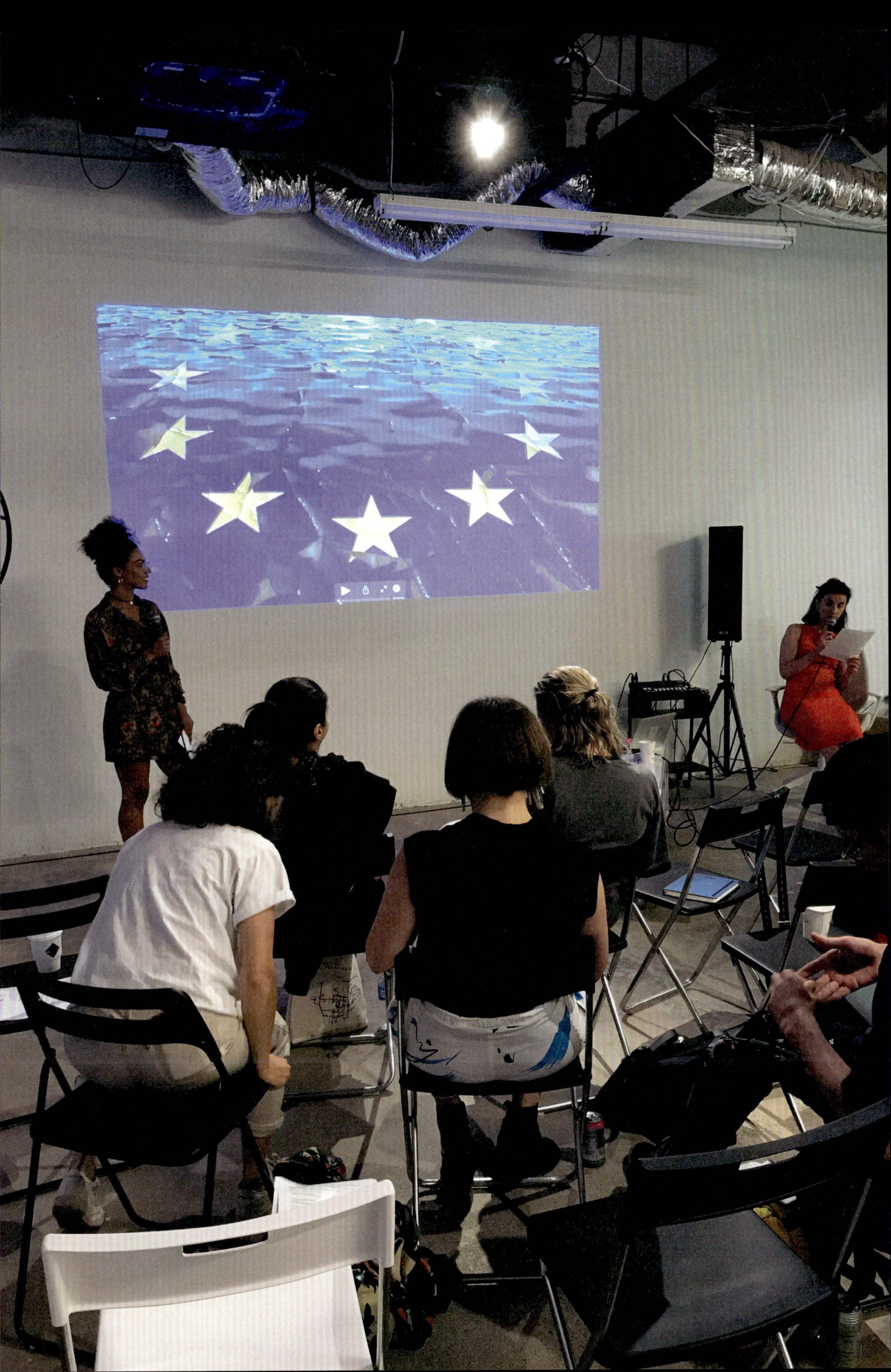

Kinga Kielczynska
Alien Species

*I saw Kinga Kielczynska's work, *How I sleep knowing*, in Palermo, at Manifesta 12, The European Biennial of Contemporary Art, in July 2018. She had filled a car with foliage waste from the Botanical Garden and the streets of Palermo. It looked like a forest was bursting out of a car, nature taking over technology, reclaiming the streets. Formally, I envisioned something similar for the skyways, a sterile environment, in which nothing "natural" or "other" is tolerated. Kinga and I started a conversation and we both became interested in the notion and language around "Invasive Species," which in fact used to be called "Alien Species." Most of the invasive plants in Minnesota have the prefix "European" or "Asian." These herbal invaders are curiously in this predicament from liberals, whose aggressive and combative language ironically picks up undertones from the conservative rhetoric many U.S. politicians use when talking about human immigrants. Formally, this project was an attraction in the skyways. People regularly stopped and peaked in. "Is this a flower shop now?," some people asked. From there we started a conversation. There are endless intriguing details that this project and its research brought to the surface, too many for this context. Plants are deep waters.

Kinga Kielczynska

Alien Species

15 July – 2 August 2019

12 July 2019, 3:30–7 pm

Happy Hour & Walking Tour

Images:
1. Installation view from outside
2. Happy Hour & Opening 3. Common Buckthorn, Russian Olive, Amur Maple, Oriental Bittersweet
4. *The Path of Least Resistance*, a walking tour through the skyways

Common buckthorn
(Rhamnus cathartica)

Appearance: Tall understory shrub or small tree up to 20' high with a spreading loosely branched crown, often multiple stems at the base. Brown bark with elongate silvery corky projections (Caution: native plums or cherries have a similar bark). Female and male plants.

Branches: Buds and leaves are sub-opposite, opposite, or alternate. Cut branch exposes yellow sapwood and orange heartwood. Twigs often end in small, sharp, stout thorns.

Leaves: Alternate, sometimes opposite; broadly elliptic pointed at the tip, smooth, dark glossy and small-toothed. Leaves stay green late into fall.

Flowers: Inconspicuous, appear in May or June, clustered in the axils of leaves.

Fruit: Clusters of black 1/4 inch fruit ripen on female plants in August and September. Seeds are viable for 2–3 years in the soil. Each berry has three to four seeds.

Roots: Extensive fibrous root system.

Ecological Threat:
– Out-competes native plants for nutrients, light, and moisture
– Degrades wildlife habitat
– Threatens the future of forests, wetlands, prairies, and other natural habitats
– Contributes to erosion by shading out other plants that grow on the forest floor
– Serves as host to other pests, such as crown rust fungus and soybean aphid
– Forms an impenetrable layer of vegetation
– Lacks "natural controls" like insects or disease that would curb its growth

Non-native bush honeysuckles
(*Lonicera tatarica*, *L. morrowii*, *L. x bella*, *L. maackii*)

Appearance: Upright deciduous shrubs, 5–12' high. Bell's honeysuckle (*Lonicera x bella*) is a horticultural hybrid. Older stems have shaggy bark and are often hollow.

Leaves: Opposite, simple, oval, and untoothed. Tartarian (*L. tatarica*) has smooth, hairless leaves. Morrow's honeysuckle (*L. morrowii*) has downy leaves. Amur honeysuckle (*L. maackii*) leaves come to a long, sharp point.

Flowers: Fragrant, tubular, bloom in May and June, white, red, but most often pink.

Fruit: Fruits are red or yellow, situated in pairs in the leaf axils.

Roots: Roots are fibrous and shallow.

Ecological Threat:
– Exotic honeysuckle replace native forest shrubs and herbaceous plants by their invasive nature and early leaf-out. They shade out herbaceous ground cover and deplete soil moisture.
– Seeds are readily dispersed by birds.
– Some research suggests that the plant inhibits the growth of other plants in its vicinity.
– Introduced to North America as ornamental shrubs and beneficial to wildlife. Commercial propagation continues with many cultivars available from nurseries.
– Bell's, Morrow's, Tartarian, and Amur honeysuckles are MDA Restricted noxious weeds in Minnesota.

Garlic mustard
(*Alliaria petiolata*)

Appearance: Biennial herbaceous plant with weak single stems 12–36" high in its second and flowering year. Only plant of this height blooming white in wooded environments in May.

Leaves: Round, scallop-edged, dark green; first year, rosettes of 3 or 4 leaves; second year plants have alternate stem leaves. Leaves and stems smell like onion or garlic when crushed.

Flowers: White, small and numerous, with four separate petals. Each plant has one or two flowering stems on second year plants.

Seeds: Slender capsules 1–2 1/2" long, containing a single row of oblong black seeds. Seeds are viable in the soil for 5 years.

Roots: White, slender taproot, "S"-shaped at the top.

Ecological Threat:
– Garlic mustard spreads into high quality woodlands upland and floodplain forests, not just into disturbed areas.
– Invaded sites undergo a decline on native herbaceous cover within 10 years.
– Garlic mustard alters habitat suitability for native insects and thereby birds and mammals.
– This European exotic occurs now in 27 midwestern and northeastern states and in Canada.
– Garlic mustard is a MDA Restricted noxious weed in Minnesota.

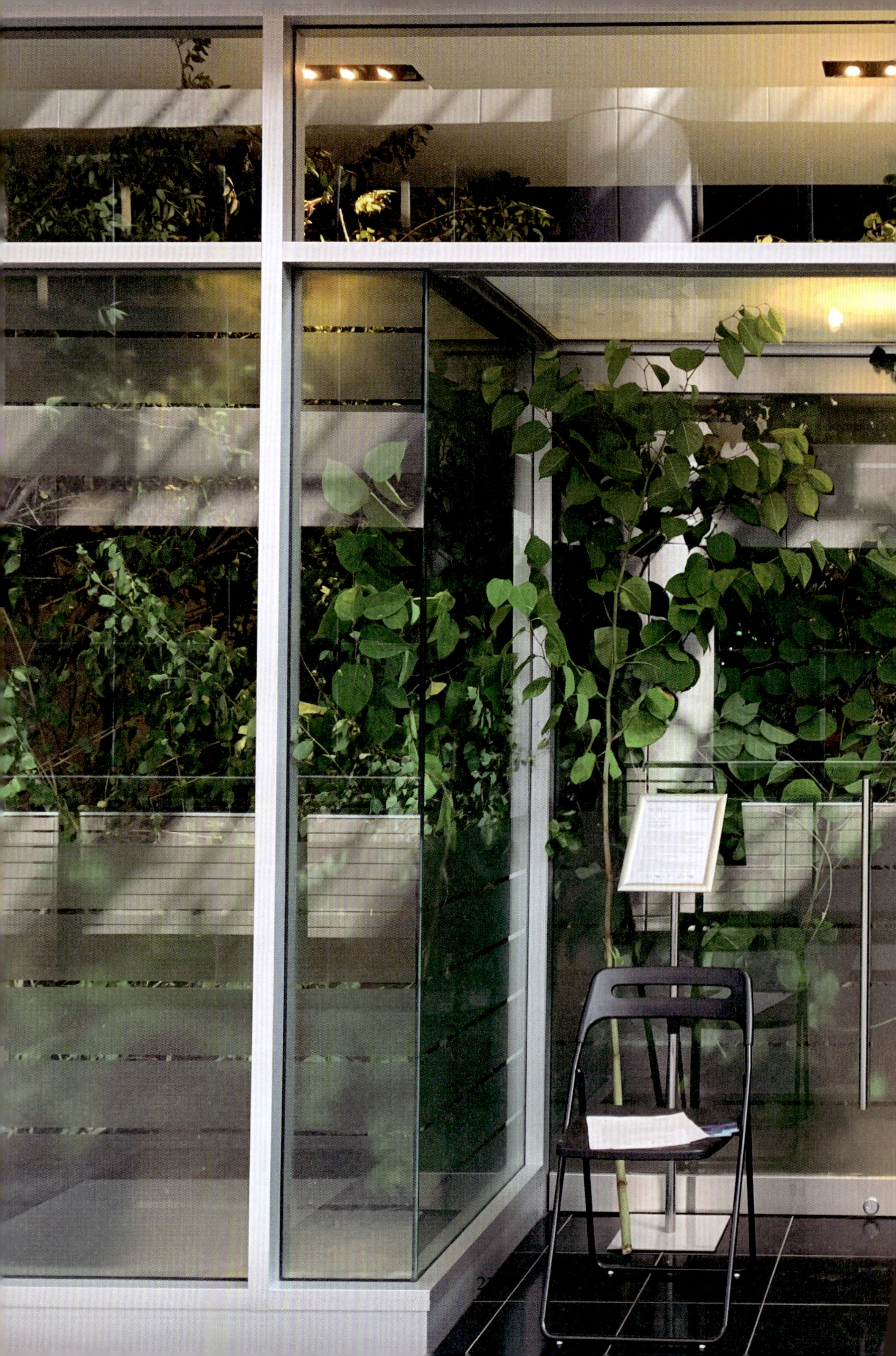

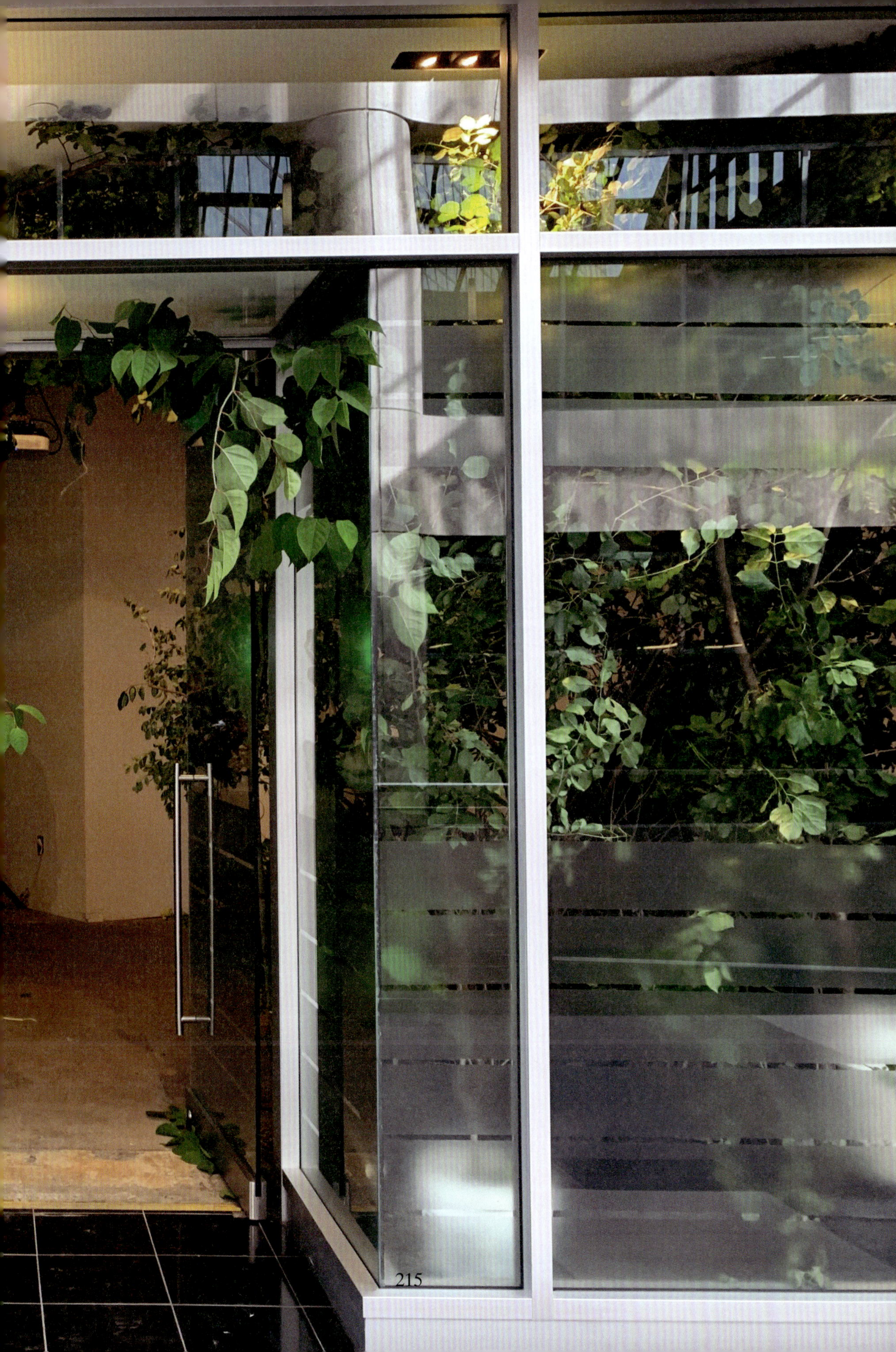

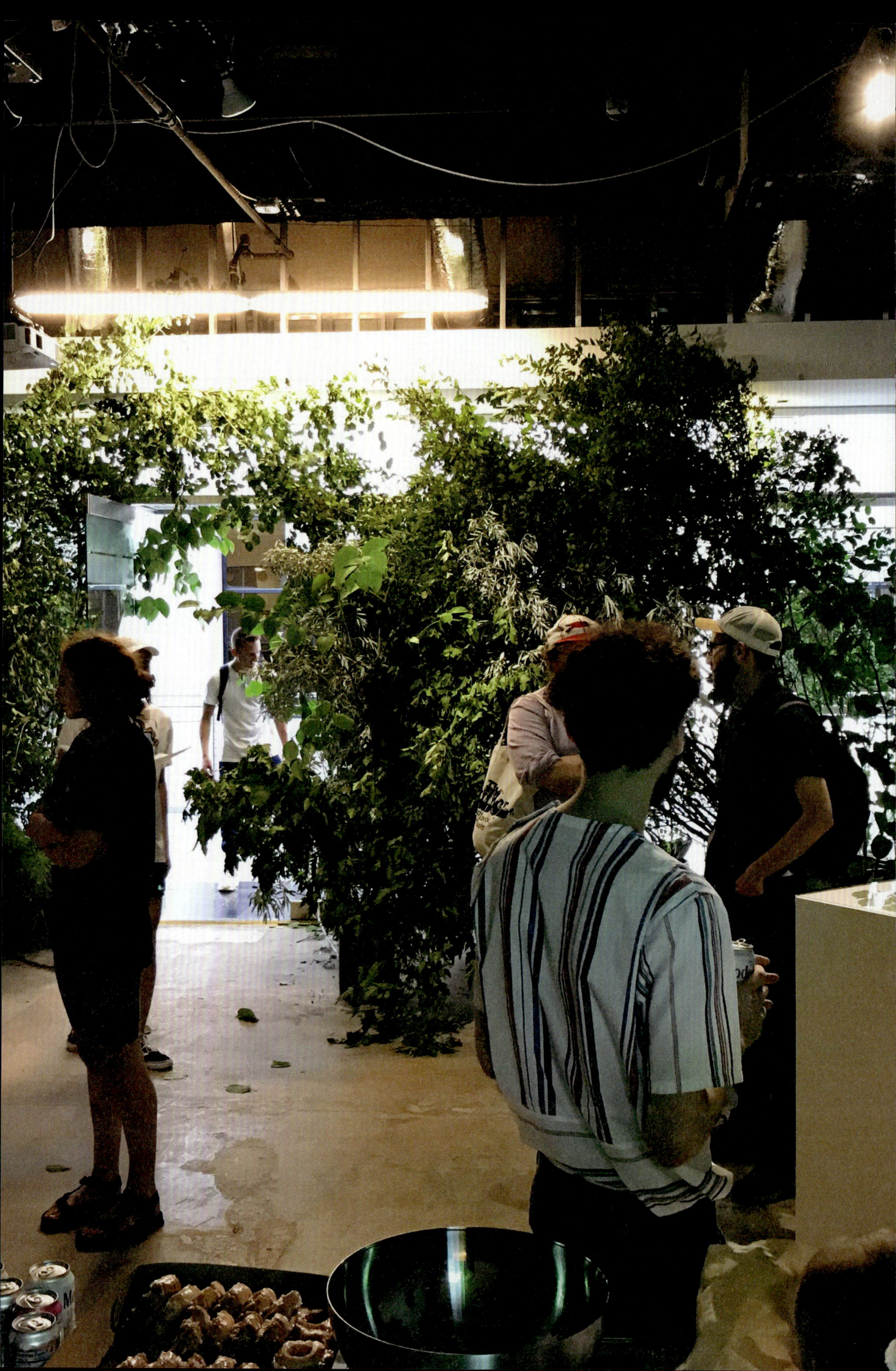

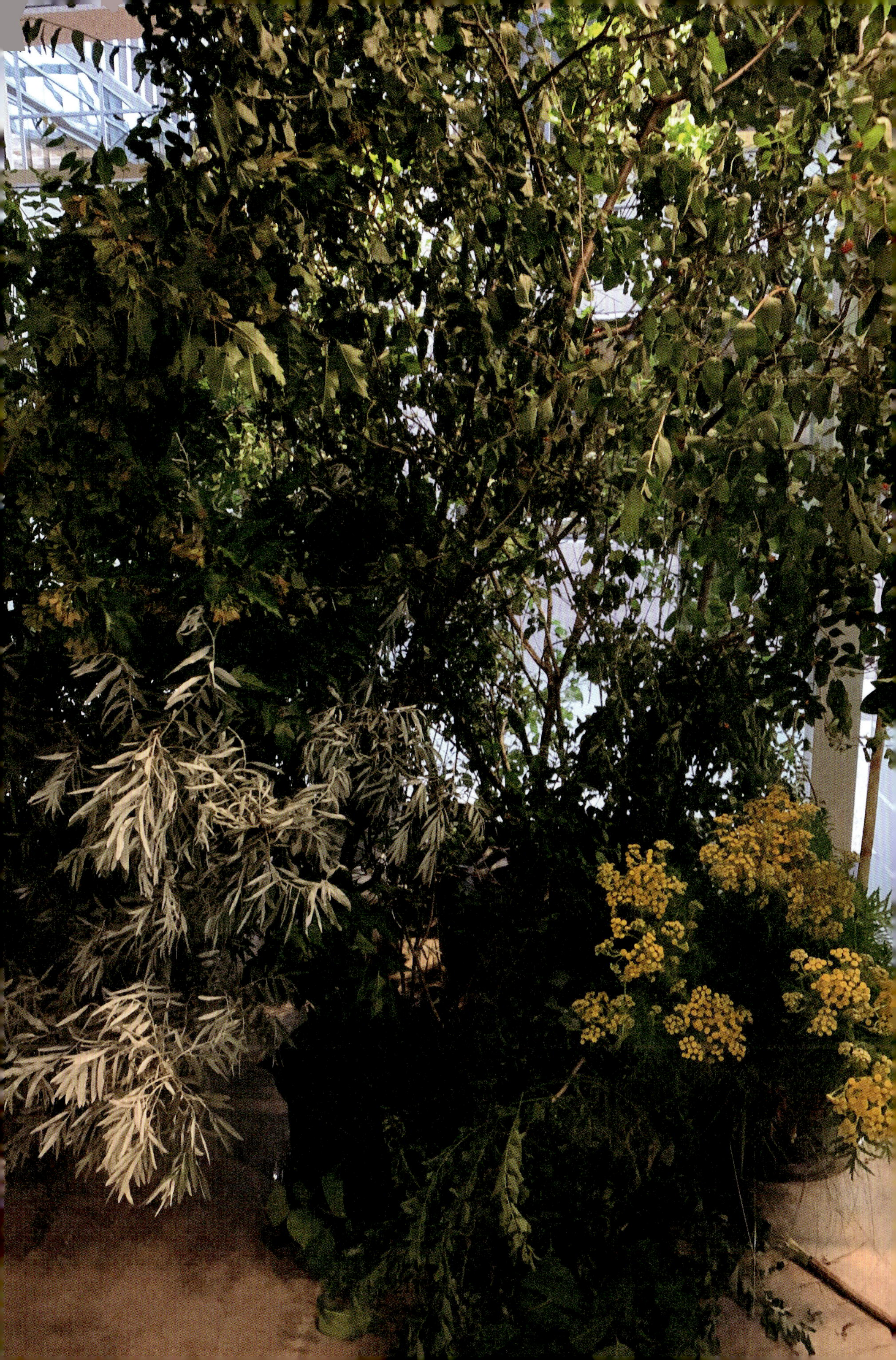

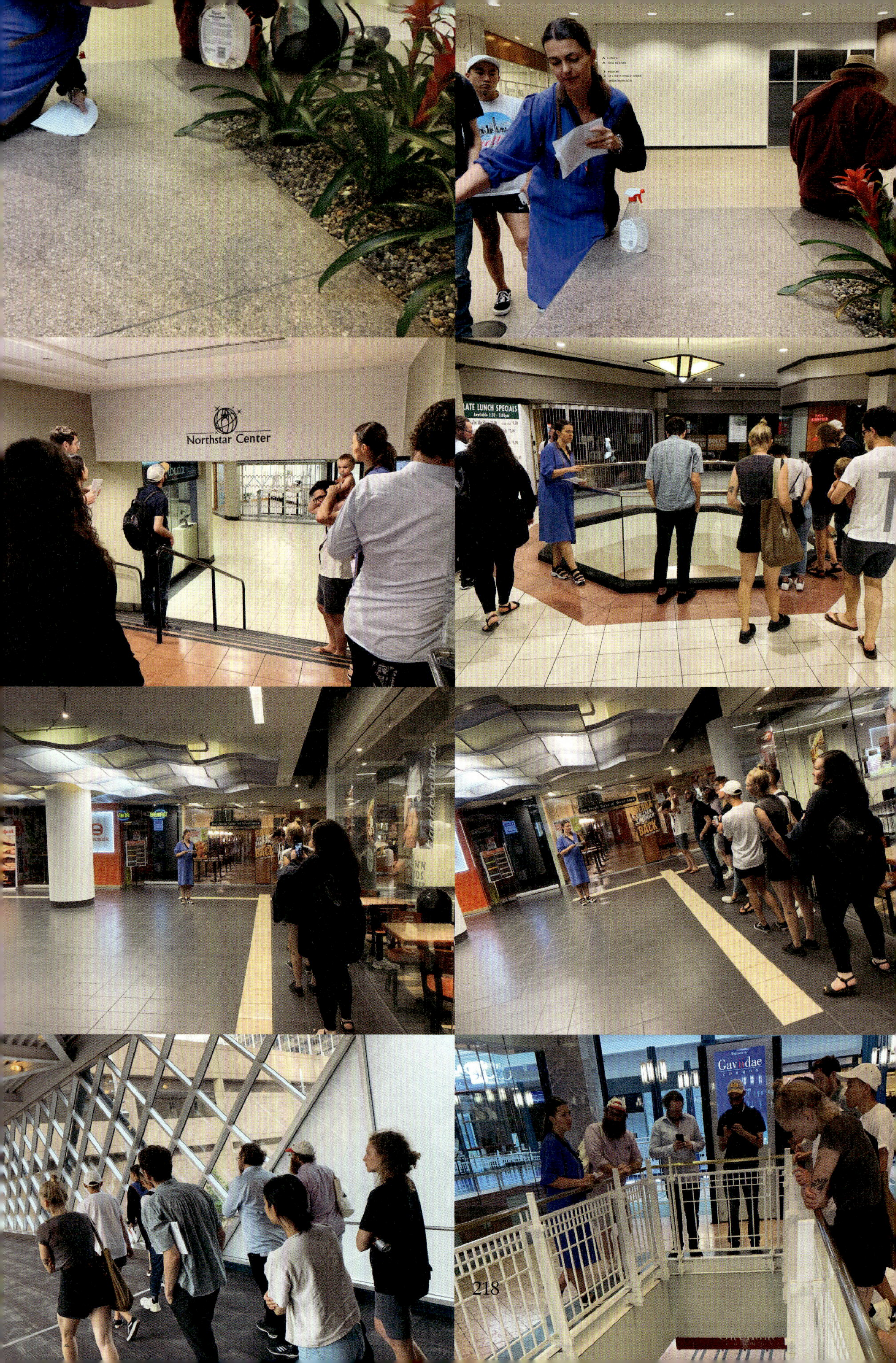
Northstar Center
LATE LUNCH SPECIALS

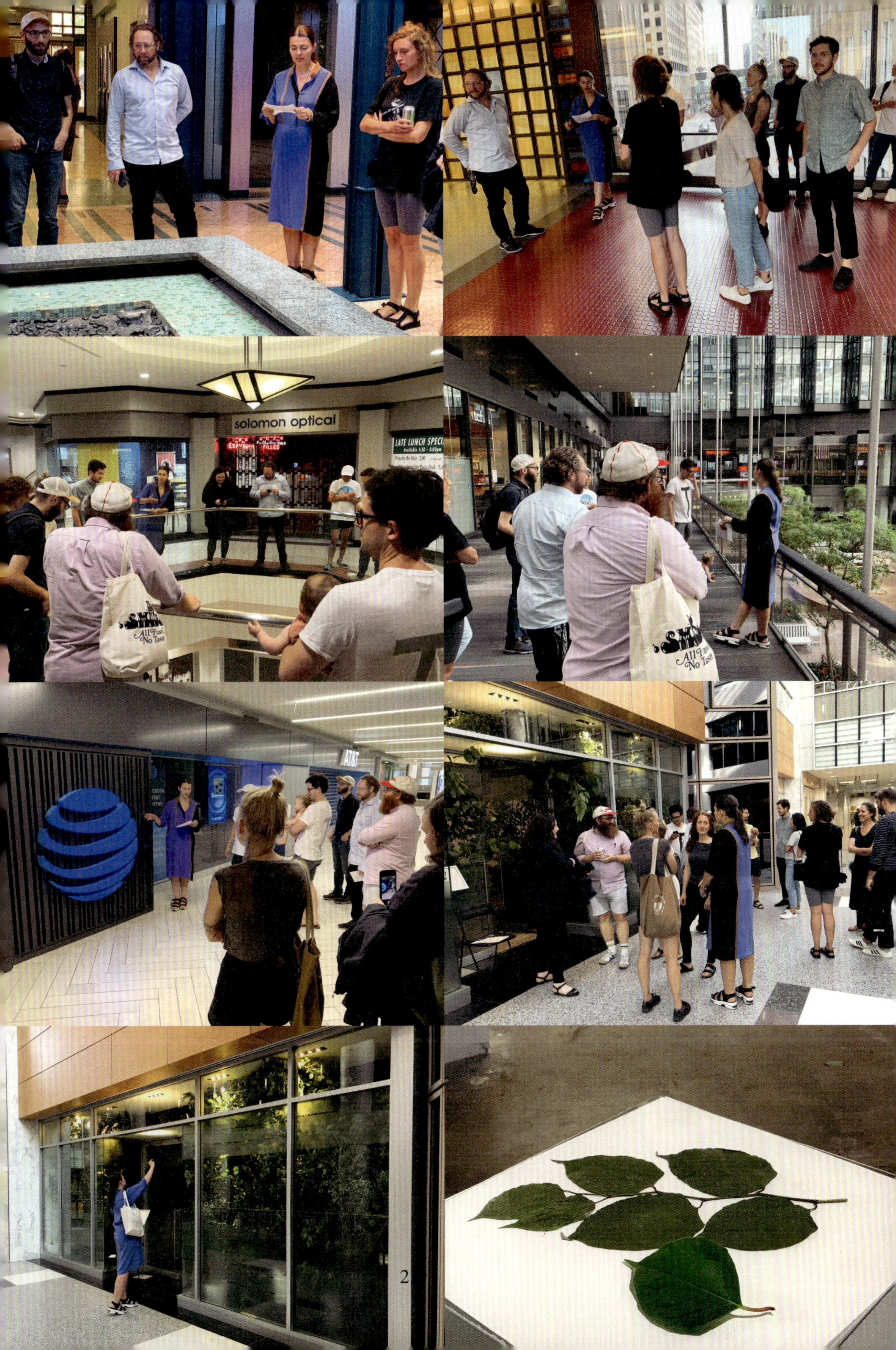
solomon optical
AT&T

Nora Spiekermann & Lee Noble
Bauhaus100 Bonanza Show

*We didn't have a "summer show" planned because we weren't sure if it would make sense in the skyways. In Minnesota, everyone is at their cabin in the summer, at least from Friday through Monday, and working hours in general are radically reduced. I had heard about the *Bauhaus100 Bonanza Show* from Nora Spiekermann who had come to numerous events at the Goethe Pop Up. I was intrigued and watched a few episodes of their series that they were producing with the local public access TV station, MTN. Since it was the 100-year anniversary of the Bauhaus, and manifold exhibitions were circulating around us, I invited Nora & Lee to set up their version of an homage to the Bauhaus in our space. The work was critical yet humorous and provided a fresh perspective towards the Bauhaus canon by pointing out its flaws in equal measure to its successes—a very timely approach that only now seems to appear.

Nora Spiekermann & Lee Noble

Bauhaus100 Bonanza Show

7–30 August 2019

16 & 17 August 2019, 10 am–2 pm

Bauhaus100 Bonanza Pop Up
Downtown Minneapolis Street Art Festival

The *Bauhaus100 Bonanza Show 2019* celebrates the 100-year-anniversary of Bauhaus, the influential German art school and cultural movement. Under the brand "Bauhaus100" numerous events, festivals, and exhibitions are happening in Germany and around the world throughout 2019.

Motivated by recently discovered Bauhaus traces in Minneapolis, Nora Spiekermann and Lee Noble are celebrating the 100-year-birthday in Minnesota's cultural metropolis, as well, in order to not only connect Weimar and Minneapolis, but to also research what Bauhaus means today.

For this special celebration, the artists are collaborating with the local public access TV station, MTN.

Inspired by the attitude of interdisciplinarity and openness that was integral to the Bauhaus's founding, the artists were drawn to the possibility of working with local public access, an inherently diverse medium predicated on access to communication technology.

Images:
1. Bauhaus advertisements
2. Installation view, featuring video from episode *The Future* with Ryan Fontaine and Kristin Van Loon
3. Installation view, featuring video from episode *Public Access* with Clair, Mother Love, and Daniel Shinbaum

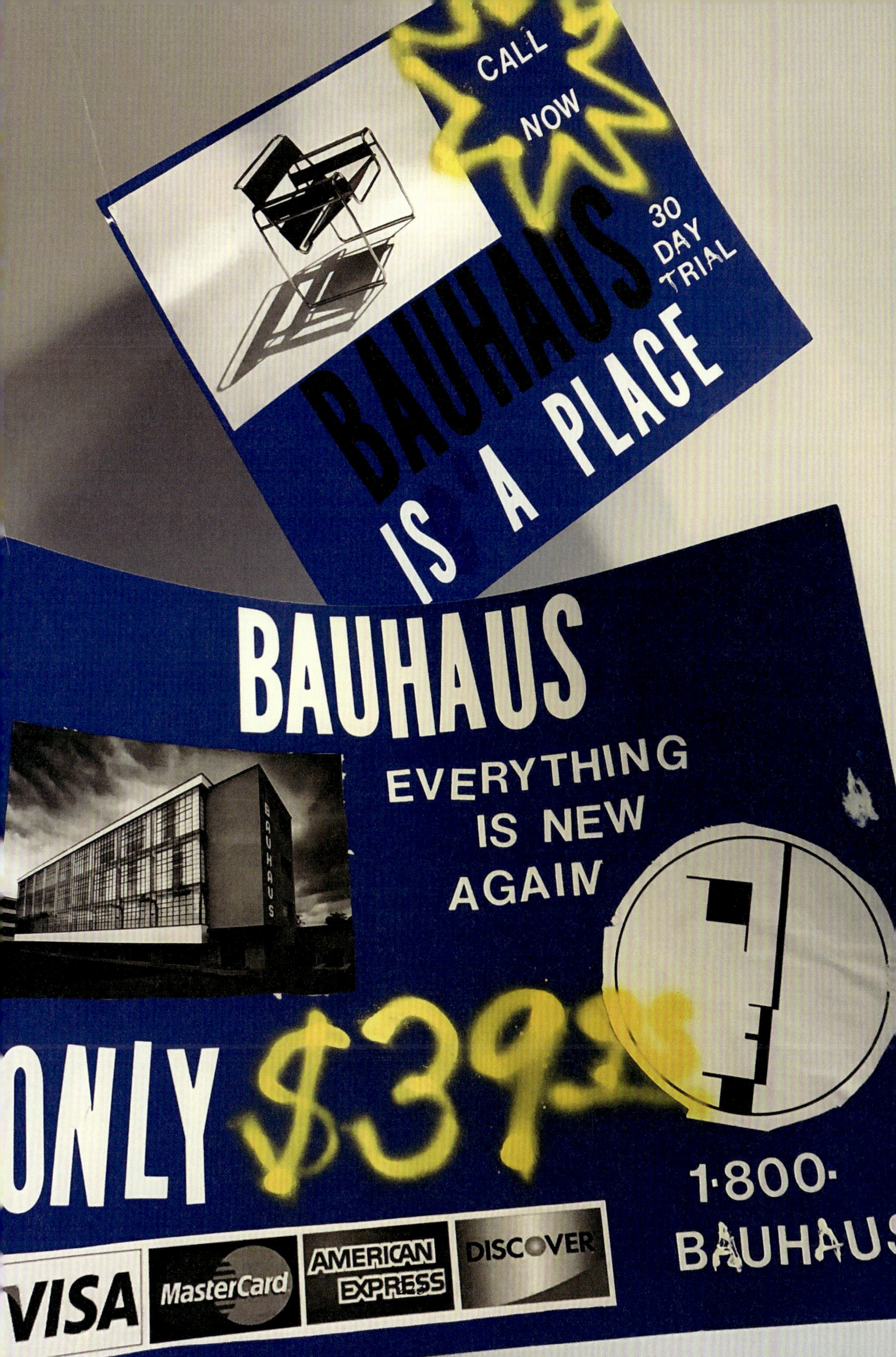
CALL NOW
30 DAY TRIAL
BAUHAUS IS A PLACE
BAUHAUS
EVERYTHING IS NEW AGAIN
ONLY $39
1·800·BAUHAUS
VISA
MasterCard
AMERICAN EXPRESS
DISCOVER

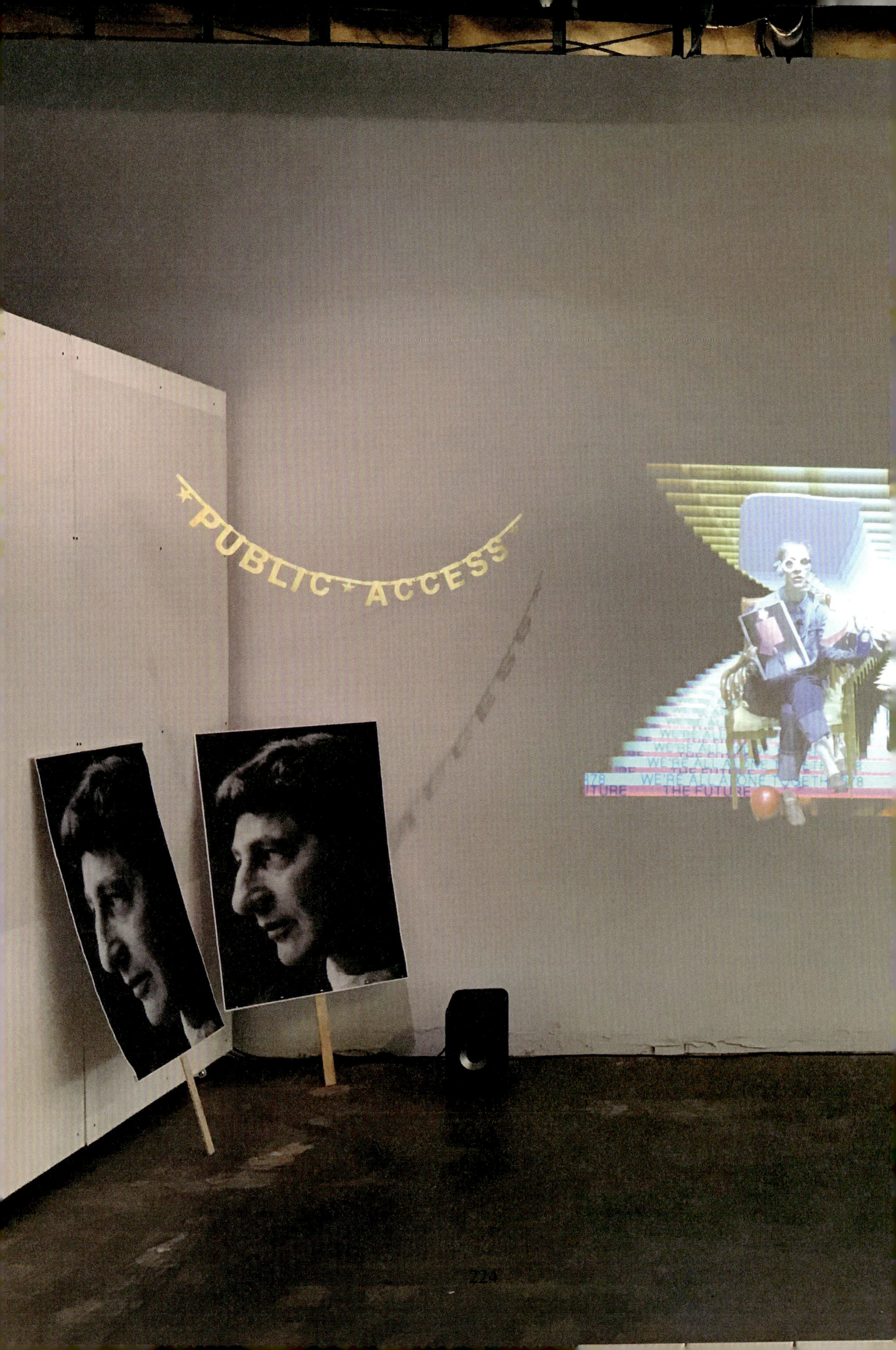
PUBLIC ACCESS
THE FUTURE

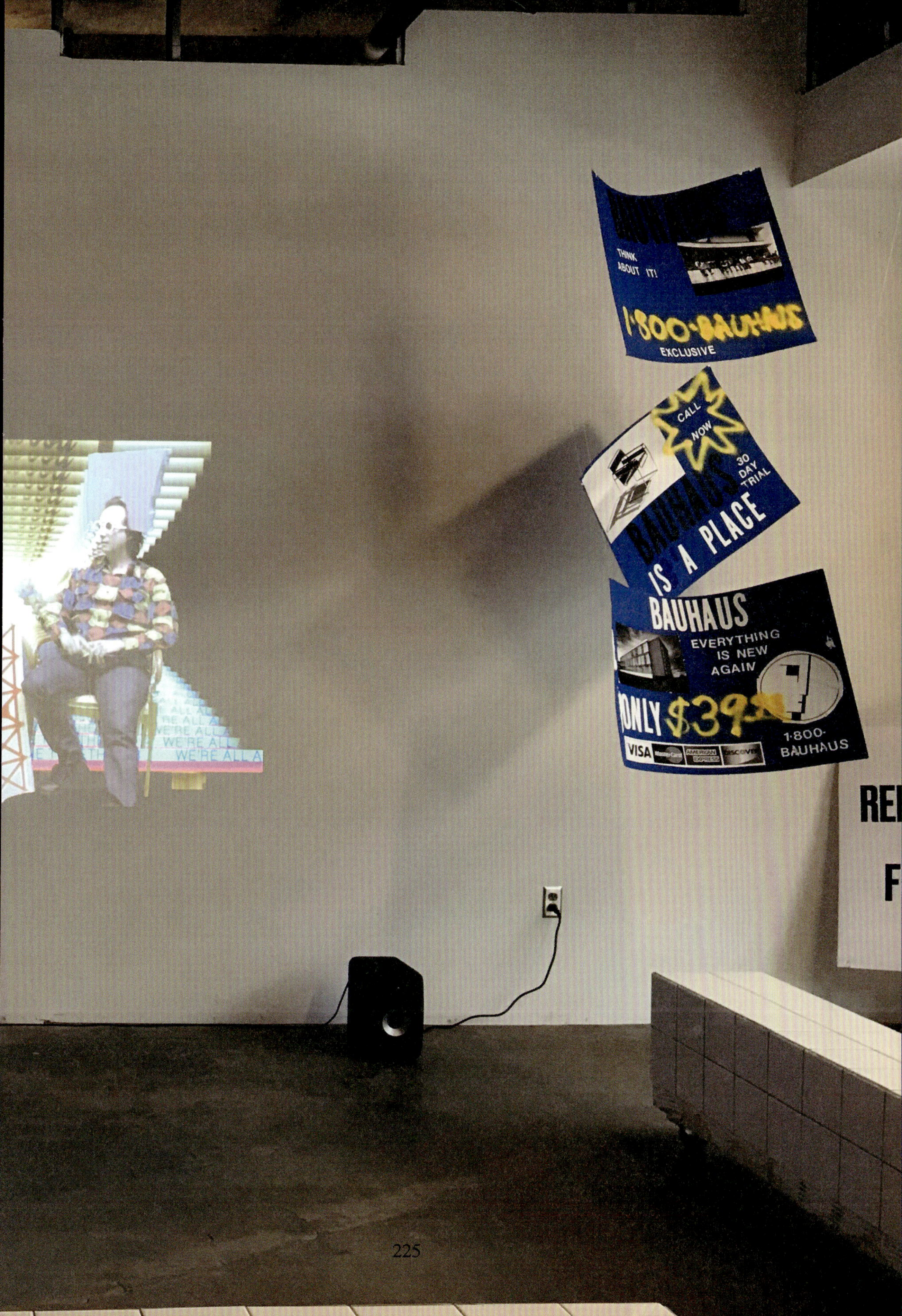
THINK ABOUT IT!
1·800·BAUHAUS
EXCLUSIVE
CALL NOW
30 DAY TRIAL
BAUHAUS IS A PLACE
BAUHAUS
EVERYTHING IS NEW AGAIN
ONLY
VISA
1·800·BAUHAUS
WE'RE ALL A

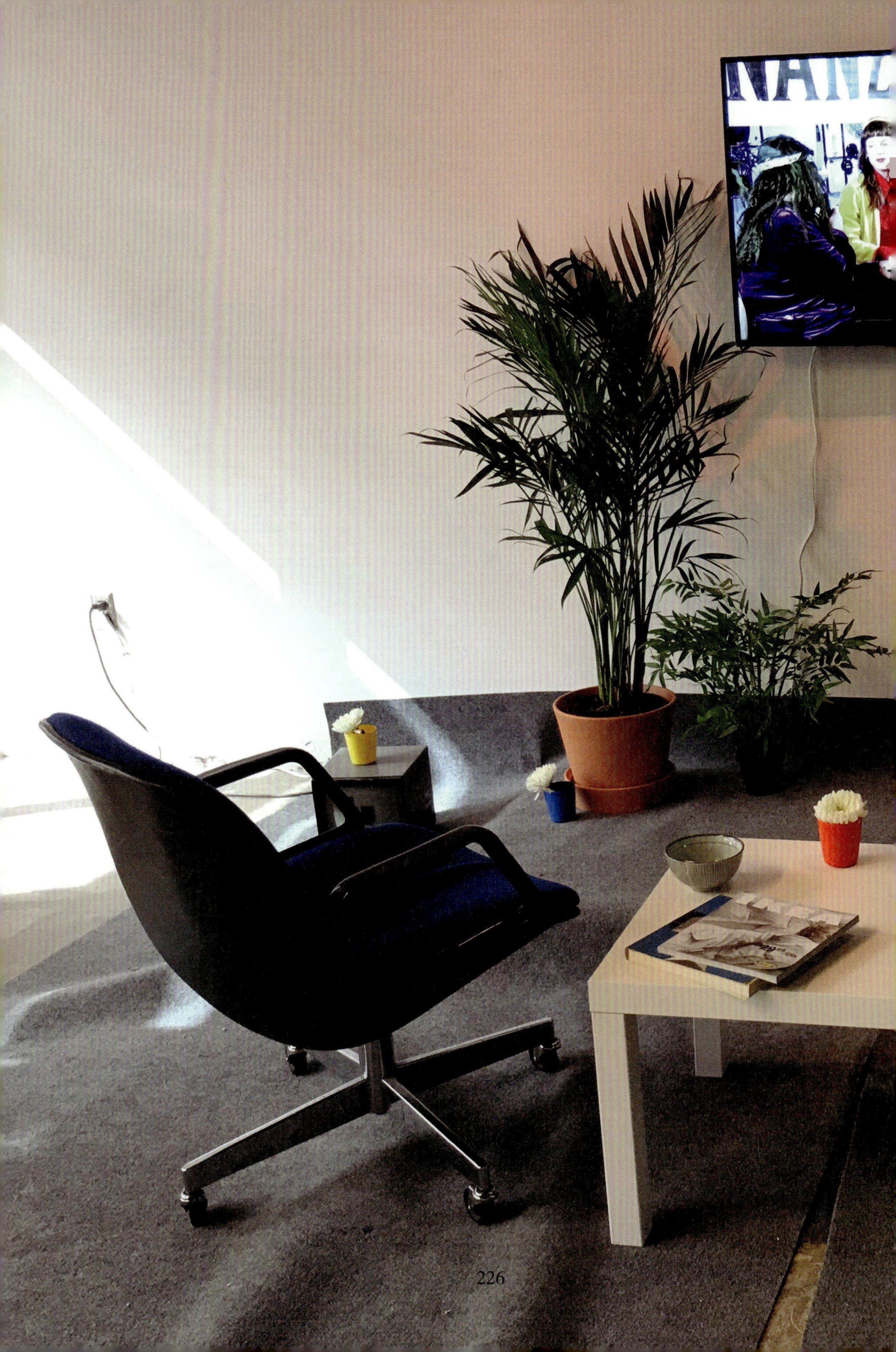

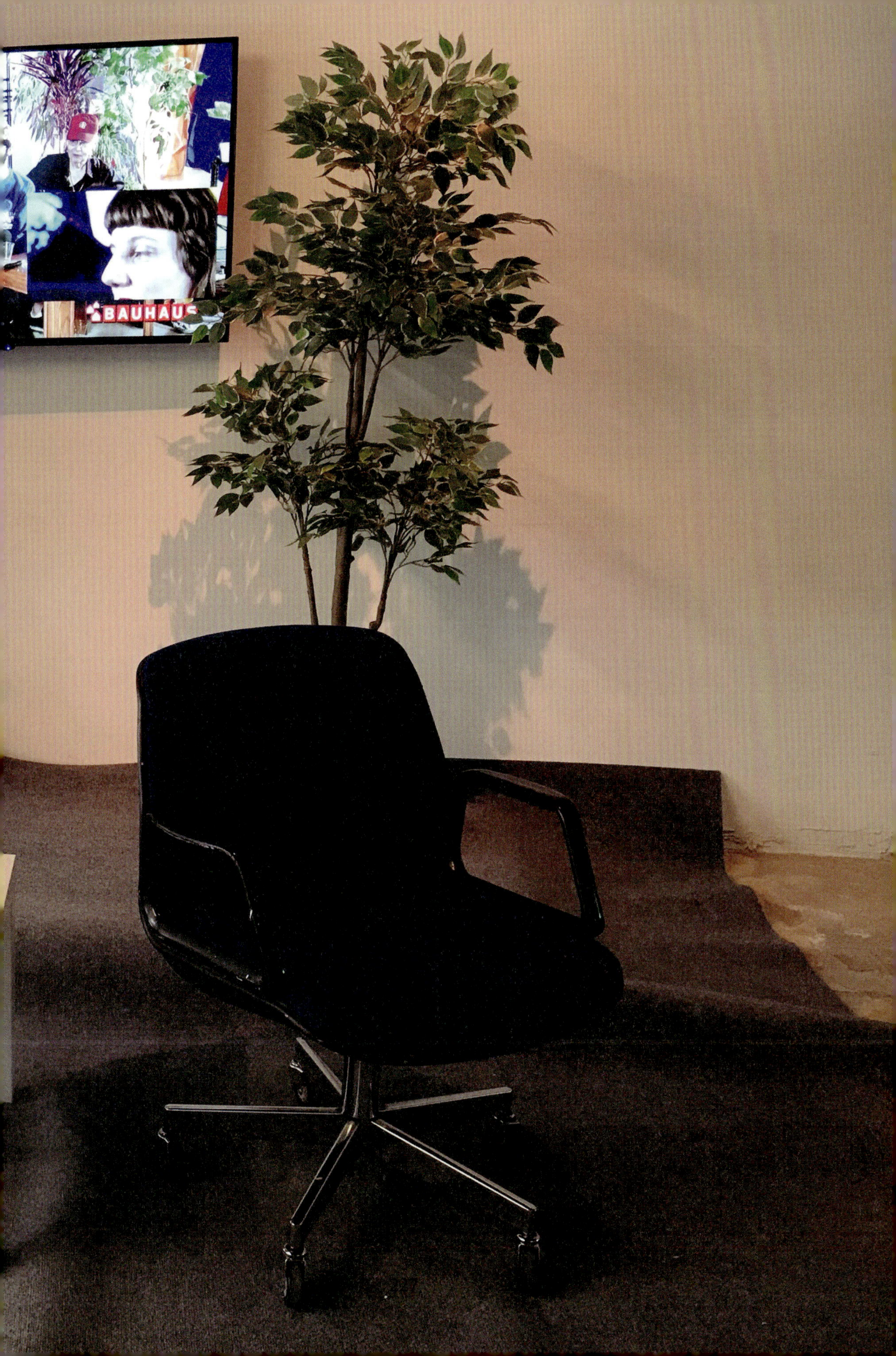
BAUHAU

On Location

Daniel Shinbaum and Sarah Petersen in conversation

Sarah Petersen: So, Daniel, I'm interested in how you would describe the public who would visit this space.

Daniel Shinbaum: That's an interesting question, because the skyways in Minneapolis are all privately owned. The entire skyway system is private and each skyway itself—the physical bridge—is jointly owned by the buildings on each side. So the skyways are a simulation of public space. It's a misnomer to call the visitors a public.

SP: It's sort of a feigned public. Technically anyone can be here as long as the skyways are open (and as long as the ever-present security forces don't find a reason to kick them out). So our baseline public is people who've managed to figure out the skyways enough or get lost in them enough to accidentally end up in front of our space. Alternatively, you could ask, how are we a "need" for people? There have been shows that people seem to find relief in visiting, like FORT's *The Calling*, their film of call center workers asleep at their desks.

DS: We installed their large-scale projection of people sleeping in an office, a grey carpet, and some boring office chairs, and it looked like an office space in disarray. One woman who visited from the media department at Target corporate, across from our space, was very excited to see art about office work, and said she would bring her whole team in. (I don't think she actually did).

SP: There are certain shows that have ended up giving people a sense of recognition. There are also a lot of people coming in who just get really excited because they have German heritage or some connection to Germany. Maybe 40 percent of visitors are suddenly telling me about their German grandmother. There were also regular visitors involved in arts communities in Minneapolis, or some who would visit from out of town specifically because they wanted to see what we were doing. But they accounted for maybe 10 or 15 percent. And then there were the people who would come for our events—they were a very loyal crew, and we were thankful for them!

laughs

DS: The public passing by is mostly either shoppers or people who work in business or service industry jobs. But our visitors tend to be people who are not on the clock—unemployed/underemployed or on vacation or retired, people who come to this skyway because it acts like a public place. There are a lot of unhomed people in the skyways, especially in the wintertime, when it gets so cold that street level is uninhabitable. So people come here to have a warm place to go and someone to talk to, where they won't be harassed. It takes time to enjoy art (or if not enjoy it, at least engage with it), and the people who pass by without stopping don't have the luxury of free time.

SP: There is a contradictory truth about the skyways: there's a socioeconomic and racialized sorting mechanism they enact, even if they don't specifically exclude anyone on the front end. But they remain, almost accidentally, a place for a diverse public. Lawyers would come in on their way to representing people at the courthouse, but so would people on their way home from a legal aid appointment, or people waiting for their friend to get out of the hospital. We'd have doctors for the Timberwolves basketball team come in and start talking about their lives, or ex-business people who had become more committed to their art practices visiting on their lunch breaks, excited to have in-depth conversations about international politics, art, etc. We were this temporary place to visit as people were wandering through, passing time while something else more important was going on in their lives. We were a break for people, an opportunity that was unexpected. We were providing a service, whether it was a place for currently unhoused people to go during the day that was friendly and open to them, or a place for people to have a minute to think about something more abstract, or something that their boss wasn't asking them to think about.

DS: Yeah, absolutely. And often the conversation had nothing to do with the art. This man came in and asked for directions to the Mayo Clinic; I told him we were an art space, but that I could help him find it. And he said, "I don't need art, I need health care!" Literally.

SP: Wow.

DS: And that makes me think about the fact that so much German money is going to these cultural projects and—

SP: —maybe because they already have health care!

DS: Yeah! And here, we don't have that yet. We don't have public funding for art or health care.

laughs

DS: How would you describe the skyways system to somebody who is not from Minneapolis or the United States?

SP: I would say the skyway system connects people to businesses and places where they can spend their money, and disconnects people from street life and the street in general. It's a physical manifestation of other power dynamics at play in downtown Minneapolis.

DS: Absolutely! When the skyways went in, it created a hierarchy where some people were inside, shopping, working, and other people were outside in the cold and waiting for the bus or just not invited inside. A lot of the stores around the skyways have rules against loitering.

SP: So do the public atriums. The security forces operating within them make people move after half an hour.

DS: We had some interesting issues with that as we tried to expand into more public space outside of the confines of the pop up itself.

SP: Hanne Lippard and I had this joke that the byline for corporate interests downtown vis-a-vis potential cultural activities within their spaces was: "Since you asked, no."

laughs

SP: So we got to the point where we just wouldn't ask permission from management anymore, because we would have to provide more information, justify the projects, and then the answer was always "No," anyway. We found workarounds, and eventually the people who worked in security at City Center looked the other way. Other than asking us to turn down our speakers sometimes, they never stopped any of our performances within the building. We relied on the goodwill of the security people, which I really appreciated over time.

DS: The fact that we weren't given official permission, though, was definitely an inconvenience and made a lot of things more difficult. During our final performance, Roseline Rannoch's *Dark Ride II: They Are Us Revisited*, since we weren't officially allowed to have our speakers outside, we had to wait until the last minute to set up. We barely had a chance to rehearse.

SP: Right. It made us very furtive. In almost every instance, our efforts had to appear last-minute, even though they'd been planned for months. And it was frustrating to not be able to confirm for artists that they would be able to do what they intended. And of course, if we went anywhere outside of City Center, artists often couldn't do what they were hoping to do.

DS: Yeah, it put us in a really precarious and uncertain position, and especially put stress on the artists. And I think the fact that we were still able to operate under these conditions… I don't know what it says about us… Maybe that it sometimes doesn't matter whether the performance actually happens. It matters that we advertise it and are able to get documentation. It's more about the archive than about the experience of witnessing.

SP: It's true, although sometimes there were events that were so beautiful, so necessarily "live," like Hanne Lippard's event when Minneapolis poets read aloud while riding the escalators, and the audience followed each of them to listen. There was something really effective about that, and affecting to me. And I think, yes, there is this "pictures or it didn't happen," evidence-based art making standard now, where if you have a document, then it happened, and that's all that matters. But I do feel like there were things that we did in time that mattered as experiences.

DS: Yes. I was out of town in Berlin for that performance.

laughs

SP: What did you expect from the experience of working here or helping to run this space?

DS: I had no idea what to expect. I had lived in the Twin Cities for four years before we opened the pop up, and my first day on the job was my first time in the skyways. I actually got lost finding my way through the skyways between the parking garage and the space.

SP: I was little when this building opened in the 80s, and it was the rowdy teenager mall downtown. It had a music store, cheap gift shops, and jewelry stores, a fast food court. It was loud here. Now it's nearly all offices, lunch restaurants, and discount stores, with a few high-end, conservative clothing stores—and a lot of empty storefronts. More generally, people used to come downtown to experience actual culture. Not only the music scene that made Minneapolis famous in the 80s, but gallery crawls every six weeks, and restaurants open late where the creative crowd would hang out, like the New French Bar and Café. That all changed not long after 2000, when sports bars, parking ramps, and stadiums took over this part of the city. I didn't spend a ton of time downtown thereafter. But inside our space, I feel like we open an opportunity to not have to ascribe to the bland, corporate, consumer culture being offered outside our door.

DS: Yeah, now there's Target Center and the Twins baseball stadium two blocks away. So there are still cultural events going on downtown, but mostly for sports culture. One woman I talked to during Albrecht Pischel's performance at Palmer's (an old dive bar) told me, "the skyways transformed downtown into a giant sports bar." That stuck with me. Of course the skyways preceded the sports monoculture, but they laid its foundation.

SP: Now, the only people who can afford real estate are corporate business entities. But there aren't enough of them to fill everything, and a higher occupancy rate means a lot in the world of commercial real estate; there may even be a tax incentive associated with subsidizing a nonprofit space. So spaces like ours are allowed to rent at a reduced rate and fill the windows as long as someone with real money doesn't show up. That was not always the case downtown. There were still hardware stores downtown, even ten years ago. There are no hardware stores downtown anymore.

DS: There are still more and more galleries, but they are all pop ups like us. There was the Better World Museum, now The Minneapolis College Pop Up Gallery in City Center. And there's a series of pop up art shows across the skyway at Alt Space. There's a mural going into the new Dayton's Project building just south of us, and lots of murals in general on the sides of buildings...
But it all feels like artwashing for corporate interests.

groans

DS: What do you think was the biggest challenge of working in the skyway space?

SP: Having to be in „host mode“ while trying to get any actual work done, while trying to manage our future projects, was really challenging. We were in a bit of a fishbowl behind the glass storefront, and as such an unexpected presence on the skyways, we constantly had to negotiate people's misrecognition of what we were. So being interrupted by the public and having to repeatedly explain our basic function, and be friendly about it—"We're an art space associated with the Goethe-Institut, Germany's cultural arm"—while trying to focus...
that was a challenge.

DS: I totally agree, and the way you frame it reminds me of the title for our opening show last October, *DISRUPTIONS, INTERRUPTIONS, MISRUPTIONS*. Often in our press releases we would allude to the fact that as a public art space, we are an interruption to regular skyway life. But the way it affected us, it was more like people would interrupt us!

laughs

SP: One of my main mentors in grad school, Harry Dodge, and I had a conversation about hosting in the context of art practices, and I remember him pointing out the dual meaning of "host." He said, "Host doesn't just mean 'the one inviting people'; it also means 'the thing that gets eaten'." So that's one of the primary contradictions of laboring inside our pop up; you're trying to give as much as you can, but correspondingly, your energies are being consumed. You're being consumed.

laughs

DS: So we're a pop up, and I think the phrase "pop up" captures a couple of different meanings. One of them alludes to a fashion pop up shop. Our final show, Philipp Rupp's *Bags From Bielefeld,* engaged with that notion. We set up the space to look like a fashion store, which was funny because throughout the past year, people would come in and see our coat rack and ask, "So what are you selling?" The other meaning of "pop up" comes from the Web. When you browse online, annoying pop up ads steal your attention (unless you block them). Online pop ups are hostile—they might be scams or viruses. Playing off that idea, Jonas Lund installed these playfully obnoxious interactive pop ups on our website to interrupt your browsing experience.

SP: There was something about our whole project that was a bit resistant and recalcitrant. I think a number of the artists Sandra invited were motivated by questioning systems and intervening in them. Even our presence as a pop up was an interference… Normally pop ups in consumer space are about entertainment or buying things. And so even as a pop up, we weren't what people expected. To name ourselves a pop up and not sell anything was a bit like, "Wait, then what are you?"

laughs

SP: "Pop up" also implies on-demand labor, which is insufficient for recognizing the amount and kind of labor that actually has to occur to produce what the space demands. There was a further contradiction in the idea of a one-year pop up: it was both long term and short term. So we were able to develop a pattern for our visitors, performing a social function for this very strange intersection of people who frequented our space, but that disperses now that we're leaving.

DS: But I also think that, despite the fact that we embody this contradiction, we aren't radically redefining what it means to be a pop up. We always knew we were going to end.

SP: I mean, everything is ephemeral. But if we're a pop up then pretty much everything is a pop up. All these corporate spaces could get bought out, too. We've seen a lot of businesses come and go in the skyways that could no longer afford rent. So it's interesting to be a pop up with no skin in the game, with no sense of needing to achieve something material or financial by being here.

DS: The fact that we're funded and backed by the German Foreign Ministry allows us to do a lot more with our programing than other artist-run spaces, because we have greater access to resources than most small galleries. We were able to bring in some of the same artists the Walker showed: Laure Prouvost, Christine Sun Kim. And the state funding allowed us to do that. But it also shows that our funding comes from the outside—it didn't emerge from the local community. So this pop up could exist anywhere. It was "popped in" to our local community.

SP: Although many of our artists—more than half—also collaborated with local creative communities, which expanded our audience and community of interest substantially.

DS: True. Even though this pop up could exist anywhere in the world, the thing that distinguished our *Goethe in the Skyways* pop up and made it unique was that we were able to use the skyways as material.

SP: It was our stake in the ground to function here, primarily, over any other space.

DS: Yes. And I do think the loss of public space in a privatized downtown results in a lot of people feeling isolated and alone. The fact that our little public bubble gathered a community, despite the limitations, despite the fact that we were only here for a year, shows that we were serving some need that isn't otherwise being met downtown.

SP: I hope, in the future, to the degree pop ups continue to be a thing, that people think of them as serving this social need. The function is to host who comes in. The need to actually be present for whoever shows up feels essential.

Elske Rosenfeld
A Vocabulary of Revolutionary Gestures

*As the program states, I wanted to include a position that reflects on the 30th anniversary of the fall of the Berlin Wall. It was very important and personal to me. In the U.S., as probably in most countries, the official (hi)story is different to what East Germans personally experienced. Most U.S.-Americans, or the ones I have met, assume that we, East Germans, were happy, grateful, indeed ecstatic about the West saving us from socialist hell, with the United States being the leader of this so-called "Free World." It is unknown to most that the majority of East Germans were fighting for a better socialism, not to be consumed by West Germany and integrated into the capitalist system. Elske Rosenfeld has worked for years, decades, on this topic. Her multi-layered films show a different (hi)story and feature pivotal figures of these turbulent times who have nowadays been forgotten for the most part, while also playing with and testing notions of repetition and re-recordings to reveal the fragility of (hi)story and its multiple layers. In addition to our programming at the Pop Up, two artist talks were organized at the local University of Minnesota in Minneapolis, and Macalester College in St. Paul.

Elske Rosenfeld

A Vocabulary of Revolutionary Gestures

9–26 September 2019

13 September 2019, 2pm

Artist Talk, University of Minnesota

16 September 2019, 4:40pm

Artist Talk, Macalester College

Elske Rosenfeld works in various formats on the history of dissidence in Eastern Europe and on the revolutions of 1989/90. Her ongoing project *A Vocabulary of Revolutionary Gestures* uses materials from 1989/90 and recent global protests and uprisings to explore how political events manifest and inscribe themselves in the bodies of their protagonists. The works of the series are centered around specific gestures—circling, standing still, repeating, interrupting—that serve as both content and methodical guidance of her investigation.

Goethe Pop Up Minneapolis *Goethe in the Skyways* presents two of Rosenfeld's films from this series.

A bit of a Complex Situation (2014) is an intervention in a recording of the first meeting of the Central Round Table of the GDR [German Democratic Republic/ East Germany] on December 7, 1989. In the scene, filmed by filmmaker and opposition member Klaus Freymuth, proceedings are interrupted by the sounds of a demonstration approaching outside. For ten minutes, members of the new movements and state representatives struggle to agree on a response. Rosenfeld amplifies and repeats movements, gestures, sounds, marking and intensifying the breaks and continuities between inside and outside, language and body, representation, and embodiment.

Versuche / Framed (2018) is based on video sketches by filmmaker Klaus Freymuth for an election spot for Bündnis 90 [Alliance 90] —an alliance of some of the new groups from the Round Table. Freymuth positions and films two protagonists of the Round Table as they view his recording of one of these meetings, one year on. In her edit, Rosenfeld plays with the different filmic and corresponding temporal frames, drawing attention to the changing contexts in which political events are given meaning. In all of these nested frames, bodies come to the fore, as language meets its limits.

Images:
1. Artist talk, Macalester College
2. Artist talk, University of Minnesota
3. Installation view *A bit of a Complex Situation*

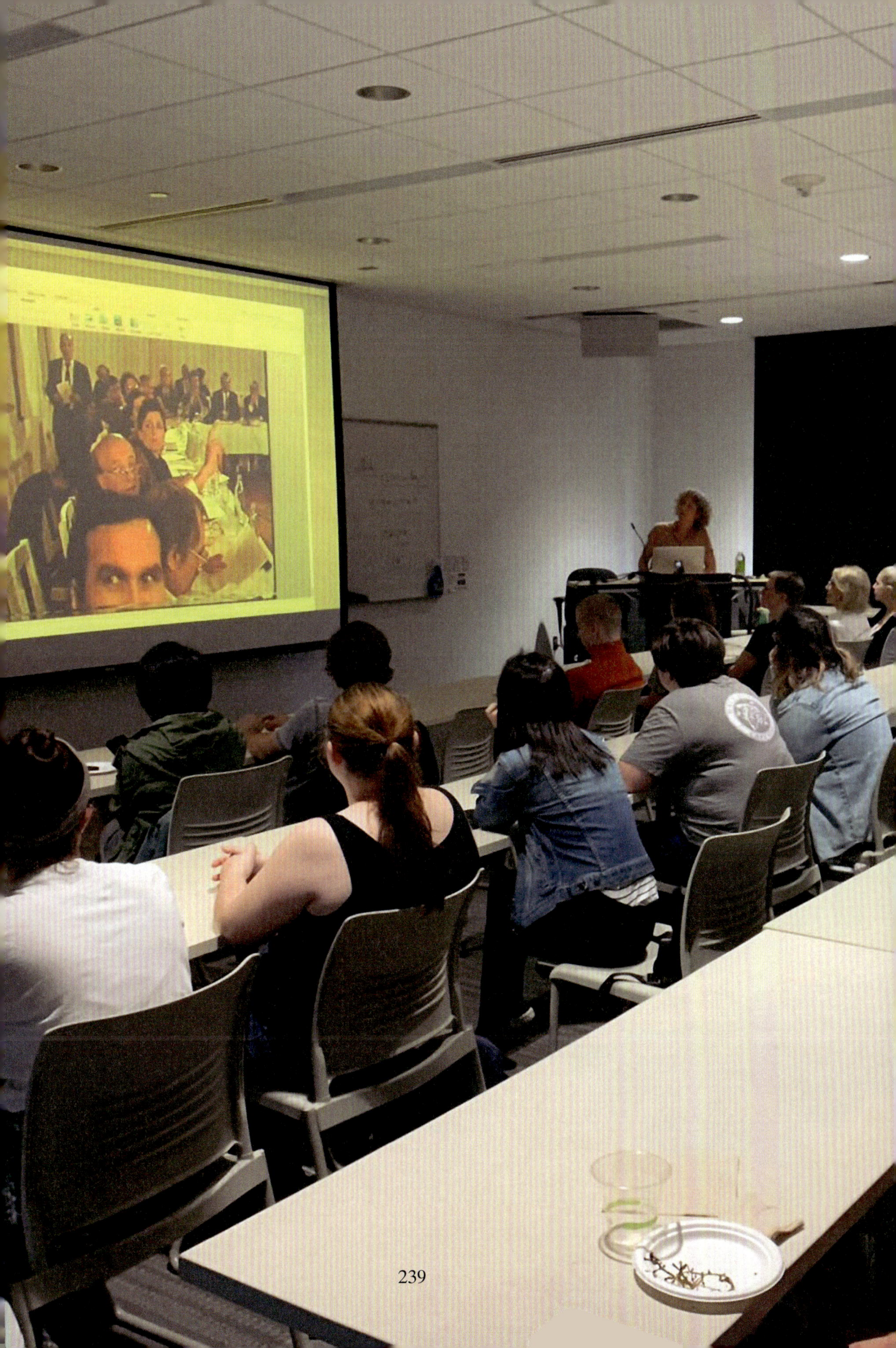

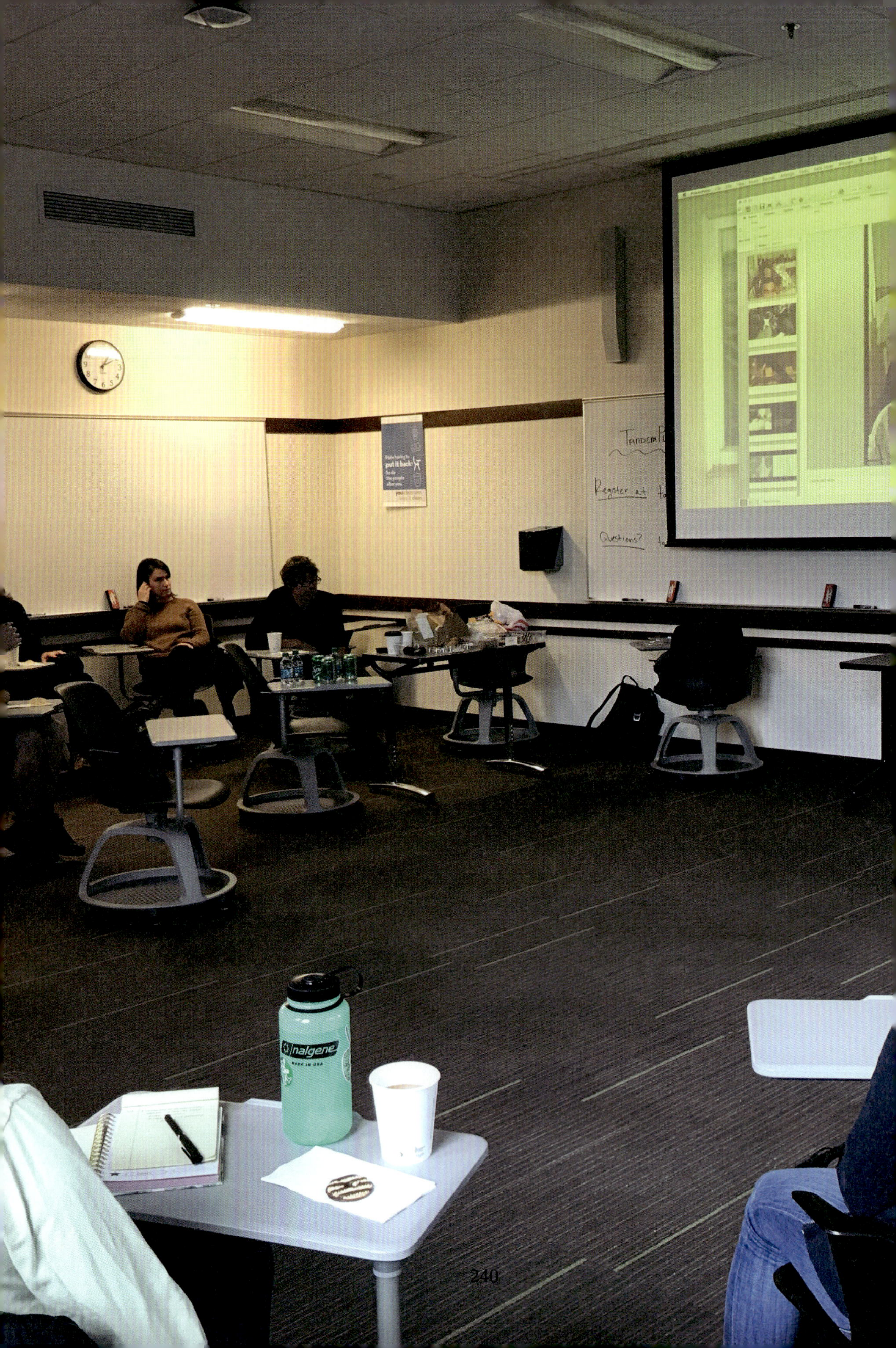
Register at
Questions?
nalgene
MADE IN USA

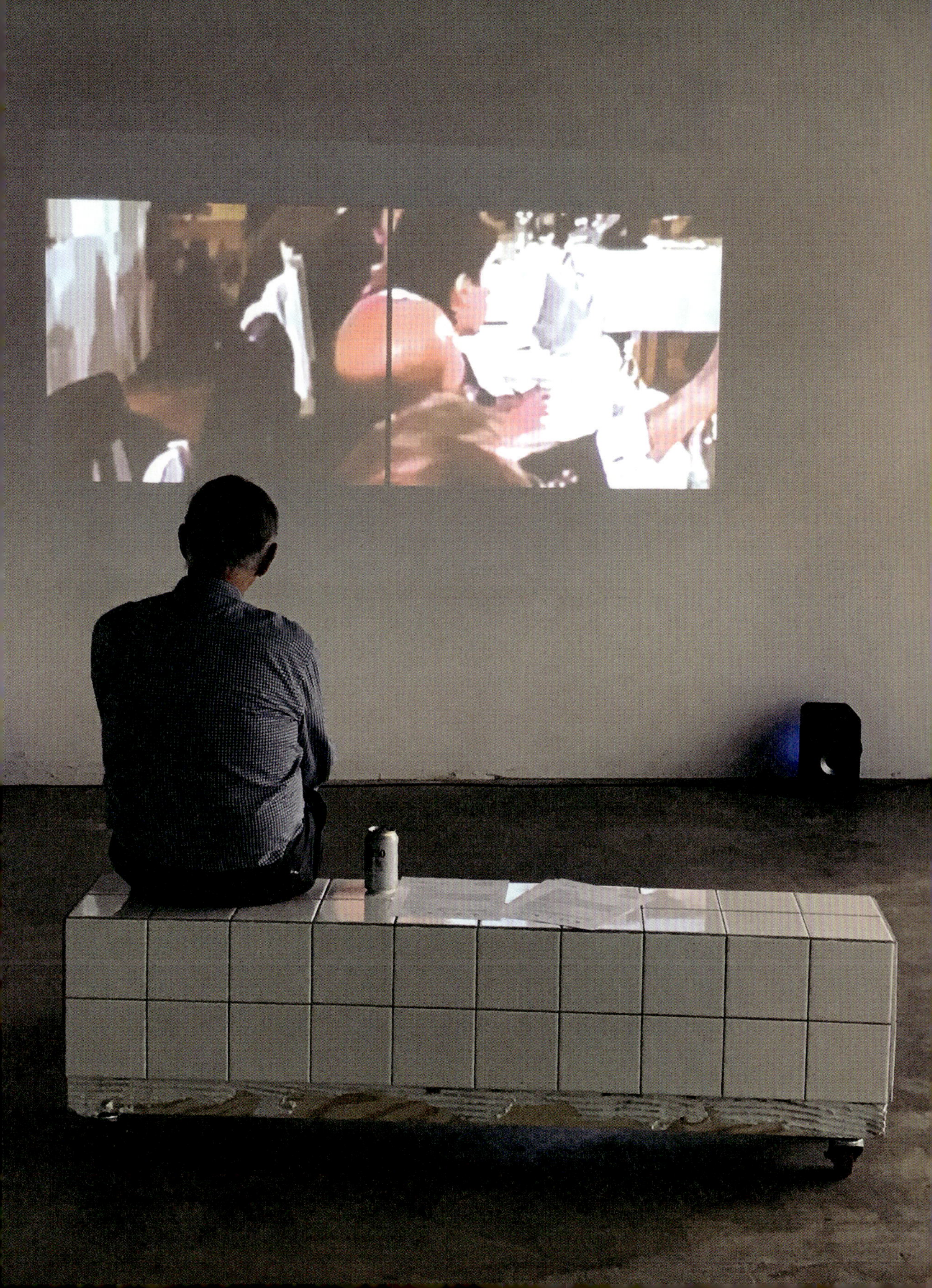

Pétunia
Passages

*At the time of our working together, Pétunia, a magazine that Valérie Chartrain had co-edited for seven years and seven editions, was transitioning into something else, and she had the idea to organize a symposium at the end of our program in Minneapolis that would address notions of legacy and transition in a both literal and abstract way, whilst using the skyways as a visualization of the notion of transition or "passage." Reflection happens too little in the cultural field due to lack of time and resources so I was very glad to have this opportunity. The resulting two-day symposium gathered an illustrious mix of Minneapolis-based and European artists, academics, architects, and dancers spread across co. (company projects) / The Third Rail and the Goethe Pop Up in the skyways.

Pétunia

Passages

27–28 September 2019

27 September 2019, 2–8pm
Passages Day 1
co. (company projects) / The Third Rail

28 September 2019, 2–8pm
Passages Day 2
Goethe Pop Up Minneapolis

Passages: a symposium including film screenings, performances, panel discussions, and many thought-bending lectures in the iconic Minneapolis Skyway System.

Featuring Jennifer Newsom / Dream the Combine, Elsa Dorlin, Non Edwards, Cameron Gainer, Erika Hansen, Brandon Hundt, Interesting Tactics, Bill Lindeke, Kaya Lovestrand, Alexandra Midal, Brenna Mosser, Lisa Middag / Mpls Downtown Improvement District, Andy Delany / OOIEE, Sarah Petersen, Emilie Pitoiset, Daniel Shinbaum, Anna Marie Shogren, Emily Stover, Sandra Teitge, Susana Vargas Cervantes, and Ramaya Tegegne.

Europe-based feminist art and culture magazine *Pétunia* organizes *Passages*, a weekend symposium of performances, screenings, readings, and discussions at co. (company projects) / The Third Rail and at the Goethe Pop Up Minneapolis *Goethe in the Skyways* in the city's iconic skyway system.

Passages, of course, refers to the skyways as physical passageways. It also, in this case, refers to passing the baton in a relay race. This handoff, or passage, is an apt metaphor for several of the contributing spaces, organizers, and magazines participating in the symposium and are themselves transitioning to new manifestations, handing over their own legacy. Finally, *Passages* refers to a book written by Walter Benjamin dedicated to the famous nineteenth-century urban Parisian arcades, one of the direct forerunners of Minneapolis's skyways. Benjamin used those urban features as a pretext to discuss other subjects, just as this symposium uses the skyways to think about legacy, traces, private and public spaces, and more.

Coinciding with the conclusion of both Goethe Pop Up Minneapolis *Goethe in the Skyways* and the relocation of co. (company projects), the aim of the two-day symposium is to invite critical feedback while reflecting on the notions of transition, transmission, commitment to the local, as well as reflecting on this peculiar architectural environment: the Minneapolis Skyway System.

Day 1

2pm Introduction
2:15pm Presentation of Pétunia by Valérie Chartrain.
2:30pm Presentation of *Goethe in the Skyways* by Sandra Teitge
2:45pm Presentation of The Third Rail & co. (company projects) by Cameron Gainer.
3:30pm Podium discussion "Crossing Practices and Questioning Legacies" with Sandra Teitge & Cameron Gainer, moderated by Valérie Chartrain.
4:30pm Lecture "Good Vibrations: Shake, Shake, Shake!" by Alexandra Midal.
5:30pm Lecture "Looking through Pigmentocracy" by Susana Vargas Cervantes.
6:30pm Film by Renate Lorenz/ Pauline Boudry, *Silent* & Lili Renaud Dewar, *Lady to Fox*.
7pm Performance *Corner* by Ramaya Tegegne.
8–10pm Launch The Third Rail Issue 13 & Finissage of *Pirouette* presented by Ouecha Ouecha.

Day 2

2pm Introduction
2:15pm "Experiences from *Goethe in the Skyways*. Shifting Perspectives" with Sarah Petersen, Sandra Teitge, and Daniel Shinbaum.
2:30pm Lecture "Skyways, a History" by Bill Lindeke.
3pm Podium discussion "Perspective on the Skyways" with Andy Delany/OOIEE, Jennifer Newsom/Dream the Combine, Lisa Middag/Mpls Downtown Improvement District, Brandon Hundt, moderated by Valérie Chartrain.
4:30pm Lecture "Tender City: feminist spatial practices in the urban commons" by Emily Stover.
5:00pm Guided tour "Who Are the Future Skyways for?" by Interesting Tactics.
5:30pm Performance *It Took The Night To Believe* by Emilie Pitoiset.
7pm Farewell and conclusion by Valérie Chartrain

The symposium is preceded by a month-long film program *There is No Neutral Space* that introduces the writers, theoreticians, and artists who have been featured in *Pétunia* or films that have been reviewed within the journal since 2009, such as Lizzie Borden, Kathryn Bigelow, Pauline Boudry/Renate Lorenz, Alexandra Midal, Caroline Mesquita, Michelle Naismith, Lili Reynaud Dewar, and Emily Wardill. *There is No Neutral Space* takes place at co. (company projects) every Wednesday in September 2019.

This project is supported by Etant Donnés Contemporary Art, a program developed by FACE Foundation and the Cultural Services of the French Embassy in the United States, with lead funding from the French Ministry of Culture and Institut Français-Paris, the Florence Gould Foundation, The Ford Foundation, the Helen Frankenthaler Foundation, Chanel USA, the ADAGP, and the CPGA.

Performance by Ramaya Tegegne with the support of the Swiss Arts Council Pro Helvetia

Clothing for the performance by Emilie Pitoiset generously partly provided by agnès b.

Images:
1. Valérie Chartrain presents Pétunia at co. (company projects)
2. Alexandra Midal, "Good Vibrations: Shake, Shake, Shake!"
3. *Passages* advertisement in The Third Rail
4. Valérie Chartrain in conversation with Cameron Gainer at co. (company projects)
5. Audience watching *Lady To Fox* by Lili Reynaud Dewar at co. (company projects)
6. Ramaya Tegegne performing *Corner* at co. (company projects)
7. Panel discussion "Perspective on the Skyways"
8. Emilie Pitoiset, *It Took The Night To Believe*

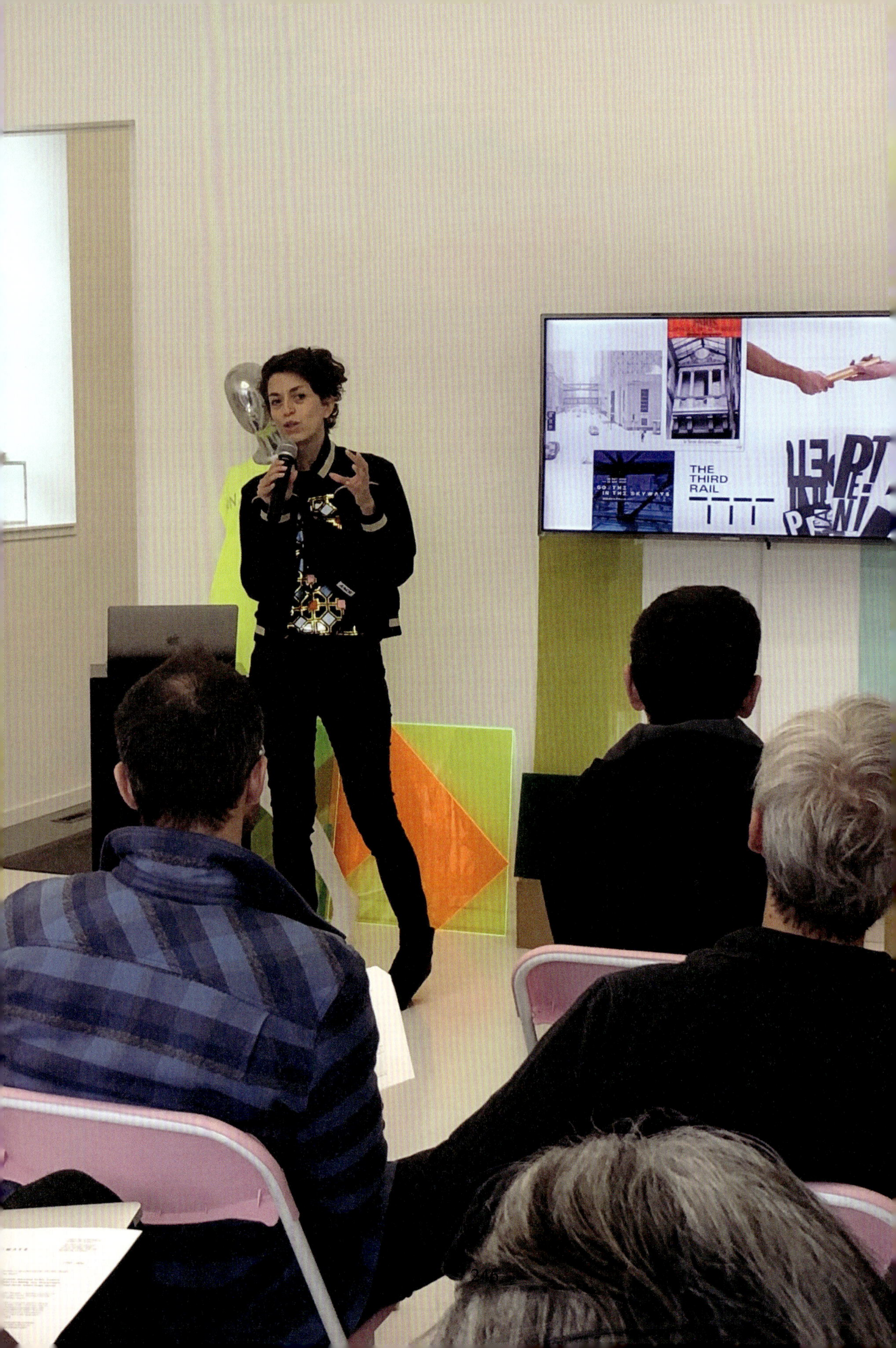
THE
THIRD
RAIL

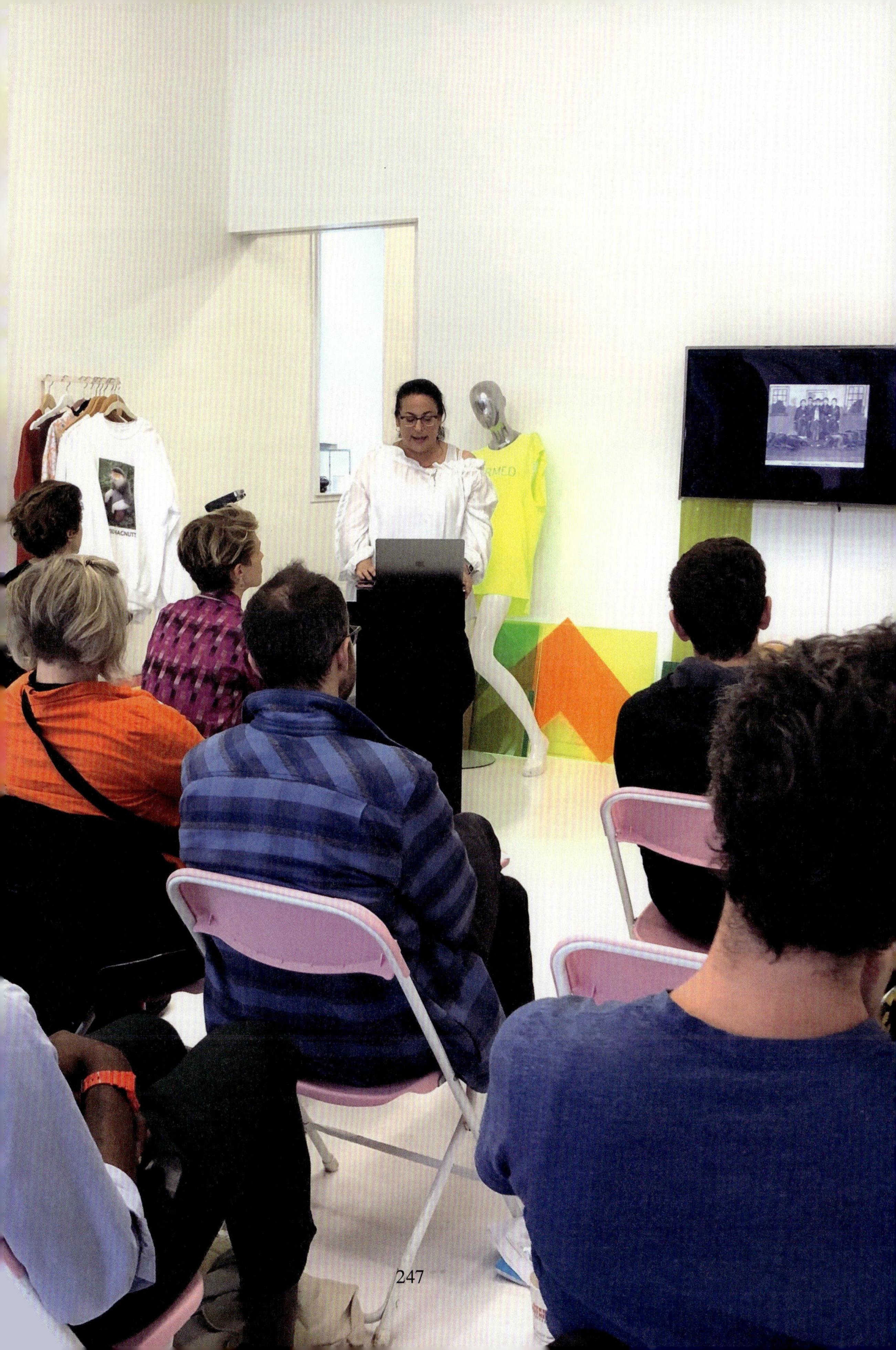

PASSAGES: a symposium

film screenings, performances, panel discussions, and lectures curated by *Petunia hosted* by *The Third Rail* and *Goethe Pop Up Minneapolis*

Friday, 27 September 2019, 2–8pm
co. (company projects) / The Third Rail
1237 4th Street NE
Minneapolis, MN 55413

Saturday, 27 September 2019, 2–8pm
Goethe Pop Up Minneapolis
Goethe in the Skyways
City Center, Skyway Level
40 South 7th Street, Suite 208
Minneapolis, MN 55402

–with Dream the Combine, Elsa Dorlin, Interesting Tactics, Cameron Gainer, Brandon Hundt, Bill Lindeke, Alexandra Midal, Matt Olson, Sarah Petersen, Emilie Pitoiset, Lili Renaud Dewar, Daniel Shinbaum, Emily Stover, Sandra Teitge, Susana Vargas Cervantes, Ramaya Tegegne, and many others

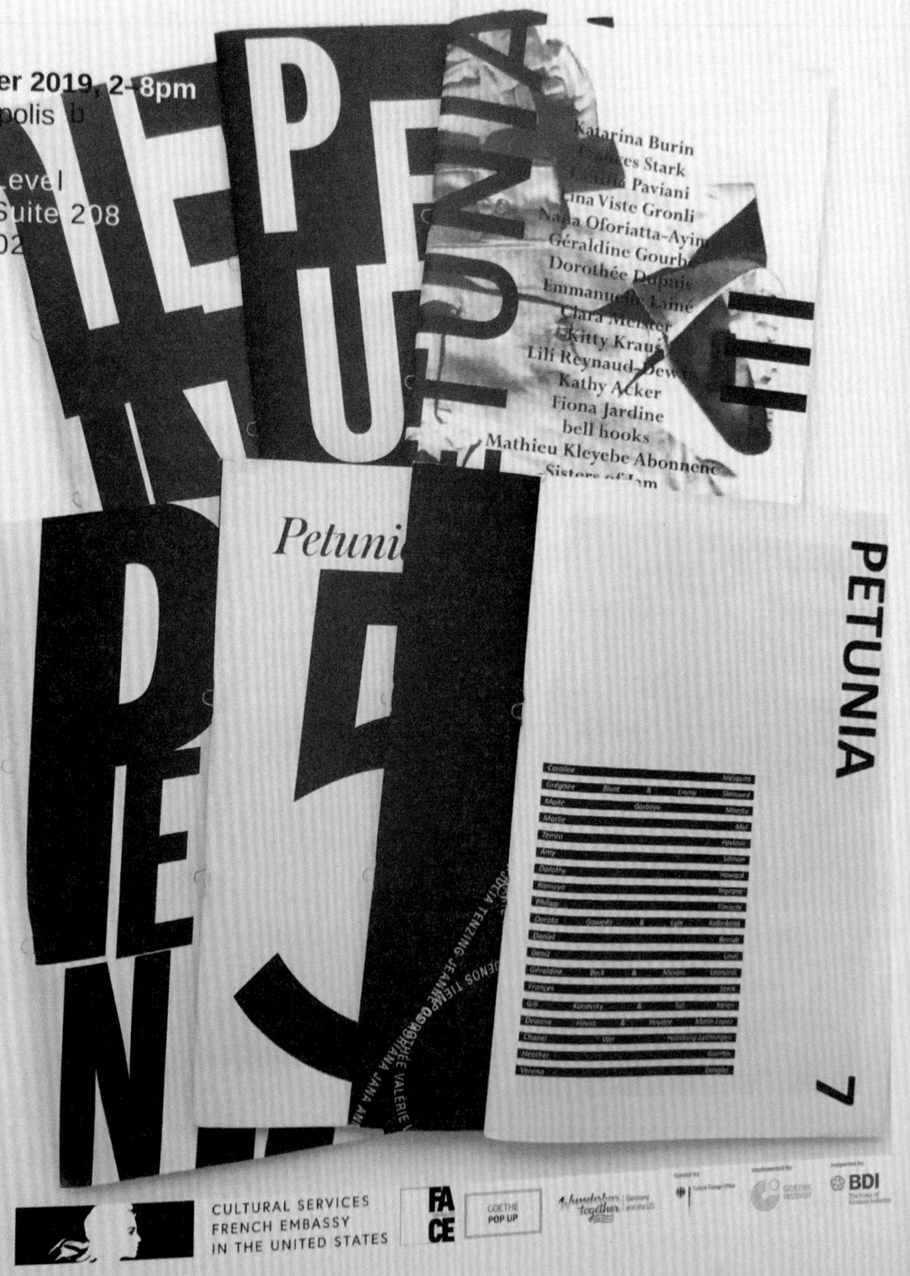

*Additional funding is provided by Étant donnés Contemporary Art, a program of the French American Cultural Exchange (FACE) Foundation.

more info:
goetheintheskyways.org
petuniamagazine.eu

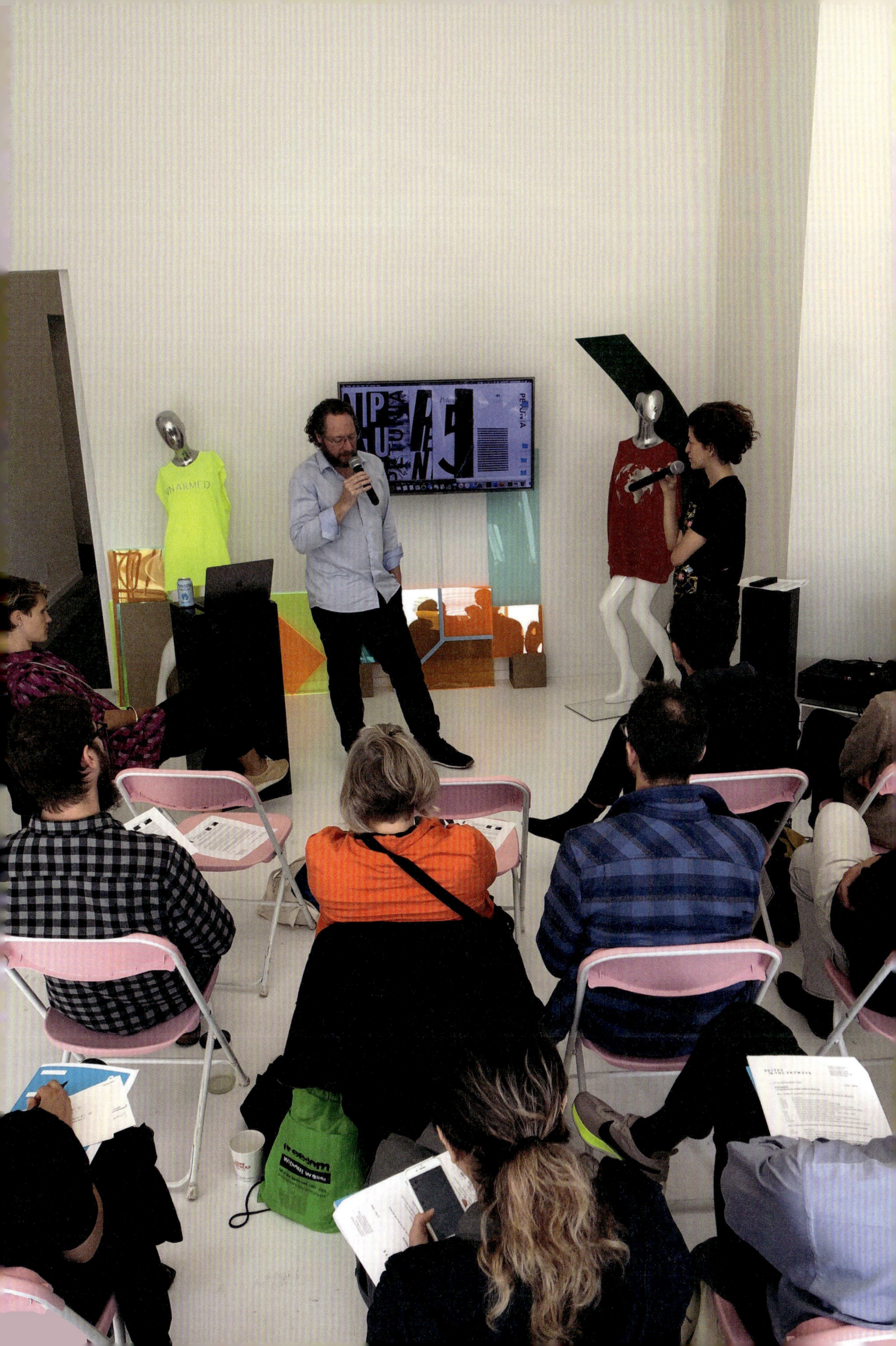

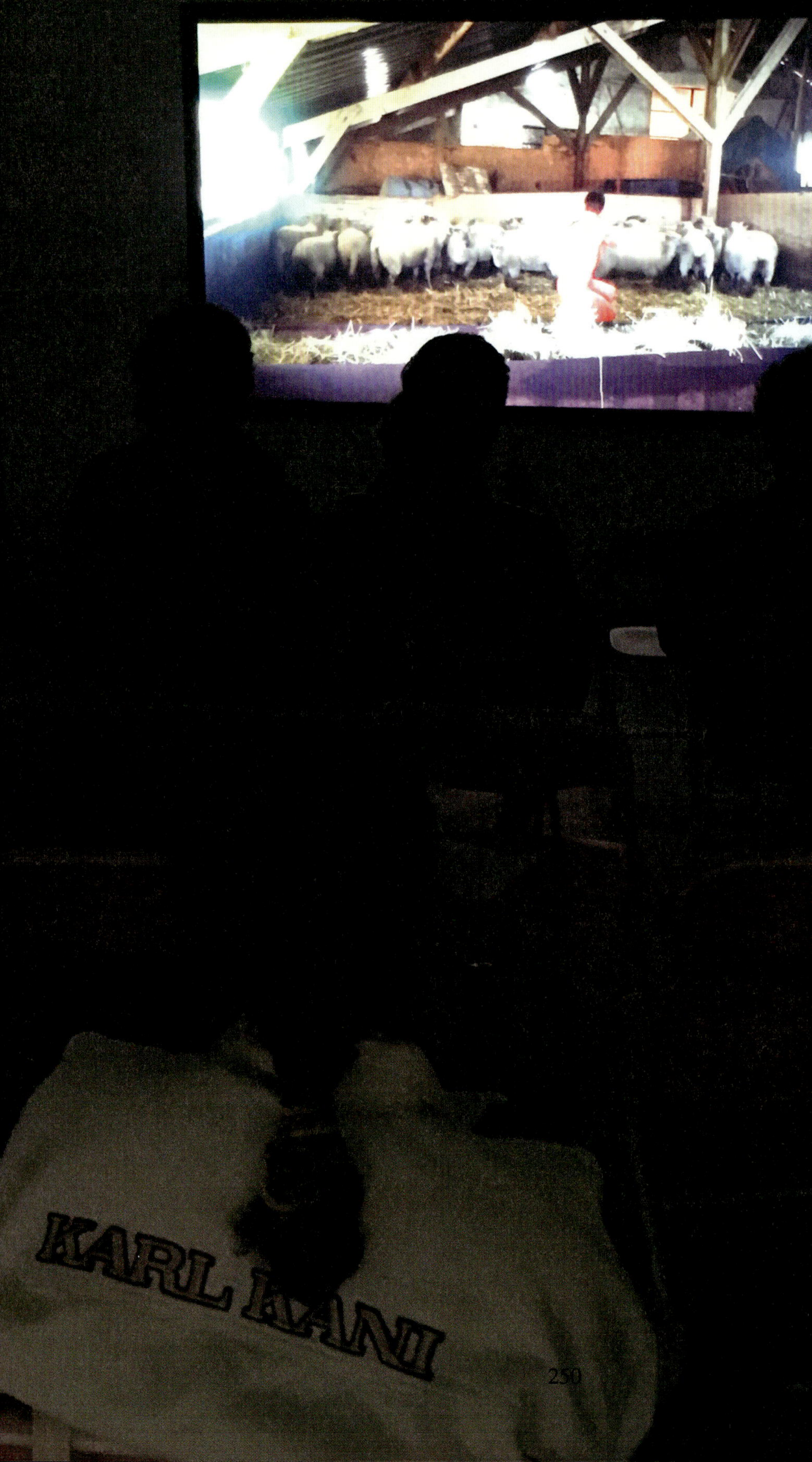
KARL KANI

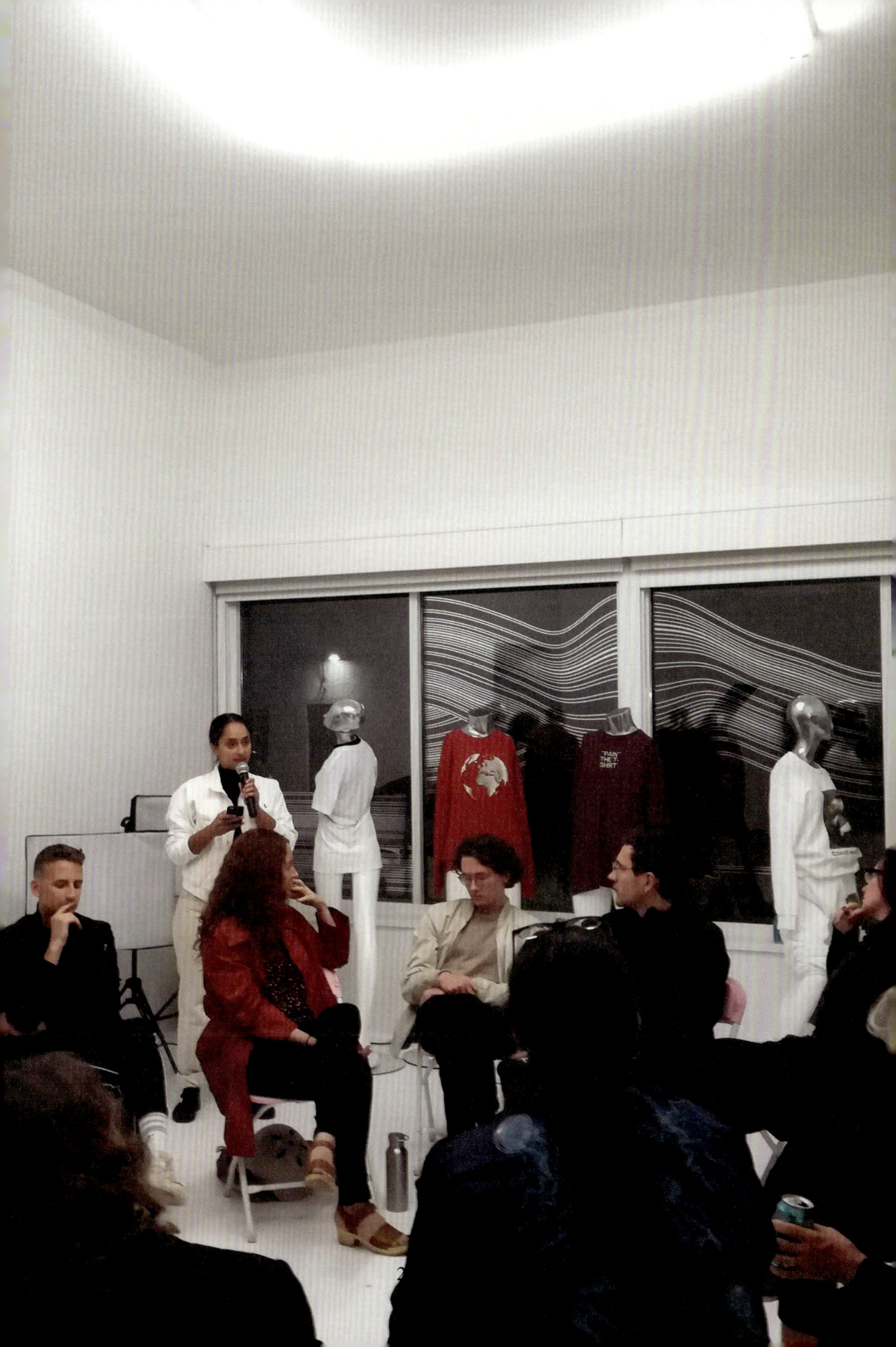
"PAIN"
THE T-
SHIRT

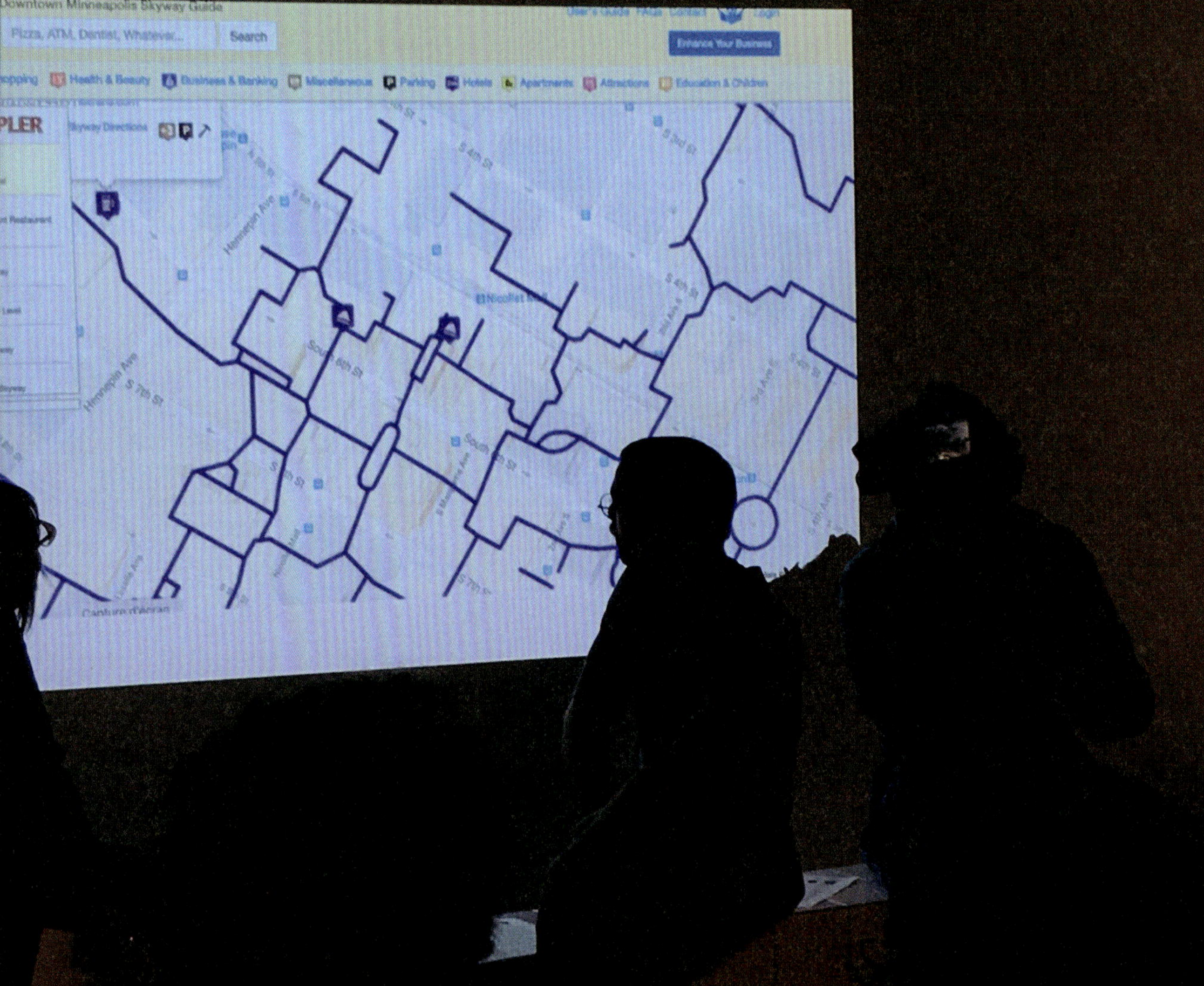
Downtown Minneapolis Skyway Guide
Search
Health & Beauty
Business & Banking
Miscellaneous
Parking
Hotels
Apartments
Attractions
Education & Children
Skyway Directions
Hennepin Ave
S 4th St
Nicollet Ave
South 6th St
S 7th St

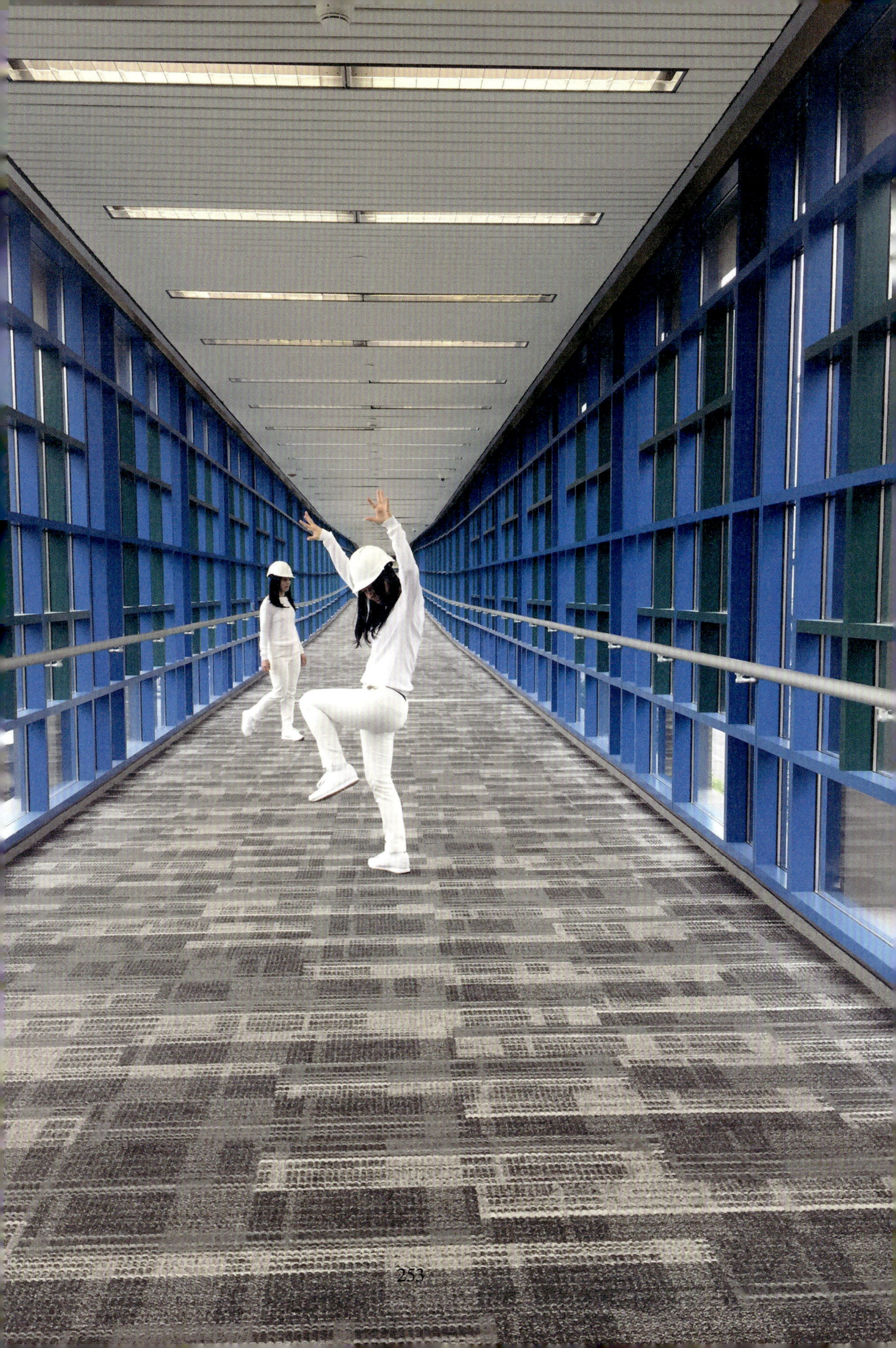

Who Are the Future Skyways for?

Interesting Tactics

Hello, this is Interesting Tactics coming from you live from beautiful Minneapolis, Minnesota. We are a utopic spatial practice and for us, utopia is not merely a place, or literally "no place"—as Sir Thomas More defined it—but a process.

Our investigation began by looking at the zeitgeist of utopian projects which shared the characteristics and genesis of the Minneapolis skyway system. The future we envision builds upon the utopian processes already present in the skyway system. Our goal is to simply continue that process.

Through an investigation into the Experimental Prototype Community of Tomorrow (better known as EPCOT), the Minnesota Experimental City, and the U.S. Highway System, we gained insight into the specific strains of post-war utopianism which created the skyway as we know it today. We chose to accelerate and reframe the ideologies which fueled each of these. That is—*to utope* by imagining a new and optimistic future of the skyways through an investigation of the system's relationship to the commons, to climate, and to technology.

CONSUMERISM TO COMMONS: EPCOT

Walt Disney's Experimental Prototype Community of Tomorrow, better known as EPCOT illustrates a retro-utopian goal to center a city around transit infrastructure and equity of mobility.

The city of the future which Disney had dreamt of in the 60's settled for a simulacra of itself to which millions buy tickets to visit for entertainment today.

The original EPCOT that Disney proposed was a city funded by private industry in which all citizens were rendered as consumers.

Not only was the city designed around a commute to the research park (facilitated by space-age tech like Monorails, PeopleMovers, and the like), but the domestic sphere itself was to be an experimental laboratory to test new consumer products.

Suggesting that perhaps the city was designed more for technology than people. EPCOT, more so than most utopias exacerbates the current questions of ownership, commons, and equity: who is the future city for?

Today, the skyways are fashioned as pedestrian malls of transit but are much more effective as a downtown, indoor commercial zone. The escalators, atriums, and food courts are borrowed from the suburban malls and entertainment districts of the 1970s, transplanted to our urban core.

The white collar workers for whom this space was built are– like the citizens of EPCOT—presupposed as consumer-producers who spend their days marketing corporate goods to spend their lunch hours weaving between the work of their peers. Citizenship begs the question—what other ways of being could exist in the skyways?

Despite the corporatism rampant within the halls of our present skyways, we can still imagine a collective commoning of the shared spaces. The consumerist bastions of the past are on the verge of collapse with the rise of Amazon and 5G. Now the white collar office worker is no longer tied to the urban core and neither are the shopping malls to transportation thoroughfares. Instead, filling the voids of both shopping districts and office space, a new cultural context may exist. The shells of city skylines might repopulate with social services, and everyday life may exist where previously only corporatism thrived.

CLIMATE CRISIS: MXC

The Minnesota Experimental City or MXC was conceived and defeated by the environmental movements of the 1960s.

MXC was the brainchild of Athelstan Spilhaus, a sci-fi cartoonist for the Star Tribune.

Spilhaus despised waste and imagined the city of the future to have immense corridors shuttling and recycling goods out of view from the rest of the city. In accordance with his predilections and with a massive budget from the Federal Government, Spilhaus designed the Experimental City.

Resources like air and water were managed, prefiguring the precarious environmental conditions of today. The design of this Experimental City was partially contained by a geodesic dome forming a vast, climate controlled interior. This interior was central to the City's utopic functions: the air inside was not only conditioned but purified. Pollution from machines that kept MXC running was either piped out or sucked deep underground, where it was rehabilitated before releasing back into the dome.

Both the Minnesota Experimental City and the skyways consider the existing climate of Minnesota inhospitable: our winters are a variable which seem to require controlling for the sake of *progress*. However, the deep irony of a climate-controlled paradise is its impact on the environment. Rising global temperatures are now manipulating the very climate these systems were designed to control.

The environmental outcry which prohibited the manifestation of MXC was the protection of natural resources. Supplanting the bucolic setting of northern Minnesota with a city of the future led environmentalists to shut down the project before any construction could begin.

The design of the skyways acts inversely. Rather than supplanting rural Minnesotans' land, the skyways took an urban core and suspended their parasitic interior above the ground level. Our projection seeks to take this inversion and apply it even further. The ground plane may become a seamless extension of the wilderness which thwarted MXC.

INFRASTRUCTURAL FUTURISM: HIGHWAYS

The Dwight D. Eisenhower National System and Defense Highways was a sociocultural infrastructure. Eisenhower, along with American Automobile Association (made up of Ford, GM, Toyota, and Standard) championed the construction of a vast network of roads for safety, defense, and the economy.

The highways themselves boosted economic activity, by creating the "greatest construction program in the entire history of the Nation," as Ike said in Detroit in 1954.

The highways also transformed the American way of life around the automobile producing both an economy and a way of being.

The highways dictate a proper kinetic. Rules are decreed by neat graphic markings, constant throughout the nation. Pass on the left and signal your turn, the golden rule of motorists.

Just like the skyways, drivers are physically separated from one another and the outside in their climate-controlled cars. Highways gave a new way to see the world; rapidly unfolding through the windshield.

Since we *know* how the highways end—a crumbling infrastructure, a sink of embodied energy, and a skeletal framework of the nation as our forefathers wanted it—we project a reoriented future for the skyways. Human infrastructure takes a new trajectory, as the skyways grow to encompass and enable a new way of living.

Could the skyways serve as an infrastructure to reorient human life towards maintenance of the earth? A new geologic layer which would scrub the Anthropocene into a thin crust suspended above the world?

The skyways enable an alternative way to see the world from above, below, and within—walking between circulatory tubes and viewing a rewilded ground from above. Skyways could connect what the highways separated, as the stuff of life is recondensed.

Come with us now, on a journey into the future!

FIRST STOP: MIRROR

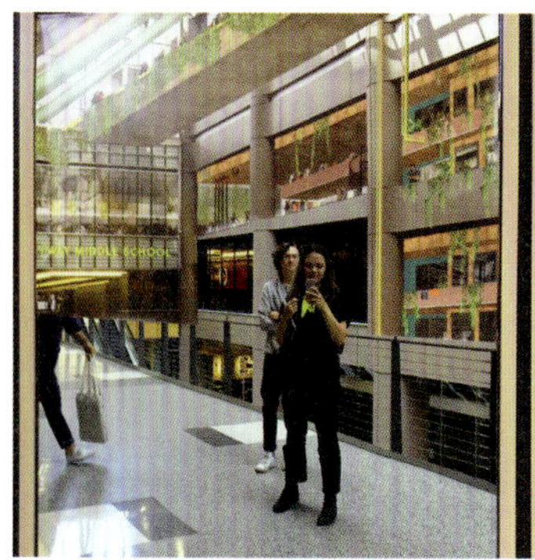

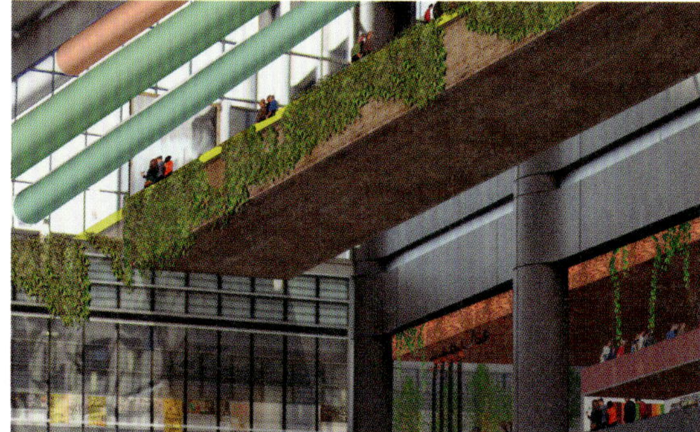

CONSUMERISM TO COMMONS: EPCOT

This is a vision of what the skyways could look like in the future, if they were centered around communal life, as opposed to working and shopping. The skyways could be a way to cultivate the commons. We imagine this taking place as office spaces and retail continue to be displaced by online networks, leaving a void in the material world. The skyways are an existing infrastructure with the potential for reorienting community life.

SECOND STOP: MOON

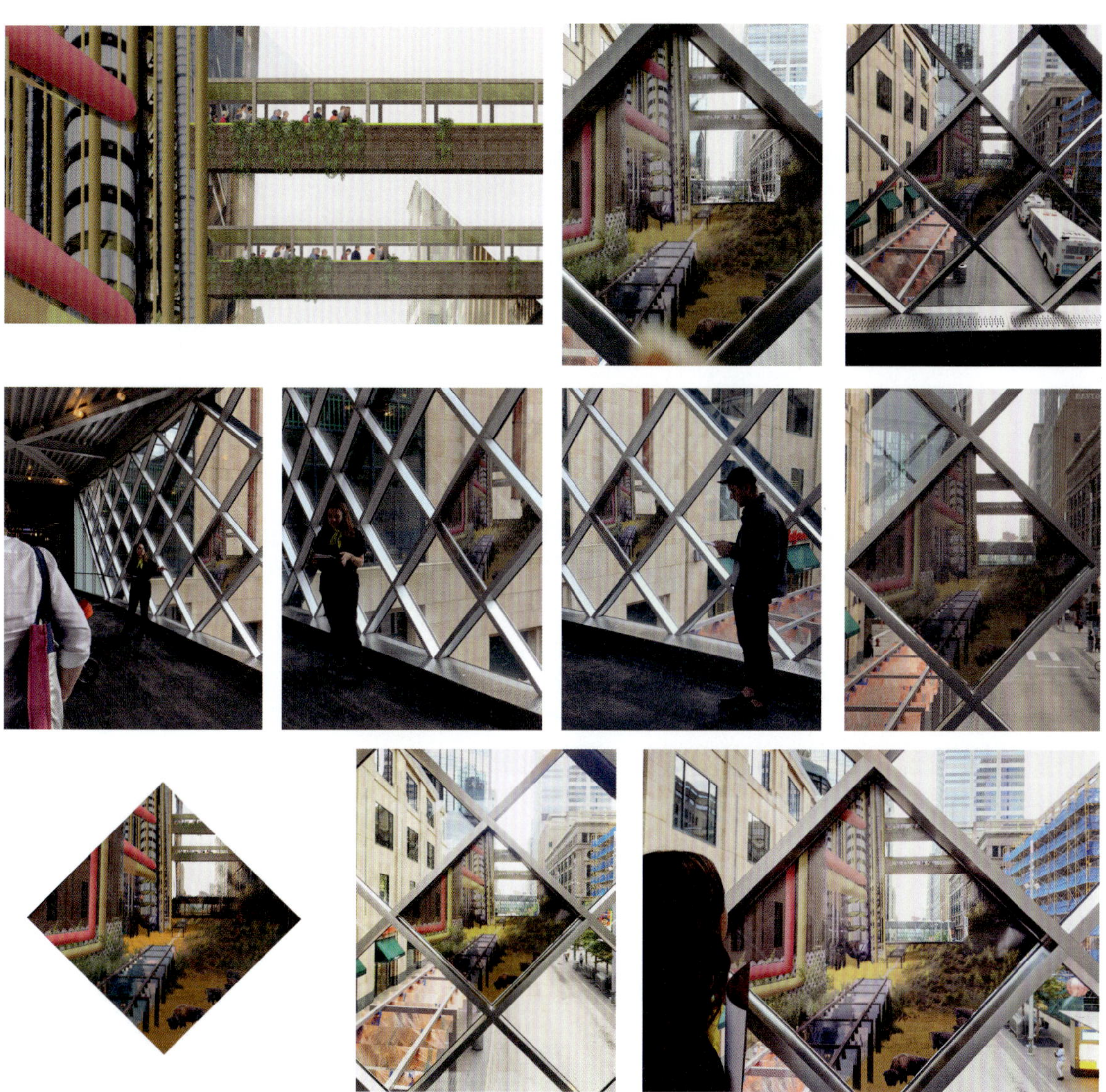

CLIMATE CRISIS: MXC

In the future, we project an elimination of this insularity, opting to intertwine the creation of microbiomes both naturally and artificially maintained. The interior use should be maximized: greenhouses which thrive due to the sealed nature of glass-filled spaces, the exterior, left to rewild.

THIRD STOP: DIAGRID

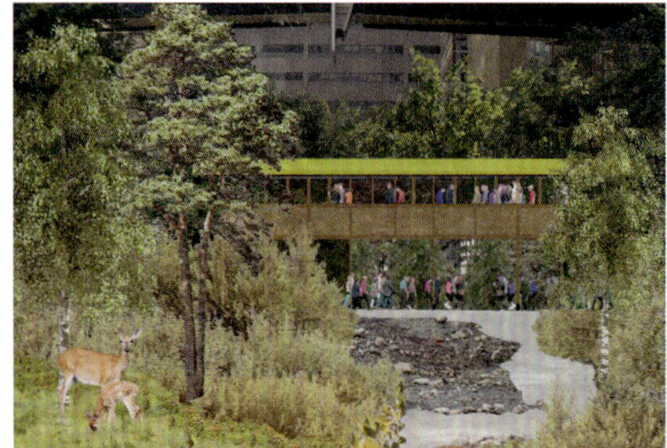

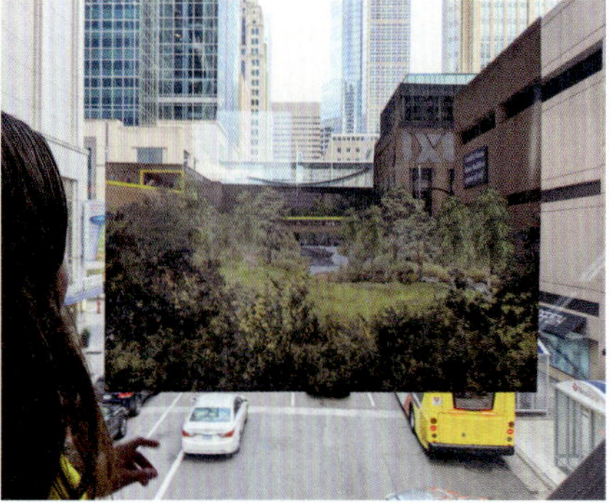

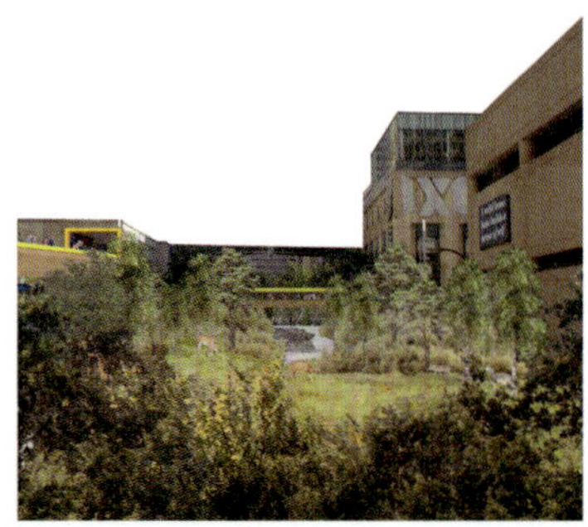

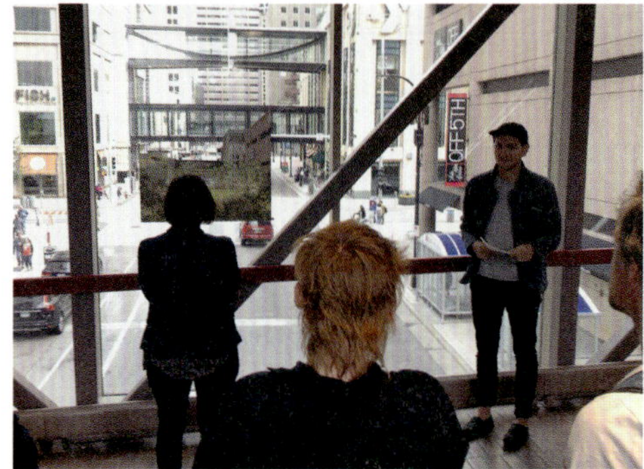

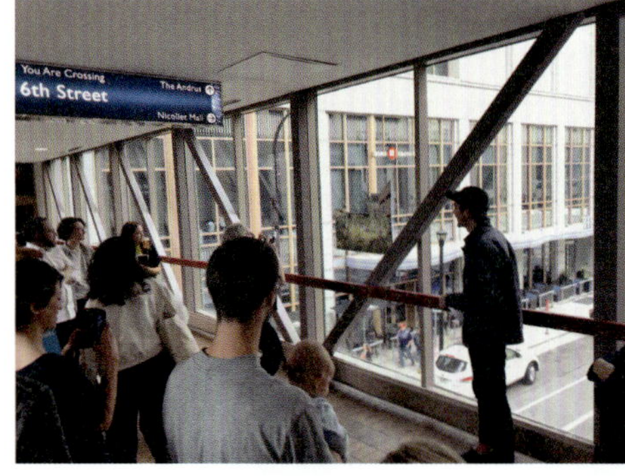

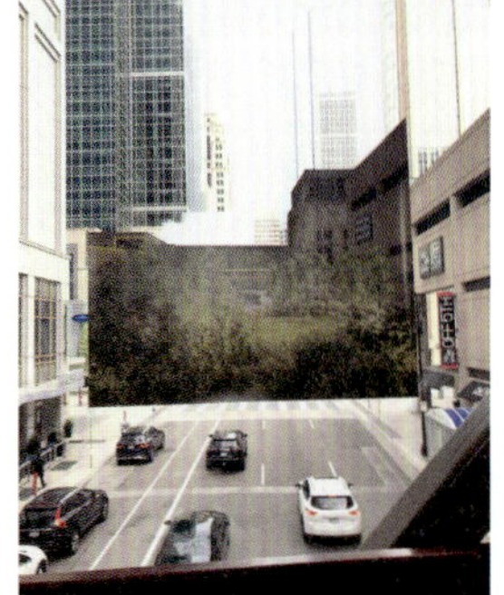

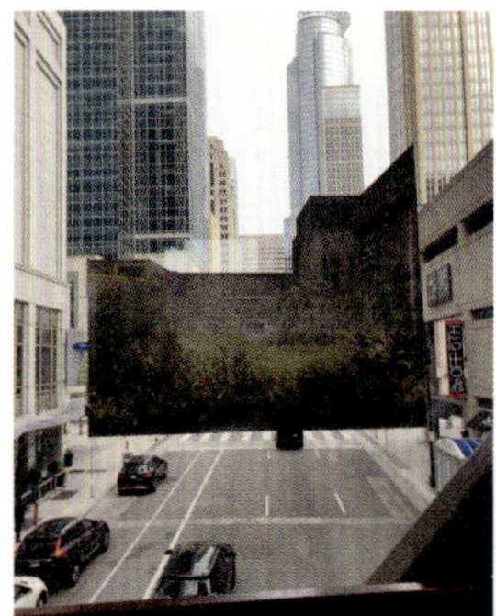

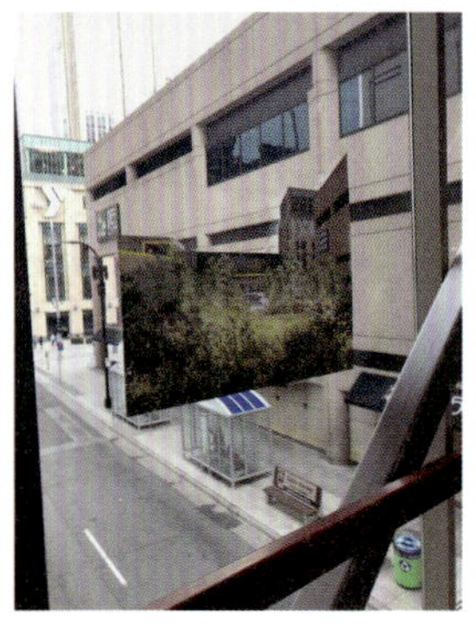

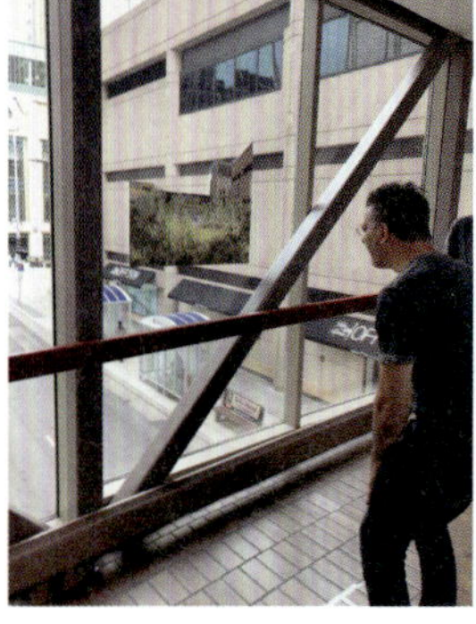

INFRASTRUCTURAL FUTURISM: HIGHWAYS

Aside from the occasional emergency, walking the skyways is fairly boring—it's a whole lotta nothing. The fun part is actually what's happening outside—the systems manages everything. So, the whole region has been optimized for maximum biodiversity, carbon responsibility, food, and water production. The skyway system and a lot of other privately owned or corporate resources have been repurposed for geo-engineering purposes. This all started after the climate crisis where there was a global paradigm shift surrounding the relationship between environment, states, and economy.

CONCLUSION

EPCOT, MXC, and the Highways are all projects that were a result of an ideology that believed that technology was the answer and that social ills were problems needing to be *solved*. The various visionary solutions that were proposed emphasized a static transportation infrastructure which was filled with modular components that could easily be adapted. Moreover, the designs also required a fictional *tabula rasa*—so existing conditions were often razed in order to make way for many of these projects. Therefore, the projects that were built often came at the cost of the destruction of working class and minority communities. The skyway is a unique case study of these visionary projects because it is the only one that was implemented a bit at a time and that it engaged with the existing city of Minneapolis. Because of its symbiotic relationship with downtown life it has thrived in ways that many malls and experimental cities have not. In conclusion, this is not *the* future but *a* future.

Students from Bielefeld University of Applied Sciences (Department of Design) with Philipp Rupp
Bags from Bielefeld

*Having been involved from the program's inception via designing the *Skyway Uniforms*, Philipp Rupp suggested an additional project that he was developing with his students in Bielefeld. We turned the Pop Up into a pseudo retail store. I thought this commercial-looking installation would be the perfect last guest, a sort of re-dedication of the space to its environment of commerce, the skyways.

Bags from Bielefeld

Students from Bielefeld University of Applied Sciences (Department of Design) with Philipp Rupp

7–10 October 2019

8 October 2019, 4:30 pm

Happy Hour

How can longing for home manifest itself in luggage?

Fashion and Graphic Design students* of Bielefeld University of Applied Sciences (Department of Design) have developed accessories that reflect the notion of navigating and living in between cultures and continents. They researched and developed forms, surfaces, materials, prints, and applications and formed them into a new fashion symbiosis inspired by pop culture and visual memories from their home countries. In a workshop, designers from the Berlin accessory label Liebeskind taught the students all the necessary processes for developing and processing bags.

The point of departure for this fashion project were themes of migration, transculturality, and the concept of mobility in the twenty-first century.

Which pieces of luggage did people have and still have with them on their journey between continents and cultures? What are the containers for their personal belongings for people when they migrate? How does the longing for the old homeland manifest itself in the luggage? How does the longing for the new home manifest itself in the luggage?

The results are being presented at the Goethe Pop Up Minneapolis *Goethe in the Skyways* as a final gesture in the form of a commercial Pop Up Shop—a gesture of handing the temporary space in City Center back over to its commercial environment.

*Greta Berghoff, Inke Borgel, Sabrina Brose, Katrin Jeworowski, Paul Kaminski, Laura Könemann, Jan König, Steffi Lahl, Fabia Meyer, Jana Meyer, Leon Pöhler, Martina Reifer, Anna Siebert, Friederike Sujeba-Roesler, Melis Uyanik, Julia Wartemann.

The project is supervised by Philipp Rupp, Professor for Fashion Design and Dirk Fütterer, Professor for Communication Design at Bielefeld University of Applied Sciences.

Images:
1. Martina Reifer & Fabia Meyer, *Kraftpaket* (inspired by Ralf Moeller & Roland Emmerich); Jana Meyer & Leon Pöhler, *Montgraf* (inspired by Steffi Graf, Sigfried & Roy); Melis Uyanik & Paul Kaminski, *Saustall* (inspired by Klaus Kinski)
2. Anna Siebert & Jan König, *Dirkules* (inspired by Dirk Nowitzki); Inke Borgel & Julia Wartemann, *Hans & Franz* (inspired by Heidi Klum+Levi Strauss); Sabrina Brose, *Marlene* (inspired by M. Dietrich)

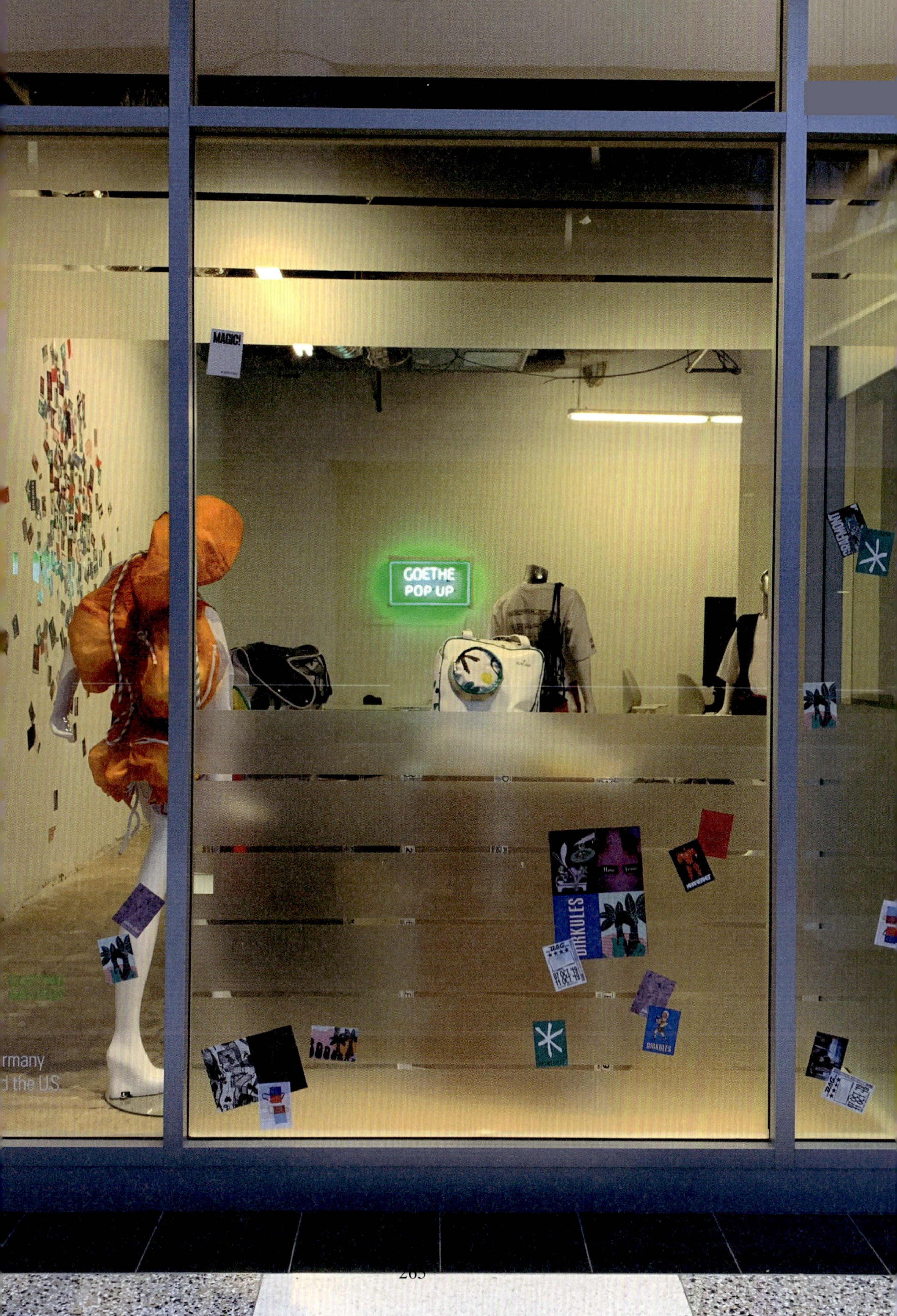
GOETHE
POP UP
MAGIC!
DIRKULES
rmany
the US

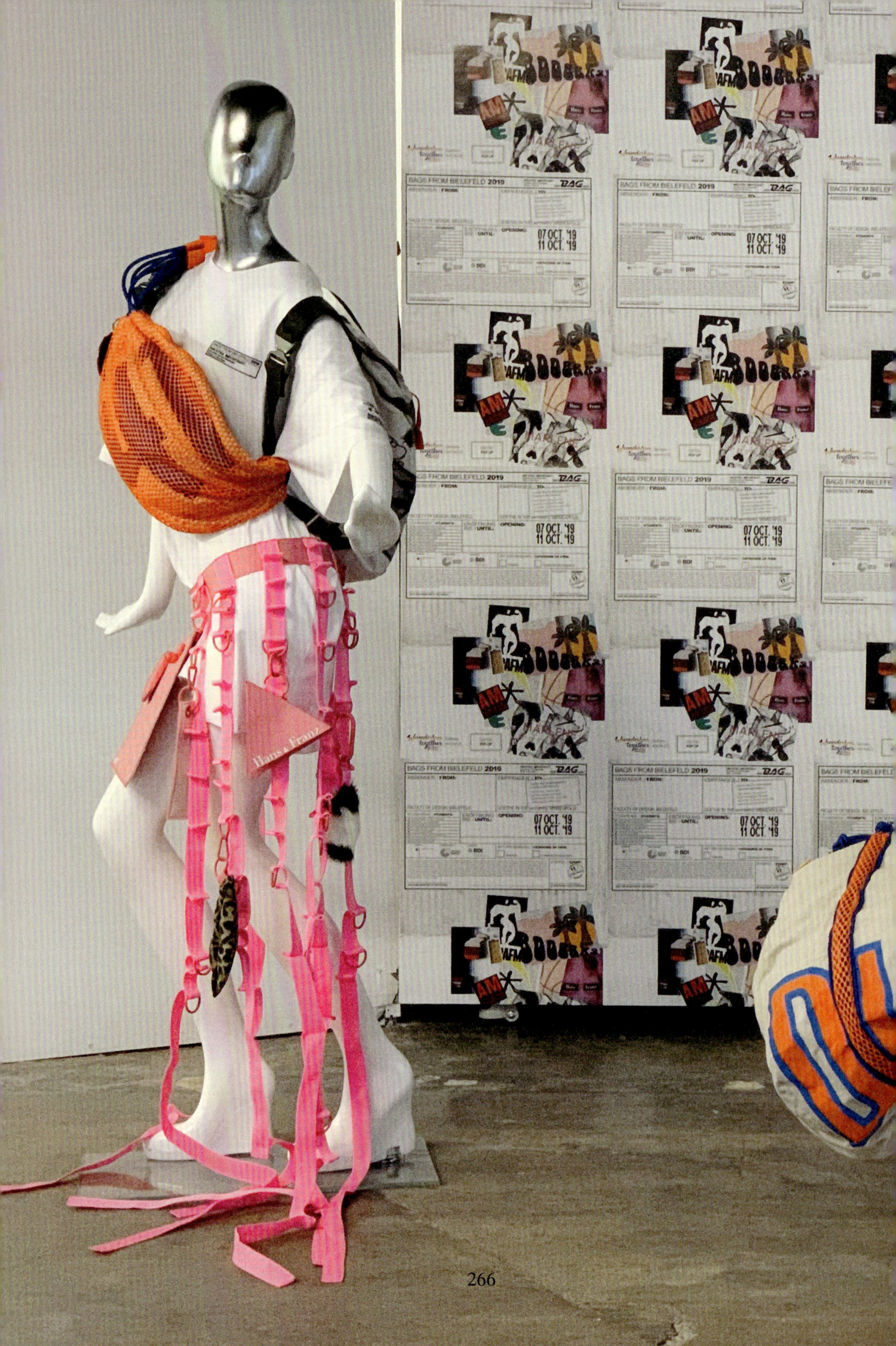
BAGS FROM BIELEFELD 2019
BAG
07 OCT. '19
11 OCT. '19
Hans & Franz

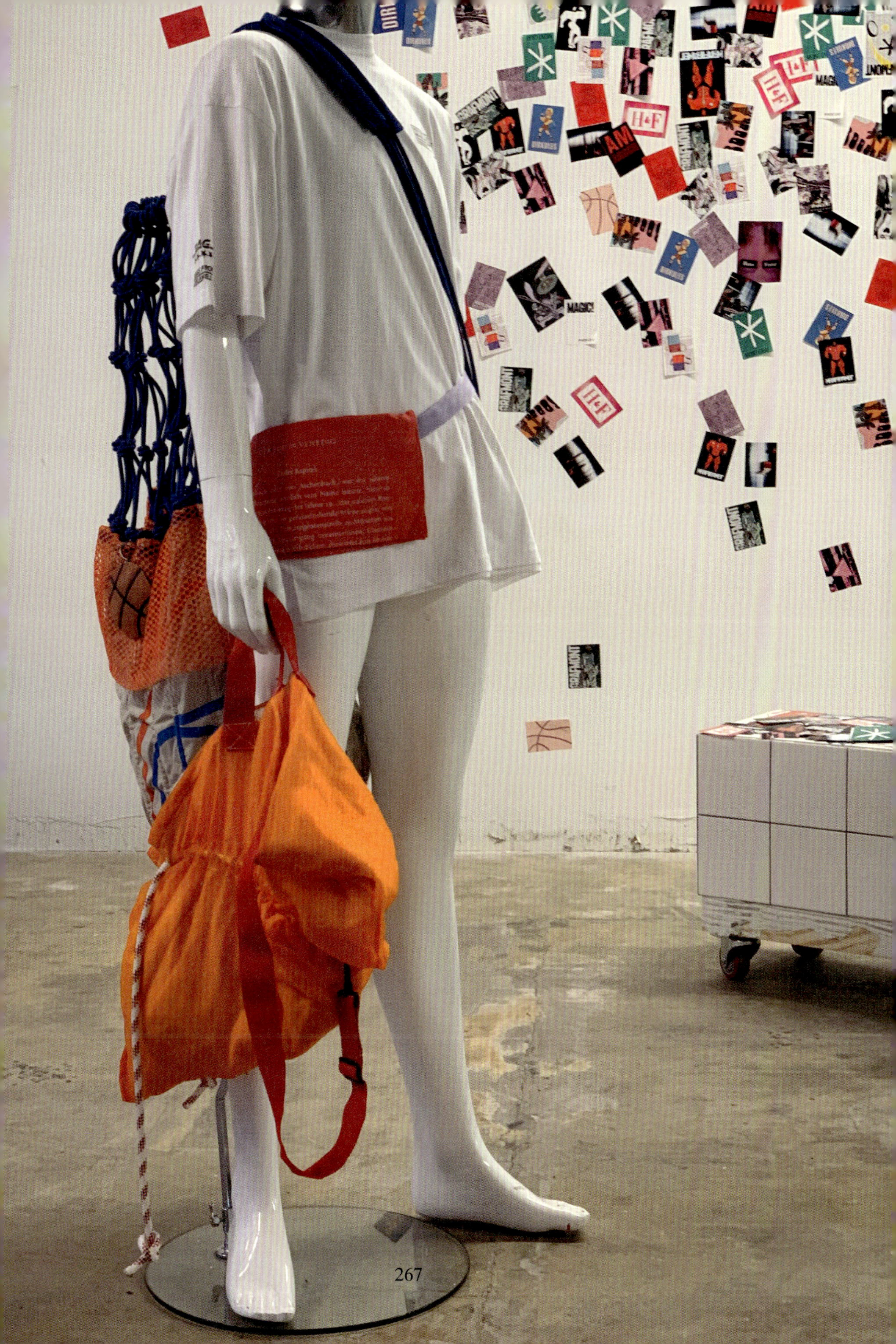

Roseline Rannoch
with Felix Profos and Philipp Rupp
Dark Ride II: They are us revisited

*Roseline Rannoch and Philipp Rupp (with Felix Profos) had organized the performance *Dark Ride* at the legendary Ku'damm Karree a few years ago. The Ku'damm Karree, a now torn-down shopping center with strange bars and shops, is the Berlin version of the skyways in Minneapolis. The zombie theme of the Berlin performance *Dark Ride* is also present in Minneapolis in the form of the annual "Zombie Pub Crawl" that takes place around Halloween inside and outside of the skyways. Roseline had actually made me aware of this phenomenon. The final *Goethe in the Skyways* event was a zombie-inspired performance with a melodramatic musical score entitled *Dark Ride II: They are us revisited*, which took place on October 8th, when the U.S. is already in Halloween fever, and thus made the ideal farewell to this year-long program.

Roseline Rannoch
with Felix Profos and Philipp Rupp

Dark Ride II: They are us revisited

8 October 2019, 6 pm

Concept, Vestimentaire, Video:
Roseline Rannoch
Music, Video Sound: Felix Profos
Vestimentaire: Philipp Rupp
Performers: Sabrina Diehl, Lydia Egge,
Christina M. Karr, Jessie Lee-Bauder

Images:
1. *Dark Ride II: They are us (Buffy)*
2–3. Performance views
4. *Dark Ride II: They are us (Turkana Boy)*

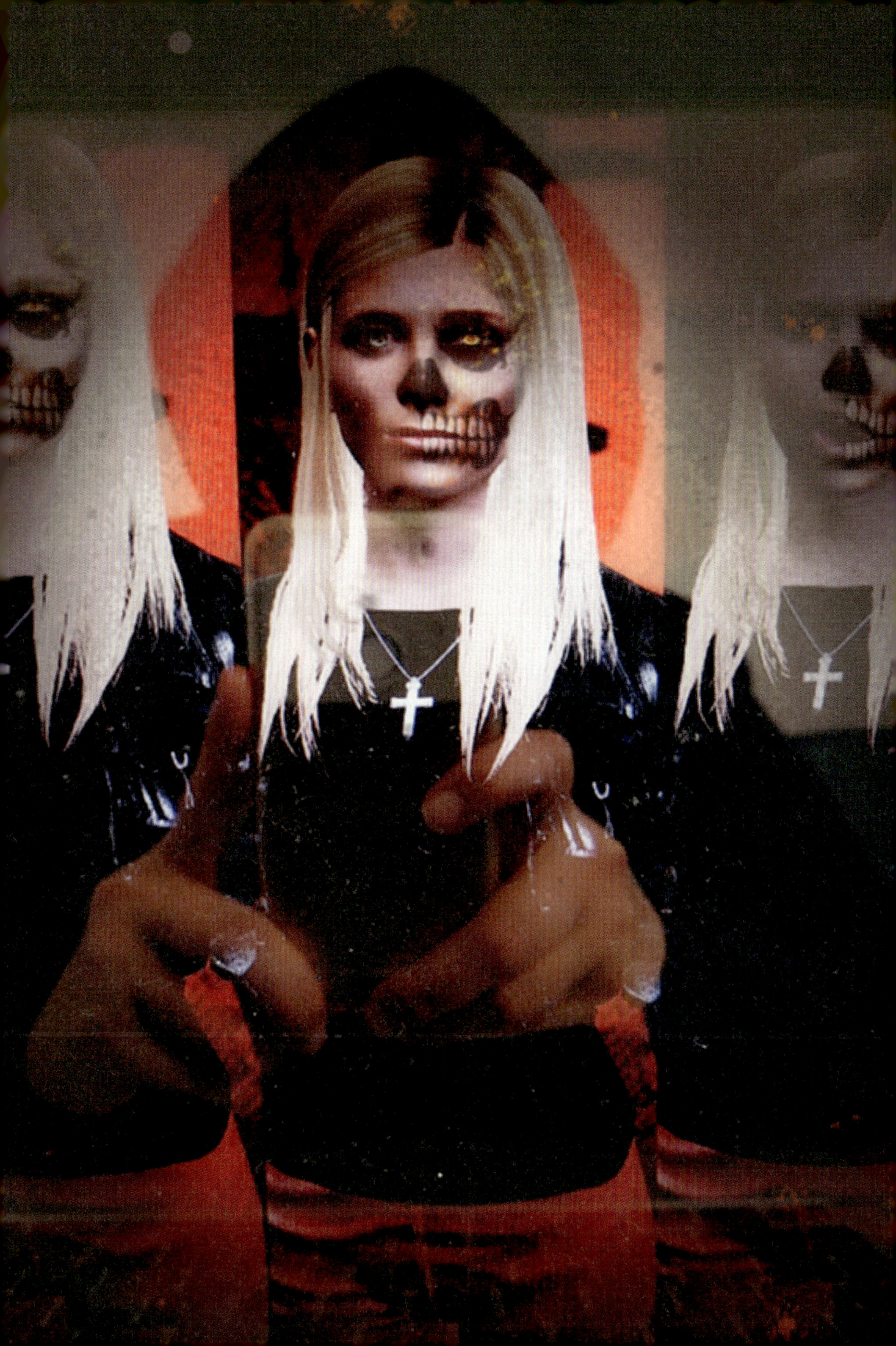

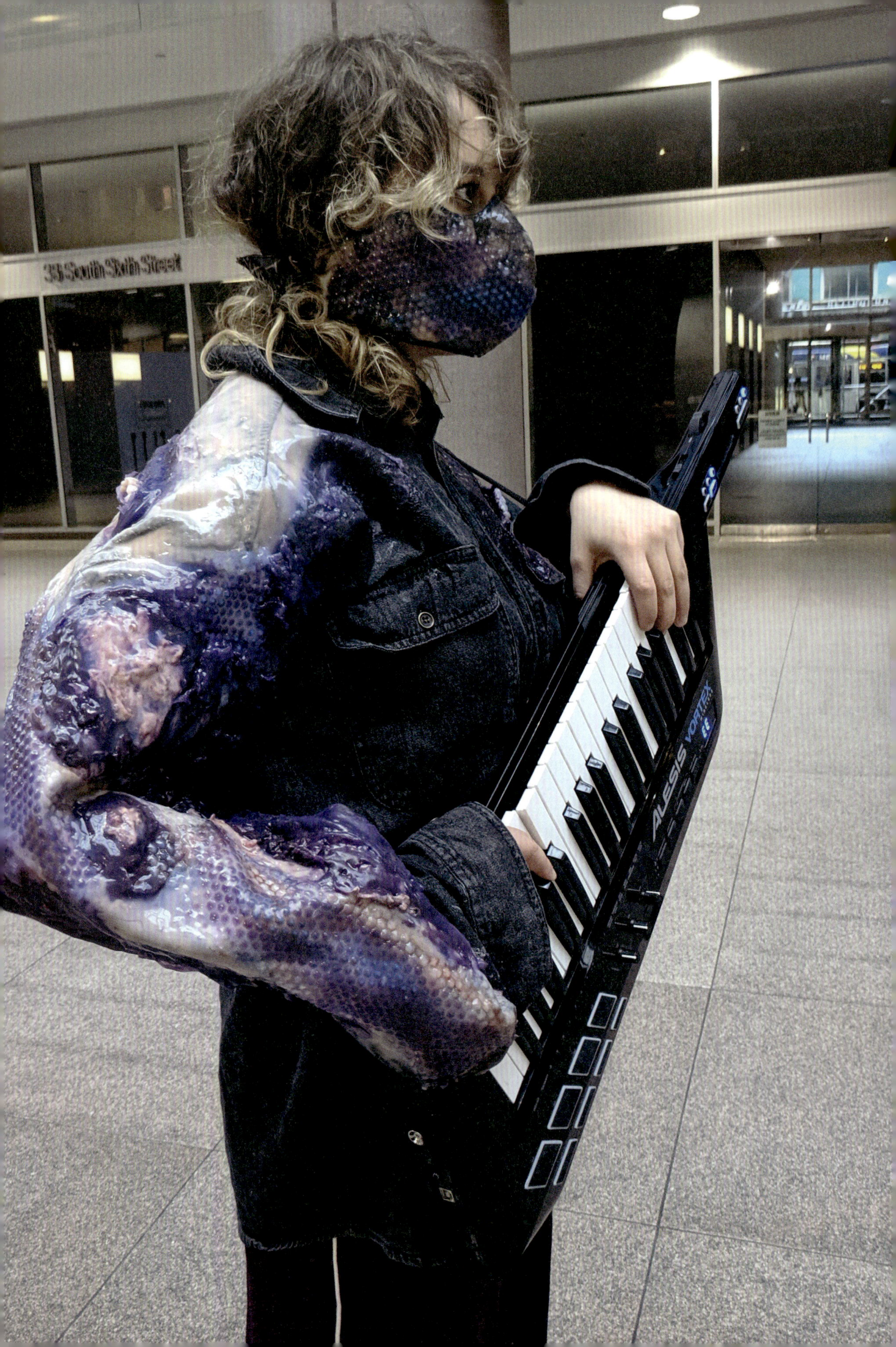
ALESIS
VORTEX

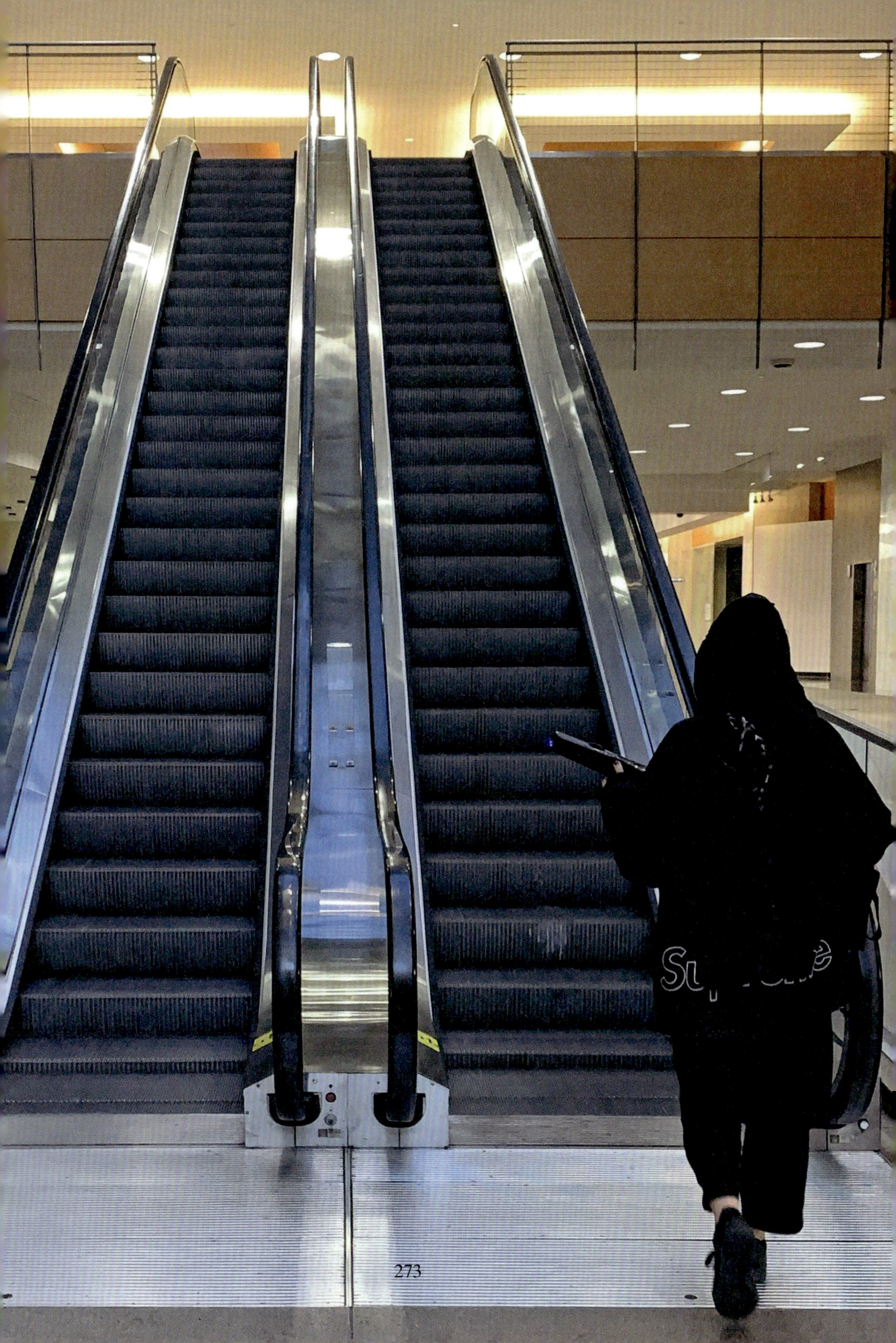

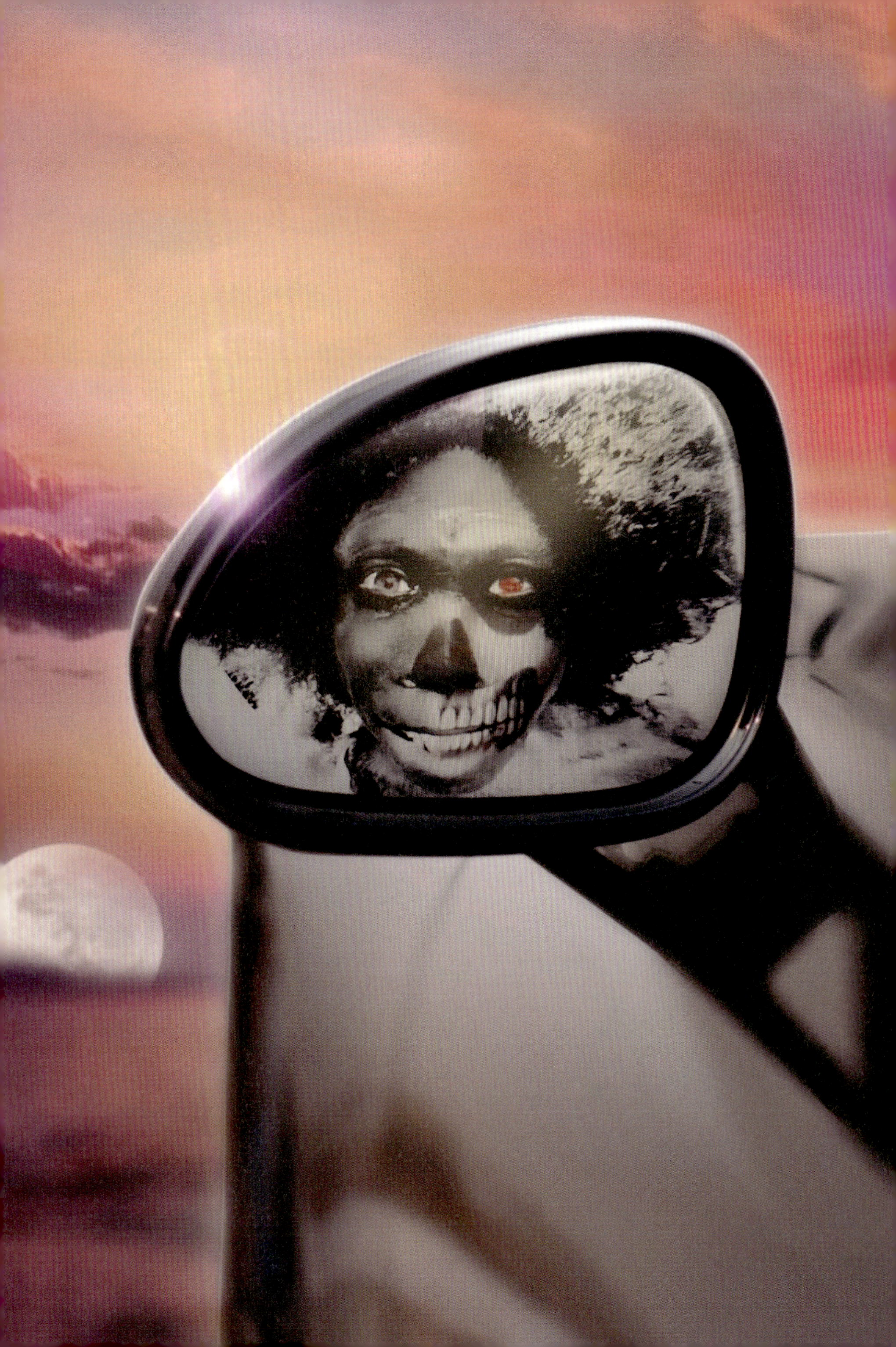

Dark Ride II: They are us revisited

Roseline Rannoch

> "All ages are ages of transition; but this is an awful moment of transition."
> —Lord Alfred Tennyson, *In Memoriam A.H.H.*

In 2005, about 150 local residents dressed as zombies met up in a park located in northeastern Minneapolis looking for fun. Every year since then, an exponentially expanding zombie horde has appeared in the Twin Cities, people from outlying suburbs no one had thought about for years. Fourteen years later, thirty-thousand zombies come crawling into the city on a single night and break Guinness World Records. Moving slowly, they stagger in the direction of what they feed on: the living; beer; things they want to buy. Every year, Google, Amazon, mega-brewer Anheuser-Busch InBev, and of course George A. Romero grant them / us (*they are us!*) permission to symbolically take over the streets and awaken dead city centers to "life." The story is full of urban masses, some of which brought down the powers that be. We are familiar with the liberating, daunting, and utopian images that flow through you at mass events and through which you flow for others. It's physical. It's okay, it can be salutary to be part of a crowd. Elias Canetti, who abhorred death but still made it the lifelong subject of his work, conceived *Das Buch gegen den Tod* [The Book against Death] as a counter proposition to *Crowds and Power.*

The figure of the zombie has a long tradition and in America (North, Central, and South) it is more than a metaphor for racial sublimation or reverse colonization. Ostensibly, today's zombie hordes, which no longer only populate films and TV series, express our concern over the inevitable collateral impacts of capitalism: loss of individuality, consumer excess and its consequences, globalization, outside control through technology and viruses. The hypnotic experience that George A. Romero had when first visiting the Monroeville Mall (where he shot *Dawn of the Dead* in 1978) is deeply rooted in the American (today globalized middleclass-) psyche.[1]

And apparently, our fixation with images of zombie apocalypses is linked to the sad conviction that there are no alternatives to capitalism as a global economic system, coupled with the realization that its logical evolution leads to nothing

1. "My impression of walking through there, going through this sort of ritualistic, unnatural, consuming experience, was that we really do become zombies here. And the way the music was lulling ... everything about it was just so hypnotic. It seemed like nothing was real in there." George A. Romero talking about the Monroeville Mall in an interview with the BBC, 1997.

but destruction. Slavoj Žižek said, with regard to our love for films depicting cataclysms of earth-threatening proportions, that we are living in a time when "it seems easier to imagine the 'end of the world' than a far more modest change in the mode of production, as if liberal capitalism is the 'real' that will somehow survive even under conditions of a global ecological catastrophe."[2]

But political resistance can also be subjected to zombification: die-ins have been a form of non-violent resistance since the sixties. The social movement Extinction Rebellion, founded in England in 2018, engages in civil disobedience against mass extinction of animals and plants and the potential extinction of humanity as a result of the climate crisis and habitat destruction. Many of the actions of the rapidly expanding, pragmatic, and global Extinction Rebellions are currently carried out by zombies.[3]

More than a few of us have a distaste for pub crawls and run away from zombie walks in the metropolitan inner cities of São Paulo, Paris, Minneapolis and, soon, Manila. But let's remember what a survivor in *Dawn of the Dead* says to others in the mall where they found refuge as they watch the advancing zombie hordes with horror: "They are us!"

Dear D.,
How are you?
I miss you and the soothing darkness as we open our eyes to go hunting. There was a time when people's freedom was marked by the distance between them and us at night. Now we have to come to terms with the fact that the vampire's age has faded and given way to the age of the zombie.
The zombie is considered an undead creature that feeds on the flesh of living humans and transforms them into its own kind. The ambivalent nature of the relationship between death and new (perverted) life, connects them to us.
I have observed them: zombies appear in groups. They are self-indulgent, conventional in their desires, and pragmatic. They behave as local, de-individualized beings. At first zombies can be an endless number of variations on a body, and then become a single body. We vampires, on the other hand, are generally considered isolated, privileged, peculiar, and intellectual. We are unique and elegant; we happily borrowed our look and demeanor from dandydom. Our proliferation has been described since the industrial revolution.
In São Paulo, I also united myself with the anthropophages. It was delicious! As with the zombies, cannibalism is what unifies us with them. Brazilian anthropophagy is at least 500 years old. It gained strength in response to the colonization that Brazil sought to impose through its identification with European culture. Its proponents take for granted that the other(s) must be physically incorporated in order to create the new (new ones).

2. Slavoj Žižek, *Mapping Ideology*, ed. Slavoj Žižek (London and New York: VERSO, 2012).
3. https://extinctionrebellion.de, https://extinctionrebellion.us

Feeding on humans is therefore productive when it extends life by ingesting and assimilating the other. In doing so, one should only devour those who can increase one's own life energies and transform oneself into something that never existed previously. It is neither about becoming like the one or the other, nor it is about destroying these.
Anthropophagic devouring is in itself anti-identitarian.
This strategy of cultural appropriation seems elegant and contemporary to me.
Also in view of our grievance of being predictable by algorithms, we need to be mindful of what we consume and what we allow to be digested. An aura of the neutral surrounds computational processes, but they and the controlling authorities behind them devour our data in accordance with turbo-vampiristic criteria. Doesn't it have to be about slowly putting us in the service of the resistance? I wish we, united with humans, zombies, and anthropophages, could transform ourselves into something new. I long for overwhelming, unstable circumstances that do not weaken or isolate us, but strengthen and animate us: mutual savoring and unification.
Micropolitics and cannibalism, assimilation of the other as self-empowerment, and liberation from subjectivity(ies). Freedom only becomes possible outside of the subject.[4]
So we're gradually turning into zombies. I view this zombification as a kind of becoming human. We are virtually transforming ourselves (back) into ourselves. We finally stand by our hunger and our FOMO (Fear of Missing Out). Our externally driven hunger is an expression of our freedom. No more fear of misrepresentation! We represent ourselves and only ourselves as a consuming, melancholic mass.
For me, it is a time of sadness and farewell to the myth of a fair vampirism and a modernism that has long nourished me, but also deceived and excluded many others. It is good that this old "New World," with its monopolies of violence, is disappearing. Do you also believe, like most of us, that in twenty years the world will be much worse off, but you will personally be doing much better? How much violence will we use in the future to secure our personal "happiness?" It will also be about that.

Greetings from Minneapolis,
R.

4. Suely Rolnik describes anthropophagy in neoliberalism as "zombie anthropophagy." It designates our eternally externally determined subjects in "cognitive capitalism" as "flexibilized, hyperactive zombie subjects," which, as long as they are only "with themselves" as closed subjects, are per se unfree. Suely Rolnik, *Zombie Anthropophagie-Zur neoliberalen Subjektivität* (Vienna: Turia + Kant, 2018).

Translation from German into English by Erik Smith.

Biographies

Alobhe (Berlin) is a musician hell-bent on gutturally stabbing each broken genre she comes across. Alobhe's visceral take on future club music combines elements of electro, black metal, dark ambient, and techno to produce foreboding sonic assaults with an underlying impulse toward the industrial dance floor. Recent releases include contributions to Warsaw's *Intruder Alert* and a debut EP called *State Space*.
Euromall, p. 205

Salim Bayri (Amsterdam) is a Casablanca-born artist whose art functions as a humorous navigational tool to sail through the contexts he left and the ones he is integrating into, touching the liminal points of what he calls "bittersweet ghorba" or "bittersweet abroad-being". Bayri takes on a multidisciplinary approach to his work, using a variety of media including CGI, drawings, wearables and sound. He is also part of the music duo BAZOGA with his brother Tayeb.
Euromall, p. 205

Pauline Boudry/Renate Lorenz (Berlin) are an artist duo who have worked together since 2006. They produce film installations that revisit recent and past material (a score, a piece of music, a film, a photograph or a performance), with a particular focus on a critical history of the photographic and moving image. The duo works with performance to create embodiments which are able to conflate different times and often create illegitimate collaborations—partly fictitious, partly cross-temporal.
Passages, p. 243

Kimberly Bradley (Berlin) has been a culture writer and editor since the 1990s. When she writes, it's often—but not always—about art or the art world. When she edits, it can be big-picture or niggling. Born in a California desert town and raised in northern Minnesota, she spent several years in Hamburg, New York, Vienna and Berlin. Bradley's work takes journalistic, essayistic, and critical forms.
The Possibilities of Negative Space, p. 119

Cardigan Donuts (Minneapolis) is the donut shop next to *Goethe in the Skyways* and arguably the best donut shop in Downtown Minneapolis. Throughout the year, Cardigan Donuts provided *Goethe in the Skyways* with donuts for all Happy Hours, Open Studios, readings, performances, and workshop sessions. For *Commission Roundabout*, Cardigan Donuts exclusively sold the "Roundabout Donut" designed by Albrecht Pischel.

Valérie Chartrain (Berlin) is a curator, editor, publisher and writer focusing on art, spirits, and probable futures. When not in the art world, she writes about spirits and curates knowledge in the wine and spirits industry while working as a strategic researcher for companies imagining their futures.
Passages, p. 243

Andy Delany (Minneapolis) is an artist who has been collaborating as a part of OOIEE since its founding in 2016. OOIEE is a cross-disciplinary, open practice with interests ranging from furniture and objects, actions and scenarios, landscape architecture related work, teaching, writing, publishing, fashion and more. He also maintains a studio practice of his own, and is co-director of Yeah Maybe gallery in Minneapolis, MN.
Commission Roundabout, p. 109

Constant Dullaart's (Berlin) practice reflects on the broad cultural and social effects of communication and image-processing technologies, from performatively distributing artificial social capital on social media to completing a staff-pick Kickstarter campaign for a hardware start-up. His work includes websites, performances, routers, installations, startups, armies, manipulated found images, frequently juxtaposing or consolidating technically dichotomized presentation realms.
Collusion, Collision, Illusion, p. 85

Creamcake (Berlin) is an open and queer platform and label dedicated to exploring the impact of the Internet on music at the intersection of music, art and technology. Founded by Daniela Seitz and Anja Weigl in 2011, they initiate and organize concerts, performances, symposiums and digital projects. Cooperating with a number of community spaces and institutions, Creamcake presents visionary, nonconformist and experimental sounds, while actively encouraging women and people of all genders to work together on an equal basis.
Euromall, p. 205

Mary Moore Easter (Minneapolis) is a Cave Canem Fellow and professor of dance emerita at Carleton College. Her chapbook is *Walking from Origins* (Heywood Press, 1993).
Inefficiencies, p. 125

Katelyn Farstad (Minneapolis) is an artist and musician. She is the drummer for Larry Wish and His Guys, and performs music solo under the name Itch Princess. As an artist she is known for a broad range of materials such as Orthodontic molds, Technicolor Easter eggs, scrawled graphite or broken toys.
Commission Roundabout, p. 109

Students from Bielefeld University of Applied Sciences (Department of Design): Greta Berghoff, Inke Borgel, Sabrina Brose, Katrin Jeworowski, Paul Kaminski, Laura Könemann, Jan König, Steffi Lahl, Fabia Meyer, Jana Meyer, Leon Pöhler, Martina Reifer, Anna Siebert, Friederike Sujeba-Roesler, Melis Uyanik und Julia Wartemann
Bags from Bielefeld, p. 263

Fauna's work (Vienna) manifests itself locally in the radical potential of art and music. The Vienna-based producer's sounds and lyrics are influenced by personal and political events, while her music takes a position and places social clichés into avant-garde beats and rap, hip hop and bass music-inspired tracks.Fauna is also co-founder of the Burschenschaft Hysteria in Vienna, and her second album was released in May 2018.

Euromall, p. 205

David Flaugher (Detroit) takes objects of American recreation, leisure, and celebration and couples them with materials of capitalist refuse. Often employing humor and pathos within the same breath, his work strikes a poignant and timely cord in an increasingly precarious era of economic and political upheaval.

Commission Roundabout, p. 109

FORT's artist duo (Berlin) consists of Alberta Niemann and Jenny Kropp. Since 2008 they have been creating installations, performances, and video works. FORT uses everyday objects that are copied, rearranged, or transformed. Seemingly banal ordinary moments are adapted and transferred to the exhibition space. The resulting settings, objects, and videos have a subtly surreal character, suggesting, despite their supposed familiarity, an atmosphere of eeriness, and abandonment. Oscillating between poetic and humorous moments, the objects frequently conflict with what the viewer normally expects to see.

The Calling, p. 133

FRZNTE (Berlin) travels the world with her MP3 collection. With her desert mix of Hip-Hop, Trap, Wave, Techno, Ghetto Tech, Disco and the most beautiful All Time Favourites she transforms art and film events, weddings, and night clubs into an extravaganza of wild parties. Her music is both trash and glam. Don't be shy! Shake your ass! As long as you dance, she is not dead!

Hyper Hyper Helium Karaoke & Dance Party, p. 161

Cameron Gainer (Minneapolis / New York) is an artist and the mastermind behind co. (company projects). He works in a broad range of media and approaches. From his Minneapolis studio emerges The Third Rail a quarterly magazine on "art, politics, philosophy, and culture" but also sculptures, films, paintings, and installation works. Cameron Keith Gainer explores the impact of natural phenomenon on human perception and its relevance to our understanding of the world around us.

Passages, p. 243

General Security Services Corporation (Minneapolis): the security officers of GSSC, Sam, Tawlet, et al. tolerated the artists' interventions into the private-public sphere of City Center and therefore made the *Goethe in the Skyways* program possible.

Sam Gould (Minneapolis) was the co-founder and editor of Red76, an expanded publication that materialized in Portland, Oregon, in the early 2000s. Instrumentalizing ideas around publication as an act of public making, Gould's work manifests publics through the implementation of ad-hoc educational structures and discursive gatherings. While these actions are often situated in what is called "public space,"—such as street corners, laundromats, taverns, and the like.

Pre-Election Poster Action, p. 71

Anna Hankings-Evans (Berlin) is a German-Ghanaian lawyer and author focusing on international economic law, its power implication, geopolitics and postcolonial theories of justice. Until recently, Hankings-Evans resided at the Centre for Chinese Studies at Stellenbosch University in South Africa as a visiting doctoral researcher. After completing her law studies, she was a research fellow at the Chair of Public Law and Public International Law of Prof. Dr. Heike Krieger in Berlin.

Euromall, p. 205

Paula Hildebrandt (Berlin) works on politics of representation, performance theory and acts of citizenship. She studied political science in Berlin, holds a MA in Global Political Economy and a Postgraduate Certificate from the University of Cambridge. In 2013 she received a doctoral degree in European Urbanism from the Bauhaus University Weimar. In her work she combines investigations of cultural phenomena with ecological and sociopolitical themes, post-disciplinary research and new curatorial approaches.

Ten Things to Take to the Sky, which Unintentionally Start with the Letter S, Except for One, and Why Again?, p. 181

Karl Holmqvist (Berlin) works with and around text and language. Since the early '90s his oeuvre has revolved around text, published in various forms: on posters, as wall drawings, in installations, videos, or readings. Holmqvist juxtaposes text material of popular songs, political phrases, literary quotes, art historical references, and individual letters of the alphabet; he is a master of the ambiguity of words and sentences that he shifts around and re-combines to create new meanings.

Collusion, Collision, Illusion, p. 85

Kolbeinn Hugi / DJ Kebab Benzin (Berlin) is an artist of a generation that emerged in the wake of the cataclysmic great rift between art and artists in the bleak neo-capitalist Reykjavík of modern times. Taking diverse motifs from 1970s techno-futurism, pseudo archeology and new-age black metal his work aims to evoke an alternate model of society and suggests that the world as it is now isn't necessarily how it has to be. Kolbeinn's stuff is simple and aims for the heart, not for the head.
Hyper Hyper Helium Karaoke & Dance Party, p. 161

Brandon Hundt (Minneapolis) is the Director of Product Management for PRI/PRX helping to design platforms in podcasting and news. He is very interested in civic design and is the mastermind behind a new map and signage for the Mpls Skyways System. Brandon has also opined on vexillology, the study of flags, for PRI.org and City Pages.
Passages, p. 243

Interesting Tactics (Minneapolis) is a utopic spatial practice comprised of Anna, Austin, Drew, Isaac, and Mary. They consider utopia a process that is both slow and tactical—a way of making do, out of necessity and naïveté.
Passages, p. 243
Who Are the Future Skyways for?, p. 255

Vincent James (Minneapolis) practiced independently and with firms in Minneapolis and New York before founding VJAA in 1995. Vincent was appointed Adjunct Professor at Harvard University's Graduate School of Design, where he taught from 2000–2006. James has authored essays on design and was co-author with partner Jennifer Yoos of a monograph on their practice published by Princeton Architectural Press as well as their book, *Parallel Cities: The Multilevel Metropolis* (2016).
On Parallel Cities, p. 141

Miriam Karraker (Minneapolis) writes, performs, and collaborates. She holds an MFA in creative writing from the University of Minnesota.
Inefficiencies, p. 125

Anton Kats (Berlin) is an artist and musician born in South-Ukraine into the family of a WWII wireless radio operators. Kats's practice derives from informal everyday relationships within the vibrant neighborhood of his hometown and is complemented through necessity and pragmatics of self-legalization in Europe via entering formal institutions of education. His work with sound and radio often unfolds in public space in form of collaborative interventions, sonic sculptures, musical compositions, and public programs.
Radio Amateur Ensemble, p. 101

Kinga Kielczynska (Berlin) first studied Spanish Philology at Warsaw University before graduating from the Gerrit Rietveld Academy and the Sandberg Institute in Amsterdam. Her multidisciplinary art practice reflects upon the relationship between nature and humans. She often exhibits her work outside of the gallery context. Past locations include a nudist beach, a night club, and a forest. In 2009, she challenged the paradigm of art-making by writing a "Reductionist Art Manifesto" which playfully proclaimed the idea of reduction instead of production.
Alien Species, p. 211

Christine Sun Kim (Berlin) uses the medium of sound in performance and drawing to investigate her relationship with spoken languages and her aural environment.
Z and be seen, p. 155

Andree Korpys and Markus Löffler (Berlin) use the methods of the modern surveillance state and reflect it back onto the state itself, focusing on its mechanisms and structures of power represented by institutions like the UN, the World Trade Center, the Pentagon, the BND, the European Central Bank, prisons, or the police. Despite these subject matters, their films remain non-judgmental and objective and don't engage in investigative journalism. Instead, the aesthetics of peripheral events, secondary characters, and details are their focus of attention.
Disruption, Interruption, Misruptions, p. 65

Cori Kresge (New York) is a NYC-based dancer, bodyworker, writer, and teacher. She graduated from SUNY Purchase with a BFA in dance and the Dean's Award. Kresge has been a member of the Merce Cunningham Repertory Understudy Group, functioning as a living archive for Cunningham works. She is a guest teacher at NYU Tisch School of the Arts and other institutions. Her debut poetry collection won the No, Dear/Small Anchor Press first chapbook contest. Kresge is currently working towards certification in Zero Balancing bodywork.
User Friendly, p. 167

Steph Kretowicz (Los Angeles) is a London and Los Angeles-based, writer, editor and journalist specialized in music, contemporary art and online culture. Her writing appears in *Flash Art*, *Dazed & Confused*, *Resident Advisor*, *The Fader* and *The Wire*, among others. Kretowicz is also co-founder and editor of London-based arts publication AQNB.com and author of novel and cross-media narrative *Somewhere I've Never Been*, published by TLTRPreß and Pool in 2017.
Euromall, p. 205

Aleksandra Lakić (Berlin) is a sociologist with a background in political science. In her current research, she focuses on the role of media narratives in shaping national identity and the problems of labor market discrimination of migrant workers in Berlin. Lakić is actively engaged in the Democracy in Europe Movement (DIEM25) and coedits Zent Magazine, an online and printed journal from Belgrade publishing works in political and social theory, art, design and architecture.

Euromall, p. 205

Larry (Berlin) is a researcher, author, and DJ from Berlin. As co-founder of Creamcake—an experimental platform dedicated to exploring the impact of the internet at the intersection of art, music and technology—she is dedicated to discovering new online music and sound cultures. Larry's sets are intended to create human expression transformed into an absurd spectacle of sound, with linguistic elements that do not communicate but are aimed instead at raw emotional effect.

Euromall, p. 205

Chris Larson (Minneapolis) has a multi media based practice that is rooted in sculpture. His work incorporates film, video, photography, performance and drawing/painting, often in installed environments. Chris Larson is currently on the faculty of the Department of Art, University of Minnesota, Minneapolis.

Commission Roundabout, p. 109

Liz Magic Laser (New York) is a video and performance artist. Her work intervenes in semi-public spaces such as bank vestibules, movie theaters, and newsrooms, involving collaborations with actors, surgeons, political strategists, and motorcycle gang members. Her recent work uses communication techniques and psychological methods appropriated by corporate and political cultures to revive their therapeutic potential.

User Friendly, p. 167

Bill Lindeke (Minneapolis) is a geographer who has spent far too many years writing about and researching the Minneapolis Skyways. He has a PhD in geography from the University of Minnesota. He is the author of Minneapolis/St. Paul: Then and Now, and the forthcoming Closing Time, a history of bars in St. Paul and Minneapolis. He was born in Minneapolis, but lives in St Paul and serves there on the St. Paul Planning Commission.

Passages, p. 243

Hanne Lippard's (Berlin) practice explores the voice as a medium. Her education in graphic design informs how language can be visually powerful; her texts are visual, rhythmic, and performative rather than purely informative, and her work is conveyed through a variety of disciplines, which include short films, sound pieces, installations and performance.

Collusion, Collision, Illusion, p. 87
Inefficiencies, p. 125

Jonas Lund (Berlin) is a designer, game master, and player all at the same time. His modus operandi involves creating systems and setting up parameters that either he or the viewers are encouraged to engage with. This results in various program-based works that encompass data and behavior analysis and apply the logics of the new economy, political mechanisms and strategies, and neural networks.

www.goetheintheskyways.org, p. 37

Patrick Marschke (Minneapolis) is a percussionist, composer, electronic musician, and writer trying to make all of those things into one thing. Recently, his work has revolved around utilizing Max/MSP to build custom project-specific sound applications exploring the boundaries of aural perception through sonic obfuscation and live electroacoustic performance.

Radio Amateur Ensemble, p. 101

Chris Martin's (Minneapolis) fourth collection of poetry, *Things to Do in Hell,* will be published by Coffee House Press in 2020. He is the Executive Director of *Unrestricted Interest*, an organization dedicated to helping neurodivergent learners transform their lives though writing. He also teaches at Hamline University and Carleton College.

Inefficiencies, p. 125

Chloë McWhirt (Minneapolis) is a painter and junior-year undergraduate student pursuing a degree in Art, German Studies, and Critical Theory at Macalester College. She was the summer intern at *Goethe in the Skyways*. In 2020, she will go on to attend Humboldt University in Berlin and the University of Vienna before graduation. McWhirt works at the Law Warschaw Gallery in St. Paul, and frequents the skyways in downtown Minneapolis.

Alexandra Midal (Paris) is a free-lance curator and Professor in the MA Spaces & Communication & Design Program at the HEAD—Genève. She combines curating and research activities in design and visual culture. She has published several books and catalogues. Her last book *Design by Accident: For a New History of Design* is published by Sternberg Press. She is also the author of a series of films of visual theory.

Passages, p. 243

Lisa Middag (Minneapolis) is an urban planner who collaborates with communities to support sustainable, and walkable public spaces through creative placemaking and community development. Lisa works for the Minneapolis Downtown Improvement District as Director of Nicollet Activation, where she is responsible for developing, directing and implementing an activation framework along the city's historic pedestrian/transit mall, assuring an inclusive range of cultural experiences for daily users and visitors.
Passages, p. 243

Lara Mimosa Montes (Minneapolis) is a writer. Currently, she works as a senior editor of Triple Canopy. Her next book, *Thresholes*, is forthcoming with Coffee House Press.
Inefficiencies, p. 125

Jennifer Newsom (Minneapolis) is the co-founder of Dream the Combine, a creative practice of artists and architects Jennifer Newsom and Tom Carruthers, based in Minneapolis. They have created site-specific installations in the U.S. and Canada. Each conflates what is real with what is imagined to create perceptual uncertainties that cast doubt on our "known" understanding of the world. Through techniques such as doubling, juxtaposition, overlay, or mimicry, they make architectural artworks that convey a multitude of viewpoints at a time.
Passages, p. 243

Lee Noble (Minneapolis) is an artist and composer working in between sound, collage, and multimedia. His work is concerned with the exponential accumulation of information in the internet age and the bleeding together of various media forms and cultural expressions. He is a graduate student at Minneapolis College of Art and Design (MCAD).
Bauhaus100 Bonanza Show, p. 221

Hanna Novak (New York) is a playwright and director from Toronto living and working in New York City. Her plays have been presented at the Frederick Loewe Theatre at Hunter College, the New Ohio Theatre, and the Performing Garage. She has collaborated with Laura Bernstein, Julia Jarcho/minor theater, and Tina Satter, among others. Hanna is a graduate of the Playwriting MFA program at Hunter College, where she received the Irving Zarkower Award for the Best New Play of the Year.
User Friendly, p. 167

Kelsey Olson (Minneapolis) received her BFA from the Minneapolis College of Art and Design in 2010 and was awarded the Jerome Emerging Artist Fellowship in 2016/17. Olson has had solo exhibitions at venues and temporary spaces in Minnesota including the Rochester Art Center, and has participated in group exhibitions at David Petersen Gallery and St. Cloud State University. She helped create and run They Won't Find Us Here Gallery in Minneapolis, which ran from 2010–2012, and has organized other publishing projects and exhibitions since that time.
Untitled Wall Project, p. 51

Noah Ophoven-Baldwin (Minneapolis) is a cornetist, composer, and improviser. As a cornetist, he has a special interest in counterintuitive and historically disregarded techniques of brass playing. His compositions incorporate elements of stillness, silence, and song. Noah is also an enthusiastic collaborator devoted to the practice and performance of all incredible sounds.
Radio Amateur Ensemble, p. 101

OOIEE (Minneapolis) is a trans-disciplinary studio that works on projects related to art, design, architecture, and landscape. Their "open practice" model is based on the belief that the world makes us as much as we make it and thus, trusting the work that emerges, whether commissioned or self-initiated, is an act of poetic surrender that gives life to something that is easy to care about. Informed by a love of research and an interest in using art history as a material, OOIEE participates in climates of knowledge with an open heart and is committed to intentions of generosity, kindness, in and around the work.
Skyway Furniture, p. 45

Sarah Petersen (Minneapolis) is an artist, educator, and the artistic producer at the Goethe Pop Up Minneapolis. Her interdisciplinary art practice includes performative, structural, sonic and textual interventions. Trained in various embodiment and material practices, she collaborates regularly with other artists, choreographers, and institutions in the production of new works and programs.
Passages, p. 243
On Location, p. 229

Drew Peterson (Minneapolis) is a painter and printmaker, and a Minnesota native best known for creating art of colorful and otherworldly spaces. Peterson received a MFA from the School of the Art Institute of Chicago and a BFA from the University of Minnesota, Minneapolis, and has received several awards and grants, such as the Minnesota State Arts Board Artist Initiative Grant and a Jerome Fellowship.
Pre-Election Poster Action, p. 71

Pétunia (Berlin) is a fine feminist publication on art and culture founded by artist Lili Reynaud Dewar, writer and curator Dorothée Dupuis and cultural producer Valérie Chartrain in 2009. A yearly journal, it presented visionary, nonconformist and radical views at the intersection of art, architecture, film, design, fiction and other cultural fields. If Pétunia ceased to exist on paper after completing a seven year cycle, the spirit remains and reappears occasionally. Since then it indeed operates as a discursive situation maker, exhibition curator and other non expected ways.

Passages, p. 243

Albrecht Pischel (Berlin) art practice comprises photography, film, installation, sound, and performance and aims at the transgression of boundaries between disparate mediums, genres, and cultures. The often self-referential works playfully reflect on the conditions of the medium in use and the cultural framework that governs the perception of art and its displays. In Pischel's carefully staged anachronisms obsolete technologies experience an unexpected return. At times he incorporates other artists' works in his projects thus opening up the confines of individual authorship.

Commission Roundabout, p. 109

Franziska Pierwoss (Berlin) is a performance and installation artist, who also works as an organizer and initiator of various cultural projects. With a strong focus on durational performance and collaborative practices, she develops site-specific installations in which personal and political boundaries are called into question. Using storytelling as an explorative methodology towards History, Pierwoss has been staging performances related to historical meals since 2014 in collaboration with Sandra Teitge.

The Art of the Deal, p. 77

Emilie Pitoiset (Paris) is an artist choreographer who works at the confluence of performance, theatre, sculpture and film and lately developed a series of work in the field of dance while pursuing a Master of advanced studies in Psychoanalysis. With a particular predilection for fragile balances, disfigurations, postures and anti-natural movements, Emilie Pitoiset reconstructs and invents situations that she confronts her audiences with.

Passages, p. 243

Felix Profos (Berlin) is a composer, classically trained pianist, and since 2002 lecturer in music theory and composition at the Zurich University of the Arts. He has performed in Doom Spa and Javascript-based projects like Eastern Shore and performed with his own band "Forcemajeure". Profos has written numerous compositions for classical orchestras, ensembles, and hardcore noise formations as well as sound installations and has created recordings for labels. In the 1990s, Profos played classical concert as pianist.

Dark Ride II. They are us revisited, p. 269

Laure Prouvost's (Antwerp) work is permeated by language—in its broadest sense. Known for her immersive and mixed-media installations that combine film and installation in humorous and idiosyncratic ways, Prouvost's work addresses miscommunication and things getting lost in translation. Playing with language as a tool for the imagination, Prouvost is interested in confounding linear narratives and expected associations among words, images, and meaning.

Collusion, Collision, Illusion, p. 85

Cole Pulice (Minneapolis) plays the saxophone, often with electronics. He enjoys improvising, composing, and collaborating in many different settings, both solo and group. Through combining extended saxophone technique with dynamic electronic performance systems, Pulice's work explores the connection between the acoustic limits of the saxophone and electroacoustic augmentation. Things influential to Cole's recent work: kaleidoscopes, prisms, holograms, sunsets, and science fiction.

Radio Amateur Ensemble, p. 101

Roseline Rannoch (Berlin) studied Latin American Literature and Philosophy at FU Berlin before graduating in Fine Arts and Media Theory from Karlsruhe University of Arts and Design. Her multidisciplinary practice manifests itself primarily in sculpture but also in complex spatiotemporal works that can be explored through various digital and analogue media.

Dark Ride II. They are us revisited, p. 269

Lili Reynaud Dewar (Grenoble) is a founding member of Pétunia. She developed a practice through performances, sculptures, videos, and installations. The heterogeneous forms question identity issues; whether they relate to the status of women or dominated communities and the icons of cultural transgression inhabit her artistic reflection.

Passages, p. 243

Elske Rosenfeld (Berlin) works in different media and formats. Her primary focus and material are the histories of state socialism and its dissidences, and the revolution of 1989/90. She recently began blogging on www.dissidencies.net.

A Vocabulary of Revolutionary Gestures, p. 237

Bartholomew Ryan (Minneapolis) is an independent curator. He served as Milton Fine Curator of Art at the Andy Warhol Museum, and prior to that he was Assistant Curator at the Walker Art Center in Minneapolis, where he co-curated the ambitious historical exhibition International Pop (2015) with lead curator Darsie Alexander. He works closely with many artists including Danh Vo.

Let's Go Outside…, p. 91

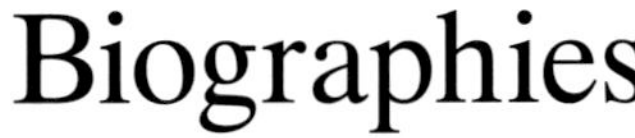

Philipp Rupp (Berlin) is a fashion and textile designer who is interested in appropriating and integrating urban imagery, such as logos of sausage stands or shop signs, into his designs reflecting on notions of class, fashion history, and the mechanisms of the fashion industry itself. Especially the phenomenon of cross-class-dressing.

Skyway Uniforms, p. 41
Bags from Bielefeld, p. 263
Dark Ride II. They are us revisited, p. 269

Nora Spiekermann (Berlin) is a Berlin-based artist who spent eight months in Minneapolis at the Minneapolis College of Art and Design (MCAD). Focusing on performance, intervention, and video, she gains her inspiration from public space, its issues and chances. While studying in Weimar, the founding city of the Bauhaus, she examined the effects of the Bauhaus Centenary and attempted her own appropriation of this event.

Bauhaus100 Bonanza Show, p. 221

Surabhi Saraf (New York) is a media artist and founder of Centre for Emotional Materiality, graduating from the School of the Art Institute of Chicago (SAIC) with an MFA in Art and Technology in 2009. Her practice explores our complex relationship with technology through multimedia works that incorporate video installations, sculptures, performances and sound compositions.

Euromall, p. 205

Setareh Shahbazi (Berlin/Tehran) studied Scenography and Media Arts to then lives and works in Beirut, Tehran and Berlin. She has been compiling notes and observations in form of found photographs: images from private collections, snapshots, film stills, postcards, newspapers, social media and daily newsfeeds. With a playful irreverence to the sanctity of a photograph as a mirror of reality, Shahbazi drains details out of images, constantly shifting perspectives to allow these observations to come together in a fictional afterlife.

Commission Roundabout, p. 109

Daniel Shinbaum (Minneapolis) is the production assistant at the Goethe Pop Up Minneapolis. He graduated from Macalester College in May 2018 with a bachelor of arts in media and cultural studies and a concentration in critical theory. Shinbaum has published many art reviews, spent a semester abroad studying metropolitan art and culture in Berlin and is also active in the Twin Cities' thriving underground techno scene.

On Location, p. 229

Jenny Schmid (Minneapolis) creates prints through her own bikini press international. Her work is densely packed with complex visual narratives. Schmid draws upon the rich print tradition of social satire and activism, notably inspired by Goya, Bruegel and Hogarth as well as the bold colors and densely packed compositions of advertisements and carnival posters, updated to respond to current social issues such as gender relations, the traps facing young girls, truth, liberty, apathy and philosophy.

Pre-Election Poster Action, p. 71

Emily Stover (Minneapolis) is an artist and design researcher at the University of Minnesota who creates architectural installations and engaging experiences in and about public space.

Passages, p. 243

Ramaya Tegegne (Geneva) presented solo exhibitions and performances in Vienna, Hamburg, Brussels, Zurich, Baltimore and New York. In 2017, she launched the campaign Wages For Wages Against, for the remuneration of artists in Switzerland and beyond.

Passages, p. 243

Sandra Teitge (Berlin) is a curator/programmer and cultural researcher, occasional writer and sporadic performer, born and raised in East Berlin. She organizes discursive events and exhibitions in the realm of contemporary art and architecture, often in overlooked locations in urban space, and is interested in the interplay of formal and informal structures. Recent projects include research on East German architects and architecture; and research and performances surrounding the notion of culinary politics. Before starting *Goethe in the Skyways*, she lived in the Twin Cities for three years and started and ran FD13 residency for the arts.

Foreword, p. 31
On Parallel Cities, p. 141
Passages, p. 243

The People's Library is an MCAD (Minneapolis College of Art & Design) student group that provides a safe space for students to discuss topics a traditional classroom may not. The organization has also been heavily involved in the Black Lives Matter movement, LGBTQIA events, and other important current issues.

Pre-Election Poster Action, p. 71

Aaron Van Dyke (Minneapolis) is an artist and teacher living in Minneapolis. He has taught art, theory, art history and mentored graduate students at the School of the Art Institute of Chicago, University of Minnesota, Minneapolis College of Art and Design, and St. Cloud State University. Van Dyke was a visiting artist at Tokyo Institute of Technology in 2012, has run the summer school at the Poor Farm (Manawa, WI) since 2009, and was Education Coordinator at Midway Contemporary Art until early 2017. He founded and helped run Occasional, a gallery in St. Paul, MN for seven years.

Untitled Wall Project, p. 51

Susana Vargas Cervantes (Mexico City) mines the connections between gender, sexuality, class and skin color. Deftly navigating between cultures and methodologies that bridge Latin South and Anglo North America, her work relates media and visual culture to theories of performative gender and sex, transnational feminisms, critical race, and postcolonial theories as well as queer and trans theories. Vargas Cervantes is the recipient of a Fullbright Scholarship and currently lives in New York.

Passages, p. 243

Wermke/Leinkauf (Berlin) is an artist duo made of Matthias Wermke and Mischa Leinkauf, who explores the boundaries of the public sphere to question common standards, constraints and the boundaries between public and private, through actions, performances, and installations. Their main interest lies in the appropriation and conquest of architecture and, more generally, urban space, especially the open spaces and gaps in the system, which in their eyes are crucial for our contemporary society. Using artistic strategies, they create temporary irritations that allow new perspectives on everyday situations and try to "open" the city by using not only their bodies but the material and the tools of urban spaces.

Disruptions, Interruptions, Misruptions, p. 65

Ruth Wolf-Rehfeldt (Berlin) started in the early 1970s to create a series of "typewritings" by combining Teutonic rigor with a subversive sense of humor. Under her fingers, the black and red characters of an Erika Schreibmaschine became patterns, butterflies, waves, abstract compositions, diagrams of fluxes, and woven lines of poetry. Wolf-Rehfeldt was employed as an office manager, and was an active participant of the international mail art movement despite the regime's strict surveillance. Her and her husband Robert Rehfeldt's studio in East Berlin's Pankow became a hub for the local and international art community in the 1980s.

Collusion, Collision, Illusion, p. 85

Jennifer Yoos (Minneapolis) practiced architecture both independently and with firms in Minneapolis and London prior to joining VJAA as a design principal in 1997. Yoos received her Graduate Diploma in Design from the Architectural Association in London and her professional degree in Architecture from the University of Minnesota. She teaches architecture, most at the Washington University in St. Louis. Yoos has authored essays on design and was co-author with partner Vincent James of a monograph on their practice published by Princeton Architectural Press as well as their recent book, *Parallel Cities: The Multilevel Metropolis* (2016).

On Parallel Cities, p. 141

Goethe Pop Up Minneapolis
Goethe in the Skyways
October 2018 – October 2019

This publication is part of the Year of German-American Friendship initiated by the German Federal Foreign Office and the Goethe-Institut, and supported by the Federation of German Industries (BDI).

Photo credits:
Wiley Hoard, Sarah Petersen, Daniel Shinbaum, and Sandra Teitge
Except:
p. 12, 27, 273, 276: Roseline Rannoch
p. 247: Emilie Pitoiset
p. 260–262: Interesting Tactics

Editor-in-Chief: Sandra Teitge
Managing Editor: Valérie Chartrain
Publisher: Spector Books
Graphic Design: HIT
Proofreading: Cassandra Edlefsen Lasch

First edition, 2020.
Edition of 1000 copies.
Printed in the EU, in Germany, by optimal media GmbH, 2020.

ISBN: 978-3-95905-358-7

Available through:

Germany, Austria: GVA, Gemeinsame Verlagsauslieferung Göttingen GmbH&Co. KG
www.gva-verlage.de

Switzerland: AVA Verlagsauslieferung AG
www.ava.ch

France, Belgium: Interart Paris
www.interart.fr

UK: Central Books Ltd
www.centralbooks.com

USA, Canada, Central and South America, Africa: ARTBOOK | D.A.P.
www.artbook.com

South Korea: The Book Society
www.thebooksociety.org

Australia, New Zealand:
Perimeter Distribution
www.perimeterdistribution.co

Thank you from the Editor-in-chief:
Petra Roggel, Thomas Rupprecht, Sarah Petersen, Daniel Shinbaum, Cameron Gainer, Joan Vorderbruggen, Cardigan Donuts, Alicia Eler, Valérie Chartrain, Bruno Freeman, Wiley Hoard, all artists, participants, collaborators, supporters, and, most importantly, our public.